D0195664

DEMOCRATIC
REFORM
IN AFRICA

WITHDRAWN
UTSA LIBRARIES

DEMOCRATIC REFORM IN AFRICA

THE QUALITY OF PROGRESS

edited by
E. Gyimah-Boadi

LYNNE
RIENNER
PUBLISHERS

BOULDER
LONDON

Published in the United States of America in 2004 by
Lynne Rienner Publishers, Inc.
1800 30th Street, Boulder, Colorado 80301
www.rienner.com

and in the United Kingdom by
Lynne Rienner Publishers, Inc.
3 Henrietta Street, Covent Garden, London WC2E 8LU

© 2004 by Lynne Rienner Publishers, Inc. All rights reserved

Library of Congress Cataloging-in-Publication Data
Democratic reform in Africa : the quality of progress /
  E. Gyimah-Boadi, editor.
    p. cm.
  Includes bibliographical references.
  ISBN 1-58826-221-9 (hardcover : alk. paper) — ISBN 1-58826-246-4
(pbk. : alk. paper)
  1. Democracy—Africa. 2. Democratization—Africa. 3. Africa—Politics
and government—1960–   4. Africa—Economic conditions—1960–
I. Gyimah-Boadi, Emmanuel.
JQ1879.A15D4618 2004
320.96—dc22   2003025709

British Cataloguing in Publication Data
A Cataloguing in Publication record for this book
is available from the British Library.

Printed and bound in the United States of America

The paper used in this publication meets the requirements
∞ of the American National Standard for Permanence of
Paper for Printed Library Materials Z39.48-1992.

5 4 3 2 1

Library
University of Texas
at San Antonio

Contents

v

Acknowledgments

This book was conceived at a workshop organized at the Calouste Gulbenkian Foundation in Lisbon, Portugal, in June 2000 on democracy and development in Africa. It owes its existence largely to Larry Diamond, who introduced the group of Africanist scholars whose work appears here to the Gulbenkian Foundation, and to the foundation's chairman at the time, the late Victor de Sá Machado, who decided to focus the attention of the foundation on Africa. Dr. de Sá Machado and his colleague, Rui Esquio, provided unstinting and generous support for this multinational project. In Ghana, the book benefited from the diligent editorial and secretarial support of Edem Selormey and Nana Adowaa Boateng at the Center for Democratic Development.

Introduction

E. Gyimah-Boadi

Auspicious political and economic developments in Africa in the 1990s no doubt provided much of the basis for the optimistic proclamations of an "African renaissance," "rebirth," and "second liberation" in the middle to latter part of that decade. Political reform and neoliberal economic reform had been considered in almost every African country by the end of the 1990s, representing a major reform moment for the continent. But protracted violent civil conflicts in Rwanda, the Democratic Republic of Congo, Burundi, and Sierra Leone, stalemate in democratic reforms in Cameroon, Guinea, and Niger throughout the decade, the eruption of an irredentist war between Ethiopia and Eritrea, and economic recession at the dawn the twenty-first century fueled dismissive assessments of Africa as a "hopeless continent,"[1] replacing much of the optimism over African prospects in the 1990s with "Afropessimism."

The surge in despair over African political and economic prospects in the beginning of the twenty-first century raises serious questions about the quality of those reforms. What has changed, and what is the quality of this change? To what extent have reforms diluted or improved the African political and economic status? Has liberalization fostered renewal or imperiled African social stability and cohesion and induced civil conflicts and wars? And what sorts of strategies are being mobilized to build institutions, reinstate the rule of law, and empower citizens along with sound economic policies and management? The authors of this book examine these and allied issues through thematic and country studies highlighting the progress and challenges of reform. The contributions come at a time when the discourse on Africa's institutional reform is mellowing from the shrill tone of optimism that hailed the maiden transitions to democracy and liberal economic systems decades ago.

The first six chapters of the book take up important thematic issues: political and economic reforms (by E. Gyimah-Boadi; Nicolas van de Walle;

and Michael Bratton and Robert Mattes), civil society (by E. Gyimah-Boadi), corruption control (by Sahr Kpundeh), and internal conflict (by Stephen John Stedman and Terence Lyons). Following the thematic chapters, the book offers four country studies: Botswana, Mozambique, Nigeria, and South Africa (by Patrick Molutsi, Brazão Mazula, Adigun Agbaje, and Steven Friedman respectively). The country studies capture the primary challenges to democracy and development in each country and highlight the interactions between the two phenomena.

Gyimah-Boadi's opening chapter and indeed many other chapters in the book suggest that the results of reforms, especially in the political realm, have been sometimes outstanding. Ruling parties have been pressured into sharing political space with rival parties and civic and interest groups. In addition, and impressively, notional commitment to democratic politics has grown in the period. African citizens appear to roundly reject nondemocratic forms of governance and express strong preference for democracy, as the rich empirical data from the Afrobarometer analyzed by Bratton and Mattes reveal. Indeed, decent dividends have been realized in some countries and in some sectors. Civil society has surged and become a key actor in reform processes in many countries (Gyimah-Boadi); major peace implementation projects centered on democratization have been initiated and are being sustained against all odds in South Africa and Mozambique (Stedman and Lyons; Friedman; Mazula); and interest in corruption control is growing (Kpundeh).

However, the chapters in this volume also confirm that success is not the only theme in the story of Africa's reform experience. Over a decade after the winds of economic and political reform came to town, the jury is still out on long-term prospects of the reform movement. What is certain is that the pace and quality of current progress have varied across states and from sector to sector. It is clear, especially from van de Walle's chapter, that progress on the economic and institutional reform front has been subpar and African countries are mired in "partial reform syndrome." Foreign exchange regimes may have been liberalized and import restrictions largely removed as import substitution advocates lose ground to the forces of globalization. But institutional renewal has continued to lag behind. Bureaucracies remain bloated, inefficient, and corrupt; legal infrastructure in most states is also still too weak to adequately supervise state business of resource extraction and allocation as well as safeguard property rights and manage the new challenges facing transforming economies; and privatization of state-owned industries is not yielding expected dividends and has largely served only to entrench avenues for rent-seeking. Above all, official corruption and neopatrimonialism persist, in spite of liberalization. It appears that largely externally driven neoliberal economic reforms are proving to have shallow roots in African countries. Not only is elite commitment to neoliberal economic reforms weak, but there is also deep popular opposition to key aspects of the reforms such as job retrenchment and removal of subsidy, as Bratton and Mattes indicate.

The chapters in this volume highlight the persistence of weak governance in spite of reforms. They also underscore the real threat that the failure of economic reform and continued weaknesses in governance poses to the medium- and long-term prospects for democracy and development on the continent. The chapter on Nigeria vividly captures the erosion of state capacity, confidence in state abilities, and perception of the value and viability of liberal democracy arising from persistent problems of economic mismanagement, bureaucratic ineptitude, institutional opacity, corruption, and social strife. The administration of Olusegun Obasanjo emerges as an example of a regime that assumed power with high approval rates (courtesy of the horrible records of departing regimes) but whose credibility is being dissipated quickly as persistent or worsening economic conditions sink mass confidence in state abilities. Botswana's impressive credentials as an African "success story" are tarnished by alarmingly high rates of HIV infection (about 40 percent of adults by mid-2002), lack of economic diversification, high unemployment, and persistent income inequalities. And while acknowledging the democratic and developmental progress in post-apartheid South Africa, Steven Friedman perceptively points to the danger posed to democratic consolidation in that country by the growing emphasis on enhancing government effectiveness, promoting economic growth, and delivering services and other managerial and technocratic aspects of governance.

The evidence presented in this volume indicates that African reform programs have only achieved less than optimum results, even by "African standards." Patronage, corruption, neopatrimonialism, and other "unprogressive" aspects of African politics persist. But the situation remains far from bleak, and there is strong evidence of progress. This books shows that these negative structures and practices have come under unprecedented pressure from the new forces unleashed by increasing openness, competitive elections, and citizen confidence as well as efficacy in demanding good governance in African political systems.

The lessons of this volume point to the various permutations for sustaining reform and highlight areas where opportunities for progress have been missed. Stedman and Lyons provide a poignant reminder of how reforms have presented both a risk of intensifying or provoking violent conflicts in Africa and an opportunity to foster peace. To be viable, reform movements must yield dividends not only in the sphere of governance but also in tangible socioeconomic terms. African states have taken only modest steps in this regard, but they are steps in the right direction. The responsibility for staying the course of "real" and "developmental" political and economic reforms remains largely in the African domestic realm. But as Larry Diamond points out in the concluding chapter, such reforms deserve and can be well served by external support and external encouragement that actively discriminate in favor of African governments that show a clear commitment to free, open, and accountable government.

Note

1. *The Economist,* May 13–19, 2000.

Africa:
The Quality of Political Reform

E. Gyimah-Boadi

Africa has been the scene of some of the most dramatic political changes since the fall of the Berlin Wall and the end of the Cold War. Within this period, some form of pluralism has been introduced or reintroduced in the politics of over thirty out of the fifty-three countries of Africa.[1] The period has also seen the departure from power of the older and first generation of political leaders (such as Julius Nyerere, Félix Houphouët-Boigny, Kamuzu Banda, and Mobutu Sese Seko) and the emergence of new leaders with no roots in the anticolonial movements (such as Jerry Rawlings, Blaise Compaoré, Yoweri Museveni, Yaya Jammeh, Meles Zenawi, and Isaias Aferworki) and leaders with no roots in the military (such as Frederick Chiluba, Bekuli Muluzi, Nicophere Soglo, Abudulaye Wade, Laurent Gbagbo, and John Kufuor). It also ushered in the spate of dramatic antiauthoritarian movements that opened the way for democratic transitions in the early 1990s. Since then, there has been talk of an African political renewal and political rebirth, even if it exists side by side with considerable political violence.[2] But how has African politics changed in past decade or so of democratization and redemocratization? What is the quality of the reforms and what are their implications for politics and governance in African countries? And what do these changes portend for governance in Africa and the future of African politics?

This chapter attempts to address these questions and examine the quality of political progress in Africa. I begin with an overview of the political changes centered around the democratic experiments of the past decade, highlighting important progress, setbacks, and outstanding problems. I follow this with an analysis of the changing nature of politics in Africa, focusing on the handling of old and new challenges such as state/nation building, HIV/AIDS, civil-military relations, and citizenship. The principal contention here is that, alongside the democratic failures, deficits, and dilemmas, there lies another reality: a positive reality of a modest but appreciable degree of improvements in the quality of governance in many African countries. In short, democratic reforms and political liberalization have helped to improve the quality of politics in Africa; they have helped to make the African state significantly less autocratic, even if it remains largely neopatrimonial.

Democratic Developments

Key developments in African politics within the last decade of redemocratization, or what others have dubbed a "second liberation," include the rather dramatic end of formal single-party rule and military dictatorship in many African countries and the emergence of multiparty politics and competitive elections after over thirty years of farcical elections with predetermined outcomes and, in many cases, no elections at all after the last one to dislodge colonial rule.[3] This trend in African political liberalization is best exemplified in the end of apartheid in South Africa in 1994 and the subsequent promulgation of a liberal democratic constitution in that country. It has manifested in the rapid expansion of Africa's thin list of "electoral" democracies from only a handful in 1989 to about eighteen in Freedom House's 2000 ranking.[4]

At the institutional level, democratic developments in Africa include the renewed interest in constitutionalism. Generally neglected in the era of single or no-party presidents, military rulers, authoritarian strongmen, and charismatic political leaders, constitutionalism came into vogue in the 1990s. The old illiberal postindependence constitutions (proscribing opposition parties, conferring permanent tenure on presidents, and suspending habeas corpus) have been jettisoned, sometimes with considerable drama as in the "national conferences" in francophone Africa,[5] and liberal democratic constitutions have been promulgated in a number of countries such as Benin, Mali, South Africa, Ghana, Malawi, and Nigeria.

The unprecedented surge in civil society, including the media, is another key development in the current African political renewal. Relaxation of media censorship has paved the way for the emergence of independent newspapers, radio, and television. It is noteworthy that Malawi obtained television capabilities only in early 1999, and that by December 2002 Ghana could boast having over forty independent FM radio and three television stations compared to none before the mid-1990s. Not only has the media sector flourished in the past decade or so, but it has also been playing a major role in the transition and posttransition phases of various countries. Independent radio, for instance, is widely credited with the relatively honest elections in Senegal and Ghana in 2000.[6]

In those countries where the transition to democracy is relatively advanced, civil societies are keeping themselves busy in the service of democratic consolidation. They are continuing their roles as watchdogs over the rights of citizens. African civil societies are gaining greater sophistication. Some are beginning to move away from the crude antigovernment and antistate confrontations of the early years and toward building consensus, fostering moderation, enriching the policy process, and other modes of constructive engagement. For instance, South Africa's nongovernmental organizations (NGOs) and "civvies" are reorienting themselves to play roles in the postapartheid social and economic reconstruction.

African civil societies have emerged as key forces in the political development of the continent. They are gaining in sophistication and building capacities. They are a major part of the change in the complexion and texture of internal African politics from unalloyed state hegemony and monopoly over power to the growing pluralism. Their growing self-awareness and determination to maintain their autonomy from both state and societal forces and to resist co-optation by government are but few of the indications that they will not disappear as their counterparts did in the aftermath of decolonization.

After years of marginalization, parliaments have begun to emerge as key institutions in African governance. Legislatures have been resurrected in many new African democracies, after a long hiatus. The legal and political status of parliaments have been substantially improved by virtue of the formal powers conferred on them in the new liberal constitutions. As products of relatively competitive multiparty elections and with stronger popular roots than their counterparts of yesteryear, the new parliaments seem to enjoy greater prestige. They also appear to exude greater confidence as key and formally autonomous bodies. Indeed, multiparty competition has made it possible for genuine parliamentary opposition to emerge; the popular image of African parliaments as rubber stamps for executive initiatives is gradually changing for the better. And there is some evidence of capacity building among African parliaments, especially in some of their specialized agencies.

Indeed, African parliaments are increasingly playing an important role in national policymaking and in the ratification of international agreements. They are attempting to enforce new and unprecedented levels of oversight over the executive and other branches of government. The Ugandan parliament, though organized on a no-party basis, has effectively confronted ministers on corruption. Zimbabwe's parliament, though dominated by the ruling Zimbabwe African National Union Patriotic Front, rejected tax proposals deemed unjust. The Public Accounts Committee of Ghana is gradually becoming a force in the auditing of the government account, building upon its success, especially in the second parliament, where the opposition parties had a strong presence.

More significant, the changes in the formal processes of African politics from mainly authoritarian systems to at least semidemocracies have also brought significant gains. Democratic developments in Africa and the new politics have offered growing opportunities and expanded capacities for popular mobilization in Africa. The new political developments have helped to expand political space and enhance opportunities for citizen participation in public affairs. As the scheduling of elections becomes increasingly regular, voting becomes increasingly meaningful and appears to be having a greater impact on the selection of representatives.[7] Moreover, opportunities for citizens to contribute to public debates through radio phone-ins and letters to newspapers have grown, even if they are largely confined to urban areas.

The recent political reforms have introduced some of the basic conditions for the establishment of rule-bound states and governments in Africa: reduction in official arbitrariness, expansion in the range of human rights enjoyed by Africans, increased spotlight on endemic public corruption, and above all, expanded opportunities for civic participation. For instance, habeas corpus laws have been revived, thereby circumscribing the power of governments to curtail the civil liberties and enjoyment of human rights by citizens. It is also noteworthy that constitutional documents are becoming the normative point of reference for African politicians, public and private institutions, and the public at large. The significant decline in the incidence of arbitrary confiscation of private property by African governments may be largely a reflection of the growing commitment to private sector–led development. But it also represents new levels of respect for property rights enshrined in new constitutions.

Moreover, human rights advocacy and elaboration of protection have been expanding beyond crucial but elite political rights (associational and media freedoms) to grassroots social issues such as customary bondage, child slavery, and female genital mutilation. For example, in Ghana the advent of constitutional and democratic rule in 1993 has seen an active campaign placing under the spotlight and targeting for abolition for the first time two of the most repressive and inhuman institutions—Trokosi and Witches Camps, rooted in traditional culture and religion and practiced over centuries. To be sure, Trokosi and Witches Camps have not been eliminated in Ghana, yet they are under assault, thanks largely to two pieces of legislation recently passed by Ghana's parliament, one criminalizing the practice of customary servitude and another protecting the rights of children, and joint monitoring by Ghana's independent human rights and administrative justice commission and a variety of civic and community-based organizations.[8]

Similarly, there has been a growing focus on the canker of corruption in the African public. The past decade has seen a significant growth in number and clout of independent anticorruption agencies. Nearly thirty ombudsman offices and anticorruption commissions have been established or reestablished, with many of them anchored in the new liberal constitutions;

there has been an explosion of independent media and the emergence of the subfield of investigative journalism (with icons such as Zambia's Fred Membe); and nonstate and civil society anticorruption pressure groups have proliferated, notably national chapters of Transparency International (the global corruption-fighting NGO). Some thirty African countries boast national chapters of Transparency International, in addition to other citizen watchdog groups.

Again, it is true that official anticorruption campaigns have been largely designed to secure public relations benefits and/or to expose misdeeds and mete out punishment to former ruling parties. The elected administration of Olusegun Obasanjo has been preoccupied with the recovery of assets looted under the previous military dictators and has canceled oil licensing contracts suspected to have been corruptly granted by the military government; the administration of John Kufuor in Ghana is trying officials of the erstwhile Rawlings government suspected to have misused or misappropriated state resources before a new "fast-track" court; and former Malian president Moussa Traoré and several of his associates in the previous government are standing trial for alleged economic crimes. In addition, despite serious legal and political complications, newly elected governments in South Africa, Senegal, and Ghana have enthusiastically embarked on "truth and reconciliation" projects in a bid to deter official impunity, foster transitional justice, and promote genuine national reconciliation.[9]

To be sure, enthusiasm for postincumbency accountability has not been matched by enthusiasm for institutional reforms that would prevent incumbents from looting assets. Typically, little attention has been paid to public sector and other institutional reforms that would promote transparency, streamline regulations, reduce official discretion, and prevent corruption. It may well be that the problem of corruption is too deep-rooted in African political cultures to be removed by popular pressure. But it is encouraging that the spotlight on the canker has been sustained, thanks largely to constitutional protection enjoyed by some public anticorruption agencies and expanding media and associational freedoms in the democratic era. It is most unlikely that the problem of corruption can escape the spotlight or be ignored without significant political costs. It is also noteworthy that corruption was a major campaign issue in elections in Benin (1996), Ghana (2000), and Zambia (2001).

Shortcomings and Failures

However, against this positive picture of African democratization and political progress lie many shortcomings, failures, and even reversals. First, the current wave of democratization has bypassed some of the large and important countries in Africa, notably Sudan and the Democratic Republic of Congo, Libya, and Morocco. Second, many of the continent's democratic transitions have been protracted and stalemated, as in Burkina Faso, Cameroon, Côte d'Ivoire, Togo, and arguably Zimbabwe. Worse still, the prospects of consolidation remain weak in all but a handful of African countries (South Africa, Botswana, Mauritius, Senegal, and possibly Benin and Ghana). In some cases, elected incumbents are busily engaged in a process of denaturing or rendering hollow the democratic content of the newly installed political systems.

It is also true that Africa's new legislatures remain deficient in physical infrastructure and basic equipment, as well as technocratic and analytical capabilities. Furthermore, constitution-making processes and amendments have not been sufficiently liberated from the hold of incumbent autocrats. It has been a source of dismay and frustration among many African democrats that some of those constitutions appear to have been designed to ensure that incumbent strongmen would retain most of their autocratic powers. Also, antidemocratic laws such as criminal and seditious libel legislation have been retained. Even in countries such as Benin, Zambia, and Nigeria, where democratic advances have been secured, the potential and real possibility for reversal cannot be ruled out. It is only in a few cases, such as Botswana, Mauritius, Senegal, and arguably South Africa and Ghana, that the prospects of democratic consolidation may be considered as better than fair.

Indeed, standards of democratic performance tend to be low, even in the best of cases. Newly installed democratic regimes in Africa insist on, and their publics largely tolerate, the self-serving excuse of newly installed democratic regimes that, being such, they only have to perform slightly better or no worse than a previous autocratic regime. The negative implications of such latitudes on African political practice are obvious: governments and public officials of what Richard Joseph refers to as Africa's newly "liberalized autocracies"[10] comply with the laws and constitution only in the most minimal way and in disregard of the democratic spirit in which such laws had been formulated; incumbent regimes use their majoritarian control over parliament to push through amendments and enact laws that contravene democratic norms, then rationalize such undemocratic actions on the untenable and backward grounds of consistency with what prevailed in a previous undemocratic regime. Thus, undemocratic amendments extending presidential terms beyond what was originally prescribed in the constitution in Namibia (under Sam Nujoma), Senegal (under Abdou Diouf), and Côte d'Ivoire (under Henri Konan Bedie), or those banning Alassane Quattara (Côte d'Ivoire) and Kenneth Kaunda (Zambia) from contesting in presidential elections in their respective countries, have been defended on the grounds that they were decided in popular legislatures.

Notwithstanding admirable African traditions of consensus building,[11] politics in democratizing Africa tends to be characterized by brinkmanship and "machismo." As an approach to national politics, it has fostered the practice of "crude majoritarianism," winner-takes-all, and neglect of minority interests instead of moderation, reciprocity, and give-and-take. It has also meant that in Africa, politicians, including self-professed democrats, regard concessions to their opponents or negotiated settlements or anything less than total defeat of opponents as tantamount to failure; and that incumbents are unwilling to ask for and to be granted forgiveness, setting the stage for messy transitional justice and national reconciliation projects.

Closely related to the "macho politics" is a gung ho attitude toward the exercise of discretionary power and display of gross impunity by power holders. In this "macho" mode, elected leaders have continued to behave brazenly by appointing hacks to key public and political offices, often as a reward for loyalty and sycophancy. This may largely reflect Africa's precolonial, colonial, and postcolonial authoritarian political heritage. But it is also a reflection of weak internalization of democratic values on the part of political actors as well as the entrenched patrimonialism in African politics, notwithstanding liberalization efforts. Evidently, the very low standards of authoritarian colonial and postcolonial rulers are still being used to judge the performance of African democrats, thereby threatening to consign African political practice to permanent mediocrity.

While elections are invested with unrealistic expectations and powers to resolve all sorts of problems (such as conflicts and resource distribution), they have tended to be rigged and bastardized. Incumbents are keen to rig elections to the extent that that they can get away with.[12] Indeed, in Africa's multiethnic and multinational states, elections have caused or aggravated social tensions and exacerbated fragility. Serious instability has followed multiparty polls in Burundi, Sierra Leone, Congo-Brazzaville, Togo, and recently Côte d'Ivoire. These may represent the worst examples of election-induced instability and violence, but in fact there are only a few African elections that have not been tainted by this problem.[13] Indeed, disappointment with electoral systems has been a source of some disaffection with politics in general and pervasive cynicism about the democratic political processes and associated institutions.

Furthermore, African democratic experiments have yet to marry the "representative" elements of liberal democratic politics with the "participatory" elements emphasized by mass-based all-inclusive single-party or "movement" systems.[14] The "movement" and single- or no-party systems may suffer from a politically unsustainable lack of engagement with the urban-based and educated/professional populace; and self-serving motives must be at work when urban-based political elites and technocrats make claims on behalf of peasants that are inherently difficult to verify or do not

provide adequate means of verification. But it is also true that Africa's multiparty systems also suffer from weak linkage with rural society (elitism)
and inadequate citizen participation in the period between general elections.

Altogether, African democratic systems suffer from weak party development.[15] For different reasons, both ruling and opposition political parties
are "plagued by weak organizations, low levels of institutionalization, and
weak links to the society they are supposed to represent."[16] Their former de
facto or de jure status as single parties shielded them from competition, and
their enjoyment of virtually unimpeded access to state resources, as incumbent "elected" governments, substantially guarantees electoral success and
political dominance. Furthermore, parties have not presented policy alternatives, and the few who have sought to win power by campaigning on
policy or an ideological platform have not been successful.[17] In addition,
internal democracy is weak. Typically, African parties are dominated by
personalities (as in Chiluba's Movement for Multiparty Democracy, Rawlings's National Democratic Congress, or Nujoma's South West African
People's Organization). Indeed, some of the most prominent parties in Africa,
such as South Africa's African National Congress and Ghana's National
Democratic Congress, exhibit Marxist-Leninist tendencies, placing a high
premium on party loyalty and frowning upon internal dissent. These failures (including the perceived failure of Western liberal democracy to foster participation and equity and the alleged tendency for multipartyism to
exacerbate ethnoregional conflicts) have led liberals and left-wing commentators to assume highly ambivalent positions about multiparty politics
and representative government and to sympathize with the no-party/"movement" system of Yoweri Museveni.[18]

These problems are serious enough. They are also for the most part a
reflection of the immaturity of African democratic systems and processes.
For instance, the tendency to appoint incompetent persons and political
hacks to key bureaucratic and technocratic positions reflects inadequate
institutionalization of meritocratic principles in new African democracies
(this aspect of politics in new African democracies recalls the flourishing of
the "spoils system" in U.S. politics and public service under President
Andrew Jackson in late nineteenth century).[19] Of course, rampant irregu-
larities in election and other problems of credibility reflect the weak development of the ballot tradition. Elections are essential to democracy, but two
or three elections do not make a democracy. It takes time to develop effective and credible electoral systems and enable them to deliver meaningful
outcomes. That recent elections in Africa are more competitive, credible,
and inclusive than those held under authoritarian single- and no-party systems of the past is yet another sign that African democratic systems can
overcome their teething problems.

At any rate, in Africa, we are looking largely at a process of transition
to democracy and not necessarily its consolidation. Indeed, African countries

have scarcely reached the threshold of democratic consolidation required in Huntington's minimalist formulation—several peaceful electoral turnovers and alternation of power; and certainly none has reached the higher threshold of having all key political actors accept democracy as "the only game in town" and in which a reversal is widely regarded as inconceivable.[20] Indeed, many of the problems listed above belong to a class of problems common to "immature" democracies, and there is nothing inherently African about them. Elements of this class of problems may even be found in some older democracies. At any rate, the shortcomings and limitations only underscore an important verity: no democracy is perfect. Democracy is never complete and needs to be improved and deepened even in the most mature contexts.[21]

Old and New Challenges

The record of democratic achievement may be mixed, but how are democratic reforms impacting African political practice? Specifically, how are they shaping national responses to critical challenges of development? A review of the manner in which African governments are handling old and new challenges provides at least an indirect assessment of improvements in the quality of politics and governance. The discussion focuses on four challenges: state and nation building, the HIV/AIDS pandemic, civil-military relations, and citizenship.

State and Nation Building

The period immediately after independence saw the initiation of state- and nation-building projects with much energy and enthusiasm and often under larger-than-life personalities such as Kwame Nkrumah, Mobutu Sese Seko, Jomo Kenyatta, Julius Nyerere, Ahmed Ben Bella, and Félix Houphouët-Boigny. These projects achieved some early successes: limited economic growth and distribution, urbanization, emergence of a national middle class, and above all, development of a sense of nationhood. But these early successes proved largely unsustainable. From the late 1970s and throughout most of the 1980s, economic crises and political decay had overwhelmed African state- and nation-building projects. Social and economic decay as well as political clientelism and patronage, at both the domestic and the international level, had become the hallmarks of African statehood and nationhood.[22] It is not surprising then that state and nation building has remained high on the African development agenda.

To be sure, state collapse has continued in a set of African countries (such as Angola, the Democratic Republic of Congo, Somalia, Sierra Leone, and arguably Liberia). In those countries, state sovereignty and the right to national self-determination are being contested, the nation-state is under siege, and the state- and nation-building project is in abeyance. Typically, domestic conflicts and civil wars in such countries have become increasingly privatized and deinternationalized, and the prospect for stability or peaceful conflict resolution appears to lie only in the eventual attrition or exhaustion of the warring groups. The Congo, Somalia, and Liberia and Sierra Leone represent the worst type of such countries, where the state has virtually disappeared and the strongmen/rogue leaders who control the various parts of the country rule largely by intimidation and force, plundering the land and acting in total disregard of international opinion and sanction.

However, state- and nation-building projects have resumed in many other African countries, such as Benin, Ethiopia, Eritrea, Ghana, Kenya, Malawi, Mali, Mozambique, Senegal, and Zambia. In these countries, an effective national leadership has been able to mobilize external and domestic resources to rehabilitate their economies and revive their "collapsing" states. Typically, they have embraced neoliberal economic reforms and thereby secured transnational resources and assistance (especially from the Bretton Woods institutions). While the process of economic recovery and state rehabilitation remains highly incomplete and long-term sustainability of renewed growth is uncertain in nearly all cases, these countries have gained international prestige as "emerging states" (i.e., states that have reversed decay and are on the rebound).[23] Such reforms have also brought significant revisions in the postindependence strategies of state and nation building.

Admittedly, state and nation building in some African countries has remained largely trapped in the old postcolonial and preliberalization mode. In Angola under José Eduardo dos Santos, the Congo (especially under Laurent Kabila Senior), Liberia under Charles Taylor, and arguably Sierra Leone under Ahmed Tejan Kabbah, the state has largely collapsed, but nominal governments with tenuous hold on power are fighting to maintain the status quo ante of an overcentralized political unit—with or without international support.[24] It is also true that rulers of African countries that have recently returned from the brink of state collapse and national disintegration (such as Museveni and Rawlings) appear to hanker after old-style politics and strategies of nation building; and many of Africa's so-called new leaders appear to seek a return to the status quo ante of the period immediately after independence—when state building was conducted principally through monopolization and centralization of power, when promises and perhaps delivery of economic development were traded for political quiescence and national loyalty secured largely through bribery, co-optation, and patronage, and when compliance was secured through fear and intimidation.

But for the most part, governments and rulers in the relatively successful African countries have wittingly or unwittingly revised their strategies of governance. To revive severely ailing economies and under intense external pressure, many African governments were compelled to beat a retreat from statist and economic nationalist policies and to embark on neoliberal economic reforms. Thus by the mid-1990s the majority of African countries were undergoing some form of World Bank and International Monetary Fund–supported structural adjustment with varying degrees of fidelity.[25] Tables 1.1 and 1.2 present a breakdown of African countries by "democratic credentials" and their human development indicators between 1970 and 2001/2002.

In addition, external and domestic pressures in the post–Cold War and postcommunist era have also brought impetus for reforms in domestic politics. The decision by the World Bank and other international financial institutions as well as bilateral donors in the late 1980s and early 1990s to emphasize governance as "the missing link in African development" (driving francophone leaders for example to issue the 1990 "Baule Declaration" by francophone leaders) signaled the end of support for dictators. It also strengthened the hand of domestic prodemocracy activists and fostered the liberalization of politics in many African countries, opening the way for the political reforms discussed above.[26] African governments had to concede a partial liberalization of internal politics, thereby opening up previously closed political systems and setting the stage for the democratic transitions of the early 1990s.

These post–Cold War neoliberal political and economic reforms have imposed severe restrictions on the use of postcolonial modes of state and nation building that feature economic nationalism, state-led economic development, centralization of political and administrative power, political patronage, emasculation of civil society, and indeed authoritarianism.[27] The loss of superpower support in the post–Cold War period, the strictures of neoliberal economic reforms (backed by stiff penalties for slippages), and state contraction (caused in part by economic retrenchment accompanying the neoliberal reforms) have caused a sharp reduction in patronage resources. At the same time, the political liberalization projects imposed by external and domestic forces have sharply diminished the ability of the same governments to rule by intimidation and force alone. State contraction has reduced opportunities to buy political compliance through patronage,[28] and internationally supervised and enforced political liberalization has restricted the use of political repression. African governments are compelled to find new ways of engaging with their citizens, private sectors, and civil societies. Thus, largely by default, a significant number of African governments effected an alteration in their strategies of mobilizing support, securing compliance, and pursuing national unity. Reliance on the techniques combining centralized control, repression, emasculation of civil society, and co-optation are gradually giving way to consultation, persuasion, bargaining, and even concessions to subnational autonomy.[29]

Table 1.1 Democratic Ranking and Human Development Indicators (1970–2001/2002)

	GNI per Capita					Human Development Index					Infant Mortality Rate (per 1,000)				
	1970	1980	1990	1999	2002	1970	1980	1990	1999	2001	1970	1980	1990	1999	2001
Democracies	220	1,235	2,580	3,390	3,415	n/a	0.61	0.69	0.67	0.70	75	51	37	38	49
Botswana	160	1,230	2,730	3,240	2,980	n/a	0.56	0.65	0.57	0.61	94.8	70.6	54.6	58.1	80
Mauritius	280	1,240	2,430	3,540	3,850	n/a	0.66	0.72	0.77	0.78	55.8	32	20.4	18.8	17
Recent Democracies	245	715	789	841	735	n/a	0.4	0.43	0.48	0.48	147	123	102	93	91
Benin	130	410	360	380	380	n/a	0.32	0.36	0.42	0.41	145.6	115.8	104.4	87.4	94
Ghana	250	430	390	400	270	n/a	0.47	0.51	0.55	0.57	111.6	93.6	66	57.1	57
Madagascar	170	450	240	250	240	n/a	0.43	0.43	0.47	0.47	153.2	119.2	103	90	84
Malawi	60	190	190	180	160	n/a	0.34	0.36	0.4	0.39	193.4	168.6	135.4	131.5	114
Mali	70	270	270	240	240	n/a	0.28	0.31	0.39	0.34	204.2	184.4	135.6	119.6	141
Mozambique	n/a	n/a	170	220	210	n/a	0.3	0.31	0.32	0.36	170.8	145.4	150.4	131.2	125
Namibia	n/a	n/a	1,800	1,890	1,780	n/a	n/a	n/a	0.61	0.63	117.8	89.6	63.8	63.3	55
South Africa	790	2,540	2,890	3,170	2,600	n/a	0.66	0.71	0.7	0.68	78.8	66.6	55	61.5	56
Semidemocracies	189	503	386	313	290	n/a	0.38	0.4	0.41	0.42	140	122	107	93	105
Central African Republic	110	340	470	290	260	n/a	0.35	0.37	0.38	0.36	139.2	117.2	102.2	95.7	115
Ethiopia	n/a	n/a	160	100	100	n/a	n/a	0.3	0.33	0.36	157.8	155	124.2	103.7	116
Gambia	110	380	320	330	280	n/a	n/a	n/a	0.41	0.46	184.6	159.2	108.6	74.8	91
Lesotho	110	490	590	550	470	n/a	0.52	0.57	0.54	0.51	134	118.6	101.6	91.7	91
Niger	160	440	310	190	170	n/a	0.25	0.26	0.28	0.29	170	135	150	116	156
Nigeria	170	710	270	260	290	n/a	0.39	0.43	0.46	0.46	139.4	99.4	86.4	83.3	110
Senegal	220	530	720	500	470	n/a	0.33	0.38	0.43	0.43	134.8	117.3	74	67.3	79
Tanzania	n/a	n/a	190	260	280	n/a	n/a	0.42	0.44	0.40	129	107.6	114.8	94.8	104
Uganda	n/a	n/a	340	320	250	n/a	n/a	0.39	0.44	0.49	108.8	115.5	104.4	88.3	79
Zambia	440	630	490	330	330	n/a	0.46	0.47	0.43	0.39	106	90.4	107.3	114	112
Autocracies	204	758	725	562	487	n/a	0.4	0.44	0.45	0.40	144	122	109	97	106
Angola	n/a	n/a	840	270	660	n/a	n/a	n/a	0.4	0.38	178.2	153.8	130.2	126.8	154
Burkina Faso	80	260	290	240	220	n/a	0.26	0.29	0.33	0.33	141.4	133.8	110.8	104.6	104
Burundi	70	220	220	120	100	n/a	0.31	0.34	0.31	0.34	138.2	121.6	118.8	104.8	114
Cameroon	160	650	970	600	560	n/a	0.46	0.51	0.51	0.50	125.8	102.6	81	77.2	96
Chad	140	240	280	210	220	n/a	0.26	0.32	0.37	0.38	171.2	123	118	100.8	117
Congo, Dem. Rep.	240	630	220	n/a	90	n/a	n/a	n/a	0.43	0.36	131	112.2	95.8	85	129
Congo, Rep.	230	880	980	550	700	n/a	0.47	0.51	0.51	0.50	101	89.2	88.2	89	81
Côte d'Ivoire	280	1,140	790	670	610	n/a	0.4	0.42	0.43	0.40	134.6	108.2	95	111.2	102
Equatorial Guinea	n/a	n/a	350	1,170	n/a	n/a	n/a	n/a	0.68	0.66	164	142.4	121	103.8	101
Eritrea	n/a	n/a	n/a	200	160	n/a	n/a	n/a	0.42	0.45	n/a	n/a	81.4	60.4	72
Gabon	650	4,750	4,750	3,300	3,120	n/a	n/a	n/a	0.64	0.65	138	116	96.2	84.1	60
Guinea	n/a	n/a	460	490	410	n/a	n/a	0.41	0.37	181	150.8	120.6	96	109
Kenya	130	450	370	360	360	n/a	0.49	0.53	0.51	0.49	102	74.8	61.8	76.5	78
Liberia	310	620	n/a	n/a	150	n/a	n/a	n/a	n/a	n/a	177.8	153.2	168	112.8	157
Mauritania	180	460	540	390	410	n/a	0.36	0.39	0.44	0.45	148	120.2	104.6	88	120
Rwanda	60	250	370	250	230	n/a	0.38	0.35	0.4	0.42	142.4	127.6	132.4	123.2	96
Sierra Leone	160	360	260	130	140	n/a	n/a	n/a	0.28	0.28	197.4	190.2	189	168	182
Somalia	90	110	120	n/a	n/a	n/a	n/a	n/a	n/a	n/a	159.8	145.4	151.8	120.7	133
Sudan	150	480	610	330	350	n/a	0.37	0.42	0.5	0.50	118	94	85.4	67.2	65
Togo	140	440	430	310	270	n/a	0.44	0.47	0.49	0.51	133.8	100	81	76.5	79
Zimbabwe	390	950	920	530	n/a	n/a	0.57	0.6	0.55	0.50	96.2	80	51.8	70.1	76
Sub-Saharan Africa	210	724	747	708	641	n/a	0.41	0.44	0.46	0.46	140	119	103	93	100

Sources: World Bank, *World Development Report 2003: Sustainable Development in a Dynamic World* (New York: Oxford University Press, 2003); World Bank, *World Development Report 2004: Making Services Work for Poor People* (New York: Oxford University Press, 2004); World Bank, *World Development Indicators* (http://devdata.worldbank.org.data-query) accessed January 22, 2004; UNDP, *Human Development Report: Millennium Development Goals: A Compact Among Nations to End Human Poverty* (New York, Oxford University Press, 2003).

Note: n/a = not available.

Table 1.2 Democratic Ranking and Human Development Indicators (1970–2002)

	Life Expectancy at Birth (years)					Literacy Rate, Adult Female					Literacy Rate, Adult				
	1970	1980	1990	1999	2002	1970	1980	1990	1999	2002	1970	1980	1990	1999	2002
Democracies	57	62	63	55	55	53	63	73	80	82	57	66	74	80	82
Botswana	51.9	58.1	56.8	39.4	38.1	47.3	59.0	70.2	78.9	81.5	46.3	57.6	68.2	76.4	78.9
Mauritius	62.4	66.0	69.6	70.8	72.5	57.7	67.2	75.1	80.8	82.3	67.0	74.1	79.9	84.2	85.3
Recent Democracies	45	49	52	49	46	25	33	42	52	52	33	42	51	60	61
Benin	44.0	48.4	51.9	53.1	52.7	5.7	10.3	16.0	23.6	25.5	10.8	18.4	28.1	39.0	39.8
Ghana	49.2	53.2	57.2	57.9	54.9	16.6	30.5	47.0	61.5	65.9	29.5	43.7	58.4	70.3	73.8
Madagascar	45.4	50.7	52.8	54.3	55.5	28.4	38.6	49.9	58.8	61.6	38.7	47.7	58.0	65.7	68.1
Malawi	40.4	44.2	44.6	39.5	37.5	19.6	27.3	36.2	45.3	48.7	37.9	44.5	51.8	59.2	61.8
Mali	37.9	42.1	45.0	42.6	40.9	3.2	8.5	18.7	32.7	17.3	6.3	13.7	25.6	39.8	27.2
Mozambique	41.9	44.0	43.4	43.1	41.1	6.6	11.2	18.4	27.9	31.4	16.6	24.5	33.5	43.2	46.5
Namibia	47.7	52.7	57.5	50.0	41.5	50.9	61.8	72.4	80.4	82.8	57.0	66.3	74.9	81.4	83.3
South Africa	53.1	57.1	61.9	48.5	46.5	68.0	74.8	80.3	84.2	85.3	69.8	76.2	81.3	84.9	86
Semidemocracies	43	46	49	46	45	19	27	37	47	50	26	35	44	53	56
Central African Republic	42.4	45.8	47.6	44.1	42.1	5.1	11.3	20.7	33.3	38.3	14.3	23.1	33.3	45.4	49.6
Ethiopia	40.1	42.0	45.0	42.4	42.1	6.0	11.3	20.4	31.8	33.8	12.6	19.6	28.1	37.4	41.5
Gambia	36.2	40.2	49.3	53.2	53.4	6.7	11.7	19.6	28.5	31.9	9.7	16.3	25.6	35.7	38.9
Lesotho	48.5	53.2	57.6	44.6	42.7	76.1	83.4	89.5	93.3	94.2	64.1	71.3	77.9	82.9	84.4
Niger	38.4	41.7	44.9	45.7	45.7	1.2	2.7	5.1	7.9	9.3	5.7	7.9	11.4	15.3	17.1
Nigeria	42.9	45.8	49.1	47.5	45.3	10.2	21.6	38.1	54.2	59.4	20.1	32.9	48.6	62.6	66.8
Senegal	40.9	45.3	49.5	52.4	52.3	6.1	11.7	18.6	26.7	29.7	14.7	21.0	28.3	36.4	39.3
Tanzania	45.5	50.0	50.1	45.0	43.1	20.2	34.3	51.5	65.7	69.2	37.2	50.1	63.8	74.7	77.1
Uganda	49.8	48.4	46.8	42.1	43.1	21.5	31.4	43.4	55.5	59.2	36.1	45.7	56.1	66.1	68.9
Zambia	46.5	50.5	49.1	38.5	36.9	32.3	46.6	58.7	70.2	73.8	47.8	58.6	68.1	77.2	79.9
Autocracies	43	46	48	47	49	15	25	38	50	53	27	37	49	59	62
Angola	37.2	41.2	45.5	46.5	46.7	n/a	n/a	n/a	n/a	n/a	n/a	n/a	n/a	n/a	n/a
Burkina Faso	39.8	44.0	45.4	44.9	42.9	2.2	4.3	8.0	13.3	15.8	7.0	10.8	16.4	23.0	39.8
Burundi	43.8	46.7	43.6	42.1	41.7	9.7	17.0	27.2	39.0	43.6	22.3	29.4	38.0	46.9	25.7
Cameroon	44.6	50.0	54.2	50.9	48.4	18.5	35.0	53.6	68.6	66.5	31.3	46.8	62.6	74.8	50.4
Chad	38.2	42.2	46.2	48.5	48.4	4.1	9.3	18.8	32.3	37.5	9.3	16.7	27.7	41.0	73.5
Congo, Dem. Rep.	45.2	49.0	51.5	45.8	45.3	11.3	20.7	34.4	48.7	53.5	22.6	33.9	47.6	60.3	64.1
Congo, Rep.	45.8	49.7	49.5	48.2	51.6	19.6	38.0	57.9	73.0	77.1	32.9	50.2	67.1	79.5	82.8
Côte d'Ivoire	44.5	49.3	49.8	46.1	45.2	6.4	13.0	23.5	37.2	39.7	15.8	23.7	33.8	45.7	50.7
Equatorial Guinea	39.9	43.2	47.2	50.6	51.7	27.7	43.8	61.1	73.3	76.9	46.0	60.0	73.3	82.2	84.8
Eritrea	43.5	44.3	48.9	50.4	51.1	10.3	17.7	28.0	39.4	46.6	24.7	33.0	43.0	52.7	57.6
Gabon	44.2	48.2	51.9	52.6	52.9	n/a	n/a	n/a	n/a	n/a	n/a	n/a	n/a	n/a	n/a
Guinea	36.7	39.8	43.7	46.4	46.2	n/a	n/a	n/a	n/a	n/a	n/a	n/a	n/a	n/a	n/a
Kenya	50.0	54.8	57.1	47.7	45.5	25.9	42.7	60.8	74.8	78.5	40.8	56.3	70.8	81.5	84.3
Liberia	46.5	50.7	45.1	47.2	47.1	7.3	13.6	23.2	36.9	39.3	18.4	27.8	39.4	53.2	55.9
Mauritania	42.6	46.7	50.7	53.9	51.0	16.9	21.0	26.4	31.4	31.3	26.0	30.7	36.4	41.6	41.2
Rwanda	44.4	45.8	40.2	40.0	39.8	16.3	28.7	43.9	59.1	63.4	27.9	39.9	53.3	65.8	69.2
Sierra Leone	34.4	35.3	35.2	37.4	37.4	n/a	n/a	n/a	n/a	n/a	n/a	n/a	n/a	n/a	n/a
Somalia	40.2	42.6	41.6	47.8	47.4	n/a	n/a	n/a	n/a	n/a	n/a	n/a	n/a	n/a	n/a
Sudan	42.9	48.2	51.0	55.5	58.4	10.3	19.0	31.8	44.9	49.1	25.5	34.9	46.3	56.9	59.9
Togo	44.5	49.3	50.5	49.1	49.6	12.5	19.5	28.9	39.6	45.4	26.2	35.5	46.0	56.3	59.6
Zimbabwe	50.5	54.9	56.2	40.4	39.0	48.9	62.4	74.9	83.8	86.3	57.5	70.0	80.7	88.0	90
Sub-Saharan Africa	44	48	50	48	47	21	30	40	51	54	30	39	50	59	61

Sources: World Bank, *World Development Report 2003: Sustainable Development in a Dynamic World* (New York: Oxford University Press, 2003); World Bank, *World Development Report 2004: Making Services Work for Poor People* (New York: Oxford University Press, 2004); World Bank, *World Development Indicators* (http://devdata.worldbank.org.data-query) accessed January 22, 2004; UNDP, *Human Development Report: Millennium Development Goals: A Compact Among Nations to End Human Poverty* (New York, Oxford University Press, 2003).

Note: n/a = not available.

The HIV/AIDS Pandemic

Undoubtedly, the HIV/AIDS pandemic presents the greatest threat to African survival in the twenty-first century. With over 17 million Africans reportedly killed by the disease in the past twenty years, rising mortality rates, declining life expectancy, rising disability, and depletion in the scarce ranks of teachers, bureaucrats, and businesspeople, HIV/AIDS threatens to overwhelm already-fragile national health systems and to wipe out the limited gains made in African social and economic development over the past four decades.

The HIV/AIDS crisis underlines severe deficiencies in the past and present of African political systems and the generally low quality of governance. Entrenched authoritarianism in African politics may not have had anything to do with the emergence of the crisis, but it certainly contributed to it. First, the prevalence of nontransparency in African political culture fostered the spread of the disease: it was dismissed as likely to disappear, limited elite discussions of the problem misguidedly focused on fighting allegations that AIDS originated from Africa, and there was a prolonged tendency to deny the reality of AIDS and to regard it as "non-African." Second, until recently, African governments tended to refuse to reveal the data of AIDS infection rates in their respective countries—partly for fear of losing tourist dollars and partly to protect national pride. And third, the prevailing culture of the "lame leviathan" (which left the government alone to deal with the problem), combined with nontransparency and denial, all but guaranteed that policymakers would sidestep the crisis. Moreover, the widespread desperation engendered by the AIDS crisis has sometimes aroused authoritarian reflexes, leading to the adoption of inhuman policies and untenable prohibitions such as mandatory AIDS tests, ostracism of people infected with HIV/AIDS, or outright bans on teenage sex.[30]

The HIV/AIDS crisis also underlines the shortcomings of African democratization and the low quality of governance even in the democratizing states, even if the epidemiological evidence and the experience of the few cases of relative success in combating the scourge contradict any claims in favor of authoritarian solutions. And while there may be little or no real correlation between HIV/AIDS and democratic development, the persistence of the pandemic poses a grave threat to the validity of African democratic experiments, especially since the period of African democratization has coincided somewhat with the onset of the AIDS pandemic. Moreover, liberal democratic Botswana and South Africa count among the countries in Africa with the highest rate of prevalence of the disease, while Uganda, a country whose strongman has managed to resist domestic and external pressure for full multiparty democracy, has won universal plaudits for its success in reducing the adult infection rate of AIDS from over 30 percent in 1983 to only 5 percent in 2001. Indeed, Botswana has the highest adult infection rate, 38.8 percent, and 20.1 percent of the adult population of South Africa were living with HIV/AIDS in 2001. At the very least, the HIV/AIDS pandemic highlights the weak quality of governance in Africa, including in its democratizing nations: the persistence of a culture of nontransparency, weak political responsiveness and accountability, and misplaced priorities. The AIDS crisis underscores the fact that democratic politics has not sufficiently translated into enhanced transparency in certain areas of African life such as death. Cultural norms continue to foster nontransparency and denial of the AIDS pandemic and help to inhibit the search for credible solutions even in democratizing states. It is instructive to note that twenty-nine members of parliament reportedly died of AIDS in the second parliament of Malawi, with three dying between June and August 2000. But in apparent conformity with prevailing cultural norms, the cause of death was never announced. The culture of secrecy and nondisclosure surrounding the death of notables in Malawi as in many other African countries has also meant that public awareness of the disease and its main causes, as well as the requisite behavioral modification to avoid it, remains low, and the urgency that must be attached to mobilizing resources for combating the epidemic is lost or poorly informed.

However, democratic politics is providing some of the political tools necessary for addressing the problem in a sustained manner. Enlightened and committed political leadership remains a sine qua non for putting the spotlight on HIV/AIDS, but openness is essential for sustaining public education on its nature, causes, and consequences, as well as preventive mechanisms. Africa's liberalized political setting is helping to break the culture of silence around the disease, promoting information flow on the subject and making it a topic for serious discussion in the media, in classrooms, and in places of worship. Similarly, the reduction in political monopoly is also proving helpful to combating the HIV/AIDS pandemic. Civil society and NGO mobilization and enhanced media involvement are augmenting scarce official resources and supplementing the efforts of government to combat the spread of AIDS and provide support for those already infected with the virus. And growing national and international effort to foster the political and economic empowerment of women is helping to attenuate the social, economic, and political pathologies that render them vulnerable to HIV/AIDS infection, such as rape, exploitation, and other forms of sexual violence and weak control over their reproductive rights. Increasing popular mobilization in politically liberalized African countries against misrule (which manifests in involvement in senseless wars, rampant looting of state assets, and misallocation of scarce resources) should in turn help to reduce poverty, stem migration, and therefore curtail the socioeconomic deficiencies that underlie the overexposure of young men and women to sexual exploitation and HIV/AIDS.[31] Altogether, it appears that the prospects of effective prevention and control of the spread of the disease are better now than ever.

Civil-Military Relations

There has been significant change in the pattern of militarization of African political processes in the past decade: a marked reduction in the incidence of taking political power by coup d'etat. Indeed, military governments have been removed in Mali, the Central African Republic, Benin, the Congo, Ghana, Mauritania, Niger, and Burundi. African rulers have had to shed their preferred sartorial style; the army khaki has given way to the attire of civilian.

However, many important setbacks have been experienced. The military has remained active in African political processes, intervening in some instances (in Burundi in 1993, Lesotho in 1994, Guinea in 1996, the Central African Republic in 1996, Côte d'Ivoire in 1999) to destabilize or hobble democratization. Typically, incumbent military rulers have hijacked democratization processes, crudely "self-civilianized" by presenting themselves as candidates in elections, and retained power by rigging elections (Togo's General Gnassingbe Eyadema, Ghana's Flight Lieutenant Jerry Rawlings, Burkina Faso's Captain Blaise Compaoré, Gambia's Major Yaya Jammeh, Uganda's Museveni, Guinea's General Lansana Conté, etc.). Moreover, Africa's new democracies are confronted with severe challenges of democratizing civil-military relations: demobilizing and disarming armed paramilitary and security forces, restoring professional discipline in armies that have been thoroughly politicized, rationalizing the costs of defense and national security and subjecting them to democratic control—in short, bringing the military-security apparatus under effective democratic control.[32]

At the same time, progress made in racial integration of the South African Defense Force, the elaboration of democratic civil-military relations in Mali and increasingly in Ghana, the emergence of civil society–based security sector specialists and organizations such as the Institute for Security Studies (South Africa) and the think tank African Security Dialogue and Research (Ghana), and increasing dialogue between national democratic institutions and security establishments[33] point to prospects to institutionalize democratic civil-military relations in some African countries. In Ghana for instance, a 2000 study on the state of civil-military relations revealed that, in general, civilians appreciate the military for protecting the territorial integrity of the country and for ensuring peace and security: 84 percent approved of a standing army, 69 percent were impressed with the character of a Ghanaian soldier, and 90 percent approved of the military's role in international peacekeeping. This goes to show that in recent times more progress is being made to promote healthy civil-military relations in some countries in Africa.[34]

Citizenship

Two notions of citizenship have competed for attention in postcolonial Africa: national and ethnic citizenship. The latter, defined around the ethnic group and demanding loyalty to the ethnic community and kin-based groups, has competed with the former, defined around the relatively more recent and often multiethnically composed nation-state.[35] It is true that the anticolonial struggles and energetic and sometimes exotic efforts at nation building embarked upon by the leaders of newly independent African countries had helped to forge a sense of nationhood where none existed before: national citizenship had begun to displace the status quo of ethnic citizenship in the putative multinational and multiethnic nations. However, C. R. D. Halitsi's notion of "dual citizenship" in South Africa has also been highly applicable to racially homogeneous but ethnically divided sub-Saharan Africa.[36] In addition, ethnic citizenship surged in the late 1970s and 1980s—largely in response to the growing predation and improvidence of the state and the abusiveness of its rulers. In the worst cases, ethnonationalist challenges were mounted against the putative multinational state; irredentist and secessionist movements emerged in the Congo, Liberia, Somalia, and Sierra Leone, among others.[37]

But a new and more nationally oriented citizenship has begun to emerge in Africa since the early 1990s. This is partly the outcome of cross-ethnic and transclass alliances built around the antiauthoritarian struggles and the sense of national pride that has accompanied success in pushing through democratic transitions. Recent experiences suggest that democratic politics has not always abated ethnic tensions in Africa and may even have aggravated the problem in some cases, notably Côte d'Ivoire. At the same time, there is evidence that a new sense of national and civic (as opposed to ethnic) citizenship has also emerged—largely as an outcome of deliberate political and constitutional arrangements that implicitly or explicitly recognize the validity of ethnic and community solidarities and citizenship and provide protections for "minority" rights, as in ethnic federalism in Ethiopia and Eritrea,[38] power sharing and semiprovincial autonomy in South Africa,[39] and Turaeg rights in Mali.[40] This in turn is helping to foster the gradual but perceptible development of closer and noncorporatist partnership across the state, the private sector, and civil society in Africa.[41]

Conclusion

Before the recent wave of democratic and other political reforms, African states could be aptly described as "patrimonial autocratic."[42] How much of this has changed in nearly a decade of liberalization? And what does the future of politics and governance in Africa look like?

I concede that African democratization and political reforms remain highly incomplete. African democracies continue to face the challenge of intense political conflict and entrenched corruption. They have yet to entrench healthy competition, moderate crude "majoritarianism," strengthen the protection of ethnic, religious, and other minorities, and promote inclusive civic participation. Indeed, democratization has yet to bring vast improvements in the quality of governance in Africa. Institutions of democratic governance are weak, and a political culture of democracy has yet to be fully established and institutionalized.

Above all, neopatrimonialism and patronage retain a strong hold on African politics, notwithstanding neoliberal and other reforms. Indeed, neopatrimonialism remains largely entrenched in the politics of both semi-democratic and semiauthoritarian African states.[43] Its inherently self-destructive concomitants such as corruption, rent-seeking behavior, and opposition to economic and administrative rationalization among ruling elites remain largely entrenched.[44] In addition, many of Africa's new leaders (democratic or not) continue to be surrounded by assorted "big men." For example, in Uganda, President Museveni's brother has been a key figure in that country's command in the war in the Democratic Republic of Congo, President Compaoré's brother is the head of the dreaded national security system in Burkina Faso, and President Rawlings's wife held sway in Ghanaian politics throughout her husband's tenure in office as an elected leader. Indeed, the prevailing understanding of how political authority is acquired or exercised remains largely colored by the legacy of neopatrimonial regimes that dominated postindependence governance in most African countries: more or less hereditary rulers rule until they die or are overthrown unconstitutionally; public and political office appears to serve a deeper "functional" (rentier?) purpose for incumbents who resist constitutional term limits, retirement, and voluntary resignation or regard such moves as synonymous with economic suicide and loss of ability to play patron in a patrimonial political culture.[45]

Nevertheless, there have been significant improvements in the quality of politics in Africa. The democratic and other political reforms of the past decade have opened up new possibilities for improved governance in Africa. They have helped to foster greater respect for or at least interest in the rule of law and constitutional rule, greater respect for human rights, institutional accountability, as well as interest in controlling public corruption. These reforms are helping to put in place the sort of facilities that Africa needs for good governance and sustained development.

Indeed, democratic reforms have opened up space for the discussion of issues long treated as taboo in Africa—such as female genital mutilation and other forms of gross abuse of the human rights of women and campaigns waged against them. It is also noteworthy that African countries such as Senegal, Uganda, and Ghana have passed laws banning female genital mutilation, in spite of entrenched opposition based on culture and religion. Indeed, the credit for what Aili Tripp describes as the "unprecedented political progress" achieved by African women in the past ten years must almost certainly go to these political reforms.[46]

Democratic and other political reforms have also opened the way for a new citizen to evolve in Africa who is neither exclusively ethnic nor monolithically national, and active rather than passive. Thanks to the liberating experience of the prodemocracy struggles and empowerment from the new liberal constitutions, these citizens are increasingly gaining a sense of political efficacy that was hitherto nonexistent. Moreover, they are quickly acquiring a sense of self-confidence, especially in their ability to countervail the power of the gun with mass protests and the power of the "thumb." Above all, the reforms have created greater opportunities for popular mobilization and hence have given greater voice to African publics. In a broader sense, they betoken the erosion of authoritarianism on the continent and prospects for improvements in the quality of governance.

To be sure, the institutions of democracy may be fragile and the process of their institutionalization is incomplete. But their simultaneous emergence in the 1990s, in addition to the increasing support they are attracting from bilateral and multilateral donors, including the international financial institutions, represents an unprecedented assault of a critical mass of institutions and process on entrenched authoritarianism, official arbitrariness, corruption, and other manifestations of neopatrimonial rule. Indeed, some of the changes represent a significant departure from patterns and processes that have characterized politics in postcolonial Africa. As African political systems become increasingly open, elections and other processes of accountability become less farcical, and citizens become increasingly forceful in demanding effective performance from their governments, even the practices of neopatrimonialism, patronage, and corruption cannot escape politically sustainable public censure.

From summits of heads of state and congresses of trades unions, African political elites have begun to express a formal commitment to democratic governance. These resolutions and protocols rejecting authoritarian rule and affirming democratic governance by the Organization of African Unity and its successor, the African Union, the Economic Community of West African States, the Southern African Development Community, and the New Partnership for African Development may be largely intended as rhetorical gestures.[47] But they also present great opportunities for mounting popular vigilance in support of democratic development or against democratic reversals. Altogether, they betoken growing recognition on the continent that democratization presents some of the crucial tools needed for addressing the challenges of development facing Africans and for creating the political and social conditions for sustained development.

Notes

1. Highly useful overviews and essays are available in Diamond and Plattner, *Democratization in Africa;* Joseph, *State, Conflict, and Democracy in Africa;* Mukum and Ihonvbere, *Multi-Party Democracy and Political Change;* Bratton and van de Walle, *Democratic Experiments in Africa;* and Diamond, *Prospects for Democratic Development in Africa.*

2. See Joseph, "Africa"; and Joseph, "State, Conflict, and Democracy in Africa."

3: This section draws heavily from Gyimah-Boadi, "The Rebirth of African Liberalism."

4. See Freedom House, *Freedom in the World 2000–2001.*

5. For an excellent discussion of the phenomenon of sovereign national conferences in francophone Africa in the late 1980s and early 1990s, see Robinson, "The National Conference Phenomenon."

6. For discussions of the political progress in Ghana's December 2000 polls, highlighting the contributions of the media, see Gyimah-Boadi, "Peaceful Political Turnover in Ghana." On francophone Africa, see Fumonyoh, "Democratization in Fits and Starts."

7. It is hardly surprising that elections in Ghana in 1996 were an improvement over those of 1992; presidential elections in Senegal and Ghana in March and December 2000 respectively had been keenly contested and produced alternation of power; and for all the monopoly it enjoys, the government of Zimbabwe lost a referendum in February 2000, and much of its control over parliament in the June 2000 polls. On Senegal, see Galvan, "Political Turnover and Social Change"; on Ghana, see Gyimah-Boadi, "Peaceful Political Turnover"; and on Zimbabwe, see Sithole, "Fighting Authoritarianism."

8 Aili Tripp chronicles the progress made by African women in the current political dispensation in "New Political Activism in Africa." See also Gyimah-Boadi, "Debating Democracy Assistance."

9. South African–style truth and reconciliation commissions have been or are being established in Nigeria, Ghana, and Sierra Leone.

10. Joseph, "State, Conflict, and Democracy in Africa."

11. For a detailed discussion of the consensual basis of politics in traditional African political systems, see Wiredu, "Democracy and Consensus in Traditional Politics"; and Owusu, "Democracy and Africa."

12. The surprising ability of African autocratic rulers to survive democratic transitions in the early 1990s is discussed in Baker, "The Class of 1990." See also Bratton and van de Walle, *Democratic Experiments in Africa.*

13. See Sisk and Reynolds, *Elections and Conflict Management in Africa.* See also Zartman, *Governance as Conflict Management.*

14. Alternative bottom-up and generally direct approaches to democracy in Africa have been advocated by leading scholars such as Issa Shivji in "The Democracy Debate in Africa"; Claude Ake in *Democratization of Disempowerment in Africa* and *Democracy and Development in Africa;* Mahmood Mamdani in *Citizen and Subject;* and John Saul in "For Fear of Being Condemned."

15. Weak party development tops Celestin Monga's list of "eight problems with African politics" in a work of the same name.

16. Van de Walle and Butler, "Political Parties and Party Systems," p. 15.

17. Ibid.

18. Many scholars remain more or less skeptical of liberal democracy projects in Africa. Among them are Thandika Mkandawire in "Crisis Management"; John Saul in "For Fear of Being Condemned"; Celestin Monga in "Eight Problems with African Politics"; Colin Leys in "Development Theory and Africa's Future"; Marina Ottaway in "African Democratization and the Leninist Option"; Mahmood Mamdani in *Citizen and Subject;* and Claude Ake in *Democracy and Development in Africa* and *Rethinking African Democracy.*

19. Frederick Mosher discusses this in context of the evolution of the principles of U.S. public administration. Mosher, *Democracy and the Public Service.*

20. According to Samuel Huntington, "a democracy may be viewed as consolidated if the party or group that takes power in the initial election at the time of transition (from authoritarianism or military rule to democracy loses a subsequent election and turns over power to those winners, and if (they) then peacefully turn over power to the winners of a later election." Huntington, *The Third Wave,* pp. 266–267. For a higher threshold for the attainment of democratic consolidation, see Linz and Stepan, *Problems of Democratic Transition and Consolidation.* For an exhaustive discussion of the concept of democratic consolidation, see Diamond, *Developing Democracy.*

21. Highly cogent critiques of democracy can be found in Sklar, "Developmental Democracy"; Dunn, *Democracy;* Schmitter, "Dangers and Dilemmas of Democracy"; and Saul, "For Fear of Being Condemned."

22. The parlous economic, social, and political conditions of the period are vividly captured in essays in Rothchild and Chazan, *The Precarious Balance;* and in Ergas, *The African State in Transition.*

23. Stories of Ghana and Uganda as examples of economic reform success are told in several volumes. On Ghana, see Rothchild, *Ghana;* and Herbst, *The Politics of Reform.* On Uganda, see Brett, *Providing for the Rural Poor;* Khadiagala, "State Collapse and Reconstruction"; and Sharer, De Zoysa, and McDonald, *Uganda.*

24. These are the countries that really fit the apocalyptic and dismissive descriptions of unreconstructed states and rulers in Africa found in Kaplan, "Was Democracy Just a Moment?" Ayittey, *Africa in Chaos;* and Bayart, Ellis and Hibou, *The Criminalization of the State.*

25. See Mkandawire and Soludo, *Our Continent, Our Future;* Lipumba, *Africa Beyond Adjustment;* Cornia, van der Hoeven, and Mkandawire, *Africa's Economic Recovery;* and World Bank, *Adjustment in Africa.*

26. On the external push for African and Third World good governance and democratization, see Mkandawire, "Crisis Management"; Mkandawire and Soludo, *Our Continent, Our Future;* Leftwich, "Governance, Democracy, and Development"; Clapham (1993); Harsch, "Democratization in Africa"; and essays in Widner, *Economic Change and Political Liberalization.*

27. On strategies and processes of state and nation building in postcolonial Africa, see Chazan et al., *Politics and Society in Contemporary Africa;* Forrest,

"The Quest for State 'Hardness' in Africa"; Wunsch and Olowu, *The Failure of the Centralized State;* essays in Ergas, *The African State in Transition;* and essays in Chabal, *Political Domination in Africa.* See also Nyangor'o and Shaw, *Corporatism in Africa.*

28. Jeffrey Herbst, in "The Structural Adjustment of Politics in Africa," undertakes a perceptive analysis of the pressures that neoliberal economic reforms impose on the status quo of African neopatrimonial politics. See also essays in Mkandawire and Olukoshi, *Between Liberalization and Oppression.*

29. See Rothchild, "Reconfiguring State-Ethnic Relations in Africa."

30. The decree in 2000 by the Swazi monarch ordering maidens in that kingdom to wear tassels and banning them from having sex before the age of twenty is another example, ludicrous as it is, of authoritarian solutions to the crisis.

31. Helen Epstein, in "AIDS: The Lessons of Uganda" and Kader Asmal and Wilmot James, in "AIDS: Losing 'The New Struggle'?" provide useful insights into the political economy and epidemiology of HIV/AIDS and its control.

32. Hutchful, "Demilitarizing the Political Process in Africa"; and Luckham, "The Dilemmas of Military Disengagement in Africa."

33. Democratization of civil-military relations in Ghana has included educational and training programs led by independent think tanks such as African Security Dialogue and Research and the Ghana Center for Democratic Development. They were aimed at enhancing the sector's professionalism and appreciation of constitutional rule.

34. See Baffour Agyeman-Duah, "Civil-Military Relations."

35. See Peter Ekeh's seminal article "Colonialism and the Two Publics in Africa."

36. Halisi, "Citizenship and Populism in the New South Africa."

37. Chazan and Azarya describe this as "citizen disengagement from the state"; see their article "Disengagement from the State in Africa." See also Rothchild and Chazan, *The Precarious Balance;* and especially Chazan, "Patterns of State-Society Incorporation and Disengagement," pp. 121–148; and Ayoade, "States Without Citizens," pp. 100–120.

38. See Cohen, *Ethnic Federalism in Ethiopia;* and, for less sanguine views, see Haile, "The New Ethiopian Constitution." See also Ottaway, *Democratization and Ethnic Nationalism;* Ottaway, "Democratization in Collapsed States"; and Mengisteab, "Democratization and State Building in Africa."

39. On power sharing in South Africa, see Lijphart, "South African Democracy."

40. See Sklar, "Finding Peace Through Democracy."

41. For an insightful discussion of citizenship in an African society, see Ndegwa, "Citizenship and Ethnicity." See also Mamdani, *Citizen and Subject;* and, for a recent general discussion, Hadenius, *Institutions and Democratic Citizenship.*

42. See Young, "The Third Wave of Democratization in Africa."

43. President Gnassingbe Eyadema, Africa's longest-serving autocrat, continues to survive on a "cult of personality" that describes him as a "force of nature," with an iron grip over an army in which 90 percent of the officer corps and 70 percent of soldiers are ethnic kinsmen (from his native Kabiye group) and two of his sons occupy key senior positions, and with repression reportedly learned largely from the North Koreans.

44. On the persistence of patrimonialism and clientelism in spite of liberalization in Africa, see Sandbrook and Oelbaum, *Reforming the Political Kingdom;* and Tangri, *The Politics of Patronage in Africa.*

45. The hold that patronage has on political processes in Africa was blatantly demonstrated when about half the members of the Ivorian National Assembly broke

ranks with the Democratic Party of Côte d'Ivoire (the former ruling party) and declared their support for the candidacy of military ruler General Robert Guei ahead of the December 2000 presidential elections—on the patently self-serving grounds that Côte d'Ivoire did not have a "culture of opposition" and that these assembly members had to stay close to power in order to influence policy.

46. Aili Mari Tripp's positive assessment of progress concludes thus: "In the past ten years, African women have made unprecedented political progress. Although daunting obstacles to their advancement remain, if the 1990s are any indication, the decade ahead is certain to see even greater political involvement on the part of women." See Tripp, "New Political Activism in Africa," p. 154.

47. The latest and clearest expression of commitment to democratic governance on the part of African leaders is found in the New African Initiative (July 2001), which merges the Millennium African Recovery Program and the Omega Plan. The principles of democracy, transparency, accountability, integrity, respect for human rights, and the promotion of the rule of law are enshrined in the initiative. The Algiers Declaration (signed at the thirty-fifth annual ordinary summit of the Organization of African Unity heads of state in 1999) specifically commits the organization to exclude new coup-makers from their meetings; the Bamako Declaration (2000) commits its francophone member nations to a path of democratic governance. The New Partnership for African Development is even more explicit in its adoption of the principles and practices of democratic governance as the cornerstone for African economic and social progress.

Economic Reform:
Patterns and Constraints

Nicolas van de Walle

At the dawn of the twenty-first century, most of sub-Saharan Africa remains mired in economic crisis despite two decades of donor-sponsored reform efforts. A handful of countries like Botswana and Mauritius are prospering, but most economies in the region have not overcome the fiscal and balance of payments deficits that have undermined economic stability since the first oil crisis. The severity of these deficits has waxed and waned over the years, but they have never completely disappeared. Meanwhile, many if not most Africans are poorer today than they were twenty years ago.

An improvement in economic indicators throughout Africa in the mid-1990s led some observers to argue that the region had finally solved its economic conundrums and could now expect sustained economic growth.[1] Conditions appeared to be favorable: several civil wars had ended and a wave of democratization had brought to power a number of new leaders who appeared resolved to address economic ills. Between 1994 and 1997, per capita growth averaged 1.2 percent a year, the fastest rate in a generation. Growth was also spread across an unusually large number of states, with all but four economies in the region recording positive growth rates in 1996. Inevitably, just as talk of an "African renaissance" was beginning to make the rounds, a sharp slowdown of the world economy followed the East Asian financial crisis, which began in July 1997, and a number of African countries suffered sharp terms of trade shocks the following year.[2] Deadly civil wars were reactivated in the Horn of Africa or in Angola, while new conflicts emerged in Central Africa. Investors closed their wallets and, by 1998, growth appeared to be slowing down again, although some countries continued to enjoy healthy growth. While the International Monetary Fund (IMF) continued to be relatively optimistic, forecasting 1.3 percent growth in per capita gross domestic product (GDP) for the region in 1998, the World Bank was more gloomy, predicting –0.5 percent growth in 1998 and only 0.4 percent in 1999.

The growth spurt may turn out to be a harbinger of things to come, but there have been several previous short bursts of growth in the past that then only sputtered out. The bottom line at the start of the twenty-first century is that the African region continues to be outperformed by all other regions and that efforts to redress this poor performance since 1980 have not been successful. Other regions of the developing world have demonstrated a much greater ability to manage their economic affairs ever since the various shocks to the world economy in the early 1970s ended the Bretton Woods system of fixed exchange rates and introduced a new volatility into the world economy.

Africa's disappointing economic performance has provided the context for the region's political debacles of the last decade. To be sure, it is even harder to generalize about the region's political situation than its economic one. On the one hand, the region has been beset by state collapse and civil war; even as the 1990s saw the end of conflicts in Ethiopia and Mozambique, long-standing civil wars in Angola and Sudan proved depressingly intractable. New conflicts have also emerged in Congo/Zaire, Sierra Leone, and Liberia. In each case, the dismal economic performance of the previous two decades could not be directly blamed for the outbreak of violence, but a decline of state capacity, the lamentable state of public infrastructure, and a rise in corruption have usually been part of the state collapse equation. On the other hand, the region witnessed a major wave of democratization in the early 1990s, which saw the fall of a dozen authoritarian systems and the more limited liberalization of a number of others.[3] While the exercise of democracy has usually fallen well short of liberal ideals in the democracies that have emerged,[4] they nonetheless constitute a factor of hope for a region in desperate need of positive change. Most observers suggest, moreover, that the prospects for democratic consolidation depend in no small measure on the economic performance of the region.[5] In sum, the dismal economic performance of the region in the past helps explain the region's political instability and will condition the prospects for peace and democracy in the future. Understanding the reasons why Africa has not overcome its long-standing economic crisis is clearly an urgent concern.

This chapter analyzes the progress of reform in Africa since 1980. As one of the current debates concerns how much actual policy reform there has been, I first examine the implementation record carefully. I then turn to explanation. Most accounts blame societal pressures on African governments for their failure to promote policy reform. Instead, my explanation of the policy outcomes we have witnessed emphasizes two sets of factors. First, I focus on factors within the African state itself, the interests of high-level decisionmakers themselves and their ideological beliefs about the economy. Second, I argue that the largely unprecedented amount of aid that has been extended toward Africa and the peculiar set of international institutions that have sprouted to manage Africa's relationship with the donors serve to protect the status quo.

The Progress of Policy Reform Implementation

I adopt the familiar distinction between *stabilization policies,* which seek to restore macroeconomic balance in the short to medium term, and *adjustment policies,* which seek to alter the basic economic institutions of the country to foster higher growth in the medium to long term. There is clearly much variation across the forty-eight African economies, but it is possible to discern trends and patterns in the record of policy implementation.

Stabilization Policies

The majority of African economies have made substantial progress on implementing basic stabilization policies, which are typically at the core of IMF programs.[6] Significant progress has been made on cutting fiscal deficits, which declined on average from well over 10 percent (excluding grants) at times in the 1970s and 1980s, to 9 percent of GDP in 1992 and to 4.5 percent in 1997.[7] Current account deficits have undergone a similar improvement and were only on average 4 percent of GDP in 1997. Exchange rate policies have perhaps undergone the most dramatic improvements. In the countries outside of the Communauté Financière Africaine (CFA) franc zone, repeated devaluations during the 1980s and movement toward a more flexible exchange rate system have resulted in a definite trend toward more reasonable exchange rates. In the CFA franc zone, in which currencies are pegged to the French franc, the devaluation of January 1994 served to bring down what had been typically fairly overvalued exchange rates. Thus, if between 1975 and 1984 eighteen of the region's economies had parallel exchange rates at least 50 percent higher than the official exchange rate, by 1995–1996 such a black market premium existed only in four countries, all with severe governance problems: Angola, Liberia, Nigeria, and Congo/Zaire.[8]

These continental averages disguise large intercountry variation, of course, but they do imply a significant amount of progress on macroeconomic policy throughout the region. It is nonetheless important to put this progress in perspective. First, much of the progress has been quite recent, occurring in the 1990s rather than the 1980s, during which there was remarkably little progress on much of the reform front. In a sense, the delay in stabilization is remarkable given Africa's absence of choices. Faced with extremely high fiscal and balance of payments crises from the late 1970s on, and generally unable to raise significant capital on private markets, African governments had little choice but to borrow from the donors, despite their policy conditions. Without the option of printing money,[9] various pressures would probably have induced equilibration of deficits in time, regardless of government policy and with or without donor pressures to do so. Indeed, donor finance and the ability to rapidly accumulate debt have served to delay this inevitable adjustment to fiscal realities, a point to which I return below.

The slow rate of initial progress is true even of the countries usually perceived today as success stories. Ghana did not liberalize its exchange rate until 1987, for example, while Uganda's fiscal deficit—in 1996 a sterling 1.6 percent of GDP according to the World Bank—was 14.4 percent of GDP as recently as 1992. In French West Africa, the devaluation of the CFA franc in January 1994, and several subsequent good rainy seasons, were the key events that account for the present apparent successful stabilization. As a result, in some countries, it is not yet clear whether the progress will be sustained or whether it is transient.

Second, progress on macroeconomic management remains vulnerable to reversals. By their nature, most stabilization measures are the policy reforms that are the easiest to achieve in the short run, but also the hardest to sustain because they are the easiest to undo. This is particularly true for measures that are in effect the subject of annual decisions. For instance, balancing the budget this year does not necessarily make it any easier to balance it next year, or less necessary to do so to maintain macrostability. In countries like Ghana, Kenya, and Gabon, past progress on stabilization was abruptly jettisoned in the months before an election by a government eager to hold on to power. Thus, Ghana's budget deficit went from 4.9 percent of GDP in 1991 to 12.7 percent in 1992, an election year in which Jerry Rawlings faced the voters for the first time. Coupled with an unexpected decline in oil revenues, Omar Bongo's campaign to retain the presidency in Gabon in 1999 led to a mushrooming of the deficit from 2 percent of GDP to an estimated 30 percent.[10] Similarly, the positive impact of the devaluation of the CFA franc on francophone West African economies will inevitably abate; even with inflation rates comfortably in the single digits, these countries typically have rates double those prevailing in the West, so that real effective exchange rates are almost sure to slowly but surely appreciate until these economies are faced with another competitiveness crisis.[11]

Third, much of the recent improvement in the basic macroeconomic picture is probably not sustainable without large amounts of external support. Balance of payments and fiscal deficits often remain too large to be sustained without external assistance or regular debt forgiveness and rescheduling. Thus, only three countries in the region had fiscal deficits of 3 percent of GDP or less in 1995–1996, if external grants are not taken into account, a level that can be viewed as a benchmark of prudent fiscal management in countries with limited access to international investment and low levels of savings. In a number of countries, progress on controlling government expenditures has been achieved thanks to high levels of donor support, creative accounting, and the deferring of core expenditures into the future. There is something profoundly disingenuous about donors and governments claiming progress on fiscal balance when it is taking place in the context of aid flows totaling a tenth of GDP, usually with a significantly high loan component. In several countries, significant debt relief largely explains ostensible improvements in macroindicators in recent years. But this can only be temporary if the underlying balance of payments and fiscal deficits have not been overturned—unless one is willing to make the unreasonable assumption that the current high aid flow is a permanent one.

In order to remain in good standing with the donors, moreover, it is not unusual for governments to resort to various budgetary sleights of hand. A favorite ploy is to accumulate arrears on civil service wages or on other obligations. In 1999, reports from francophone Africa were indicating that Gabon had accumulated seven to eight months of salary arrears since 1995, while they had reached eleven months in Niger.[12] Such salary arrears have long been endemic in the CFA franc zone countries, given strict rules limiting government financing of deficit spending. Since civil service wages are invariably the biggest single item in the budget, including these financial obligations in the deficit would significantly worsen the fiscal situation. Yet the international financial institutions (IFIs) typically look the other way to keep adjustment programs officially on track. Some oil exporters like Cameroon and the Congo have similarly sold forward oil several years into the future, despite strict IFI rules against the practice. According to the World Bank's statistics, Congo's fiscal deficit averaged 10.8 percent of GDP in the 1990–1996 period, excluding donor support, but the precise meaning we are to attach to these numbers is unclear when rumors suggest that the government has sold forward five years' worth of national oil production—which provides well above 90 percent of government revenues—in secret agreements with private oil companies.[13] Countries like Tanzania, Uganda, and Zambia adopted "cash budgets" in the 1990s, whereby expenditures are monitored and strictly controlled throughout the year relative to available revenues, in order to achieve a balanced budget.[14] Cash budgets have been widely praised for the fiscal turnaround in these countries. But in all three countries it has led to the accumulation of arrears, as line ministries pay for goods and services with promissory notes. In Zambia in 1997, the Ministry of Finance itself admitted that arrears accounted for the equivalent of 1.5 percent of GDP.[15] Typically, these arrears are not included in fiscal statistics.

Fiscal adjustment has been held back by the stagnation in revenue levels that has characterized the adjustment pattern of most African economies.

The impact of adjustment on government revenues is the subject of some disagreement. Carl Jayarajah and William Branson find that state revenues declined from 18.7 to 17.7 percent of GDP during the course of Bank adjustment programs in their sample of Africa countries from 1980 to 1991.[16] This accords with the findings of several studies that tax revenues and levels of foreign aid have had a significant negative correlation.[17] On the other hand, the IMF has usually argued that its own adjustment operations have not resulted in systematic changes in the government's tax effort.[18] No one, on the other hand, has argued that adjustment programs have resulted in a large increase in government revenues, despite the IMF's stated intention in virtually all of its adjustment operations to increase them. According to published World Bank data, across Africa (excluding South Africa and Nigeria) government revenues declined from an average of 16.3 percent of GDP during 1975–1984 to 15.8 during 1990–1996.[19] Clearly, in many countries, the weakness of revenue collection constitutes a real handicap for sustained macroeconomic stabilization.

Most problematic, macroeconomic stabilization may have come at the expense of long-term development. All across Africa, investment budgets have been sacrificed in order to protect the more politically sensitive recurrent budget from the cuts in expenditure made necessary by the economic crisis and mandated by reform programs, particularly in cases in which revenue generation does prove stagnant. The donors have recognized that reshaping the patterns of public expenditures to favor development is just as important in the long run as cutting the fat out of budgets, but the Bank itself recognizes that its efforts to do so have largely failed.[20] Thus, in the 1990s, gross public investment declined to an average of less than 6 percent of GDP. The proportion of expenditures devoted to public infrastructure declined sharply.

Skimping on maintenance and investment is an inevitable feature of macroeconomic stabilization programs and not a cause for alarm in the short run. Over time, however, the prolonged nature of the African crisis is turning what could be justified as a necessary short-term expedient into a critical obstacle to renewed economic growth. Twenty years of accumulated inadequate maintenance in effect represents significant obligations on future budgets. The World Bank thus estimated in 1995 that additional outlays of over U.S.$1.5 billion a year for a decade were needed simply to restore the existing road network in the region to an appropriate level, following decades of woefully inadequate maintenance.[21] Similar levels of maintenance expenditures are likely to be necessary for other government assets, from buildings to public utilities and enterprises.

Without making these essential expenditures, it is difficult to see how many of these economies can sustain growth. There is already some evidence that inadequate public investment has had an impact on growth and poverty alleviation. During the 1980s, Africa was the only region of the developing world where agricultural labor productivity actually declined. According to Azizur Rahman Khan, between 1980 and 1990 it declined by 0.4 percent a year, while increasing by 2.7 percent in South Asia and 3.9 percent in the Middle East and North Africa.[22] The decline appears to have quickened starting in the 1990s. There are complex causes for this decline, but the dismal condition of rural infrastructure is surely a primary one. For example, in 1997, only 4.6 percent of agricultural land in sub-Saharan Africa was irrigated, compared to 38.4 percent in Asia.[23] Africa's road network is by far the most poorly developed and the least satisfactorily maintained. In turn, declining productivity is one cause of the production stagnation that characterizes the region's agricultural sector. Ali Abdel Gadir Ali and Erik Thorbecke link all these factors to striking patterns of growing rural poverty in Africa, with 59 percent of the region's rural population living below the poverty line. The region, they conclude, "in comparison with other regions, suffers from greater, more severe and more persistent poverty, more unequal distribution of income, declining food production per capita and agricultural labor productivity; and a continuing population explosion."[24]

These various lacunae almost certainly also explain why the reasonably positive economic climate of the mid-1990s has not produced more than a small increase in investment, which remains too low in most countries.[25] In 1996 the African region received less than 1 percent of global foreign direct investment (FDI), and two-thirds of that went to Nigeria and Angola for oil exploration.[26] The enormous capital flight that has characterized Africa since 1980 has not reversed despite the apparent improvement of the mid-1990s. In 1999 the United Nations Economic Commission for Africa estimated the amount of African capital kept outside of the region to be the equivalent of 39 percent of the region's GDP. Nigerians alone held an estimated U.S.$50 billion outside of the country.[27] In surveys, businesspeople cite the dismal condition of the infrastructure and the cost implications of poor health conditions on labor productivity to explain their reticence to invest in the region.[28] Economic studies suggest that malaria cost the region the equivalent of 1 percent of GDP a year in the mid-1990s, and HIV/AIDS lowered GDP in some countries by 0.25 percent a year, a testament to the dismal state of the public health system in the region.[29]

There has been a slight increase in investment in a minority of countries like Uganda and Ghana that have courted the private sector. The problem is that the perception that the progress on stabilization is not sustainable will tend to be a self-fulfilling prophecy; if private sector agents do not view the reforms as fully credible, they will take a wait-and-see attitude before changing their economic behavior. Even these relatively successful countries have underinvested in basic public goods. The conclusion that the belated progress on macroeconomic stabilization witnessed in the 1990s will be difficult to sustain is inescapable, given its shaky foundations and Africa's pressing developmental needs. A small number of countries appear to have put their economies on a solid footing, but in most, improved statistics in the late 1990s will likely prove short-lived.

Structural Adjustment Policies

Structural adjustment policies are reforms that may not have a direct effect on macroeconomic stability in the short run but that are designed to affect the long-term prospects for economic growth. In general, they can be thought of as "stickier" reforms than stabilization policies, with more complex implementation issues, but with a lower chance of reversibility once they have been pushed through. The record here is even more ambiguous and uneven across the economies of the region. On the one hand, widespread progress has occurred in certain areas. Almost all countries have undergone extensive price liberalization, with significant progress on the elimination of domestic price controls and the liberalization of bank credit and interest rates.[30] Liberalization measures were almost invariably at the core of the World Bank's conditionality in its first-generation adjustment programs. The 1980s witnessed considerable deregulation in the banking sector, which had long been a privileged site for government interference. Banking services had constituted a public monopoly in well over a third of the countries in the region in the late 1970s; today, no country retains such a monopoly. In the agricultural sector, governments have done away with many of the agricultural marketing boards that had statutory monopolies over the commercialization of export crops and that often fixed producer prices at excessively low prices.[31] Elimination of these marketing boards, or the encouragement of private competition in the commercialization process, was designed to improve incentives for farmers.

This process of liberalization of the domestic economy is nonetheless far from complete. Key elements of the old apparatus of state control have survived in some countries. Often, the policies have changed on paper, but in practice, something resembling the status quo ante continues to prevail.[32] Governments often continue to ignore the spirit of their own liberalization efforts by continuing to interfere in deregulated markets. In Senegal, for instance, Elliot Berg has concluded that much deregulation and price liberalization has little impact on private sector investment, which continues to be undermined by "skepticism about the government of Senegal's commitment to liberalization; the lack of transparency in decision making and implementation coupled with a generalized suspicion that the playing field is uneven; and the persistence of administrative delays, weaknesses and harassment."[33] Similarly, Zambia's liberalization reforms in the 1990s were widely heralded, but the local business magazine pointed out in 1998 that it still took licenses from eleven different public institutions to open a tourism lodge.[34] A 1995 report on Tanzania, often cited as an example of successful investment liberalization, sounds a similar tone: the authors recognize that the country has made "substantial progress on economic reform," but argue that "the government continues to exhibit the laxity and indifference to performance of the socialist era" and note that "virtually every interaction with the government (by private businessmen) seems to require some sort of side payment to assure that necessary licenses, approvals or clearances are processed favorably."[35]

The agricultural sector is often emblematic of this tendency. Although policy reform appears to have advanced more in southern and eastern Africa, and less in western and central Africa,[36] nonetheless much has changed throughout the region. The expensive fertilizer, seed, and pesticide subsidies of the past have been almost universally withdrawn,[37] while the many parastatals that had once promoted a crop or region with extension services, input delivery, and other activities have typically been closed or seen their activities sharply curtailed. Typically, the agriculture sector reform programs that oversaw these reforms also mandated price liberalization, but here reform implementation has been much more ambiguous. It is important to distinguish export from food crops. Many key export crops have not seen their prices completely liberalized. In some countries, poorly informed farmers remain at the mercy of unscrupulous local officials keen to retain their central role in the marketing chain, or of newly empowered private purchasing agents, often in some degree of collusion with state officials. Thus, in Cameroon's cocoa belt, the adjustment program of the early 1990s resulted in the old price-fixing system being eliminated in favor of an annual "minimal indicative price," which theoretically established a floor below which now purely private transactions could not go. In practice, the latter prices were more or less enforced as the fixed price.[38] A World Bank review of the agricultural sector suggests that this practice is not limited to Cameroon, but is widespread throughout Africa.[39] Reviewing the experience in six countries, Peter Gibbon and colleagues find that the prices actually received by farmers probably declined during the 1980s in half of the cases.[40]

The policy environment for export agriculture has improved more significantly in countries like Kenya and Zimbabwe in which farmer organizations with long histories stretching back to before World War II have effectively pressured governments for favorable treatment. In Zimbabwe, however, the policy regime has hardly moved in the direction of *liberalization* as large commercial farmers have fought for and retained significant subsidies.[41] In West Africa, on the other hand, the absence of a European settler history has resulted in a much slower and haphazard reform process for export agriculture. Cotton, usually the leading export crop in the Sahel, continues to have its farm gate prices fixed by a state marketing board throughout French West Africa. In Senegal, so do the politically sensitive groundnut prices.[42] Governments usually acceded to donor demands to improve price incentives to farmers, long viewed as significantly too low, but have proved extremely reticent to allow markets to set prices themselves, preferring to maintain their power to fix prices annually.

Trade policy reform has seen even less progress.[43] It has long sought to lower and simplify tariffs, eliminate nontariff barriers, make customs procedures more transparent, and lower export taxes. Trade reform has been a staple of all reform programs since the early 1980s, despite the fact that tariffs constitute a significant source of revenue for most states in the region. Yet in a majority of cases, reforms have been left unimplemented or, when undertaken, have often been subsequently reversed. Officially, as a result, trade protection remains significantly higher in Africa than in other regions of the developing world, with tariff rates averaging about 25 percent, roughly four times the non–Organization for Economic Cooperation and Development (OECD) average.[44] Table 2.1 provides data on trade restrictions. Africa is the only region in the world in which the degree of openness has not significantly increased during the course since 1980.[45] The actual situation on the ground is much harder to assess, however, given the extremely uneven manner with which trade policy is implemented. In some countries, governments have undone the impact of policy by tolerating high levels of corruption within the customs services or extending exemptions from prevailing rates to favored firms. Michael Lofchie and Thomas Callaghy argue that in Tanzania "corruption in the customs bureaucracy is so extensive that Tanzania is, for all practical purposes, a duty-free zone."[46] In other countries, the trade sector continues to face red tape and excessive interference from government bureaucracy, so that reform may not have changed the effective rate of protection faced by business given various transaction costs that appear to have increased. The uncertainty and randomness of the situation in many countries, even when the effective levels of protection are quite low, is almost certainly a strong deterrent to potential trade growth.

Public enterprise reform offers an interesting contrast; after proceeding at a snail's pace during the 1980s, it picked up speed in the 1990s.[47] Over time, privatization has become more prominent in the reform agenda, as various schemes to improve the management of public enterprises invariably failed to stem their thirst for costly subsidies. Nonetheless, during the 1980s, privatization appeared stalled by a combination of political opposition and the technical difficulties of arranging for sales. Governments worried about the implications of large retrenchments. In the more recent past, however, privatization transactions have been completed in a number of

Table 2.1 Trade Restrictions in Africa

	Unweighted Tariff Rates (%)		Unweighted Nontariff Restrictions (%)	
	1984–1987	1991–1993	1984–1987	1991–1993
Côte d'Ivoire	23.3	—	6.6	—
Ethiopia	29.0	29.6	—	22.5
Ghana	29.6	—	48.4	—
Kenya[a]	39.2	43.7	67.3	37.8
Malawi[a]	16.7	15.2	96.1	91.3
Mauritius[a]	34.9	27.6	—	35.2
Nigeria	23.8	32.8	17.0	8.8
Tanzania[a]	32.1	29.8	62.2	79.7
Zimbabwe[a]	8.7	10.1	2.5	93.6
All Africa	26.3	25.7	43.7	42.9
Sub-Saharan Africa[b]	26.3	25.3	44.0	47.1
Latin America[b]	26.6	12.3	30.2	8.6
South Asia[b]	61.7	47.5	47.6	20.4
East Asia[b]	17.9	16.7	21.2	3.6
All Countries	27.0	22.1	37.7	23.7

Source: UNCTAD, cited in *The Africa Competitiveness Report, 1998* (Geneva: World Economic Forum, 1998), p. 41.

Notes: a. Data are from 1984–1987 and 1988–1990.

b. Regional averages are taken from fifteen sub-Saharan African states, eleven Latin American states, five South Asian states, and seven East Asian states.

countries. According to Paul Bennell, the period 1980–1987 witnessed some 227 privatization transactions, while there were some 657 transactions between 1988 and 1995 and over 300 in 1994–1995 alone.[48] Initial resistance to privatization appears to have been overcome primarily by the growing unwillingness to bear the burden of subsidizing loss-making parastatals combined with the attraction of the revenues to be generated by selling off public assets. Bennell thus points out that privatization transactions raised almost U.S.$2 billion in the region between 1990 and 1995.

In many cases, however, governments remain unwilling to part with the biggest of their public enterprises. Zambia, for instance, has undertaken a large privatization program since 1992, but did not completely divest itself from the Zambia Consolidated Copper Mines (ZCCM) until spring 2000, after the once extremely profitable giant copper-mining concern had started to lose over a million dollars a day.[49] In some cases, the fear that privatization will benefit certain ethnic groups, or foreign business interests, has stalled divestiture, or the process has stalled following accusations that the transactions were leading to a nontransparency that appeared to benefit members of the political class, usually through a significant undervaluation of assets and sales at fire-sale prices.[50] As Peter Lewis comments about the privatization process in Nigeria, much of which was conducted through offerings on the national stock market: "The dispersal of government assets, especially in a tight economy, created numerous opportunities for windfall gains. The weak regulation of securities transactions facilitated the use of insider information for substantial profit . . . private placements and closed bidding provided easy avenues for directing favors to friends and clients."[51]

Finally, there has been little progress on civil service reform, which has long been discussed but rarely implemented. The objective of reform is both to cut down on unnecessary staff and to improve the conditions of service for the remaining staff. Virtually every country in the region has undergone some kind of civil service reform program, supported by international finance.[52] The donors have long recognized the need for reform, but have hesitated to promote it, given its likely cost, complexity, and perceived political sensitivity. As a result, it has rarely been at the forefront of adjustment programs, relegated instead to a back burner. Governments have been willing to commission studies on the civil service, to institute costly and largely ineffectual donor-funded programs of voluntary retirement or campaigns to get rid of ghost workers, but very few have been willing to lay off sizable proportions of the civil service or to increase salaries to keep up with inflation. For their part, the donors have rarely focused their conditionality on civil service reform progress. Three notable exceptions to these patterns are Uganda, Guinea, and Ghana, where programs resulted in the civil service being cut by 20,000, 30,000, and 60,000 persons respectively in the late 1980s.[53] Elsewhere, there has been noticeably little progress. It would have been remarkable if more than two decades of fiscal crisis had not served to cut the size of the civil service relative to the population, as appears to have happened; on average, civil servants amounted to 1 percent of the population in 1996, down from 1.3 percent in 1991, belying the image of an overdeveloped state.[54] Nonetheless, the best available estimates from the IMF suggest that between 1986 and 1996, the number of civil servants actually increased in eleven out of the eighteen countries for which there are complete data. The more ambitious elements of the reform agenda, focusing on increasing civil service professionalization and effectiveness, have progressed even less. The same IMF data indicate that average real salaries increased in only seven countries during this same period, suggesting that in most countries working conditions are not improving.[55]

This section has so far focused on the agenda of reform defined by the IFIs since the late 1970s. It has not addressed an array of other issues African governments need to address, in all likelihood, for their economies to have a chance at sustained, rapid growth. These issues include law and order reform, technical and university training, infrastructure development, and so far in a minority of countries, effective AIDS/HIV prevention and treatment policies. In each of these areas, the average African country has made little progress over the last two decades, and without major efforts, the current situation will constitute a definite constraint on growth for the foreseeable future. Foreign direct investment will not be forthcoming to economies in which so much of what makes for an "enabling environment" is not in place.

The uneven implementation of reform policies is summarized in Table 2.2. With the caveat that it is difficult to generalize across all the cases, it is

Table 2.2 Policy Reform in Africa: Patterns of Implementation, 1980–2000

Reform	Degree of Probability	Implementation of Reversals	Comments
I. Stabilization			
a. Fiscal Adjustment	Mediocre–Good	High	Belated progress in mid-1990s. Sustainability questionable.
b. Exchange Rate Policy	Good–Excellent	Medium	Early focus of International Monetary Fund. CFA countries devalue in 1994, maintain fixed rate.
c. Monetary Policy and External Balance	Mediocre–Good	High	Uneven progress across time. Reliance on large aid flow.
II. Adjustment			
a. Domestic Liberalization	Poor–Excellent	Medium	High variance across cases, sectors.
– Banking/Credit	Good–Excellent	Low	Early focus of adjustment programs.
– Investment	Mediocre	Low	Large gap between de jure and de facto situation.
– Export Agriculture	Mediocre	Medium	Prices still set by state, particularly in ex-CFA countries.
– Food Markets	Mediocre–Good	Medium	Consumer prices liberalized more than producer prices. Less continuing regulation in West and Central Africa.
b. Trade Policy	Poor–Mediocre	High	Little progress, often subverted in practice.
c. Public Enterprise Reform	Poor–Mediocre	Low	Privatization quickens in 1990s, biggest public enterprises remain.
d. Civil Service Reform	Poor	Low	Consistently deferred, high cost and complexity.

possible to broadly summarize the course of reform in the following manner. While there has been some undeniable progress on changing economic policies, it is uneven across the region's economies, given to partial implementation and to reversals. Basic stabilization reforms have a better implementation record, but have proven more likely to suffer quick reversals. Fiscal adjustment, in particular, has suffered dramatic setbacks after bouts of clear progress. Exchange rate reform has usually been sustained with greater consistency. Structural adjustment reforms have proceeded more slowly but appear less vulnerable to reversal. In some areas, reform appears to have taken hold. In particular, privatization, though slow to start, has not been questioned once it has been implemented. There are no examples of renationalization in the region. A broad array of domestic markets have been liberalized. In other areas, there has been virtually no sustained progress. Civil service reform is one such glaring example. Why has there not been more progress on policy reform? How can we explain why certain types of reform have been implemented across the region and not others? Why has the speed of reform varied across policy areas? The next section addresses these questions.

The Politics of Reform Implementation

The conventional explanation for the failure of economic policy reform has always been that African governments have not been able to overcome the pressures of powerful societal forces organized in interest groups, which support the policy status quo.[56] Governments are thus viewed as prisoners of the social forces that maintain them in power. Reform was unpalatable to rulers because they worried it would result directly in political instability. Julius Nyerere is alleged to have said that he opposed an agreement with the IMF in 1985 because the price of such an agreement "would be riots in the streets of Dar es Salaam."[57] Much anecdotal evidence was adduced to confirm that, in fact, economic reform amounted to political suicide for governments. In countries as varied as Morocco and Tunisia in 1984, Egypt in 1979, Zambia in 1986, and Venezuela in 1990, observers noted that government attempts to eliminate subsidies on consumption goods such as bread or gasoline had been met with massive urban unrest.[58] In Sudan in 1984, such attempts even led to the overthrow of the Niemiri regime. In an often cited statistic, in 1968, Richard Cooper noted that for the Third World as a whole, in the year following a devaluation, the responsible finance minister's risk of being replaced was three times higher and the government's risk of falling from power was doubled.[59]

The analysis of interest groups and the politics of economic reform was strongly influenced by events in the developed countries following the first oil crisis. The political understanding of the economic crisis in the Third World was swayed by the literature then emerging on the politics of stagflation in the Western social democracies, with their powerful trade unions, big state bureaucracies, and vulnerable coalition governments. Interestingly, in this context, the very term "structural adjustment" entered the public policy lexicon in reference to the adjustment industrialized countries had to undergo after 1973 in response to the dramatic increase in the price of energy.[60] Particularly influential was Mancur Olson's work, which purported to demonstrate that the rise of entrenched economic interest groups, in particular trade unions, doomed industrialized states to economic stagnation.[61]

This analytical framework was adapted to the developing countries by Latin Americanists, for whom it resonated in the countries they studied, with their highly mobilized labor organizations defending entrenched positions in the public and import substitution industrialization sectors and governments that had responded with unsustainable inflationary spending and monetary policies. Latin American "populism" appeared readily explainable in terms of these same interest group models, though they were soon adapted to fit local circumstances and the Latin Americanists' own analytical frameworks.[62]

Yet even a cursory comparison between Africa and the industrialized West reveals how woefully organized societal interests are in the former compared to the latter. Long repressed or co-opted by government, unions, business associations, and other groups are smaller, more poorly organized, and underfunded compared to their Western counterparts. Even most of the societies in Latin America can claim much more powerful interest groups. The size and structure of African economies serve to further weaken interest groups. Given very low population densities, there is no historical tradition of strong private landed interests outside of southern Africa. The weakness of the private sector and the recent development and small size of the industrial sector, as well as the preponderance of the civil service within formal sector employment, weaken labor organizations. Senegal, for example, has one of the oldest industrial sectors in West Africa, with a textile industry going back to the 1940s, yet total union membership probably never exceeded 40,000 during the 1980s out of a formal sector labor force of between 160,000 and 190,000 and a potential labor force of perhaps 5 million men and women.[63] Ghana has perhaps the largest and traditionally the best-organized labor movement, with some 467,000 members in the national Trade Union Congress, or 13 percent of the labor force. Yet in Ghana, as in Senegal, the 1980s witnessed a decrease in membership and political influence, as governments clamped down or co-opted union leaders, and rank-and-file workers grew discouraged by sharply declining real incomes.[64] It is difficult to argue with Elliott Berg and Jeffrey Butler's assessment right after independence that, across the continent, the striking characteristic of African trade unions was "their limited political impact."[65]

In fact, an interest group approach to reform would predict that policy reform was likeliest in Africa, since societal groups opposed to reform are weaker and less well organized than their counterparts in Latin America or Eastern Europe. Exactly the opposite proved true, and there has been less progress on economic reform than elsewhere in the developing world. Despite this empirical record, much research on economic reform has continued to assume the determinant influence of interest groups in shaping economic policymaking in the Third World.[66]

Instead, I wish to argue that the main obstacles to policy reform are to be found within the state itself, rather than within societal actors. At the domestic level, there are three sets of related obstacles to policy reform within the state apparatus itself: first, a set of political obstacles having to do with the material interests of senior state elites; second, ideological obstacles; and third, the low and declining capacity within the state. These factors are interrelated through negative synergies. Low capacity reinforces the neopatrimonial tendencies within the state, which in turn maintain a long-standing tendency to underinvest in capacity. The political interests of state elites often dovetail with an ideological proclivity for state intervention in the economy. The evolving nature of adjustment politics must also be emphasized. The dynamics described here have unfolded over time, with new and changing issues emerging as a result of the failure to undertake reform and restore macroeconomic equilibrium in the previous period.

The Exigencies of Neopatrimonialism

My first argument is that the nature of political power in the low-income countries of Africa holds the key to an understanding of the course of policy reform attempts in the region. The exercise of power operates through pervasive clientelistic practices and the logic of neopatrimonialism.[67] Political authority is based on the giving and granting of favors in a continual series of dyadic exchanges that go from the village level to the highest reaches of the central state. The Weberian-influenced notion of neopatrimonialism captures the thesis that most African states are hybrid regimes in which patrimonial practices coexist with modern bureaucracy.[68] Outwardly, the state has all the trappings of a Weberian rational-legal system, with a clear distinction between the public and the private realm, with written laws and a constitutional order. However, this official order is constantly subverted by a patrimonial logic in which office holders almost systematically appropriate public resources for their own uses and political authority is largely based on clientelist practices, including patronage, various forms of rent-seeking, and prebendalism, all of which again rely on state resources.

These regimes are highly *presidential,* in the sense that power is centralized around a single individual with ultimate control over most clientelist networks. The president personally controls a big share of the state's resources and has discretional power over most of these resources. This is true not only in the smallest, most backward states of the region, but also in some of the bigger, allegedly more institutionalized states, like Côte d'Ivoire and Nigeria.[69]

I wish to emphasize the hybrid and essentially dual nature of neopatrimonial regimes. The public policy community usually downplays the patrimonial dimensions of these regimes. It views the pervasive clientelism as little more than an odd atavism, which a couple additional "capacity-building" projects promoting greater administrative hygiene and technical expertise will soon entirely do away with. It refuses to accept the idea that clientelism in these states is more than incidental. For example, it is striking that most anticorruption strategies being devised in the policy community simply assume that there is a rational-legal logic at the apex of these states that will be available to carry out the strategy.[70] In fact, all too often, leaders at the apex of the state choose to undermine these strategies, which threaten practices they find useful and profitable.

On the other hand, many academic students of neopatrimonialism downplay the rational-legal dimension in these states. They argue that formal structures do not matter at all, that all the meaningful decisionmaking takes place within a parallel "shadow state" that is entirely patrimonial.[71] They do not believe that policies or ideologies matter at all, except as a posteriori justification for state predation. Both of these views are excessive. Even in the least-institutionalized states in the region, there are rational-legal pockets attempting to assert themselves. The intellectual debates about policy are meaningful and cannot be reduced to rent-seeking motivations. On the other side of the spectrum, no state in Africa can claim to have entirely avoided the neopatrimonial tendency in its highest reaches. In most states, the two tendencies coexist, overlap, and are engaged in what amounts to a struggle for control of the state. The balance of power between the two obviously varies, and it is easy to believe that the prospects for the rational-legal tendencies to win out are better in, say, relatively bureaucratic Côte d'Ivoire than in the decrepit and brutal personal dictatorship that is Equatorial Guinea.

Neopatrimonialism undermines economic policy reform in contemporary Africa in at least two ways. First, because clientelism is based on the extensive use of state resources for political purposes, clientelist regimes almost inevitably produce highly interventionist economic policies. Economic liberalization is viewed as anathema to regimes that rely on the politically mediated distribution of access to state resources. Clientelism is viewed as critical in countries with little sense of nationhood and a tendency toward multiple ethnic and regional divisions, and in which few regimes can count on either a successful economy or electoral mandates for their legitimacy. Richard Sandbrook is right in asking about what will hold these societies together when the rulers have little in the way of patronage to distribute.[72]

Second, it is argued that neopatrimonialism results in a systematic fiscal crisis. As Thomas Callaghy has argued about the Zaire of Mobutu, "finances is the Achilles heel" of these regimes.[73] At the outset of the African crisis, the World Bank and the IMF typically accused African states of being "too big," but that is not really the case: relative to the economies they govern, the size of African states is roughly comparable to the size of states in other middle- and low-income regions.[74] True, patronage needs swelled the ranks of the civil service too rapidly following independence, but salaries were also allowed to decline precipitously in real terms, so that the cost of the civil service was not unusually high. In Tanzania, for example, salaries in the civil service were allowed to fall by an incredible 90 percent in real terms during the first two decades of independence, even as the size of the civil service more than tripled over the same period.[75] States also devoted little expenditure to transfer payments or entitlement programs, unlike states in the West or in some of the richer middle-income states of Latin America. Instead, the real cause of the endemic fiscal crisis that has plagued most African states following independence has been on the revenue side. Despite extensive state intervention in the economy, cronyism and rent-seeking have siphoned off potential state revenues. Taxes are not collected, exemptions are granted, tariffs are averted, licenses are bribed away, parking fines are pocketed. As a result, revenues always lag behind expenditures. It is often said that these regimes have low levels of *extractive capacity,* but the problem is not one of capacity so much as it is one of the political logic of a system in which the authority of the state is diverted to enhance private power rather than the public domain. In sum, theorists of clientelism viewed the onset of unmanageable fiscal and balance of payments crises as an entirely logical and predictable outcome of the manner in which politics was conducted south of the Sahara, and they were extremely skeptical about the ability of these political systems to give up these practices.

Observers too often assume that this pervasive clientelism reflects a fundamental absence of state autonomy. Clientelism is viewed as weakening the state by overwhelming it with particularistic demands and lessening its ability to act according to its own preferences or carry out a developmental project in the public good. In fact, pervasive clientelism is not necessarily evidence of the absence of autonomy. Outside of a small political elite, which Callaghy has aptly referred to as a "political aristocracy"[76] and which may not total more than a couple hundred people in any single nation, the low-level beneficiaries of clientelism do not have much influence over policy. The obstacles to reform in Africa have always been in these elite arrangements within or very close to the state apparatus rather than in the broader version of clientelism. When push comes to shove, states have much more willingly cut back on the latter than the former. In the same way that they are willing to directly attack the purchasing power of urban populations or of the civil service, they prove willing and able to cut back on, for instance, patronage practices or small time rent-seeking by low-level officials (e.g., trader licensing and permits).

In Latin America and the West, clientelism has been associated with low levels of state autonomy, and this relationship has been wrongly extended to Africa. Yet patronage practices in the former coincide with relatively strong labor unions, professional associations, and long-standing corporatist traditions. As a result, the beneficiary of patronage has some job security, even when clientelist networks may have originally secured the position. But when it is not relayed by organizational power, as it is not usually in Africa, the client position is much weaker. While not denying the reality of ethnolinguistic or regional solidarities that cut across stratifications of power and wealth, in sum, I argue that they are not ultimately constraining to state elites. Instead, a relatively autonomous state elite, long used to exploiting public resources to paper over its own internal differences, has found it difficult to change those habits. They have also found the reform process easy to manipulate to gain new avenues for enrichment, as I argue below.

Elite Beliefs

A second factor that is too often ignored in the literature explaining the course of economic reform is the ideological predilections of policy elites. Arguments about the role of economic ideas in governments' commitment to adjustment policies must be based on the premise that economic ideas can be at least partly autonomous from material interests. For much of the policy reform literature, on the other hand, the preference for state intervention in the economy is explained almost entirely by the patronage possibilities thus afforded to leaders. Many analysts argue that an international consensus has in fact emerged around the IFI economic policy reform package, including among African policy elites.[77] In this view, the unwillingness of African states to adopt structural adjustment ideas reflects their understanding of the political difficulties of implementing those reforms, and not their rejection of the intellectual logic behind adjustment policies. The socialist orientation officially chosen by African regimes, their vocal attachment to planning, or their concern for equity issues are viewed, then, as anachronisms from an earlier era, which African policy elites retain

largely as a posteriori and disingenuous uses of ideology for political purposes, rather than as the sincere affirmation of deeply held beliefs. Economic liberalization is unpopular not because of its ideological implications, but because it strips African rulers of key instruments of political
stability. It is true that egalitarian and socialist rhetoric in the mouth of a
Mobutu or a Moi ring false. It is also probably true that adjustment policies
may in many cases be less socially regressive than the policies they replace,
since few governments could in fact claim a progressive orientation to public expenditures before reform.[78]

But does this imply that economic ideas in fact have not played an
autonomous role in the rejection of adjustment policies? Very little attention as been devoted to understanding why the economic ideas embodied in
policy reform programs have not found more fertile ground in Africa. Yet if
it is true that African states are more autonomous than usually believed,
then the economic ideas of decisionmakers will matter to policy outcomes,
and we need to focus on them.

There are in fact several reasons to believe that a purely self-interested
understanding of these ideas is not warranted. First, it is rather striking that
the dislike of adjustment policies is widely shared across the political spectrum. Far from being limited to African politicians in power, they are
opposed by many if not most local intellectuals and academics, many of
whom are otherwise extremely critical of government. Much the same could
be said of the opposition press or of Africa-wide news magazines such as
West Africa, or *L'Autre Afrique,* and *Jeune Afrique.*

In part, this opposition reflects and is in turn reinforced by Africa's relative isolation. African intellectuals have been somewhat cut off from the
global public policy debates that have generated support for economic policy reform elsewhere in the world. Relatively few of them have been able
to follow policy developments in regions of the world where these reforms
have been carried out. They are less likely to have received public policy
training or had professional experience in the West.

In other regions of the world, the literature has identified technocrats
within government as the vehicle through which adjustment ideas get disseminated in government. In this process, foreign-trained technocrat civil
servants untainted by local politics influence the policy process and, with
luck, convince the politicians. However, it is not clear that, as a general
rule, technocrats in Africa do support the entire adjustment package of policies. Callaghy makes much of the commitment to reform of Kwesi Botch-
wey, Ghana's secretary of finance and economic planning in the mid-1980s,
who led the reform effort.[79] Others have pointed to the impeccable "neoclassical" credentials of Mamadou Touré, a reformist minister of finance in
Senegal from 1986 to 1988.[80] Yet much impressionistic evidence suggests
that technocratic support for policy reform is uneven. In countries like

Cameroon, Tanzania, and Kenya, senior staff whom donors had at one point labeled as technocrats did not prove able to sustain a reform impulse.

It could be argued that ambivalence about adjustment demonstrates that all these intellectual and technocratic elites belong to the same social class as the politicians who also oppose these policies. It could thus be argued that intellectuals in the capital city oppose devaluation, say, because their consumption tastes and lifestyles make them major beneficiaries of the overvalued currency. Surely there is some truth to this argument, but I would suggest that, in addition, opposition to key elements of the adjustment package is rooted in intellectual or ideological motivations that are not reducible to social predispositions.

I reject the notion that a policy consensus has emerged in Africa around structural adjustment. Instead, decisionmakers across Africa more typically do not believe that "adjustment will work," for a variety of reasons, and that for the most part, adjustment programs have been imposed from the outside on dubious governments. African governments are highly dependent on external public finance and cannot afford to disagree too vocally with donors and their policy prescriptions. They agree to reform programs to gain access to the external cash needed for crisis management, and may actually implement parts of the reform program, but often remain unconvinced by the intellectual logic behind these programs.

Skepticism about economic policy reform has been reinforced by the failure of IFI-supported structural adjustment programs to restore growth. In Ghana, the unsatisfactory nature of early reform results apparently led Rawlings to increase his commitment to reform.[81] In most countries, however, partial and mostly unsuccessful implementation of the first generation of programs has served to erode commitment to reform. Many people blame the reform program for the general economic crisis and come to doubt the validity of reform policies. Partial implementation of a reform program is thus doubly negative; the program is almost surely to fail, requiring further sacrifices, yet the people's patience and tolerance for austerity are also eroded. Moreover, the absence of a clear adjustment success story across the continent increases the sense that these policies will not provide economic solutions. African elites see that even reformist Ghana has not attracted significant new capital or investment, and the limited progress that this country has made is not nearly attractive enough to convince them to adopt the same risky policies.

Political leaders derive a second lesson from the uneven record of the last decade: that the economic costs of nonimplementation of adjustment are minimal and that nonreform is sustainable. In 1980, at the outset of adjustment programs in countries like Côte d'Ivoire and Senegal, it was possible for leaders to believe that nonimplementation would have dramatically negative results for the economy and state. International capital would dry up, the state would go bankrupt, social systems would fall apart, and so on. Now, two decades later, state elites view nonimplementation with more confidence. They understand that conditionality has turned out to be largely toothless, aid continues to flow, and debts continue to be rescheduled; the fiscal crisis has continued to worsen but the state has adapted and socio-political stability seems less threatened by the status quo than by reform.

Unlike Latin American leaders who have at one time or another seriously believed in the possibility of a heterodox program of stabilization and adjustment, in Africa no coherent alternative to a "Washington consensus" style of adjustment has emerged that politicians can rally around. Structural adjustment is the "only game in town," but when leaders compute the relative cost/benefit ratios of serious reform and the current muddling-through, they increasingly opt for the latter.

State Capacity

At independence, most countries in Africa could count only a handful of native college graduates. The colonial administration was almost entirely in the hands of Europeans, with Africans holding at most clerical posts. Since then, Africa has witnessed a dramatic increase in the number of individuals with skills and training. Nonetheless, somewhat paradoxically, most observers agree that state capacity has not improved and has actually declined in many cases. This was certainly the opinion of the African Governors of the World Bank when they presented a report on capacity issues in 1996: "Almost every African country has witnessed a systematic regression of capacity in the last thirty years; the majority had better capacity at independence than they now possess."[82]

The signs of this progressive loss of state capacity in the region have been much reported.[83] African civil services are characterized by pervasive absenteeism, endemic corruption, politicization, declining legitimacy, and low morale. The public policy literature often depicts state capacity levels as exogenously determined, somewhat like a country's level of natural resources,[84] or it makes vague references to the legacy of colonialism and underdevelopment. The message has been that more training programs and foreign experts can get African countries over the hump. Yet after four decades of independence and tens of billions of dollars in state capacity projects, low state capacity in Africa cannot be viewed as the unfortunate if inevitable by-product of underdevelopment. It should instead be perceived as the direct consequence of the formal policies and informal practices of governments for which a developmental state apparatus is not a high priority.

In fact, neopatrimonial political practices have had a profoundly corrosive effect on technocratic competence. In most countries of the region, there are inadequate professional incentives for graduates to demonstrate technical competence within the bureaucracy. Ambitious young technocrats with the appropriate training are quickly dissuaded from taking policy initiatives that risk rocking the boat. They find there is little institutional demand in such ventures as improving the ministry database and that their efforts to do so will generate at best indifference. The technical skills they brought to their positions atrophy over time, or they find that they are more appreciated and much better remunerated in the private and donor sectors and tend to emigrate from the public service over time. In sum, by the early 1980s the state administration had already begun a long process of decay. Technocratic pockets battled with politicians to assert rational decision-making, but more often than not found themselves on the short end of the stick.

In addition, the fiscal difficulties of African states undermined state capacity from the early years of independence by decimating the wage incentives facing civil servants in the region. In real terms, civil service salaries collapsed over the course of the 1970s and 1980s. In anglophone countries, it was not unusual for salaries to lose more than 80 percent of their real value as they failed to keep up with inflation. In the francophone countries, the situation was somewhat more ambiguous; real salaries officially fared better thanks to the lower levels of inflation within the CFA franc zone, but governments often accumulated substantial salary arrears in response to their substantial fiscal deficits, so the effective wage incentives to employees may in some cases have declined as much as that of the anglophone countries.[85]

The International Context

International factors might have altered the domestic dynamics I have just described. In fact, Africa's relationship with the donors has on balance reinforced these obstacles to policy reform. The onset of Africa's economic crisis was met by a massive increase in foreign aid. Overall aid levels to the region as a whole grew by an astounding annual average of over 5 percent in real terms between 1970 and 1995. By 1995, excluding South Africa and Nigeria, the average African country received the equivalent of 13.2 percent of its GDP in annual aid, an amount simply unprecedented in historical terms. In comparison, all other regions of low- and middle-income countries received less than 1 percent that same year.

During the 1980s, foreign aid progressively became a visible and massive force in the African political economy. In the typical country, some thirty official donors in addition to several dozen international NGOs provide several hundred million dollars in assistance a year, through over a thousand distinct projects and several hundred resident foreign experts.

Other than the state itself, the aid business is today the biggest single employer in most African economies. Most graduates can thank aid resources in some way for the education they have received. Many now consider working for the aid business as more prestigious than employment in the public sector. Aid has taken over many of the state's key functions; for instance, aid accounts for somewhere between a third to half of all education and health expenditures in the region.[86]

Most observers agree that the objective of public capital flows is to reintegrate Africa into the world economy, from which it has become increasingly marginalized. For much of the policy community, donor support of structural adjustment programs will provide the necessary incentives for African governments to undertake the policy reforms needed to attract foreign investment in their economies and to increase African exports to the rest of the world.[87] Moving from an inward to an outward orientation in its economic policies is viewed as a sine qua non of renewed economic growth. Conditioned foreign aid is designed to facilitate what is recognized as a difficult policy shift.

NGO and left-wing critics of the IFIs have long agreed that the objective of donor efforts in Africa is to increase the links between Africa and the global economy, but they oppose what they view as an attempt to secure African economies in a subaltern position relative to world capitalist forces.[88] They view integration into the world economy as undermining African economies unless it is limited and carefully regulated.[89] The conditionality attached to donor support of reform programs is viewed as a coercive form of blackmail, with disastrous consequences for African society.

In sum, both sides agree that IFI structural adjustment programs are leading Africa down the path of integration into the world economy. Both sides view aid as a *change agent* in the region. On the contrary, aid resources and in particular the aid given for the purpose of structural adjustment have served an essentially conservative function in the region, by lessening the incentives African governments have to undertake policy reform. The combination of massive aid increases and uneven or ineffective policy conditionality, I argue, has ensured the sustainability of policies that otherwise would have been disciplined by market forces.

In brief, aid has made policy reform less likely, not more. Similar arguments have been made in recent years by Tony Killick and Paul Collier, among others.[90] But I make a broader argument that links the overall aid relationship to the peculiar combination of political stability and state decay that we observe in the region. Aid has had a powerful effect on state institutions in Africa, simultaneously sustaining them and stripping them of decisionmaking power. First, the foreign aid system has undermined the development of state institutional capacity by externalizing policymaking. It is not unusual for forty-odd bilateral and multilateral donors plus twice that many Western NGOs to be implementing over a thousand distinct aid activities and essentially dominating if not taking over key governmental functions.[91] Entire ministries have been marginalized from their own areas of responsibility, with sectoral policy increasingly designed in aid missions and donor capitals and implemented "off budget" by self-standing project units outside of central government, which has lost much of its sense of accountability and responsibility.

Whatever government attention and much of the resources that had once been devoted to national budgeting and planning are now committed to the World Bank–inspired Public Investment Program and/or Public Expenditure Review processes, while governments worry about meeting IMF letter of intent benchmarks rather than budgetary targets. These processes are dominated by IFI staff and are typically undertaken with some kind of ad hoc structure, a special "Ministry of Stabilization" or a section of the presidency, rather than being integrated into the government's already existing structures.[92]

One result of donor dominance over decisionmaking has been to arrest the processes of *policy learning* among African policy elites. Because governments have largely implemented policies designed in Washington and European capitals by Western experts, African decisionmakers have been largely passive, at least until the implementation stage. No viable heterodox alternative to the IMF/World Bank's orthodox reform plans have emerged, and few countries in Africa have made a serious attempt at a heterodox stabilization plan during the last decade.[93] As a result, "counterfactuals," or in other words the relative merits of different approaches, have only rarely been tested and a dialectical process of comparison, confrontation, and mutual learning between orthodoxy and heterodoxy has not happened in Africa to the same extent as in Latin America. That process of learning in other parts of the world has resulted in the adoption of growth-oriented policies. In Africa, by comparison, there has been little policy learning.[94] Indeed, many technocrats may have grown hostile to reform policies precisely because the reform process seems to emasculate them to the benefit of foreign experts.

At the same time, aid has comforted if not reinforced the state's neopatrimonial tendencies by turning the decisionmaking process into a series of largely uncoordinated projects with tangible and excludable benefits controlled by state agents. As state capacity has waned and the fiscal squeeze increased, growing rent-seeking and indiscipline on the part of political elites have become evident. The responsibility of the aid system in this evolution, while only partial, is clear—even if, as I wish to emphasize, aid is also responsible for a large proportion of the development work that does take place and does improve the welfare of target populations. But aid's complicity in the current institutional devastation can clearly be linked to its role in sustaining weak governments in power while at the same time emasculating their developmental institutions.

The Partial Reform Syndrome

The length of the African economic crisis is one of its truly distinctive features. The failure to sustain reform over such a long period of time has created a series of unintended effects or feedback loops that today condition the nature of African political economy and pose distinct problems for the renewal of growth. Three of these unintended effects can be identified. Together, they make up what can be called the *partial reform syndrome.*

First, prolonged nonreform has resulted in a striking erosion of state capacity, which now complicates the renewal of growth. Again, this varies across countries and time, but all observers agree that in virtually all African countries, the state's ability to get things done has weakened since 1980. On one level, the persistent economic crisis during this time inevitably led to resource cutbacks for public sector infrastructure, civil service salaries, and recruitment. Sustained rates of high inflation, fiscal deficits, and stagnant economic growth have clearly had a devastating effect on the state. On another level, however, the decline of state capacity cannot be blamed entirely on the economic crisis and should also be understood at least in part as the outcome of political dynamics within Africa during the process of partial reform.

The perpetuation of austerity for an extended period of time, and the manner with which the adjustment process has been managed, serve to weaken bureaucratic rationality and reinforce the patrimonial tendencies of these regimes. Some state actors have found this decline in capacity quite useful, if and when they have themselves not precipitated it. States have certainly underinvested in state capacity because they did not view it as a priority.

The style of management of the reform process weakens the state everywhere. Foremost, the resources available to the state apparatus have simply been inadequate. Two decades of woefully small operations and maintenance budgets have cumulatively deeply cut into the ability to implement policy. Second, permanent large fiscal deficits have brought about a constant recourse to crisis management, which has weakened the rational management of public resources. Finally, the disempowerment of the central state bureaucracy serves to benefit the presidency or ad hoc structures dominated by the president, the donors, and NGOs. For all these reasons, the state's ability to undertake a reasonable reform effort has almost certainly weakened over time.

The underinvestment in state capacity by state elites has strengthened the relative power of neopatrimonial interests within the state; these prevent extraction and thereby weaken the state apparatus further. As a result, over time, the ability of rational-legal elements within the state to control events and force accountability on the political class atrophies. The sum result after two decades of this downward cycle is that the prospects for reform are far worse than they were at the onset of the crisis. Even leaders who want to undertake reform find that the state has been hollowed out—it is unable to implement even the most basic policies and has been taken over by rent-seeking and corrupt practices.

A second and related unintended effect of partial reform is that it has produced a specific political economy, with winners and losers, which early observers of reform had not anticipated but which may make future reform less likely. More specifically, there is much evidence that the reform process has often been manipulated to generate new opportunities for rent-seeking, in a manner that undermines rather than enhances economic efficiency. There are many reasons for the partial implementation of reform in Africa since 1980, but the peculiar nature of policy change in the region can often be linked to the interests of state elites as they seek to adapt the course of reform in such a way that clientelist networks are maintained or allowed to be reinvented. Note that, here too, the main beneficiaries of partial reform tend to be elites, who are close enough to the policy process to take advantage of the illicit opportunities around the process of policy change. The classic example of this is in privatization, where low-level parastatal employees have been laid off even as their managers and patrons in the administration have engineered sweetheart deals to benefit from the divestiture. Privatization is usually delayed by factional infighting within the elite as to who will be allowed to access state assets at bottom rates and/or protected markets, rather than by a fear of the reaction of parastatal employees.

Standing in between their own societies and their donors, top state elites have sought to use the policy reform process to gain maximum autonomy from both. Even as the course of partial reform is used to recentralize public resources and restore greater discipline to clientelist networks, it has also kept the donors at bay. Governments can always point to one area or sector in which some progress is being achieved, even as the previous progress in another area is being eroded. With little knowledge of local politics, remarkably little institutional memory, and a bias toward optimism about the course of reform, donors are easily fooled. The big losers are of course to be found among the vast majority of Africans, whose welfare continue to decline.

One tendency that is becoming increasingly clear at the beginning of the twenty-first century is the progressive withdrawal of the state from developmental activities, often with the blessing of the donors. This is the third unintended effect of partial reform. Despite much heated rhetoric about a "neoliberal assault on the state," the African state has not as a rule become smaller. As a proportion of the economy, the average African state's expenditures have actually crept upward by one or two percentage points of GDP since 1980.[95] Indeed, when foreign aid is factored in, the major proportion of which takes the form of goods and services provided to states, in effect the size of African government expenditures relative to their domestic economy has grown, not shrunk, despite two decades of devastating economic crisis.

At the same time, the process of structural adjustment has legitimated the retreat of the state apparatus from what were once considered central developmental functions. In effect, African states are no smaller than before, but now they spend less on development. Thus there is considerable variance across countries and across sectors, but the best estimates suggest that somewhere between one-third and two-thirds of education and health services now completely bypass the state and are the result of a combination of donor, NGO, and private sector efforts.[96] As Mark Robinson and Gordon White note, in many countries there is a de facto return to the situation during the colonial period, when the state's role in social sector provision was peripheral to the effort of the Christian missions.[97] The current fiscal crisis is also leading many governments to forsake the dominant postcolonial ambition and minimize state provision. In Uganda, for example, donors financed 77 percent of health spending in fiscal year 1992/1993, while the government's share was 23 percent. In the case of expenditures on hospitals, however, the government's share was 64 percent, suggesting the often noted preference of governments in the region for city-based curative care that benefits the better-off.[98] In Tanzania, 58 percent of secondary school enrollments were accounted for by NGO and church organizations by 1997, up from 28 percent in 1965. In Zimbabwe, in 1997, church missions provided more than two-thirds of all hospital beds in rural areas.[99]

On the other hand, African states are spending increasing resources on nondevelopmental expenditures that shore up political stability. Thus, African armies have actually substantially increased in size since the mid-1980s.[100] Seemingly impervious to austerity, African government cabinets continue to be egregiously inflated. Between 1979 and 1996, the average cabinet in the region increased from 19.1 ministers to 22.6.[101] Public offices of all kinds continue to increase. National legislatures, for instance, grew from an average of 89.5 seats following the first postindependence election in the early 1960s, to 140 seats in 1989, and to 149 in 1997.[102] I do not wish to imply that big cabinets or large armies are invariably a bad thing. But the growth of these nondevelopmental activities that typically benefit a very small political elite, even as the government retreats from the provision of central public goods, is one of the more striking recent products of the policy reform process in Africa.

Conclusion

The process of economic policy reform in Africa is now over two decades old. At any given time during this period, there have been plausible reasons to believe that African governments had begun to undertake real reform. A breakthrough on reform and the renewal of growth have been predicted more than several times. Always, however, these hopes have been dashed, and the region has remarkably little to show for its official commitment to reform.

I have argued in this chapter that African governments have never been convinced of the need for policy reform, which did not fit easily with their conception of their own political needs, or of what might, in practical terms, be effective in an African context. The international community's efforts to assist the process of reform with generous amounts of aid have ironically served to maintain the very institutions that had brought about economic stagnation. What we have witnessed as a result in the region is the political instrumentalization of the reform process by governments that increasingly came to view the donor-led process of structural adjustment as compatible with the survival of the status quo. This is not necessarily a safe long-term choice. The possibility of state collapse represents a real risk in economies in which state capacity has been allowed to wither away, to the point that even the most routine tasks are problematic for the state apparatus. On the other hand, two decades of failed reform leaves most African economies less capable of engineering reform in the future, even in countries where the political class has come to be convinced of the desirability of new policies. That in the end may turn out to be the biggest failure of the reform process.

What are the policy implications of the foregoing analysis? It is sometimes argued that the economic policies embodied in structural adjustment have been tried and have failed. The first half of this chapter sought to show that reform implementation has been partial, uneven, and rarely sustained. Many of the policies that prevented economic growth in the early 1980s still do so more than twenty years later. Thus a first clear implication of my analysis is that African governments still need to reduce fiscal deficits, liberalize their domestic economies, privatize public enterprises, and pursue trade reform. This narrow structural adjustment agenda is assuredly not sufficient, however, to resume economic growth by itself. After two decades of failed reform, it is clear in particular that state decay represents a significant obstacle to growth. Thus a second implication is that both governments and donors need to pay special attention to improving the professionalism and capacity of the civil service, to rehabilitating the public infrastructure, which has been allowed to atrophy for so long, and to reinforce the rule of law, notably through the strengthening of the judiciary.

Third, the relationship between donors and African governments has proven increasingly counterproductive, as a substantial resource flow has not promoted policy change and may indeed have thwarted it. This suggests the need for a significant change in the nature of donor conditionality that would serve to alter the incentives that African governments face. Foremost, donor support of policy reform should be more selective, focusing only on governments that have demonstrated commitment to policy reform. It is simply unfathomable that governments that have routinely deceived donors for two decades continue to receive support. Next, conditionality should be narrowed, focusing only on a small number of issues that are easy to monitor. Related to this, it should be less intrusive. Regular missions from Washington by small armies of international bureaucrats and their consultants who do everything from prepare the budget to massage national statistics and devise sectoral policy should be a thing of the past. Governments should be obliged to come to the negotiating table with policies they have developed themselves. Finally, conditionality should focus on governance issues. This is in part a contradiction with my recommendation to narrow the scope of conditionality, but the devastating impact of rent-seeking, corruption, and political clientelism on policy seems hard to deny. The donors have been much too complacent about high-level corruption in the past, even when it undermined their reform programs; explicit and tough-minded conditionality on governance issues is now necessary to change the perception that African leaders have of their incentives to pursue reform.

Reforming the donor-government relationship along these lines will not be easy.[103] There are difficult tradeoffs between different desirable objectives. For example, the goal of selectivity in donor lending is likely to be incompatible with need-based allocation. It is unfortunately true that the countries that most need aid are those that are also least likely to use it effectively. In addition, donor organizations are deeply wedded to their current approach and there will be intense bureaucratic opposition to significant change. Nor is it clear that an effective constituency for change will emerge soon. African governments could most benefit from a new regime in the long term, but they have come to terms with the present one, which they believe promotes stability. The status quo described here may thus well end up continuing through a third decade of economic crisis and state decay.

Notes

1. See, for instance, the optimistic assessment of the IMF in Fischer et al., *Africa.* For an optimistic U.S. perspective, see Gordon and Wolpe, "The Other

Africa"; and the more measured assessment by Deborah Bräutigam in her essay "Economic Takeoff in Africa."

2. Harris, "Impact of the Asian Crisis on Sub-Saharan Africa."

3. Africa's democratic transitions are surveyed in Bratton and van de Walle, *Democratic Experiments in Africa.*

4. On these issues, see Diamond, "Is the Third Wave Over?"

5. A clear link between economic performance and democratic consolidation in low-income countries is well established in Przeworski and Limongi, "Modernization."

6. Killick, *IMF Programmes in Developing Countries.*

7. Fischer et al., *Africa.* For a broader assessment of fiscal adjustment, see Datta-Mitra, *Fiscal Management in Adjustment Lending.*

8. Calculated from World Bank, *African Development Indicators 1997,* p. 51. Unless otherwise indicated, the statistics attributed to the World Bank throughout the chapter are from this volume.

9. It is interesting that, with the notable exception of Zaire, African governments on the whole did not resort to the expedient solution of printing money. In the CFA franc zone, strict rules apparently served as an effective deterrent. Elsewhere, governments appear to have been dissuaded from doing so by the examples of disastrous hyperinflation in other regions, notably in Latin America. Perhaps as important has been the influence of extensive and long-standing technical assistance to central banks and finance ministries from the IMF, the French treasury, and other Western donors.

10. Calculated from Economist Intelligence Unit, *Country Report: Gabon.*

11. A recent assessment of the CFA franc zone is provided in Cabrillac, "La situation macroéconomique." See also Clement et al., *Aftermath of the CFA Franc Devaluation;* and an earlier essay by van de Walle, "The Decline of the Franc Zone."

12. On Gabon, see *Marchés Tropicaux,* April 16, 1999, p. 797. On Niger, these arrears are reported in "Niger: Lassitude pre-electorale," pp. 40–41.

13. These sales have been widely reported. See, for instance, "Les milliards en l'air du Congo," which mentions the conservative estimate of 3.5–3.75 billion French francs in sales to oil companies on production through 2004. See also various Economist Intelligence Unit country reports on the Congo in the mid-1990s.

14. See Stasavage and Moyo, *Are Cash Budgets a Cure?* and Bolnick, "Establishing Fiscal Discipline."

15. Stasavage and Moyo, *Are Cash Budgets a Cure?* p. 13. My own interviews of officials and businessmen in Lusaka in May 1999 suggest that this figure may be a significant underestimate.

16. Jayarajah and Branson, *Structural and Sectoral Adjustment,* p. 134.

17. For example, White, "Foreign Aid, Taxes, and Public Investment."

18. For instance, Nashashibi et al., *The Fiscal Dimensions of Adjustment,* which provides data suggesting that government revenues went up in nine African cases and down in nine, relative to a "base year."

19. World Bank, *African Development Indicators 1997,* p. 194. These data are made suspect by the obviously incorrect values provided for certain countries. Kenya, for example, is listed as having revenues that never exceed 1.6 percent of GDP during this entire period.

20. World Bank, *The Impact of Public Expenditure Reviews.*

21. World Bank, *A Continent in Transition,* p. 58.

22. Cited in Ali and Thorbecke, "The State of Rural Poverty," p. 10.

23. Ibid., p. 13. In fact, this grim statistic is further reinforced by database statistics from the Food and Agriculture Organization (FAO), which reported in 2001 that only 0.6 percent of agricultural land in sub-Saharan Africa was irrigated, compared to 11 percent in Asia. The FAO figures were obtained by dividing the total irrigated agricultural land, 5,221 (sub-Saharan Africa) and 187,655 (Asia), by the total agricultural area, 910,134 (sub-Saharan Africa) and 1,649,684 (Asia).

24. Ibid., pp. 9, 11. Of course, these totals disguise wide variations across the region, from Côte d'Ivoire, with a poverty head count ratio of 38 percent, to the Central African Republic, with an incredible 78 percent.

25. Fischer, *Africa*. See also Bost, "L'Afrique Subsaharienne."

26. See Sachs, "Foreign Direct Investment in Africa," p. 37.

27. Cited by Lewis Machipisa, "Africa Loses Millions Through Capital Flight," Interpress Service, May 12, 1999, found in a Lexis Nexis Internet service search.

28. See Sachs, "Foreign Direct Investment in Africa," p. 37.

29. Cited in Ramachadran, *Investing in Africa.*

30. A good, if biased summary of the progress achieved up to the early 1990s is provided by the World Bank in *Adjustment in Africa*. The country case studies on which much of that assessment is based have been published as Husain and Faruqee, *Adjustment in Africa*. See also Sahn, Dorosh, and Younger, *Structural Adjustment Reconsidered;* and Jayarajah and Branson, *Structural and Sectoral Adjustment.*

31. Adjustment in the agricultural sector is reviewed in Meerman, *Reforming Agriculture;* Shepherd and Farolfi, *Export Crop Liberalization in Africa;* and Seppälä, "Food Marketing Reconsidered." See also Gibbon, Havnevik, and Hermele, *A Blighted Harvest.*

32. In her excellent book on the informal sector in Dar es Salaam, Aili Tripp documents cases in which old laws were so consistently evaded by the citizenry that public officials stopped trying to enforce them. In such cases, as well, the actual policy regime is quite ambiguous. See Tripp, *Changing the Rules.*

33. Berg et al., "Sustaining Private Sector Development," p. 17. For a slightly different emphasis focusing specifically on the import sector, see Thioub, Diop, and Boone, "Economic Liberalization in Senegal," which is in agreement with the Berg source that despite official trade liberalization, infighting between business and "old-style politician businessmen" continues to exist over the lucrative imported manufacturing market, but which emphasizes the state's declining ability to control rent-seeking networks in a context of declining administrative capacity and political legitimacy.

34. Cited from *Profit Magazine* to me in interviews with Jon Lomoy at the Norwegian embassy, Lusaka, May 1999.

35. Lofchie and Callaghy, *Diversity in the Tanzanian Business Community,* pp. 1, 20, 22.

36. So concludes an excellent recent review of agricultural adjustment: Binswanger, Townsend, and Tshhibaka, "Spurring Agriculture," pp. 13–15.

37. Meerman, *Reforming Agriculture,* pp. 74–83, covers the record for all input subsidy programs.

38. Courade and Alary, "Les planteurs camerounais," p. 79 and passim. See also Losch, "Les agro-exportateurs."

39. Meerman, *Reforming Agriculture,* pp. 70–71. See also Shepherd and Farolfi, *Export Crop Liberalization,* pp. 13–19.

40. Gibbon, Havnevik, and Hermele, *A Blighted Harvest,* pp. 107–109.

41. Tor Skalnes makes this argument convincingly for Zimbabwe in his book *The Politics of Economic Reform.* Zimbabwe is also marked by growing rural inequality, as all farmers are far from benefiting from the same level of political

influence. See also chap. 5 of the fine but now somewhat dated study Herbst, *State Politics in Zimbabwe;* and Bratton, "The Comrades and the Countryside."

42. Rouis, "Senegal."

43. The progress of trade policy reform is discussed in Nash, "Trade Policy Reform Implementation"; Ng and Yeats, "Open Economies Work Better!"; and Hibou, *L'Afrique est-elle protectioniste?* Charles Soludu focuses on a sample of countries with a somewhat better trade reform record in his essay "Trade Policy Reforms." On the political economy dimension of trade policy reform, see Rodrik, "Why Is Trade Reform so Difficult in Africa?" and Bienen, "The Politics of Trade Liberalization."

44. Ng and Yeats, "Open Economies Work Better!"

45. This is the conclusion of Sachs and Warner, "Economic Reform"; and World Bank, *Global Economic Prospects.*

46. Lofchie and Callaghy, *Diversity in the Tanzanian Business Community,* p. 2.

47. A useful survey is provided in Bennell, "Privatization in Sub-Saharan Africa." See also World Bank, *Bureaucrats in Business;* and Berg, "Privatization in Sub-Saharan Africa."

48. Bennell, "Privatization in Sub-Saharan Africa," pp. 1789–1790.

49. The ZCCM's belated privatization is chronicled in "Zambia Finalizes Sale." The general Zambian context is explored in Rakner, van de Walle, and Mulaisho, "Aid and Reform in Zambia."

50. This argument is well made by Mkandawire, "The Political Economy of Privatization."

51. Lewis, "Economic Statism," p. 446.

52. See the excellent collection of essays in Lindauer and Nunberg, *Rehabilitating Government.* In her own contribution, Barbara Nunberg cites fifty-five World Bank loans with a civil service reform component extended to Africa between 1981 and 1991. See Nunberg, "Experiences with Civil Service Pay." See also Olowu, "Redesigning African Civil Service Reforms."

53. De Merode and Thomas, "Implementing Civil Service Pay." The Ugandan numbers are ambiguous, given the high number of ghost workers and the distinction between general public employment and the civil service. The overall public employment rolls were cut by an amazing 160,000 employees between 1990 and 1996. See Lienert and Modi, "A Decade of Civil Service Reform," tab. 9.

54. Lienert and Modi, "A Decade of Civil Service Reform," p. 44. The size of the African state and its economic implications were recently analyzed in Goldsmith, "Africa's Overgrown State."

55. Lienert and Modi, "A Decade of Civil Service Reform," p. 43.

56. The political economy literature on policy reform includes such works as Nelson, *Economic Crisis and Policy Choice;* Haggard and Webb, *Voting for Reform;* Bates and Krueger, *Political and Economic Interactions;* Rodrik, "Understanding Economic Policy Reform"; and Mosley, Harrigan, and Toye, *Aid and Power.*

57. Quoted in Tripp, *Changing the Rules,* pp. 79–80. Note that when an agreement was finally reached in 1986, there were no such riots.

58. See for example Walton and Seddon, *Free Markets.*

59. Cooper, *Currency Devaluations,* pp. 28–29.

60. The intellectual history of structural adjustment is recounted in Mosley, Harrigan, and Toye, *Aid and Power,* pp. 27–38.

61. Olson, "The Rise and Decline of Nations." See also Lindberg and Maier, *The Politics of Inflation;* Berger, *Organizing Interests;* Goldthorpe, *Order and Conflict;* and Katzenstein, *Between Power and Plenty.*

62. See, for instance, Kaufman and Stallings, "The Political Economy of Latin American Populism."

63. See Bergen, "Unions in Senegal," p. 1.

64. On Ghana, see Herbst, *The Politics of Reform in Ghana,* pp. 64–68.

65. Berg and Butler, "Trade Unions," p. 340. For a somewhat more sanguine appraisal, see Sandbrook and Cohen, *The Development of the African Working Class.*

66. For example, Frieden, "Classes, Sectors, and Foreign Debt"; or Bardhan, *The Political Economy.* Robert Bates himself has moved away from such a society centric view, notably in his book *Beyond the Miracle of the Market.* On the other hand, the approach remains a favorite among economists; see the comments in the recent review essay Collier, "Explaining African Economic Performance," pp. 105–106.

67. Among a large Africanist literature that theorizes and describes these practices, a short list of vital works would include Bayart, *L'etat en Afrique;* Boone, *Merchant Capital;* Fatton, *Predatory Rule;* Callaghy, *The State-Society Struggle;* Chabal and Daloz, *Africa Works;* Joseph, *Democracy and Prebendal Politics;* Reno, *Corruption and State Politics;* and Sandbrook, *The Politics of Africa's Economic Stagnation.* A review of this literature and an analysis of the key characteristics of neopatrimonialism is presented in chap. 2 of Bratton and van de Walle, *Democratic Experiments.*

68. Weber, *Economy and Society.*

69. On Côte d'Ivoire, see Fauré and Médard, *Etat et bourgeoisie.* On Nigeria, see Joseph, *Democracy and Prebendal Politics.*

70. A good example of this tendency is provided in Klitgaard, *Controlling Corruption.*

71. The shadow state is theorized in Reno, *Corruption and State Politics.* An extreme version of this argument has recently been presented in Chabal and Daloz, *Africa Works.*

72. Sandbrook, *The Politics of Africa's Economic Stagnation.*

73. Callaghy, *The State-Society Struggle,* p. 194.

74. See, for instance, World Bank, *World Development Report 1997.*

75. Stevens, "Public Expenditure and Civil Service Reform," pp. 66–69.

76. Callaghy, *The State-Society Struggle,* pp. 184–194.

77. Ravenhill, "Adjustment with Growth"; and Biersteker, "The 'Triumph of Neoclassical Economics."

78. Sahn, "Public Expenditures in Sub-Saharan Africa."

79. Callaghy, "Lost Between State and Market," pp. 271–286.

80. See Ka and van de Walle, "Senegal."

81. See Rothchild, *Ghana,* especially the essay by Nugent.

82. African Governors of the World Bank, *Partnership for Capacity Building,* p. 5.

83. The multiple deficiencies of African administrations are well documented and explored from multiple perspectives. In addition to the materials already cited, see, for example, Adamolekun, *Public Administration in Africa;* Mutahaba, Baguma, and Halfani, *Vitalizing African Public Administration;* Leonard, "The Political Realities"; Hirschmann, "Institutional Development"; Dia, *Africa's Management in the 1990s;* and Sadig and Luke, *Development Management in Africa.*

84. A good example of this tendency is the World Bank's *World Development Report 1997,* which focused on the state and governance issues. Though sometimes compelling on the prescriptive side, the report is entirely silent on the causes of

poor state performance. This is akin to a doctor who prescribes medication without first learning the nature of illness the patient is suffering from.

85. On the evolution of civil service wages, see the data provided in Robinson, *Civil Service Pay;* Lindauer, and Nunberg, *Rehabilitating Government;* and Lienert and Modi, "A Decade of Civil Service Reform.

86. See van de Walle, *The Politics of Permanent Crisis,* chap. 5.

87. For example, World Bank, *Adjustment in Africa,* esp. pp. 61–98.

88. See, for instance, Hoogvelt, *Globalization and the Postcolonial World.*

89. Such a view is summarized in Mkandawire, "Crisis Management."

90. Collier, "The Failure of Conditionality"; and Killick, *Aid and the Political Economy.*

91. Van de Walle and Johnston, *Improving Aid to Africa.*

92. Berg, "Aid and Public Sector Reform."

93. I would argue that Tanzania in the early 1980s and Zambia in 1986–1988 represent the only true heterodox experiments in Africa during the decade.

94. See Mkandawire and Soludo, *Our Continent, Our Future,* for a similar argument.

95. See, for instance, World Bank, *World Development Report 1998,* tabs. 4–12 and 4–13.

96. See Semboja, and Therkildsen, *Service Provision Under Stress;* and Robinson, "Privatizing the Voluntary Sector."

97. Robinson and White, "The Role of Civic Organizations," pp. 9–13.

98. Ablo and Reinikka, "Do Budgets Really Matter?" p. 24.

99. These last two statistics are provided in Robinson and White, "The Role of Civic Organizations," pp. 12–13.

100. For the forty countries on which the Stockholm International Peace Research Institute reports data, the number of soldiers had grown by an average of 67 percent between 1985 and 1996. Recognizing the great variety of defense needs across African countries between these two dates, I excluded six countries that had been involved in significant military activities during this period (Angola, Burundi, Rwanda, Senegal, Sierra Leone, and Uganda) as well as three countries in which defense needs had enormously declined during the period (Ethiopia, Mozambique, and South Africa), and recalculated the rate of increase. For the remaining thirty-two countries, the number of soldiers had still increased by 28 percent during this period.

101. I calculate this from data provided in Europa Publications, *Africa South of the Sahara.* Data for 1979 are mostly from April (n = 46); data for 1996 are mostly from September (n = 47).

102. The first two numbers are cited in Bratton and van de Walle, *Democratic Experiments,* p. 71. I calculated the numbers for 1997 from various sources. They concern lower houses of parliament, and exclude ex officio members.

103. I discuss the difficulties in my essay "Aid's Crisis of Legitimacy."

What "The People" Say
About Reforms

Michael Bratton and Robert Mattes

Africa is a latecomer to globalization. In terms of timing, African countries have followed rather than led the reform movements that installed democratic and market systems around the world. And, as foreign aid dependencies, African countries experienced considerable external pressure to liberalize. One should not automatically conclude, however, that the impetus for reform originated from outside Africa rather than from within.

This chapter measures whether, and to what extent, mass popular constituencies exist for democratic and market reforms within selected African countries.[1] If political and economic liberalization are Northern ideas that are being imposed on an unwilling South, then certain empirical facts should follow. We would expect that most Africans would (a) be unaware of democracy and markets, (b) have distinct cultural understandings of their meanings, (c) be unsupportive of regimes based on democratic and market principles, (d) prefer alternative political and economic regimes, and (e) be unsatisfied with what these regimes have delivered in practice. Alternatively, if we find popular awareness of, support for, and satisfaction with recent reform initiatives in African countries, we can conclude that reforms have some sort of indigenous base. It is important to know this because democracy and markets can contribute to the alleviation of Africa's developmental problems only if they are embraced by African people themselves.

To measure public attitudes, we employ an original set of data from a large-scale, cross-national survey research project (the Afrobarometer), which is designed to systematically map mass attitudes toward democracy, markets, and civil society in about a dozen African countries and, ultimately, to track the evolution of such attitudes in selected countries over time. This chapter reports results from a first round of surveys implemented between July 1999 and February 2000 in Botswana, Ghana, Malawi, Namibia, Nigeria, and Zimbabwe.[2] Face-to-face interviews were conducted by trained interviewers in local languages with a total of 10,398 respondents using a questionnaire instrument that contained a core of common items.

A caveat is in order about generalization. Because country samples were each drawn randomly, they represent national voting-age populations.[3] But the six countries selected, which are all English-speaking territories that have recently undergone political transitions to electoral democracy, are not fully representative of the sub-Saharan subcontinent. We do not allege that the findings in this chapter can be extended to francophone Africa, to the continent's remaining authoritarian regimes, or to states that are imploding through civil war. If we occasionally refer to "Africans," we have a more limited populace in mind.

To anticipate our findings, this chapter reports that Africans (so defined) overwhelmingly support democracy and reject alternate, authoritarian regimes. They are much less happy with the way that democracy actually works, however, though a majority are satisfied in five out of the six countries studied. Against this mass domestic constituency for political reform, we find greater ambivalence about market principles and economic adjustment. The Africans we interviewed are especially dissatisfied with the consequences of structural adjustment, which they associate with widening gaps between the rich and the poor.[4] Thus the two modes of reform do not form a coherent whole. There may be a consensus about the compatibility of political and economic reforms in Washington, D.C., but this consensus has not penetrated public opinion in Africa.[5] While adherents of the free market in Africa tend to support democratization, sympathizers of democracy do not necessarily support markets.

Popular Attitudes Toward Democracy

Awareness of Democracy

Because democracy means different things to different people,[6] we began by asking, "What, if anything, do you understand by the word 'democracy'? What comes to your mind when you hear the word?" Although the question was posed in the local language of the respondents' choice, the word "democracy" was always presented in English. To all survey respondents who ventured an opinion on the meaning of the concept, we attributed an awareness of democracy. All those who replied that they didn't know— or had never heard of the word—were held to be unaware of democracy.

By this criterion, the concept of democracy is recognizable to most Africans interviewed. Across six countries, an average of almost three-quarters of all respondents (74 percent) were able to volunteer a definition of the term.[7] By no stretch of the imagination can democracy be described as a strange and incomprehensible construct in these parts of the continent.

Even though democracy seems to be a familiar idea to many Africans, interesting cross-national variations nonetheless exist (See Table 3.1). The level of public awareness of democracy ranges from a low of 65 percent in Namibia to a high of 88 percent in Malawi. We speculate that the diffusion of political ideas occurs more easily in geographically small countries with high population densities than in large, underpopulated countries. Neither Malawi nor Namibia is highly urbanized, however, a factor that probably helps to increase awareness of democracy in Ghana (72 percent aware, 36 percent urban) and Nigeria (77 percent aware, 43 percent urban). Also, education undoubtedly enables awareness, a fact we document later.

The Meaning of Democracy

Beyond recognizing democracy, what do people think it means? Because we used an open-ended question, respondents were free to offer answers in their own words. Rather than trying to fit diverse interpretations into predetermined categories, we transcribed all answers verbatim and coded responses after the fact. This inductive procedure was adopted so that we would not overlook any distinctive meanings that Africans might attach to democracy. We were particularly concerned to resist an imported, Western framework and to leave room for indigenous conceptions. As it happens, though, the Africans whom we interviewed seem to have arrived at understandings of democracy that are more universal than culturally specific.

First, with few exceptions, the survey respondents attached a *positive* value to democracy. Among those people aware of the concept,[8] more than nine out of ten (91 percent) volunteered a laudatory connotation: democracy was a public "good" that in some way would make conditions "better." Fewer than one out of a hundred (0.8 percent) saw democracy as in some way "bad." This small minority thought that democratic reforms brought elite corruption, conflict among social interests, or "confusion" in political life. The remainder (8 percent) saw democracy in neutral terms, usually as a "change of government" or as "civilian politics or government" without inferring whether a new regime would be better or worse than what had gone before.

Second, respondents regarded democracy in *procedural* as well as *substantive* terms. This finding runs counter to much of the literature, which paints democratization in Africa as a quest for equal social and economic outcomes. This portrayal is usually accompanied by a critique of procedures like constitutional reform and multiparty elections as mere formalities. In Claude Ake's words. "The democracy movement in Africa gets its impetus from the social and economic aspirations of people in Africa."[9]

Our findings show otherwise. Among the positive meanings of democracy offered by survey respondents, almost seven out of ten (69 percent) referred to political procedures like the protection of human rights, participation in

Table 3.1 Popular Attitudes Toward Democracy, Selected African Countries, 1999–2000
(percentages of national samples, including "don't knows")

	Botswana (n = 1,200)	Ghana (n = 2,004)	Malawi (n = 1,208)	Namibia (n = 1,183)	Nigeria (n = 3,603)	Zimbabwe (n = 1,200)
Knowledge of Democracy						
What, if anything, do you understand by the word "democracy"?	69	72	88	65	77	70
(percentages able to supply a meaning)						
Support for Democracy						
Democracy is preferable to any other kind of government.	82	76	66	57	81	71
In certain situations, a nondemocratic government can be preferable.	7	9	22	12	9	11
For someone like me, it doesn't matter what form of government we have.	6	14	11	12	10	13
(percentages choosing these options)						
Rejection of Nondemocratic Alternatives						
Military rule.	85	89	82	59	90	70
One-party state.	78	80	77	63	88	74
Traditional leaders.	74	—	71	55	—	63
All alternatives.	61	52	53	36	76	49
(percentages disapproving these alternatives)						
Extent of Democracy						
[My country is:]						
Completely democratic.	46	—	34	30	17	9
Democratic, but with minor problems.	36	69	28	42	33	18
Democratic, but with major problems.	8	—	23	15	46	17
Not a democracy.	5	12	12	3	1	38
(percentages choosing these options)						
Satisfaction with Democracy						
Overall, how satisfied are you with the way democracy works in [your country]?	75	54	57	63	84	18
(percentages saying "fairly" or "very" satisfied)						

decisionmaking, and voting in elections. Only one out of five respondents (17 percent) referred to substantive outcomes like peace and unity, social and economic development, and equality and justice.[10] Thus, when left unprompted, the majority of Africans interviewed saw democracy as a limited, political process rather than as an expansive socioeconomic transformation.

Moreover, the rank order of substantive interpretations was revealing: more respondents associated democracy with *political* goods (such as peace, unity, equality, justice, or national independence, which together account for 11 percent of responses) than with *economic* goods (social and economic development, which accounts for just 5 percent). The "peace or unity" responses are particularly interesting since none of the countries in the sample, with the possible exception of Namibia, employed democratic elections to implement a peace agreement.[11] One would expect an even closer identification of democracy with peace in countries emerging from civil war.

But the popular meaning of democracy cannot be so easily laid to rest. An alternate question about the components of democracy gave rise to dissonant results. Noting that "people associate democracy with many diverse meanings," we asked respondents to say whether a list of political and economic features were "essential . . . for a society to be called 'democratic.'" The list included (procedural) political features like "majority rule," freedom to criticize government, and "regular elections"; but it also added (substantive) socioeconomic features like "jobs for everyone," "equality in education," and "a small income gap between rich and poor." In two countries (Botswana and Zimbabwe), respondents rated political and economic attributes as equally essential to democracy. In three other countries (Malawi, Namibia, and Nigeria),[12] however, respondents rated economic components as significantly more essential than political ones. This finding suggests that African conceptions of democracy include important substantive components of economic delivery and social justice.[13]

Third, popular African conceptions of democracy are, perhaps unexpectedly, quite *liberal*. When open-ended responses are analyzed, people cite civil liberties and personal freedoms more frequently than any other meanings of democracy (34 percent). These represent a conception of democracy based on individual rights that stands in marked contrast to the less than one in a thousand respondents (0.1 percent) who make reference to group rights. Contrary to those who would have us believe that Africans conceive of democracy and associated rights in a different way than Westerners, our survey respondents are telling us that they place individual rights uppermost.[14] And to the extent that they claim such rights as a means of resisting repression at the hands of an authoritarian ruler, Africans are beginning to think more like citizens of a constitutional state than clients of a personal patron.

Nevertheless, people use very general terms when they speak of political freedoms, for example referring to "freedom as a birthright," "the right to everything," "living freely," and "control over one's own life." These vague associations—expressed by more than half (56 percent) of those citing civil liberties—suggest that the popular conception of human rights remains highly undifferentiated. When people do mention specific rights, they overwhelmingly define democracy in terms of freedom of expression, including the freedoms of speech, press, and dress. Freedom of expression accounts for 35 percent of the references to civil liberties. All other specific freedoms—of movement, association, property, and religion—together account for only 9 percent. The notion of democracy as a system allowing free speech was particularly prevalent in Ghana, where respondents referred to "being free to talk about the government," "allowing people to bring out their own views," and "the ability to say what you think." Several referred to a democratic system as a deliberative one in which "you say some and let me say some," which is a direct translation of a well-known Akan saying.

Are there cross-national variations in the way citizens understand democracy? Botswana stands out as the most liberal country, with more than half of its citizens (55 percent) identifying democracy with civil and political rights. Nigerians are distinctive insofar as they are almost twice as likely as any other Africans to see democracy as "government by the people" (38 percent).[15] That they also associate democracy with voting rights (14 percent) is surely attributable to the recency of the historic transition elections there. Malawi, for its part, is the only country in this sample in which more than one in ten persons (11 percent) offer a substantive definition of democracy. Interestingly, like other Africans, they see democracy's substance not so much in terms of the delivery of socioeconomic development but in term of guarantees of political order and social harmony, which, given the country's regional rivalries, may reflect wishful thinking.

Finally, the meanings imputed to democracy help us interpret the contrasting levels of democratic awareness noted earlier for Namibia and Malawi. In 1989 a dominant political party came to power in Namibia in a negotiated transition from colonialism that marked the achievement of state sovereignty. As such, Namibians are significantly more likely than other Africans to associate democracy with national independence. By contrast, Malawi's 1994 transition signaled the collapse of an indigenous single-party monopoly and local demands for open multiparty competition. Thus Malawians (as well as Nigerians and Ghanaians) associate recent events with the installation of democracy rather than with decolonization.

Support for Democracy

To assess support for democracy, the Afrobarometer poses a standard question that has been employed in Barometer surveys in Western Europe, Latin

America, and the former Soviet bloc. It asks, "Which one of these statements do you most agree with? A. Democracy is preferable to any other form of government; B. In certain situations, a non-democratic government can be preferable; or C. For someone like me, it doesn't matter what form of government we have." Those persons who find democracy to be the best form of government (Option A) were deemed to support democracy.

By this measure, more than seven out of ten people interviewed in six African countries (75 percent) identified themselves as supporters of democracy. This average figure is high by global standards, for example, when compared with mean scores recorded in 1995 for six Eastern and Central European countries (65 percent) and four Latin American countries (63 percent).[16] The apparent strength of public commitment to democracy in Africa can be explained in good part by the exceptional levels of support in just two countries: Botswana and Nigeria. If these two countries are excluded, and South Africa is brought into the sample, then support for democracy is almost identical in sub-Saharan African countries and in other new democracies.[17]

Botswana has the highest levels of popular support for democracy so far found in any African country (82 percent) (see Table 3.1). This appreciative public mood probably reflects a mature and rational assessment that the country's stable political regime based on regular elections has served it well over a period of almost forty years. By contrast, the high level of public support for democracy in Nigeria (81 percent) is hardly based upon an extended experience with competitive elections and good governance. More likely, it reflects popular euphoria over the restoration of civilian rule after the country had suffered through a particularly corrupt and repressive interlude of military dictatorship. While a jubilant mood prevailed at the time of the survey (January 2000)—just half a year after the inauguration of an elected government—there is no guarantee that high levels of support for democracy can be sustained indefinitely. Note also that support for democracy in Nigeria varies by region, reflecting a power shift in 1999 from the north to the south. While support for democracy is high throughout the country, it is markedly higher in the south (86 percent, higher even than Botswana) than in the north (75 percent, which matches the continental standard).[18]

Other country features stand out. For example, Malawians display much more nostalgia for authoritarian rule than other Africans in the sample: fully one out of five respondents in Malawi (22 percent) agree that "in certain situations, a nondemocratic government can be preferable." These longings for the past vary significantly by region; they are most prevalent in Malawi's central region (30 percent), the homeland and political base of Hastings Kamuzu Banda, the country's former strongman.[19] Also notable are the Namibians who admit that they "don't know" whether they support democracy (20 percent), a figure four times higher than for other African countries in the sample. This finding confirms not only the limited mass awareness of democracy in Namibia, but also the existence of popular doubts about whether the de facto one-party regime that is emerging there is really a democracy at all.

Ghana and Zimbabwe are in the middle range of popular commitment to democracy. Yet at the time of the surveys, each country was embarked on a very different political trajectory. Ghana was in the process of completing an extended transition from military to democratic rule on the basis of increasingly open elections; and Zimbabwe was descending into political crisis at the hands of a dictator bent on retaining power by openly flouting the rule of law. Under such divergent circumstances, it is perhaps surprising that the mass electorates in these countries would express such similar levels of commitment to democracy. This finding (together with the finding about high levels of public support for democracy in the contrasting cases of Botswana and Nigeria) suggests that African citizens make separate judgments about democracy as a preferred political system and the imperfect democratic status of their governments of the day.

Opposition to Nondemocratic Alternatives

To explore this issue further, we probed popular appraisals of alternative political regimes.[20] Democracy was presented as a concrete regime form, described as "our present system of government with regular elections and many parties," and was contrasted to the "previous regime," whether colonial, one-party, or military. Using such comparisons, Ghanaians rated democracy well above "the former system of military rule" (6.7 versus just 3.6 on a scale of 1–10). Malawians, however, granted the new regime, which permits multiparty elections, only a slightly higher rating than the old one-party system (6.1 versus 5.4 on a scale of 1–10).

We also asked about future alternatives. In the Afrobarometer surveys, respondents were informed that "some people say that we would be better off if the country was governed differently" and were asked: "What do you think about the following alternatives to our current system of government?" A list of statements was then presented about military rule ("the army should come in to govern the country"), one-man rule ("we should abolish parliament and political parties so that the president can decide everything"), one-party rule ("candidates from only one political party should be allowed to stand for elections and hold office"), rule by traditional leaders ("all decisions should be made by a council of elders, traditional leaders, or chiefs"), and rule by technocrats ("the most important decisions, for example on the economy, should be left to experts"). Clear patterns emerge when regime preferences are probed this way. Generally, we can reconfirm that Africans who live in new democracies wish to retain their current political regimes. And they roundly reject nondemocratic alternatives (see Table 3.1).

Military government is the least popular form of rule, being rejected by an average 81 percent of respondents in the six countries surveyed. This average is pulled up by Nigeria, where fully 90 percent said "never again" to a form of government that they now associate with the abuses of General Sani Abacha. The prospect that "the army should come in to govern the country" was eschewed with almost equal vehemence in Ghana (89 percent) and Botswana (85 percent). By contrast, only a modest majority of Namibians (59 percent) opposed the prospect of soldiers seizing political power. This suggests that, while neither Botswana nor Namibia have ever experienced a coup, citizens of Botswana would be much less likely than their Namibian counterparts to tolerate one if it ever occurred.

Africans also disavow rule by big men and single parties. Generally, they seem to see one-man rule and one-party rule as inseparable regime forms; very similar majorities shun these options (both 76 percent).[21] But cross–country comparisons reveal interesting differences. In Botswana, Ghana, and Zimbabwe, slightly more respondents oppose one-man rule than oppose one-party rule. This may indicate that, in these countries, all of which have relatively well developed political institutions by African standards, citizens are becoming more attached to political institutions than to individual leaders.[22] Malawi, Namibia, and Nigeria display a different pattern, with slightly more respondents opposing one-party rule than opposing one-man rule. Indeed, only a slim majority of Namibians (56 percent) oppose a strongman option. Other things equal, these seem to be places in Africa where personalistic politics are most deeply entrenched and pose the biggest threat to the health of new democracies.

In searching for political regimes appropriate to Africa, we asked about the contemporary relevance of traditional authority. Would citizens countenance a return to decisionmaking by chiefs or a council of elders? Interestingly, in all countries where this question was asked, survey respondents were less resistant to this option than to military or one-party rule. Opposition to traditional rule tended to be weakest in countries where citizens were either geographically isolated or politically alienated from central authority (namely Namibia and Zimbabwe). Opposition to traditional rule was strongest where chiefs actually retained practical powers, formal or informal, over decisionmaking (e.g., Botswana and Ghana). Ironically, therefore, those who had experienced the involvement of traditional leaders in modern governance were most likely to express reservations. And overall, twice as many respondents repudiated a traditional regime as supported it.

The most demanding measure of antiauthoritarian sentiment is the summary percentage of citizens who rejected *all* the nondemocratic alternatives put to them. There was considerable variation in the sub-Saharan region on this measure. At the time of the first round of Afrobarometer surveys, Nigerians were most dismissive of the full range of authoritarian alternatives (76 percent). By this measure, Botswana (61 percent) resembled the citizens of consolidating new democracies in Eastern and Central Europe, whereas Namibians (36 percent), like the denizens of various former Soviet republics, were the most willing to flirt with hard-line alternatives. Public opinion in the remaining African countries (Malawi, Ghana, Zimbabwe) was essentially split on whether to accept or reject any nondemocratic alternative. As such, one cannot be completely certain that public support for authoritarian restorations could not, at some future time, be revived.

Apart from the widespread popular rejection of military rule, the most striking finding concerns another form of technocratic governance. In almost all countries surveyed, African citizens consistently favored a system of government in which "the most important decisions, for example on the economy, should be left to experts." Rule by civilian technocrats won majority approval in five out of the six countries, the only regime form, apart from democracy, to gain such support. And indeed, unlike other alternative regimes, technocratic governance of the economy is not inconsistent with democracy. But this finding indicates that African citizens do not feel confident in their understandings of the operations of the national economy, a realm of endeavor that they would rather leave to others who they deem more qualified. It also suggests that if national leaders choose to pursue an orthodox economic management strategy that requires the insulation of technical decisions from popular pressures, they will encounter little mass objection.

The Extent of Democracy

Do Africans think that their own countries are governed democratically? To find out, the Afrobarometer surveys asked respondents whether their countries were "completely democratic," "democratic, but with minor problems," "democratic, but with major problems," or "not a democracy."

Nowhere did a simple majority of respondents think that the current regime in their country was completely democratic (see Table 3.1). Even in Botswana only a plurality (46 percent) perceived democratization to have been fully achieved, but the overwhelming majority thought that democracy was either "complete" or incomplete only in "minor" respects (82 percent). In Ghana, where the question was asked in a more compact form, 69 percent thought that the country was a democracy, whereas 12 percent thought that it was not.

These cases, which show some evidence of gradual regime consolidation, stand in marked contrast to Namibia and Nigeria. In Namibia, a plurality of respondents (42 percent) thought that the country was "democratic, but with minor problems." In Nigeria, the largest group (46 percent) was less optimistic, finding the country "democratic, but with major problems." This last assessment strikes us as intuitively reasonable, especially given the tremendous challenges of recovery and development that an elected Nigerian government must confront with untested democratic institutions. While Nigerians say they support democracy at almost the same levels as Botswana, perceptions of the extent of democracy are exactly inverse. To wit, the same proportion of Nigerians see "major problems" with their democracy as Botswana who see their democracy as "complete."

This brings us to Zimbabwe, the exception among the countries studied here. A majority of citizens here (55 percent) either think that Zimbabwe is "not a democracy" or say they "don't know" or "don't understand." The proportion of Zimbabweans who think that their country is not a democracy (38 percent) is three times larger than in Malawi (12 percent) and almost forty times larger than in Nigeria (1 percent). And the proportion of Zimbabweans who "don't know" (17 percent) far exceeds the equivalent proportion in Namibia, a country already noted for having the lowest levels of popular awareness of democracy in the sample. We suspect that, far from being oblivious to the meaning of democracy, many Zimbabweans simply have a hard time thinking of their own country in these terms during a period of enforced one-party dominance.

Satisfaction with Democracy

At best, then, most of "the people" regard democracy in Africa as a work in progress. Because actual regimes imperfectly reflect citizen preferences, their performance may or may not induce popular satisfaction. Much depends on whether individuals judge the accomplishments of the new order against recollections of a previous regime's record or against a yardstick of future expectations. If the former, democracy may appear as the lesser of two evils; if the latter, democracy is destined to always fall short.

At this juncture, we draw a sharp distinction between *support* for democracy and *satisfaction* with democracy. Support refers to a judgment in the abstract about one's preferred form of political system. Satisfaction refers to an assessment of the concrete performance of elected regimes. We also note that, because satisfaction with democracy is a much more corporeal standard, it almost always lags support for democracy wherever it has been measured around the world. The Afrobarometer surveys track satisfaction with democracy by asking the standard question, "Overall, how satisfied are you with the way that democracy works in [your country]?" Respondents are offered the options of "very satisfied," "fairly satisfied," "fairly unsatisfied," and "very unsatisfied." (In the discussion that follows, we describe as "satisfied" all those who answered either "fairly satisfied" or "very satisfied.")

These results reveal the widest variation in attitudes reported so far. At one extreme is Nigeria, where 84 percent of adults interviewed were satisfied with democracy; at the other extreme stands Zimbabwe, where only 18 percent were satisfied (see Table 3.1). This stark antithesis is best interpreted as a contrast between populations either celebrating a long-awaited transition to democracy or bemoaning the intransigence of an entrenched autocracy. Expressions of satisfaction with democracy are subject to the exigencies of regime life cycles and must be regarded as much more volatile than other, more stable attitudes like support for democracy. The level of satisfaction in Nigeria could gradually erode, for example, if the administration of Olusegun Obasanjo fails to live up to popular expectations. Similarly, if Robert Mugabe's Zimbabwe African National Union Patriotic Front had been defeated in the June 2000 elections, Zimbabweans might now be willing to express more satisfaction with democracy.

Other countries are arrayed between these extremes. In terms of the proportion of people professing themselves "very satisfied" with democracy, Botswana (32 percent, the highest in the sample) actually exceeds Nigeria (26 percent). Again, this points to a populace whose attitudes toward democracy are based upon an accumulated set of positive experiences. And Ghana scores lower on satisfaction than its relatively high scores on awareness of, and support for, democracy would lead one to expect.

When calculated as a mean for all respondents across six countries, popular satisfaction with democracy averages 64 percent. This cross-national average is inflated by the presence of Nigeria, with its high satisfaction scores and large sample size. Satisfaction with democracy drops to 59 percent if sample sizes are standardized by calculating satisfaction as an average of aggregate country scores (that is, controlling for the large size of the Nigeria sample). And satisfaction declines further still to 51 percent if we set aside the two countries (Nigeria and Namibia) where, countering global patterns, citizens report more satisfaction than support. Most important, satisfaction with democracy lags support for democracy in the African cases. And the gap is wider in Africa than in Eastern and Central Europe and in South America.[23] We interpret this to mean not only that African citizens have inflated expectations of democracy but also that African governments often are unable to satisfy them.

From Satisfaction to Support

Does satisfaction with democracy help to shape overall support for democracy? One might expect that popular assessments of an elected regime's performance would deeply influence whether citizens opt for democracy as their preferred form of government.

The African data support this proposition, though less strongly than expected. Support is positively related to satisfaction in five out of the six countries surveyed (see Table 3.2). If "don't knows" are excluded, 58 percent

**Table 3.2 The Relationship Between Support for Democracy and
Satisfaction with Democracy, Selected African Countries, 1999–2000
(percentages of national samples, excluding "don't knows")**

	Support Democracy		Support Any Alternative Regime[a]		
	Satisfied with Democracy	Unsatisfied with Democracy	Satisfied with Democracy	Unsatisfied with Democracy	Pearson's r
Botswana	70	17	7	6	0.136***
Ghana	53	26	10	11	0.170***
Malawi	53	22	13	13	0.337***
Namibia	54	18	17	11	0.181***
Nigeria	72	11	14	6	0.133***
Zimbabwe	15	59	8	17	−0.142***
All	58	21	12	10	0.149***

Notes: Figures may not agree with Table 3.1 because "don't knows" are removed in this table. Row percentages may not sum to exactly 100 due to rounding.

a. Includes those who support nondemocratic alternatives and those for whom the type of regime "does not matter."

*** p < 0.001.

of all respondents are both supportive of, and satisfied with, democracy. Yet although this relationship is statistically significant in all of these five country cases, it is strong only in Malawi.[24] And in Zimbabwe (where the sign on the correlation coefficient is negative), the relationship runs counter to the predicted direction, with high levels of support coinciding with low levels of satisfaction.

We interpret these data as follows. On the surface, popular support for democracy in at least five African countries appears to have an instrumental component. Citizens seem to extend support to the regime in democracy in good part because they are satisfied with its performance at delivering desired goods and services. But 21 percent of all survey respondents (and 59 percent in Zimbabwe) say that they support democracy *even though* they are dissatisfied with the performance of their own regime. These citizens value democracy intrinsically, that is, not so much as a means of delivering development but as an end in itself.

These results cast new light on the quality of the democracy emerging in African countries. Take Zimbabwe, for example, which harbors the most "dissatisfied democrats." Zimbabweans apparently cling intensely to democracy precisely because their current government has broken most of the rules of the democratic game. Thus intrinsic support for the principle of democracy is best revealed in regimes in crisis, when citizens have abandoned all pretense of instrumental support for an underperforming incumbent government. There is also evidence of intrinsic support for democracy in Ghana. Three-fourths of Ghanaians endorse democracy even though only one-half of them are satisfied with the way it works in practice. In other words, the quality of the "democracy" they have experienced under soldier-turned-civilian Jerry Rawlings falls short of the ideal regime they would prefer. Such intrinsic attachments suggest that the quality of democracy is relatively well-established in Ghana, a country that once led Africa to political independence.

Table 3.2 should not be read as raising reservations about Botswana, which our surveys portray as the paragon of African democracies. Even though this country has the highest levels of expressed support for democracy in the sample, most of this support appears at face value to be instrumental. At this time, we do not know if high levels of instrumental satisfaction in Botswana (or any other country) mask high underlying levels of intrinsic support. Nor can this issue be resolved unless the regime undergoes a period of crisis. Should economic or political performance ever take a serious turn for the worse, and should public attachments to democracy falter in response, then democracy in this country would have been revealed to be less secure than commonly thought. More likely, as in Zimbabwe, citizen attachments to democracy in Botswana will then be revealed as being deep-seated.

Finally, Nigeria and Namibia are interesting anomalies. They are the only two countries in Africa—and possibly the world—where more citizens reported satisfaction with democracy than support for it. In these countries, even people who do not support democracy in principle stand ready and willing to consume the products of a regime that calls itself democratic. Citizens here seem to be instrumentalists par excellence. Many of them apparently care less about the form of government than about the capacity of rulers—any rulers—to deliver the goods. Under circumstances where the attachments of citizens to democracy are largely conditional, we are tempted to conclude that the consolidation of democracy is a distant prospect in both these countries.

Popular Attitudes Toward Markets

Awareness of Adjustment

We have established that the Africans we interviewed know a good deal about democratization reforms. But are they also alert to the second strand in the dual transition? Are they aware of the economic reform package commonly referred to as the structural adjustment program (SAP)? To find out, we asked, "Have you ever heard anything about the government's structural adjustment program, or haven't you had a chance to hear about this yet?" The most common name for this program, (e.g., the economic recovery program [ERP] in Ghana, the economic structural adjustment program [ESAP] in Zimbabwe) was inserted for each country. If respondent's seemed uncertain, a prompt was added: "you know, the reforms to the economy introduced in the 1980s/1990s."

We found considerable diversity across countries in awareness of adjustment (see Table 3.3). At the low end, only four out of ten Nigerians (40 percent) could remember ever having heard about structural adjustment, compared to more than twice as many in Zimbabwe (85 percent). The Nigerian results are somewhat surprising considering the extensive public debate that surrounded the introduction of a market-oriented policy program by the government of Ibrahim Babangida in 1986. The ESAP was introduced more recently in Zimbabwe (1990) and the ESAP terminology has become incorporated into public discourse, including pop songs.[25] Moreover, the Zimbabwean government repeatedly blamed the country's economic downturn on the Washington-based international financial institutions, a smoke screen that could not be blown by the Nigerian government, which claimed that its reforms were homegrown.

On average, in the four countries where this question was asked, respondents were evenly split on awareness of the national economic reform program: 49 percent had heard of it and 51 percent had not. From the perspective of policymakers, this must be read as a disappointing result. After two decades of a sustained international effort to induce African governments to reorient African economies toward the market, one-half of intended beneficiaries claim to be ignorant that such a strategy even exists.

Of course, low levels of name recognition may reflect the shifting and cryptic labels attached to adjustment programs, such as the change from ERP to SAP in Ghana (with a detour into a social safety net program called PAMSCAD). A lack of mass familiarity with economic policies may also reflect the fact that some African governments have only partially adopted market reforms and implemented them inconsistently. Or the economic reforms and accompanying public discourse that occurred in the mid-1980s may have become, for some citizens, historical events. In Ghana, for example, which in 1983 was first among present countries to launch a comprehensive adjustment program, young people are less economically conscious than their elders.[26] Moreover, because SAPs address complex macroeconomic policy questions, awareness also varies greatly by education.[27]

From the perspective of policy elites, low levels of awareness of SAPs may be read in a more positive light. Since these agreements are usually negotiated under international pressure and behind closed doors, SAPs may constitute a constraint on democratic choice, which in turn can undercut a government's legitimacy.[28] Thus governments may find it to their advantage to conceal the concessions on economic policy they have made to international investors or bankers and to undertake adjustment by stealth, a strategy apparently adopted by the government of South Africa. Even if

Table 3.3 Popular Attitudes Toward Markets, Selected African Countries, 1999–2000
(percentages of national samples, including "don't knows")

	Ghana (n = 2,004)	Malawi (n = 1,208)	Nigeria (n = 3,603)	Zimbabwe (n = 1,200)
Knowledge of Adjustment *Have you ever heard about the government's [SAP name] structural adjustment program?* (percentages saying "yes")	42	51	40	85
Responsibility for Well-Being *People should look after themselves and be responsible for their own success in life.*	56	73	42	37
The government should bear the main responsibility for ensuring the well-being of people. (percentages agreeing "somewhat" or "strongly")	44	25	56	59
Support for User Fees *It is better to raise educational/health standards,[a] even if we have to pay fees.*	72	48	69	58
It is better to have free schooling/health care[a] for our children, even if the quality is low. (percentages agreeing "somewhat" or "strongly")	28	44	27	34
Support for Institutional Reform *The government cannot afford so many public employees and should lay some of them off.*	28	21	19	51
All civil servants should keep their jobs, even if paying their salaries is costly to the country. (percentages agreeing "somewhat" or "strongly")	72	73	73	41
Perceived Equity Effects of Adjustment *The government's economic policies have helped most people; only a few have suffered.*	32	11	34	7
The government's economic policies have hurt most people and only benefited a few. (percentages agreeing "somewhat" or "strongly")	68	32	60	78
Satisfaction with Adjustment *How satisfied are you with the [SAP name] structural adjustment program?* (percentages of knowledgeable respondents saying "somewhat" or "very" satisfied)	34	19	16	4

Note: a. The question referred to education services in Ghana and Nigeria and health services in Malawi and Nigeria.

SAP terminology is not broadly recognizable, citizens may still know what sectoral policies are supposed to achieve. Moreover, to the extent that particular reforms are actually implemented, people have experienced the effects of adjustment at firsthand.

Knowledge of Adjustment

In Ghana and Nigeria we asked people, "What, in your opinion, is the SAP[29] supposed to do?" Only one-third of respondents in either country (35 percent in Nigeria, 34 percent in Ghana) could venture an answer. These figures stand in marked contrast to the 74 percent of citizens (the average for six countries) who could attach a meaning to democracy.

Like democracy, however, adjustment is viewed positively. Among those persons who are aware of SAPs, less than one out of fifty (2 percent in Ghana, 1 percent in Nigeria) made reference to negative purposes. To be sure, a handful of people thought that the objects of adjustment were "to bring hardship and difficulties," "to increase inflation," or "to benefit the rich." But over 98 percent cited positive goals, a remarkable finding in light of emotional debates about the appropriateness of market reforms to Africa. Contrary to the conventional wisdom that "the people" regard adjustment in a derogatory light, we find that most knowledgeable Ghanaians and Nigerians seem to associate adjustment reforms with affirmative economic objectives.

What are these affirmative objectives? Two stand out: "to improve the economy" and "to improve living conditions." Whereas Ghanaians name improvements in the macroeconomy (46 percent) ahead of improvements in the conditions of individuals (31 percent), Nigerians put these purposes in reverse order (25 percent and 29 percent respectively). On one hand, these responses suggest that most well-informed citizens recognize that, even if the medicine of adjustment is bitter, SAPs are designed to bring about economic recovery. On the other hand, these responses also indicate that popular comprehension of the purposes of adjustment is loose at best. Respondents usually described the purposes of adjustment in terms that were even sketchier than their sometimes vague interpretations of democracy. Very few respondents associated SAPs with specific measures like fiscal stabilization, the liberalization of prices, the promotion of exports, privatization, and public sector reform. Fewer than 3 percent of the adults in either country tendered any one of these goals. An impression arises from these figures of extremely low popular levels of economic literacy.

Support for Market Values

Even if hazy about the exact content of adjustment policies, people still hold basic economic values. We wondered where Africans position themselves in the great debates about state and market. Do they see themselves as autonomous economic actors or do they rely on government as the chief provider of public well-being? In this regard, respondents were asked to make a choice on a standard survey item that is used in values surveys worldwide: either "People should be responsible for their own success in life," or "Government should bear the main responsibility for ensuring the well-being of people." Because this item is the core correlate in an economic values scale, it neatly summarizes the orientation of citizens to economic values generally.

By this criterion, Africans seem to be caught between state and market. On average, in the six countries surveyed, 52 percent believe in individual responsibility and 44 percent think that government is accountable for public well-being.[30] These figures can be usefully compared with the responses to a similar item posed in seven former Soviet republics in 1989, where the surveyed population was also of two minds. But their preference order was reversed, with a slight majority of Soviet citizens (51 percent) favoring government provision over individual responsibility (49 percent).[31] Thus, even during an era of democratization, significant proportions of the population in both world regions continue to turn to the state in the hope of obtaining socioeconomic welfare. At the margins, however, Africans seem slightly more willing to entertain the prospect of individual self-reliance than Russians, Ukranians, Belorussians, and the residents of Baltic and Central Asian states.

Beneath the African averages, however, lie sharp cross-national differences (see Table 3.3). Support for individual responsibility is highest in Malawi (73 percent) and lowest in Zimbabwe, where a clear majority (59 percent) regard the government as responsible for public welfare. This distinction in popular attitudes may reflect the recent fiscal health of each government. In some African countries (like Malawi and Ghana), the government has long lacked the budgetary capacity to deliver mass benefits, whereas in others (like Zimbabwe and Nigeria) it has enjoyed access to reliable flows of foreign exchange. Thus citizens are responding rationally when they say they prefer to fend for themselves in the former countries but prefer to make claims on the state in the latter countries.

The more we probed into general economic values, the more that attitudes of self-reliance and entrepreneurship were revealed. More people consider that "the best way to create jobs is to encourage people to start their own businesses" (54 percent) than who think that "the government should provide employment for everyone who wants to work" (42 percent).[32] Fully 77 percent agreed that, in order to make a business succeed, people "should invest their own savings or borrow," against just 18 percent who felt that "there is no sense in trying to start a new business because it might lose money."

At the same time, questions about the division of public-private responsibility in various sectors revealed a persistent statism. This was particularly true in relation to the distribution of investments in socioeconomic development. Across all countries, respondents were agreed that government had the prime responsibility for providing agricultural credit (66 percent) and building schools and clinics (65 percent). Respondents also supported, though more equivocally, a lead role for government in marketing the country's main export commodity[33] (53 percent) and controlling crime (52 percent). Only with regard to the construction of housing did they consistently prefer the private sector (individuals and companies) or public-private partnerships rather than the government (26 percent).

In almost all sectors of all countries surveyed, people expressed doubt about the ability of private enterprise to replace public provision. Only tiny minorities thought that market-based institutions should be held responsible for delivering export marketing services (14 percent), agricultural credit (6 percent), or schools and clinics (3 percent). Given the abject failure of state marketing boards across the continent, it is surprising that more Africans have not embraced private sector solutions in the export commodity sectors. Solid minorities support open markets for agricultural inputs and products only in Malawi and Botswana (30 percent and 19 percent respectively), perhaps because private entrepreneurs are available to service at least some rural areas in these countries. Elsewhere, only a handful of respondents are willing to put faith in open markets for agricultural outputs (9 percent in Ghana and 5 percent in Botswana), probably due to a fear that private buyers will either not materialize, or pay only low prices, when farmers have produce to sell. In short, while respondents know that the state lacks administrative capacity, they consider that the private sector is less reliable still. As such, at least in the six countries surveyed, Africans remain ambiguous at best about the viability of markets.

Support for Adjustment Policies

This does not mean that the debate about structural adjustment in Africa should be cast in black-and-white terms. Without the benefit of much empirical evidence, commentators often assert that Africans are either "for" or "against" (usually "against") adjustment. But structural adjustment is a complex package of reforms that citizens need not accept or reject wholesale. Accordingly, we wondered whether survey respondents would support some policy items in the adjustment program but reject others.

We framed four straightforward questions on particular adjustment policies that ordinary folk might have encountered. The first concerned user fees. "Is it better to raise educational/health standards even if [you] have to pay fees?" Or, "Is it better to have free schooling/healthcare for [your] children, even if the quality is low?" The results are striking and consistent (see Table 3.3). In every country, more people supported the payment of user fees for improved services than opposed them (on average over six countries, 62 percent versus 33 percent). Willingness to pay one's own way was most evident in Ghana (72 percent) and least evident in Malawi (48 percent). This discrepancy is partly explicable in terms of the contrasting policies adopted in each country; for example, President Jerry Rawlings of Ghana began to introduce charges for junior secondary schooling as early as 1986, whereas President Bekuli Muluzi of Malawi campaigned as recently as 1999 on a platform of free primary education.

Second, we asked about market prices for consumer goods. Is it "better to have goods available in the market even if the prices are high"? Or is it "better to have low prices even if there are shortages of goods"? A similar pattern emerged of support for market-based policies, though more ambiguously and at lower levels of support. On average, more persons preferred the free play of market forces in setting consumer prices (54 percent) than wanted to retain consumer subsidies (36 percent). But quite a few people were undecided on this question, especially in Namibia (15 percent). Moreover, Malawi and Zimbabwe bucked the general trend, with more people preferring low consumer goods prices, even at the risk of shortages. Again, the formation of these opinions probably derives from the recent economic history of each country. Malawi and Zimbabwe have never experienced shortages as a consequence of the oversubsidization of basic commodities in a centrally planned economy. By contrast, Ghana and Zambia experienced repeated policy-induced shortages of consumer goods during the 1980s. The memory of these interludes of deprivation is apparently sufficient to induce citizens in these two countries to now opt strongly for allowing the market to set prices (an identical 72 percent in Ghana in 1999 and in Zambia in an earlier survey in 1996).[34]

Third, we quizzed respondents about privatization. The question was again worded as a choice. Should the government "retain ownership of its factories, businesses and farms," or should it "sell its businesses to private companies and individuals"? On this question, the pendulum of public opinion swung away from the market and back toward the state. In five out of six countries, more people favored state ownership over privatization, the only exception being Botswana, where a plurality favored privatization (48 percent versus 36 percent). On average, 57 percent of the Africans interviewed wanted to retain state ownership and only 35 percent supported the sale of public corporations. In contrast to earlier results, however, Malawians now resemble Ghanaians in their strong rejection of privatization. To explore the issue of privatization in greater depth, further disaggregation may be necessary by sector. Focus groups conducted with opinion leaders in Ghana in March 2000 suggest that these citizens favor privatization in some sectors (e.g., broadcasting) but resist it in others (e.g., electricity).[35]

Finally, we asked about the restructuring of the public service. Should "all civil servants keep their jobs, even if paying their salaries is costly to the country"? Or, since "the government cannot afford so many public employees, [should it] lay some of them off"? This choice evoked the most ardent antireform reaction (see Table 3.3). Across six countries, two out of three respondents (an average of 67 percent) rejected retrenchment of the public service and only one-quarter (25 percent) extended support. The strongest prostate sentiment was found in Botswana and Malawi, both small countries with long-standing traditions of public employment on which many extended family networks depend. The only exception was Zimbabwe, where more people (a slim majority of 51 percent) support retrenchment than oppose it (41 percent). This unforeseen finding indicates that Mugabe's party-state machine has become so bloated that even his erstwhile supporters now think that he has distributed too many patronage posts.

A comment is in order about the intensity of opinions on economic adjustment policies. We know that "the people" in selected sub-Saharan countries are not broadly aware of the existence of official macroeconomic adjustment programs and have little intimate knowledge about the objectives of these programs. But they have little difficulty in recognizing policies that have a direct impact on their own economic interests. Most respondents were able to express an opinion when faced with the range of practical policy choices listed above; only a few said they "didn't know" (between 5 and 10 percent, depending on the question). Instead, respondents felt strongly about adjustment, as evidenced by the clustering of responses (whether "pro" or "con") toward the "strongly agree" ends of the spectrum.

To close this section, let us summarize the bifurcated attitudes toward structural adjustment that have been revealed to date. Far from being wholly for or against economic reforms, most Africans interviewed express discriminating views. In some respects, they support market liberalization. Like the independence generation before them, currents cohorts of African citizens continue to place a lofty value on education and health care, to the point of even being willing to pay school and clinic fees. To a lesser extent, most citizens will even accept market pricing for consumer goods perhaps because, under adjustment policies, so many more of them have become private traders in the small-scale, informal economy.

Against this toleration for "getting the prices right," we note also a strong resistance to the reform of economic institutions. The majority of respondents in our surveys expressed strong attachment to the supply of developmental goods and services by the state. The key issue here is the persistent role of the state as the principal provider of employment in African

countries. Even if public sector salaries are in decline, the rents and per-
quisites associated with public office are apparently still attractive. Through
opposition to privatization and public service retrenchments, citizens indicate that they do not believe that the private sector, whether driven by
international investment or small-scale enterprise, can deliver a reliable
supply of remunerative jobs. Until the free market can demonstrate that it
will perform better at job creation than even an enfeebled state, Africans
would rather seemingly stick with the devil they know.

Satisfaction with Adjustment

How, then, do citizens judge the performance of structural adjustment programs?[36] Most Africans interviewed (68 percent across the four countries
where the question was asked) are unsatisfied with the changes they attribute to the government's economic reform program. An absolute majority in
every country in the sample—ranging from a bare 53 percent in Ghana to
a stunning 92 percent in Zimbabwe—expressed dissatisfaction with SAPs.
To be sure, a substantial proportion (13 percent) claim to be undecided or
neutral in their judgments about the effects adjustment. But, on average,
fewer than one in five (18 percent) say they are satisfied, though in Ghana
one out of three persons (35 percent) expressed some measure of satisfaction. Thus, though some Ghanaians are cheered by recent economic reforms,
almost all Zimbabweans are distressed by them.

On a cautionary note, we wonder whether this indictment of SAPs is a
case of mistaken identity. Are people conflating structural adjustment with
economic crisis, thereby blaming the medicine for the disease? On one
hand, possible evidence exists of this kind of misdiagnosis: in five out of
the six countries surveyed, people who are dissatisfied with the condition
of the economy are also very likely to be dissatisfied with SAPs.[37] On the
other hand, when we asked people "Who is responsible for . . . current economic conditions?" we found that people could distinguish between crisis
and adjustment. Almost all people blamed economic decline on mismanagement by a previous or current government (83 percent in Ghana and 76
percent in Nigeria). Fewer than 9 percent in Ghana and fewer than 2 percent in Nigeria chose to attribute current economic woes to the SAP or the
international financial agencies. Indeed, almost as many people in Nigeria
blamed supernatural forces!

Nonetheless, the survey respondents held the view that adjustment has
uneven social effects. When asked whether the government's economic
policies had helped or hurt "most people," most respondents saw increasing
inequality (see Table 3.3). On average, 62 percent of those able to offer a
valid answer agreed ("somewhat" or "strongly") that structural adjustment
has *hurt* most people and benefited few.[38] In no African country did a

majority of respondents think that adjustment had assisted most folk. The largest vote of confidence in SAPs was mustered in Nigeria, where just 34 percent saw broad-based benefits. Even in Ghana, only 32 percent thought that most people had gained, suggesting that prosperity was not trickling down even from the continent's longest-running economic reform program.

On this theme, respondents thought that, across a range of public tasks, reformist governments did worst of all at "narrowing the income gaps between the rich and the poor." For example, whereas 64 percent saw the Obasanjo government in Nigeria doing "well" at combating corruption, only 40 percent said the same about its performance at closing income gaps. In Ghana, an even smaller proportion (32 percent) praised the Rawlings government's handling of income distribution in a context where they gave it much higher marks for controlling crime (57 percent). Caution must be exercised in interpreting the results for Malawi. In this country, more than half the respondents (55 percent) admitted that they "didn't know" or "couldn't say" about the social consequences of adjustment. This finding helps to underline the remoteness of the adjustment debate, particularly when it refers to the macroeconomy rather than to the lives of ordinary individuals. But among those who had an opinion, dissatisfaction was closely correlated with perceptions that adjustment had had an unequal social impact.[39]

When we delved into exactly "who benefits," the answer was clear. Overwhelming majorities of Nigerians (84 percent) and Ghanaians (74 percent) reported that the benefits of adjustment accrued to "people close to government." Mentioned in this group were the president, cabinet ministers, senior officers in the party or junta, regional barons appointed by the top leadership, and individuals in the informal circles of power around such leaders. No other category of supposed beneficiary came close. Foreign businesses and "the rich" were cited by only 3–5 percent of respondents in either country. Interestingly, the unequal impact of adjustment was seen to occur along class rather than communal lines. Only 4 percent of Ghanaians and 3 percent of Nigerians portrayed unfair gains from adjustment in terms of rural-urban or interregional differences. When they (rarely) mentioned a region, Ghanaians cited Volta, the homeland of President Rawlings and Nigerians pointed to Hausaland or "the north." Instead, a new class of beneficiaries was perceived to have arisen through access to the offices and functionaries of the state.

Thus, in the final analysis, "the people" have strong reservations about structural adjustment. The willingness of Africans to support selected reform policies is not extended to the economic strategy as a whole. We propose that the Achilles heel of a market-oriented development strategy in Africa is its association in the popular imagination with the intensification of politically based social inequalities, an issue that we explore further in the next section.

Relating Political and Economic Attitudes

To close this chapter, we consider how democracy and markets interact in African public opinion. And we explore several reasons why people accept or reject various reforms. Four lines of inquiry are followed:

- Are attitudes toward political and economic reform *related?*
- Is support for reform affected by the *meanings* that people attribute to democracy and markets?
- Are mass attitudes influenced by demographic factors, especially *education?*
- Do popular concerns about *inequality* undermine support for adjustment and democracy?

No African Consensus

The Washington consensus about the complementarity of democracy and markets is not mirrored by a parallel African consensus. For the most part, attitudes toward the two types of reform are unrelated in our surveys. Where a relationship does exist, it points to a process of dual transition whose dynamics are more contradictory than coherent.

To begin with, *support for democracy* in six African countries cannot be predicted from the main economic attitudes examined in this chapter. For example, popular attachments to democracy are largely unlinked to mass support for "getting the prices right." More than seven out of ten respondents regard democracy as the ideal form of government, regardless of whether they support market pricing (79 percent) or oppose it (74 percent). Any observed differences are not statistically significant.[40] We suggest that support for democracy is sufficiently widespread that it occurs among *both* adherents *and* opponents of free market reform.

Nor is support for democracy much affected by respondent reactions to the impact of adjustment. More than eight out of ten respondents prefer democracy to authoritarian rule, regardless of whether they are satisfied (84 percent) or unsatisfied (80 percent) with their country's structural adjustment program. Again, any observed differences are statistically insignificant.[41] Thus the legitimacy of democracy is not only widespread but also relatively robust. So far, at least, the popularity of the democratic principle in six African countries has withstood the potentially corrosive effects of adjustment fatigue.

An affinity appears between the two types of reform, however, once one moves beyond abstract political values to concrete assessments of regime performance. We find a strong, positive, and statistically significant relationship between *satisfaction with democracy* and *satisfaction with*

SAPs. Fully 83 percent of respondents who are satisfied with their country's economic reform program are also satisfied with democracy. But only 53 percent who are dissatisfied with SAPs are also satisfied with democracy.[42] Thus the survey respondents hinge their judgments of the performance of democracy in good part on their comfort level with the implementation of adjustment. Widespread disgruntlement with the impact of economic policy reform (on average, only 20 percent across six countries are satisfied with SAPs) is a major factor pulling down the public's assessment of the performance of democracy.

Adjustment's chilling effect on satisfaction with democracy is observable in every country for which data are available (see Table 3.4). The effect is strongest in Malawi, where discontent with SAP cuts satisfaction with democracy almost in half. The effect is weakest (but still statistically significant) in Nigeria, where, shortly after a landmark political transition, satisfaction with democracy was so widespread that it permeated virtually all social, economic, and opinion groups. The pattern is consistent even in Zimbabwe, despite the markedly lower levels of public satisfaction with democracy there. In short, everywhere we looked, we found that economic dissatisfaction depressed political satisfaction.

Thus, in some African countries, public opinions about democracy and markets are connected, but not quite in the harmonious and productive ways that advocates of democratic capitalism contend. To be sure, those citizens who report satisfaction with the implementation of structural adjustment measures are likely to say that they are also content with the way democracy works. But so few Africans are satisfied with SAPs that the introduction of adjustment measures actually undermines democratic satisfaction. Thus the

Table 3.4 The Relationship Between Satisfaction with Democracy and Satisfaction with Adjustment, Selected African Countries, 1999–2000 (percentages of national samples, excluding "don't knows")

	Satisfied with Democracy		Unsatisfied with Democracy		
	Satisfied with SAP	Unsatisfied with SAP	Satisfied with SAP	Unsatisfied with SAP	Pearson's r
Ghana	33	32	7	29	0.381***
Malawi	23	29	4	44	0.432***
Nigeria	16	67	2	15	0.077**
Zimbabwe	2	20	2	76	0.228***
All	17	42	3	38	0.322***

Notes: Figures may not agree with Tables 3.1 and 3.3 because "don't knows" are removed in this table. Row percentages may not sum to exactly 100 due to rounding.
   ** p < 0.01.
   *** p < 0.001.

only reason that democracy and markets can coexist in Africa is because democracy has intrinsic legitimacy of its own, earned quite independently of the performance of economic policies. This feature of democracy is reflected in the significant majorities of Africans across numerous countries who say they *support* democracy *regardless* of what they think of adjustment.

The Eye of the Beholder

To state the obvious, support for reform begins with awareness of the purposes of reform. Individuals who cannot define democracy are much less attached to it as a preferred form of regime. Compared to politically conscious citizens, they are twice as likely to say that "it makes no difference to me what form of government we have."[43]

More interesting, support for democracy and markets is related to the content of popular understandings. In Nigeria, for example, a subset of citizens comprehend structural adjustment to involve measures to instill fiscal discipline, including cutbacks in the government's budgetary outlays.[44] Those who conceive of SAPs this way are also likely to welcome a role for the market in determining the prices of consumer goods (65 percent). By contrast, those who think that adjustment aims to increase the provision of government services are significantly less likely to favor market pricing (53 percent). Thus individuals who correctly identify economic reform with a reduced role for the state are more prepared to accept the consequences of economic reform.

Similarly, citizens' support for democracy increases if they conceive it in procedural rather than substantive terms.[45] For instance, whereas 81 percent of those who see democracy as "government by the people" name it as the best form of regime, the comparable figure is 73 percent for those who define democracy as "social and economic development," a small but statistically significant difference. Moreover, support for democracy is lowest among those who associate democracy with "social and economic hardship" (56 percent).[46] Thus support for democracy seems to be centered solidly among minimalists, for whom democracy's scope is limited to setting the rules of the political game, but more tentative among maximalists, who hope that democracy will herald sweeping socioeconomic change.

The same applies, but with greater force, to satisfaction with the way that democracy actually works. The most satisfied citizens are those who define democracy in terms of the procedural notion of electoral choice (73 percent). The least satisfied are those who expect democracy to deliver economic equality or social justice (59 percent), social or economic development (58 percent), and security from crime (57 percent), all substantive desires. We conclude that citizens who have modest expectations—namely, that democracy will enable them to choose leaders and participate in other decisionmaking procedures (and not much more!)—are relatively likely to be satisfied with democracy. If, however, they believe that democracy will automatically provide jobs, redistribute income, and ensure social peace, then they are candidates for rapid disillusionment. In short, the perceived performance of democracy and adjustment are partly in the eye of the beholder.

The Impact of Education

A standard prediction in social science is that demographic attributes such as gender, age, and income shape mass beliefs. We find that, with the exception of education, such factors have relatively little influence on attitudes toward reform in six countries in Africa.

Take gender. Men and women display very similar levels of support for, and satisfaction with, key political and economic reforms, differing only in their awareness of democracy and, especially, markets. Whereas 21 percent of males in the six countries had never heard of democracy, some 31 of females were similarly uninformed.[47] And whereas 56 percent of men had never heard of their country's structural adjustment program, fully 69 percent of women were similarly uninformed.[48] These differences survived a statistical control for the respondent's level of education, thereby suggesting a genuine *gender* gap in awareness of the political and economic worlds.

Neither were there any meaningful urban-rural distinctions in attitudes toward democracy and markets. Urban and rural dwellers in the six countries support democracy in roughly equal proportions. In five countries (especially Botswana, Nigeria, and Zimbabwe) urbanites were more likely to express dissatisfaction with the way democracy was working. But this general finding is offset by results from Malawi, where urbanites were more satisfied with democracy than their country cousins. Given that economic reform programs were intended to correct imbalances in urban-rural terms of trade, one might expect to find greater support for markets and satisfaction with adjustment in rural areas. But urbanites are just as likely as rural dwellers to support market pricing for consumer goods and to be unsatisfied with the performance of SAPs. We found a significant difference in these attitudes only in Nigeria, where, contrary to forecasts, rural dwellers were more dissatisfied with SAPs than city folk.

Of all demographic factors, education has the greatest observed effects on attitudes toward reform. Not surprisingly, the higher their educational attainment, the more likely Africans are to be aware of democracy and markets.[49] For example, nine out of ten persons with university education say they know something about democracy, whereas six out of ten persons with no formal schooling make the same claim. More striking still, 91 percent of university postgraduates have heard about an SAP, compared to only 13 percent of persons without schooling.

Unlike in the West, however, education does not seem to build support for democracy in Africa. Postgraduates are no more likely than people who have never been to school to say that democracy is "always preferable." Indeed, the very highly educated in Africa seem to have qualms about democracy precisely because it endows nonliterate citizens with political rights that they fear may be exercised unreflectively or irresponsibly.[50] Moreover, educated Africans are critical of democracy in practice. Only 10 percent of university postgraduates are "very satisfied" with democracy, compared to 32 percent of those without formal schooling. If educated people are satisfied at all, they are likely to damn with faint praise by saying they are only "fairly" satisfied.

Nevertheless, education does increase sympathy for some aspects of economic reform. The educated elite are more likely to support market pricing for consumer goods and to accept user fees for social services; for example, a strong majority of those with university degrees (71 percent) applaud market pricing compared to a minority of those with some primary schooling (45 percent). Nonetheless, educated people are no more likely than anyone else to support privatization or civil service retrenchment, indicating that this key group of opinion leaders has yet to be convinced of the merits of these institutional reforms. And while educated people are clearly not satisfied with adjustment, they are somewhat more satisfied than the lesser educated. For instance, some 22 percent of university graduates say they are satisfied with SAPs compared with 14 percent of those with some primary schooling.

In the absence of household income data for all countries, we do not know whether these putative educational effects are actually due to income differentials. The evidence from Ghana and Nigeria is inconclusive. Income and education are not as closely correlated as one would expect.[51] And income displaces education in explaining support for market pricing only in Ghana. More research is required.

The Challenge of Equity

We arrive, finally, at the public demand for distributive justice, an issue central to African political cultures. One might guess that, in settings where traditional social values emphasize egalitarianism, community, and reciprocity, the legitimation of political and economic regimes would depend on how equitable they are perceived to be.

As noted earlier, public opinion holds that SAPs hurt more people than they help. And citizens clearly associate economic adjustment with perceptions of emerging social inequality. For example, Malawians show above average satisfaction with their country's adjustment program (46 percent) as long as they think that their new government is treating everybody "equally and fairly." By contrast, they are far less satisfied with the SAP if they think that, now, people are treated less equally than before (8 percent).[52] Take another example. The majority of Ghanaians (61 percent) who think that the government is doing "well" in reducing rich-poor income gaps are also satisfied with the ERP. But only 25 percent who think that the government is handling income gaps "badly" hold a favorable opinion about adjustment.[53] These are among the strongest relationships found in this study.

Even more critically, perceptions that SAPs widen the gap between the rich and the poor have a negative spillover effect on attitudes toward *political* reform. Respondents who think that SAPs help most people are very likely to be satisfied with democracy (84 percent); by contrast, those who think that SAPs hurt most people display much lower levels of political satisfaction (63 percent).[54] This relationship is particularly strong in Malawi and Zimbabwe.[55] And whereas those who think that the government is handling income gaps "well" are usually satisfied with democracy (72 percent), those who think that income gaps are being handled "badly" rarely find democracy satisfying (47 percent). This relationship is based on observations from Ghana and Nigeria.[56]

Finally, a multivariate analysis of satisfaction with democracy was conducted for all six countries, using as predictors the variables discussed so far (education, meaning of democracy, satisfaction with SAPs, and perceived equity effects of SAPs). All reported relationships remained highly significant even when controlled for one another.[57] Even more important, the strongest explanatory factor was satisfaction with SAPs, closely followed by the perception that SAPs have hurt more people than they have helped.[58]

These findings lead us to reverse the conventional argument about the tension between political and economic reform.[59] The threat is not so much that democratization will expose leaders to popular pressures, which prevent them from taking the tough measures that economic recovery requires. Rather, popular satisfaction with democracy will be undermined if economic adjustment programs are only partially implemented and, instead, become frozen at a point where the mass public perceives that benefits are accruing unevenly.[60]

Conclusion

We end this chapter with a summary and interpretation of attitudes toward democratic and market reforms in Africa. "The people" in the six countries surveyed in the 1999–2000 Afrobarometer research project say they are much more aware of political than economic regimes, of democracy rather than markets. Democratic values have been absorbed into popular political attitudes and discourse. But market liberalization (as a comprehensive strategy for economic recovery) has yet to fully capture the popular imagination.

Democracy, broadly defined, has already attained wide legitimacy, with more than seven out of ten African respondents naming it as their preferred form of government. Because previous regimes of military and one-party rule are no longer popular in large parts of the continent, support for democracy is not presently compromised by large pockets of authoritarian nostalgia. While perhaps a mile wide, support for democracy in Africa may be only an inch deep. Many people express extremely vague understandings of democratic values and procedures, regard the new regimes in their countries as seriously incomplete, and express low levels of satisfaction with the practical performance of elected governments.

Nor is economic adjustment endorsed with anything like the same exuberance as expressed for democracy. While a majority of survey respondents support "getting the prices right," the Africans we interviewed generally abjure reforms to the existing architecture of economic institutions. Resistance to market liberalization is unusual given the African genius for trade, whether in its historical long-distance form or its contemporary guise as the informal sector. But such resistance is driven by a deep-seated popular conviction that market institutions, especially in their current globalized form, cannot provide employment and development services with the same effectiveness and equity as even corrupt and hollowed-out states.

We conclude that Africans participate in the global shifts toward democracy and markets for dissimilar reasons. Support for political liberalization is a primarily indigenous sentiment that arose as a popular quest for accountable government quite independently of political conditions attached to foreign aid.[61] Economic liberalization, by contrast, remains a largely exotic project, promoted more feverishly by Africa's donors and lenders and negotiated only with African elites. And while educated people within Africa have acted as vectors for the dissemination of awareness about democracy, they remain too ambiguous about adjustment to serve as opinion leaders in this realm.

Will skepticism about market reforms undermine democracy in Africa? The jury is still out on this important question. On one hand, the Afrobarometer surveys point to an intrinsic core of popular support for democracy in many countries that is unaffected by instrumental judgments about regime performance. The intrinsic core is most vividly revealed in countries in political and economic crisis, but it underpins support for democracy in many other places too. Moreover, opponents of market principles and adjustment reforms do not denigrate democracy; in fact they support democracy at unexpectedly high levels. Thus, for the moment, it is hard to identify an economically based social segment on which an antidemocratic movement could be mounted. Perhaps a constituency of this sort will arise in time among democracy's initial supporters who become disillusioned with regime performance at economic delivery. As of 1999, however, even those persons who were unsatisfied with economic reform were still likely to report satisfaction with democracy.

But the surveys also show clearly that satisfaction with democracy declines when citizens disdain the content and consequences of official economic policy. To the extent that it has an instrumental base, support for democracy is therefore susceptible to erosion if adjustment measures are introduced ahead of the pace at which citizens feel comfortable. Even if citizens express tolerance for a measure of price reform, they still want state institutions to provide employment and essential services. They also insist loudly that policy reform should broadly benefit common people rather than accumulate in the hands of state elites. In principle, democracy puts in place the procedures for holding state elites accountable. Governments that are responsive to "the people" should in turn be relatively more effective at alleviating equity concerns. Through the course of our survey research, we have come to believe that, reciprocally, the very survival of infant democracies requires that elected leaders attend closely to the popular demand for social justice.

Notes

1. We situate our African survey results in the grand tradition of comparative empirical research on mass political attitudes. The revived debates in this field are skillfully summarized in Norris, *Critical Citizens.*

2. The sample sizes for each country are as follows: Botswana = 1,200, Ghana = 2,004, Malawi = 1,208, Namibia = 1,183, Nigeria = 3,603, and Zimbabwe = 1,200. We are grateful for research funding from the National Science Foundation and the U.S. Agency for International Development.

3. The samples were designed using a common, multistage, stratified, area cluster approach. Random selection methods were used at each stage, with probability proportional to size where appropriate. Sampling frames were constructed in the first stages from the most up-to-date census figures or projections available, and thereafter from census maps, systematic walk patterns, and project-generated lists of household members. In each case the samples were sufficiently representative of national characteristics on key socioeconomic indicators (gender, age, region, etc.) that statistical weighting of the data was not necessary. For details of the sampling methods used in each case, see country survey reports available from the Institute for Democracy in South Africa, the Center for Democratic Development (Ghana), or Michigan State University.

4. For a succinct current statement on the political implications of the neglected equity issue, see Karl, "Economic Inequality."

5. See Williamson, "Democracy and the Washington Consensus."

6. For recent empirical contributions to a vast literature on the exegesis of democracy, see Miller et al., "Conceptions of Democracy"; Simon, "Popular Conceptions"; and Luckham, "Popular Versus Liberal Democracy."

7. Except where noted, all "average" figures are calculated as the raw mean of aggregate country distributions. This has the effect of weighting each country sample as if it were the same size. Mean scores are not corrected for the country's population size.

8. That is, excluding "don't know," "can't explain," and "never heard of the word 'democracy,'" plus all refusals and missing responses.

9. See Ake, *Democracy and Development*, p. 139.

10. The proportions in the "procedural" and "substantive" categories depend in part on how one classifies the response that defines democracy as "government by, for, or of the people." If they voiced this interpretation, most respondents cast it as "government *by* the people," which together with "government *of* the people" is probably best interpreted in terms of political procedure. The figures reported here so classify it. But even if one excludes this response from analysis, or reclassifies it as "substantive," a majority of respondents still opt for procedural interpretations (76 percent and 56 percent respectively).

11. Namibians actually chose the "peace or unity" option less frequently (5 percent) than all respondents (6 percent).

12. The question was not asked in Ghana.

13. At first we wondered whether respondents were led by the closed-ended list, being prompted to choose substantive attributes that they did not freely associate with democracy when asked in a completely undirected way. But factor analysis shows that political and economic responses cluster along separate dimensions and that people who emphasize democracy's political procedures are not necessarily those who emphasize its economic substance.

14. For a recent exposition on "the primacy of the collective," see Chabal and Daloz, *Africa Works*, p. 130.

15. Whereas 22 percent of Ghanaians opt for "government by the people," only 3 percent of Namibians do so.

16. *New Democracies Barometer IV* (1995), cited in Mishler and Rose, "Five Years After the Fall," p. 13; and *Latinobarometro* (1995), cited in Linz and Stepan, *Problems of Democratic Transition,* p. 222.

17. See Bratton and Mattes, "Support for Democracy." The unstandardized average score for Ghana, Malawi, Namibia, Zimbabwe (1999), and South Africa (1997) is 65 percent.

18. Contingency coefficient = 0.142, sig. = 0.000.

19. In the north, where residents have seen control of the state pass from the central region to the southern region, people were twice as likely as Malawians countrywide to say that the form of government "makes no difference" (19 percent versus 11 percent).

20. This approach heeds the advice of Richard Rose, William Mishler, and Christian Haerpfer to measure "real" rather than "ideal" conceptions of democracy. See Rose, Mishler, and Haerpfer, *Democracy and Its Alternatives,* esp. chap. 2.

21. Bivariate Pearson's r correlation coefficient = 0.536, sig. = 0.000.

22. In Ghana and Zimbabwe, however, opposition to big man rule also surely reflects popular disaffection with sitting leaders who have outstayed their welcome.

23. With data from *New Democracies Barometer IV* (1998), we estimate an average support-satisfaction gap for Eastern and Central Europe (six countries) of

about 5 percentage points. With data from the *Latinobarometro* (1995), we estimate an average gap for South America (four countries) of about 13 percentage points. Depending on how it is measured, the average gap for sub-Saharan African countries in 1999–2000 is between 11 and 21 percentage points.

24. The correlation coefficients for the rest of the countries are sufficiently modest that they might disappear if we controlled for other factors simultaneously associated with both variables.

25. See Vambe, "Popular Songs," p. 80.

26. Whereas almost one-half (48 percent) of Ghanaians over forty-five years of age were familiar with the ERP, only one-third (35 percent) aged eighteen to twenty-six were similarly aware.

27. In Nigeria, for example, education and awareness of the SAP are closely related. Contingency coefficient = 0.505, sig. = 0.000.

28. See O'Donnell, "Do Economists Really Know Best?" pp. 38–40; and Bratton and van de Walle, *Democratic Experiments,* p. 133.

29. The actual name of the country's economic program was inserted here.

30. Because the data set is not complete for all market attitudes, Table 3.3 reports results for only four of the six countries surveyed on this and several other items. The sample is even more evenly divided if we use total distributions (n = 10,398), which overweight the impact of the large Nigeria subsample (n = 3,603). By this measure, 50 percent support individual responsibility and 47 support government responsibility.

31. See Finifter and Mickiewicz, "Redefining the Political System."

32. When asked, "Who has responsibility for creating jobs?" however, the results came out differently: 54 percent public sector, 6 percent private sector (individuals and businesses), and 28 percent joint public-private responsibility.

33. Oil in Nigeria, cocoa in Ghana, diamonds in Namibia, and tobacco in Botswana, Malawi, and Zimbabwe.

34. See Bratton, "Political Participation," p. 559.

35. Center for Democracy and Development, "Elite Attitudes."

36. The question was posed somewhat differently in the four countries where it was asked. In Ghana and Nigeria we asked, "How satisfied or unsatisfied are you with the [SAP]?" In Malawi and Zimbabwe we asked, "What effect do you think [the SAP] has had on your life?" For purposes of comparison, those who thought the SAP had made life worse were assumed to be unsatisfied, and those who thought it had made life better were assumed to be satisfied. Since either question was asked only to the minority who were aware of SAPs, the sample size was reduced to 3,614 across four countries.

37. Pearson's r correlation = 0. 414, sig. = 0.000, for the four southern African countries (0.430, sig. = 0.000 for Ghana). The variables were only weakly related in Nigeria.

38. Percentages exclude "don't knows."

39. In Malawi and Zimbabwe, perceptions of the negative impact of SAPs on people's lives were almost perfectly associated with perceptions that only a few had benefited (Pearson's r = 0.984, sig. = 0.000).

40. Pearson's r correlation = 0.006, sig. = 0.531. Calculations exclude "don't knows." All statistics quoted in this section of the chapter are simple bivariate coefficients. Except in one instance (see endnote 53), regression analysis was not used, since (a) causal direction was not known and (b) various aspects of political and economic reform are examined (i.e., with a different dependent variable each time).

41. Pearson's r correlation = 0.022, sig. = 0.182. Calculations exclude "don't knows."

42. Pearson's r correlation = 0.322, sig. = 0.000. Calculations exclude "don't knows."

43. A difference of 9 percent versus 20 percent.

44. We report results for Nigeria here because data on "what adjustment [is] supposed to do" were not available for all countries.

45. A difference of 79 percent versus 74 percent.

46. Caution is warranted with this finding, since the subsample size on which it is based is rather small.

47. Contingency coefficient = 0.113, sig. = 0.000.

48. Contingency coefficient = 0.136, sig. = 0.000.

49. Contingency coefficients = 0.215 (for democracy) and = 0.355 (for economic reforms), sigs. = 0.000.

50. Among Zambians, for example, educated persons are less likely to agree with the principle of universal franchise. They are also less likely to vote. See Bratton, "Political Participation," p. 564.

51. Pearson's r = 0.279 and 0.192 for Ghana and Nigeria respectively, sigs. = 0.000.

52. Contingency coefficient = 0.458, sig. = 0.000.

53. Contingency coefficient = 0.406, sig. = 0.000.

54. Contingency coefficient = 0.349, sig. = 0.000.

55. Contingency coefficient = 0.376, sig. = 0.000.

56. Contingency coefficients = 0.322 and 0.246 respectively, sigs. = 0.000.

57. All sigs. = 0.000.

58. Though ordinary least squares regression explained little total variance, just 14 percent.

59. See Przeworski, *Democracy and the Market.*

60. For a definitive discussion of the political dynamics of partial economic reform, see Hellman, "Winners Take All." For Africa, see Chapter 2 in this volume, and van de Walle, *The Politics of Permanent Crisis.*

61. The finding about democracy's internal dynamics echoes at the micro level what we demonstrated at the macro level in Bratton and van de Walle, *Democratic Experiments.*

Civil Society and
Democratic Development

E. Gyimah-Boadi

The term "civil society" has come to occupy a central position in the contemporary discourse on African development in general and democratic development in particular in recent times. Nevertheless, considerable debate has raged over its conceptual usefulness in the African context.[1] Indeed, the relevance and quality of civil society (especially the types favored by international donors) to African political renaissance has been seriously questioned.[2] This chapter contributes to these discussions by addressing issues such as the exact contributions that civil society makes to African democratic development, the drawbacks and limitations associated with civil society in the context of African democratization, and its prospects for helping to deepen and consolidate African democratization. The chapter ends with suggestions for reducing the weaknesses and reinforcing the strengths of African civil societies.

I argue that nascent civil society can contribute and has contributed significantly to African democratization. And given Africa's huge institutional deficits, it must do so. I attempt to show that its organizations played central roles in the African democratization projects of the early 1990s. Having moved from crude antistate activities to complex engagement, they continue to play key roles in the posttransition and in nominally democratic regimes of the respective countries. However, I also argue that civil society must overcome many internal and external obstacles and deficiencies that bedevil it, if it is to sustain its effectiveness as an agent of African democratic development. In this sense, I share some of the critical concerns of scholars and analysts,[3] but remain far more sanguine about the performance of civil society and prospects for African democratic development. I write not only as a scholar and a researcher on African democratization and civil society development but also as a practitioner, and when I write about the organization that I lead—Ghana Center for Democratic Development (CDD-Ghana)—I do not pretend to be able to be objective.[4]

The Contributions of Civil Society

Civil society involvement in African politics and democratic development is not completely new.[5] Nascent civil society was a major component of the nationalist movements that fought against colonial rule and brought independence to their respective countries in the 1960s—in the form of trade unions, youth and literary clubs, and hometown improvement associations emerging in the interwar years.[6] To be sure, the development of civil society was severely curtailed and the sector's ability to foster democratic development was circumscribed by the hegemony-seeking and authoritarian regimes that prevailed in Africa in the first thirty years of independence,[7] even if some key groups in the embattled sector, notably bar associations/law societies, student unions, and Christian organizations, managed to sustain some types of antiauthoritarian projects in their respective countries.[8] However, civil society appears to have made its most significant contribution to democratic development in Africa in the post–Cold War and postcommunist wave of democratization, or what some have termed as Africa's "second liberation." Below, using Larry Diamond's checklist, I outline the contributions of civil society to African democratic development.[9]

Helping to Pry Open Authoritarian Systems

Civil society organizations have helped to pry open previously closed political systems. The late 1980s and early 1990s saw associations of teachers, students, and market traders leading the struggle to end years of autocratic rule in Benin. Similarly, in Ghana, the Bar Association, Christian Council, and National Union of Ghana Students played key roles in ending the quasi-military dictatorship of Jerry Rawlings and the Provisional National Defense Council. And in Zambia, the labor movement led the way to redemocratization, just as the "civvies" did in South Africa.

The trend continued in the middle to late 1990s. In Liberia, the local chapter of the West African Women's Association and its dynamic leader Theresa Leigh-Sherman mobilized women to play a crucial role in ending the civil war and returning to constitutional rule in that country in 1997. In the late 1990s the National Democratic Coalition, the Transitional Monitoring Group, the Constitutional Rights Project, the Civil Liberties Organization, and Center for Democracy and Development, as well as prominent Christian clergymen such as Archbishop Paul Okogie and Father Matthew Kukah, were on the front lines of the prodemocracy movement of Nigeria. They demonstrated extraordinary tenacity and made heroic contributions to the protracted transition to democratic rule. Additionally, individuals from civil society, especially prelates such as the late Isodore de Souza of Benin and Archbishop Fanoko Kpodro of Togo, were instrumental in the transition process in their respective countries—deploying their broad credibility, political skills and commitment to broker agreements in bitter political conflicts between intransigent autocrats and impatient democrats.

Civil society's contribution to African democratic development during the 1990s has been equally crucial in the process of sustaining democratic transitions and working toward their consolidation. For example, the Institute for Democracy in South Africa (IDASA) played a key role in conceptualizing and modeling a truth and reconciliation commission in South Africa consistent with the country's commitment to national unity in the postapartheid era. The Cotonou-based Groupe d'Étude et du Recherche sur la Démocratie et le Développement Économique et Sociale en Afrique (GERDDES-Afrique) helped to resolve the impasse over power alternation from President Nicophere Soglo to President Mathieu Kerekou, the winner of the presidential ballot of 1995.

It is also noteworthy that in contexts where the transition to democracy has reached an advanced stage or consolidation has begun, civil society organizations are moving away from the crudely confrontational style of their early years in favor of a focus on consensus, moderation, more thoughtful policy debate, and other modes of constructive engagement. Thus, South African nongovernmental organizations (NGOs) and "civvies" are reorienting themselves, albeit with difficulty, to engage in the work of postapartheid social and economic reconstruction. IDASA is working on a new generation of innovative programs, including those designed to reduce racial and ethnic prejudice among South Africans, to safeguard the rights of non–South African Africans, and to support improvements in governance at both the national and provincial levels. CDD-Ghana is delivering support to the parliament of Ghana by mobilizing civil society inputs into and helping to review draft bills. CDD-Ghana is also collaborating with the constitutionally grounded Commission on Human Rights and Administrative Justice (CHRAJ) to build a national coalition to combat corruption.

Limiting the Power of the State and Challenging Abuses of Authority

An emergent independent press and a host of liberal civil society organizations (human rights advocacy groups, civil liberties organizations, middle-class professional bodies, especially law societies/bar associations) have joined fledgling opposition parties to monitor and keep governments on their toes. Research think tanks such as IDASA and CDD-Ghana have been monitoring governments and public authorities in South Africa and Ghana respectively, and civil liberties organizations have been doing the same in Nigeria. In Burkina Faso, the Coalition of Human Rights Organizations, led by the Burkinabè Movement for Human and Citizens Rights, has been giving the authorities sleepless nights with its persistent demand for a credible official inquiry into the December 13, 1998, death of crack investigative journalist Norbert Zongo. In Liberia, pressure from the Catholic Church, the media, and other local civic bodies, combined with international pressure, compelled then-elected strongman Charles Taylor in 2002 to back down from a decision to close private radio stations. These are some of the ways in which civil society activism is helping to countervail the power of government in Africa today.

Where old illiberal constitutions have prevailed, as in Kenya and Zimbabwe, civil society organizations such as Kenya's Citizens' Coalition for Constitutional Change and the trade unions have continued their frontline roles in campaigning for liberalization. But where liberal constitutional dispensations have become available, as in Benin, Ghana, South Africa, and Nigeria, bar associations and journalist associations, independent think tanks, and other civil society groups are taking full advantage of the opening to perform vital watchdog functions.

In addition to an emergent investigative media, many African countries can now boast of national chapters of Transparency International or other civil society–based anticorruption bodies working with official agencies to promote transparency and accountability to combat official corruption. For example, the independent press in Ghana, most notably the *Ghanaian Chronicle,* was instrumental in getting the ombudsman body (CHRAJ) to conduct a probe of top state and ruling-party functionaries, leading to their resignation from office in 1996. This unprecedented development was triggered by sustained research-backed exposure in the media of corrupt behavior on the part of a number of well-placed officials. Moreover, at great financial expense and political risk to itself, the *Chronicle* provided assistance to CHRAJ in the investigation. It supplied important leads and incriminating forensic evidence that helped the underresourced commission conclude the investigations successfully.

NGOs are also becoming increasingly involved in championing fiscal discipline and the elimination of waste and official corruption. IDASA, for example, has a program that undertakes critical analyses of budgets and their social justice implications. Of late, propoor advocacy NGOs are turning their attention to reviewing budgets and monitoring expenditures as ways to check official abuse and promote equitable distribution of scarce national resources.

Monitoring Elections and Enhancing the Credibility of the Democratic Process

Pioneered on the continent by GERDDES-Afrique in the Benin elections of 1990, independent election monitoring by domestic civil society has become a key feature in contemporary African elections. GERDDES-Afrique, which also observed the elections in Benin in 1995, has been on hand to undertake poll-watching in many francophone African countries. In Zambia, the Foundation for Democratic Process in Zambia played a key role in monitoring the transition elections of 1991, and both the Independent Monitoring Team and the National Committee for Clean Campaign played key roles in monitoring the elections of November 1996. In Ghana, a coalition of prominent civic bodies, religious groups, and NGOs going under the name Network of Domestic Election Observers and another local NGO (Ghana Alert) mounted a highly successful watch over the polls of 1996, helping to make the election more transparent and its outcomes broadly accepted. Similarly, in Kenya, an alliance of the Catholic Justice and Peace Commission, the National Council of Churches of Kenya, and the Institute of Education and Democracy monitored the elections of 1997. Nigeria's Transitional Monitoring Group, comprising sixty-three organizations drawn from all over the country, deployed over 1,000 observers for the 1999 elections, which returned the country to democratic rule.[10] It is also noteworthy that under domestic civil society groups, poll-watching is a much broader process, covering preelection scenarios (access to the media, opportunity to campaign without intimidation, integrity of the voter's register, etc.) as well as the conduct of elections on voting day. With their deeper knowledge of local conditions and greater familiarity with the preelection scenario, these local groups constitute a vital component of a credible poll-watching effort. Indeed, the efforts of domestic poll-watching bodies are highly complementary to those of their international counterparts.

It is now fairly safe to assume that alone or along with their international counterparts, domestic civil society groups will be available to undertake credible observation in any African election. It is not surprising, therefore, that another independent coalition of civil society organizations, the Coalition of Domestic Election Observers—comprising over twenty civic bodies—recruited, trained, and deployed over 5,000 people to monitor the first- and second-round polls in Ghana in December 2000.

Educating Citizens and Building a
Culture of Tolerance and Civic Engagement

Civil society bodies such as Civitas, Street Law, and legal literacy groups, as well as advocacy groups, are increasingly involved in civic education, thus helping to break the longtime monopoly of state and parastatal civic education agencies. For example, in Ghana, the Ghana Legal Literacy Resource Foundation, the Christian Council of Churches, and Civitas-Ghana have been active alongside constitutional bodies such as the National Commission on Civic Education and CHRAJ. The Lawyers for Human Rights and the local chapter of the U.S.-based National Institute for Citizen Education have collaborated to run a Street Law program aimed at providing civic education for postapartheid South Africa. And civic education programs, specifically public debates staged by the Uganda Human Rights Education and Documentation Center, have given Ugandans a chance to critically examine the official no-party doctrine.

Most significant, these nonstate civic education bodies, Street Law programs, and human rights advocacy groups are helping to effect a much needed change in the content of African civic education. They are moving civic education toward the development of democratic citizenship and away from the traditional overemphasis on citizen responsibility, political education (indoctrination), and agitprop (along the lines of Kwame Nkrumah and Kamuzu Banda's Young Pioneers and Jerry Rawlings's Defense Committees) and the resultant political docility.

Incorporating Marginal Groups and Enhancing Responsiveness

Incorporating marginal groups into the political process and enhancing societal responsiveness to their interests and needs are the preoccupation of some of the most ardent activists in the civil society sector in Africa today. Some of these issue-oriented advocacy and developmental NGOs have emerged to fill the gap in meeting the social and economic needs of marginalized groups arising from the breakdown of state and traditional social support systems. Others have been provoked by perceived marginalization arising from the implementation of neoliberal economic and structural adjustment reforms. And yet others have been formed in response to recent crises on the continent, notably civil wars and other violent conflicts as well as famines and natural disasters. Thus, in addition to the traditional international NGOs such as Oxfam, Care, Catholic Relief Services, and Action Aid, there are multitudes of small and medium-sized community, national, and regional NGOs operating in African countries today. Together, they are supporting grassroots community groups, demanding safeguards for the rights of community groups, tackling violence, and helping to rebuild societies.

The growing impact of these nonstate agencies in promoting the welfare of marginalized groups was manifested in Ghana in the late 1990s when a number of NGOs, notably International Needs and the International Federation of Women Lawyers (FIDA), as well as the media and some Christian bodies collaborated with CHRAJ to mount a successful campaign against the traditional institution of Trokosi (a form of "customary female servitude"). Thanks to the campaign, the existence of this inhuman practice became widely known to the Ghanaian public and received widespread condemnation and inspired parliament to pass a bill outlawing such practices. Similarly, gender advocacy groups have helped to expand the representation of women in African legislatures and participation in public life as well as competitive elections.[11] These issue-oriented civil society bodies are helping to give voice to the otherwise voiceless in society and to bring the plight of marginalized groups to the attention of policymakers and politicians. They help not only in the immediate material rehabilitation of marginalized groups but also in their integration into the economic and political process.

It also worthy of note that in recent years, some of these Africa-based propoor NGOs have collaborated closely with NGOs in developed countries to influence the policies of the Bretton Woods and other international financial institutions as well as bilateral donors. Similarly, a collaboration between global environmental advocacy groups, notably Friends of the Earth International, and their national chapters as well as other grassroots NGOs in the countries affected by the proposed West African Gas Pipeline Project has mounted steady pressure on the investment consortium of Chevron, the Nigerian Petroleum Corporation, Sobegaz of Benin, Sofogaz of Togo, and Ghana's Volta River Authority. These activist groups are lobbying in favor of environmental protection and monitoring social equity issues arising from the giant project. It will be valid to contend that the inclusion of issues of environmental protection, poverty alleviation, gender equity, and debt relief on the agenda of the World Bank and other major development partners is a measure of the growing influence and success of such NGOs in giving voice to the traditionally marginalized.[12]

Providing Alternative Means for Material Development

Civil society has always held a high promise in African economic development. In the form of kinship and ethnic groups or clans, it has been a key form of social capital similar to what Francis Fukuyama describes about Asian societies.[13] The example of bands of "migrant planters" and indigenous capitalist farmers playing midwife to the nascent cocoa and oil palm industries in southern Ghana in the colonial period documented by Polly Hill stands as testimony to the efficacy of civil society as a vital agent in private sector–led economic development.[14] Indeed, the initial interest of international donors in the sector was largely grounded in the expectation that it would facilitate the rekindling of African economic and social development.[15]

It is true that years of colonial and postcolonial authoritarian rule and the ascendancy of statist economic policies (especially after independence) did much to kill the economic development potential of civil society in

Africa.[16] However, some of that developmental potential of civil society has been restored, by default or by design, following the near collapse since the late 1970s of the African state and its economic development structures and the accompanying upsurge in informal sector activities.[17] The proliferation of a wide range of grassroots and development NGOs in the 1980s and 1990s was a key manifestation of this restoration. This phenomenon, combined with the growing emphasis on private sector-led development as well as the emergence of private sector development groups and revamping of business associations, presents renewed possibilities for the development of the private sector and economic decentralization, which can only enhance the prospects of African democratic development in the twenty-first century.

Opening and Pluralizing the Flow of Information

The emergence of a vibrant media, advocacy groups, and especially independent research think tanks is helping to break the monopoly African governments have held over the production and dissemination of information in Africa. The independent print and electronic media are providing alternative nonstate outlets for opposition parties to broadcast their messages. They are making it possible for information unflattering to government or not sanctioned by state authorities to reach the public. Thanks to the independent media, it is most unlikely that the virtual news blackout imposed on the monumental antiauthoritarian and prodemocracy developments in the former Soviet Union, Eastern Europe and China in the late 1980s can be repeated in Africa in the twenty-first century. Moreover, democratic struggles in other parts of the world, including the prosecution and punishment or disgrace of deposed autocrats, are able to receive widespread coverage in the African media (to the chagrin of local tyrants), giving encouragement to local prodemocracy activists.

Publications, opinion surveys, and studies of independent research think tanks such as the Center for Policy Studies (CPS) and IDASA in South Africa, Institute of Economic Affairs (IEA) and the Center for Policy Analysis (CEPA) in Ghana, the Center for Basic Research in Uganda, and Kenya's Research on Poverty Alleviation and IEA provide some of the best information on specialized subjects. And in their efforts to state their respective cases and to win the hearts and minds of the public, issue-oriented and advocacy groups are helping to pluralize the information regimes in Africa. Typically, these publications are relatively more accessible than academic ones and are often targeted to the policy community, thereby enriching the information base for public policy. They also offer academics outlets and opportunities to pursue locally relevant academic work and to influence the domestic policy dialogue.

Building a Constituency for
Economic and Political Reforms

The contribution of civil society to the building of a constituency for economic reform in Africa is rather ambiguous—especially since labor unions, propoor and grassroots developmental NGOs, as well as human rights and democracy-promoting civil society bodies, tend to be vehemently opposed to neoliberal economic reforms and advocate left-leaning/populist economic policies. However, the emergence of donor-funded liberal economic think tanks such as the Nairobi-based Africa Economic Research Consortium, Ghana's CEPA, IEA, and CDD, Kenya's IEA, and South Africa's Free Market Foundation, as well as business bodies such as the Private Enterprise Foundation in Ghana, represent new prospects for the development of a constituency for liberal economic reforms.[18]

The Structural Adjustment Participatory Review Initiative, launched in Washington, D.C., in July 1997, represents donor acknowledgment of the importance of civil society in development policymaking, implementation, and monitoring. The initiative, which includes four African countries (Uganda, Ghana, Mali, and Zimbabwe) out of seven pilot countries, may have been motivated by a desire to co-opt domestic critics of the World Bank and structural adjustment programs. But it does present an opportunity for civil society to dialogue with the World Bank, other donors, and national governments over economic reforms. It also has the potential to foster civic participation and local ownership of neoliberal reforms.

Indeed, it is the new trusteeship types of NGOs and advocacy groups (and not the traditional civil society organizations such as labor unions, religious bodies, and trader associations) that occupy the front lines when it comes to pushing for reforms that would move the democratic process beyond elections. The traditional civil society groups tend to retreat to their traditional and noncivic concerns. Church bodies devote their attention to ecumenical matters, unions deal with labor issues, trader cartels focus on official regulations, and so on.

Some of the most innovative reforms with a potential to deepen democracy have come from prodemocracy NGOs. For instance, IDASA and others have worked to get the South African parliament to pass a law requiring public office holders to declare their assets in a reasonably open manner. IDASA and civil society organizations were also instrumental in getting South Africa to pass a new "freedom of information" law. In Ghana, civil society organizations such as the Ghana Integrity Initiative (the local chapter of Transparency International), the IEA, the Media Foundation of West Africa, and CDD-Ghana are collaborating with public agencies to push for the passage of "freedom of information" legislation, and FIDA has initiated actions to get parliament to pass a bill criminalizing violence against women.

The new democracy-promotion, human rights advocacy, and policy think tanks may lack the social roots of labor unions or even political parties,[19] but they represent a nascent and highly important constituency for democratic development.[20] Their emergence has brought energy, dynamism, and professionalism into a sector whose effectiveness has often been hampered by amateurism and apathy. By liaising with traditional civil society bodies such as trade unions, business and professional associations, as well as key public institutions of democratic governance such as independent election authorities, ombudsmen, parliaments, and judiciaries, the new trusteeship types of civic bodies are helping to create formidable networks of public and private institutions that can facilitate democratic development.

Continuing Problems and Weaknesses

Notwithstanding the above-mentioned achievements, the potential of civil society to contribute to African democratic development is severely hampered by a number of weaknesses and limitations. The sector is constrained by an extremely weak material base. This is largely a reflection of the miserable economic conditions of contemporary African states. It derives also from the weakness of the domestic private sector and the related problem of weak to nonexistent possibilities for local corporate sponsorship. While this constraint is true for civil society in general, it is particularly acute for the new types of nonmembership "trusteeship" NGOs. Whatever the causes, severe material handicaps present stark options to civil society organizations in Africa, leaving them heavily dependent on politically problematic and volatile extraorganizational sources of funding: the state and international donors.

Local funding for civil society is severely circumscribed in African countries. There is hardly a local philanthropic sector to speak of in Africa (with the possible exception of South Africa, where domestic private corporations provide limited funding to NGOs). This leaves the state as the only source of domestic funding for most civil society organizations. But state funding for civil society is bound to be highly inadequate for all but a handful of highly privileged civil society organizations, given the usually precarious economic conditions of African states and the near fiscal bankruptcy of its governments. Moreover, state funding compromises the independence and autonomy of civil society organizations. It also renders them highly susceptible to co-optation by hegemony-seeking African regimes and distorts accountability.

Of course, rising levels of external support are helping to reduce huge resource gaps faced by civil society in Africa. Indeed, in many cases donor funding is the sole means of survival for the new trusteeship NGOs. An article in *The Economist* in 2000 reported that all but 9 of the 120 NGOs established in Kenya between 1993 the end of 1996 received all their income from foreign governments, which is fairly typical.[21] But external support renders NGOs suspect in the eyes of nationalists and reinforces the prevailing notion that they are local agents of foreign interests. Moreover, external funding (or even the likelihood of external funding) has sometimes provoked destructive turf battles and one-upmanship among local NGOs. Worse still, it has often distorted the accountability owed by NGOs to domestic constituencies and to society at large. It also leaves civil society bodies open to blackmail by governments that manipulate their "gate-keeping" positions with international donors to direct assistance away from assertive and independent civil society organizations in favor of progovernment NGOs. To reduce dependency and increase sustainability, donors have been pushing African civil society organizations to undertake income generation activities. But paid consultancies, contract research, and other directly productive ventures expose such organizations to the risk of being diverted from their civic action and democracy-promoting mandate.

Attitudes toward civil society in Africa remain highly ambiguous. Government and community leaders welcome developmental NGOs as partners in development. But they also see these nonstate entities as potential competitors for donor funding and public affection. Moreover, official attitudes toward the independent think tank and advocacy subspecies, as well as toward the media, are often hostile. Such NGOs are constantly disparaged in official discourse. They are wont to be viewed as instruments of external subversion, even among relatively liberal political and bureaucratic elites. The statement made by Nelson Mandela (widely regarded as the most liberal of contemporary African leaders) on South Africa's "Day of National Reconciliation"—that the challenge is to weed out the real NGOs from the phony and, in doing so, avoid the liberal-imposed agenda that could be furthering the aims of their financiers—is very instructive in this regard.[22]

The rise in the profile of NGOs and attainment of relative prominence in the political lives of their respective countries has triggered two reactions among key domestic actors. Opposition parties have become eager to court democracy-promoting and antiauthoritarian NGOs and to co-opt them; governments have become determined to co-opt and control them. Either way, the autonomy, independence, and integrity of civil society organizations are threatened. Civil society bodies, especially those focused on democracy promotion and the defense of human rights, have been targeted with predatory official regulation, often in the name of rationalizing and preventing abuse, and strident application of existing illiberal laws. For instance, an NGO bill initiated by the elected Rawlings National Democratic Congress government in the Ghanaian parliament in the early 1990s included pernicious provisions requiring mandatory registration of NGOs with the proposed

National Advisory Council of NGOs overwhelmingly dominated by government appointees. It also stipulated that NGOs must be "willing and able
to work in cooperation with any agency of the state that the minister may
direct." Similarly, Niger's National Assembly passed a law in 1997 imposing tighter restrictions on the press than what had prevailed under direct
military rule. Despite the fact that Niger does not have a university, the
press law imposes a minimum of four years of postsecondary education as
a condition for becoming accredited to practice journalism. The arrest and
jailing in Egypt in June 2000 of a prominent civil society leader and human
rights advocate on the charge of "accepting external funding without official permission" is another example of escalating crude attempts by African
governments to cripple civil society.[23] Perhaps the murders and rising spate
in recent years of politicians and public officials suing journalists under
criminal libel and sedition laws, and at times securing jail sentences, represent the most virulent manifestation of this antipathy for the burgeoning
independent media.

The prominence of civil society organizations in the process of economic and political development at both the national and the international
level has also inspired the emergence of bogus NGOs seeking to cash in on
the relative prestige of the sector and credibility of the others. Some of
them are set up to organize rackets for securing visas to the developed
countries; others provide tax shelters for crooked entrepreneurs; and yet
others are simply chasing donor dollars. In some instances, NGOs have
been set up to front for key political actors in government or opposition.
Notable examples include the erstwhile Better Life for Nigerian Women (of
Miriam Babangida); the Youth Earnestly Asking for Abacha (YEAA); and
the Association for a Better Nigeria (ABN), set up to promote the self-
succession goals of Nigerian military rulers; and Ghana's 31st December
Women's Movement (DWM), led by the first lady of Ghana (Nana Konadu
Agyeman Rawlings) and dedicated to the mobilization of women and donor
funding in support of her husband, Flight Lieutenant Jerry Rawlings, and
his ruling National Democratic Congress. As self-described NGOs, the
YEAA, ABN, and DWM are problematic in the sense that they compete for
the limited local and international resources available to African civil societies. Worse still, they serve to undermine the credibility of the sector as
a whole.

African civil society organizations suffer from low levels of institutional development. Many of them have been founded only in the past
decade and have been preoccupied with political activism. They may have
a strong passion for promoting good governance at the levels of national
governments and international bodies, but that is hardly matched by their
willingness or ability to promote similar values in their own organizations.
Indeed, far from being paragons of democratic behavior, civil society

organizations are sometimes leading violators of the democratic principles of accountability, transparency, and internal democracy. In fact, "bureaucratized" NGOs such are IDASA are the exception rather than the norm in Africa. The rest tend to suffer from weak internal management, poor levels of corporate governance, and weak internal democracy; they are personality-driven, run as personal fiefdoms and patronage machines, and their leaders are not accountable to members or any governing board. Self-proclaimed good governance and democracy-promotion NGOs have suffered credibility problems, as they have left accounts unaudited and have sought refuge in some vague notion of "struggle accounting," Allan Boesak style![24] Yet another factor limiting the impact of civil society on African democratic development is its overconcentration in national capitals and exclusiveness to the middle-class elites based there. Typically, grassroots constituencies, rural areas, and even provincial cities are largely excluded from the activities of the democracy-promoting NGOs and advocacy groups.

The period immediately after the overthrow of a dictatorship and/or the first transition elections or even the first electoral turnover has presented peculiar challenges to civil society organizations in general and the democracy-promoting types in particular. First, it has been difficult if not impossible to sustain the levels of excitement prevailing in the period of agitation for democracy and the national conferences. Second, key groups in civil society have returned to their "traditional" and primary concerns as religious bodies, professional associations, labor unions, and youth activists. Third, there has been a loss of key members to political society and public administration. Of course the latter development is a double-edged sword. On the positive side, it has the potential to reduce the prevailing antipathies and create greater empathy between civil society and politicians in a context where relationships between the two have tended to be characterized by mutual suspicion and mistrust. Indeed, if prodemocracy civic bodies are providing some of the leadership of fledgling African democracies, and especially if such leaders recruited from civil society consistently exhibit democratic behavior in their new offices, then for the larger project of democratization this may also represent a net gain and the realization of the Tocquevillian ideal of civil society as "free schools for democracy." But at the same time, the exodus of civil society leaders to the political, bureaucratic, and business sectors has deprived the civil society of some of its ablest leaders.

Auspicious Dynamics

The upsurge in the activism of civil society groups reflects the considerable prestige they are deriving at least in part from the collapse of the state and associated institutions and from the heroic roles played by the sector in the democratic openings of recent years. It is also a reflection of the unprecedented enhancement of associational and media freedoms enshrined in the new liberal democratic constitutions and the inauguration of formal democracy in many countries of Africa in the aftermath of the Cold War and the end of communism. However, it is the dynamic developments within and without the sector on the whole, and the democracy-promoting developments in particular, that provide much hope for civil society's long-term survival and ability to contribute to democracy building on the continent.

Potential to Develop Crosscutting Density

Civil society, in particular the NGO fraction, is a veritable growth industry in Africa today. Growth has been exponential for all categories of NGOs— from the so-called niche and cross-sectoral types to the grassroots/community development types as well as the relatively new human rights advocacy and direct democracy promotion types.[25] South Africa's record of having between 30,000 and 80,000 NGOs may be exceptional,[26] but it is likely that the numbers have been growing in all African countries too. In Ghana, for instance, there were 80 NGOs registered with the Ministry of Social Welfare in the early 1980s. By 1990, the number was over 350; and over 300 registrations were recorded between January and June 1996 alone. A 1999 publication by the European Platform on Conflict Prevention and Transformation and the African Center for Constructive Resolution of Disputes listed 120 Africa-based NGOs involved in peacebuilding alone,[27] and many of them had been founded only since the mid-1990s.

While the number of civil society organizations and NGOs directly involved in democracy promotion is relatively small, it appears to be growing fast. At any rate, the growing density and crosscutting nature of the sector as a whole is good for democratic development. Combined with the growing number of human rights and political NGOs, the nonpolitical and apolitical NGOs provide a formidable nonstate network for promoting counterhegemonic projects nationally and regionally.

Attracting African Talent

Another sign of the growing vitality of African civil society is the attraction of talent to the sector. The decade of the 1990s began with the emergence, under exceptionally energetic leadership, of independent, nonpartisan national and continental NGOs dedicated to the promotion of democratic governance and human rights. The sector has continued to attract some of the best and the brightest sons and daughters of Africa who would have gone into careers in government or the private sector in an earlier period.

An example is Sadikou Alao, a lawyer by profession who resigned from a very senior position as deputy general counsel at the African Development Bank to found GERDDES-Afrique. Other examples include Yao Graham, a lawyer, social scientist, and journalist who has forgone a career in academia or government to run the Third World Network and operate as a "public intellectual" editing the *Public Agenda,* and Shyley Kondowe, a social scientist who founded and has been running the Malawian Institute for Democratic and Economic Affairs. The presence of such well-credentialed individuals on a full-time basis has brought energy, dynamism, and professionalism into a sector whose effectiveness has often been hampered by amateurism and apathy.

Attracting Donor Support

The civil society sector is also receiving favorable attention from international donors, which have began to look for ways to correct the prostate focus of development assistance of previous years. While actual figures are hard to come by, there is growing anecdotal evidence that bilateral and multilateral donors are beginning to devote an increasing amount of their funding, especially the fraction earmarked for democracy and human rights assistance, to civil society bodies. The United Nations Development Programme and other multilateral agencies, as well as bilateral donors, have introduced direct funding for civil society; assistance to civil society has also come under the rubric of support for democracy, governance, and human rights.

In addition, many development agencies and international NGOs have established partnership arrangements with local civil society bodies or adopted the latter as "implementing agencies." International bodies—ranging from the World Bank to the African Union—have granted consultative status to African NGOs. The granting of limited participation to domestic civil society groups at the "Consultative Group" meetings between the World Bank/donors and governments is one manifestation of this new trend.

Opportunities for direct funding, networking, and collaboration between Africa-based civil society organizations and international civil society have been vastly expanded in recent years. The emergence of political foundations such as the U.S.-based National Endowment for Democracy and the UK-based Westminster Foundation, as well as expanded support by private philanthropic bodies such as the Ford Foundation and George Soros's Open Society Foundation,[28] has introduced diversity into sources of funding for civil society. International civil society organizations such as Chapter 19, Amnesty International, Global Witness, and Transparency International have been veritable sources of technocratic and informational resources for cognate African civil society. Chapter 19 has provided invaluable materials for media advocacy groups; Transparency International has provided moral, political, and technical support for its local chapters. Taken together, they help to reduce the opportunity for national governments to manipulate their gate-keeping roles to the detriment of assertive and autonomy-seeking domestic civil society.

Active Networking

Evidence abounds of active networking among African NGOs at the national, regional, and international levels. This is taking place at conferences, workshops, and seminars as well as through "virtual networking" made possible by the spread of new information technologies and has helped to enhance self-consciousness of the sector and provided valuable opportunities for sharing experiences and learning best practices.

Networking among prodemocracy NGOs and civic bodies has seen the Media Foundation of West Africa, based in Accra, liaising with human rights bodies in Burkina Faso to keep the pressure on the Burkinabè government for a proper investigation into and action on the murder of Norbert Zongo. Indeed, the recent trial in Senegal of Hissein Habre, the former dictator of Chad, on charges of torture and other human rights atrocities has been brought about by a formidable array of national, regional, and international human rights bodies—Human Rights Watch, the Dakar-based African Assembly for the Defense of Human Rights, Senegal's National Organization for Human Rights, the London-based Interrights, the International Federation of Human Rights Leagues (FIDH), the Chadian Association for the Promotion and Defense of Human Rights, Chad's League for Human Rights, and the French organization Agir Ensemble pour les Droits de l'Homme. Similarly, local and international human rights environmental NGOs are collaborating to block a World Bank project to construct an oil pipeline from Cameroon to Chad. As these auspicious developments present great possibilities for the endurance of civil society, it is difficult to see a complete and successful closure of the sector in the short run.

Accentuating the Positive Aspects of Civil Society

African civil societies have emerged as key forces in the political development of the continent. They are gaining in sophistication and building capacities and are a major part of the change in the complexion and texture of internal African politics from unalloyed state hegemony and monopoly over power to the growing pluralism. The growing self-awareness, determination to maintain their autonomy from both state and societal forces, and determination to resist co-optation by government are some of the indications that they will not disappear as have their counterparts in the aftermath of decolonization. The above-mentioned achievements may confirm the universally acknowledged positive attributes of civil society as a great source of dynamism and energy, focus and specialization, and as a veritable source of information and expertise. They also affirm the contention that the involvement of civil society is key to building ownership, legitimacy, and democracy.[29]

However, in thinking of civil society in Africa and, in particular, its role in democratic development, it is important to keep in mind that, as elsewhere in the world, it has a vicious and uncivil side. Negative traits universal to civil society, such as exclusiveness and selfishness, tend to be rather pronounced among African civil societies. A common but antisocial manifestation of this "selfish factor" is the tendency for members of vertically composed civil society organizations to protect and reward "native sons and daughters" who commit atrocities or engage in gross corruption and abuse of public office, saying to the effect, "He is a rogue, but he is our rogue."[30] Indeed, the contemporary African experience suggests that this tendency is not confined to primary organizations of civil society. The trade unions in many African countries have disregarded atrocious human rights records of incumbent regimes, supported bankrupt and corrupt governments, or refused to join prodemocracy movements against regimes when they are perceived to be "prolabor." For example, in Ghana, the Trade Union Congress (TUC) largely excluded itself from the middle-class opposition to gross economic mismanagement, corruption, and political repression under the military rule of General Acheampong and the Supreme Military Council. The quiescence of the TUC at this time was apparently an expression of gratitude to the Acheampong regime for overthrowing the Busia regime and thereby saving the TUC from persecution by the Busia regime.[31] For the leadership of the TUC at this time, quiescence also represented a tactical move not to support opponents of a regime that was pursing policies of economic nationalism and nominal full employment.

Similarly, the National Union of Ghana Students readily aligned itself with the coup-makers who overthrew a democratically elected government in 1972 and who confessed that it was essentially an "officers' amenities coup" because the coup-makers promised to restore student allowances. Prominent religious bodies have sometimes exploited their enormous clout to cut deals with governments. Thus the Catholic Church has used its influence with governments to get them to abandon family planning programs—in total disregard of the impracticability of abstinence or the "rhythm method" and negative social implications of unregulated births on the larger society; and Muslim groups have lobbied impoverished African states to sponsor the faithful to make trips to Mecca for the Haj—to the detriment of national economies and at the expense of many pressing social needs. Of course, pilgrimages to Mecca or Jerusalem may be great for the spiritual development of the faithful, but they constitute an additional burden on the resource-poor African state.

Moreover, in some notable instances, civil society itself is the repository of nonliberal values of hierarchy, gerontocracy, male chauvinism, and patriarchy.[32] In some cases, civil society organizations set the lead in illiberal politics. Some have deified their leaders by raising statues in their honor or giving them "life" tenure. The Ghana Private Road Transport Union of Ghana's TUC provides an example of this tendency. When he was alive, the chairman of the Ashanti regional branch of the union was given life tenure and members wore tee shirts embossed with his photograph. When he died, a statue was erected in his honor![33]

It is also particularly important to recognize that the sector is dominated by vertically composed organizations or penetrated by primordial structures—ethnic, racial, caste, and clan groups, as well as some religious groups—based on *the exclusion* of others.[34] It is instructive in this regard to note that when Tutsis and Hutus engaged each other in a genocidal conflict, they did so, at least in part, as civil society groups.[35]

The above observations underscore several points. Civil society is a mixture of good and bad; its presence may only present a potential for democratic development; civil society organizations have varying degrees of validity and utility for democratic development; and certain types of civil society organizations—specifically civic and public interest advocacy groups, human rights organizations, independent think tanks, and media and other civic subspecies of civil society—are more directly relevant to democratic development than others. The question then is how to accentuate the positive and minimize the negative in civil society for the democratic development of Africa.

The factors that could help to minimize the vicious and strengthen the virtuous side of civil society include:

- Increasing the number, variety, and quality of civil society organizations, thus creating the possibility for them to moderate each other, and in so doing, helping to moderate society and the state and to generate broader types of social capital.[36]
- Fostering the independence and autonomy as well as organizational and other capacities of the various civil society organizations. This will put them in a stronger position to undertake their various society enrichment/welfare promotion activities while resisting co-optation and countering the monopolistic and hegemonial orientations of the state.
- Generating at least a percentage of funding from members and other local sources. This would help to reduce dependency on politically

compromising sources of funding and enhance accountability to domestic stakeholders.

- Promoting transparency, accountability, and internal democracy as well as adherence to the rules of corporate governance among civil society organizations. This would help to internalize and diffuse the same values into the society at large.
- Fostering public-mindedness, sacrifice for the community, and civic consciousness among civil society organizations. This is key to securing a virtuous civil society.
- Above all, establishing and protecting a legal and constitutional framework that effectively guarantees fundamental human rights and liberties, especially freedom of association. This would also include a regulatory framework that is not predatory and that allows civil society organizations to flourish as well as constitutional and legal reforms that will foster the development of an indigenous modern philanthropic sector.

Conclusion

The unprecedented surge in civil society is a key factor in African political renewal at the present time. The sector has flourished in the past decade or so and is playing a major role in the transition and posttransition phases of the various countries. But it is also true that civil society is largely nascent in Africa. Its emergence in Africa as part of the anticolonial protest movement was interrupted by postcolonial authoritarianism. And while the sector has surged tremendously in recent years, it continues to be dogged by severe problems and weaknesses. This presents major challenges: how to minimize the weaknesses and vicious aspects of civil society and what to do to reinforce its positive aspects.

In the specific context of democratic development in Africa, this requires concerted efforts by supporters of African democratization to protect and expand the legal and constitutional space for associational life, improve the material base of the civil society sector, and strengthen the autonomy of its institutions. It also requires that civil society organizations themselves, in particular those directly involved in democracy promotion, impose effective self-regulation and establish and abide by a credible code of conduct. Given the reality of limited external assistance to civil society, it would be useful to discriminate in favor of African civil society organizations that demonstrate a commitment to the defense of human rights, gender equity, nonviolence, transparency, accountability, anticorruption, and the protection and expansion of domestic associational space.

Notes

1. Excellent discussions on this are found in Harbeson, Rothchild, and Chazan, *Civil Society and the State;* see especially contributions by Harbeson, Young, and Callaghy. See also Kasfir, "The Conventional Notion of Civil Society"; Makumbe, "Is There a Civil Society in Africa?"; Hutchful, "The Civil Society Debate"; Landell-Mills, "Governance, Cultural Change, and Empowerment"; Fatton, "Africa in the Age of Democratization"; and Post, "State, Civil Society, and Democracy."

2. See, for example, Ottaway and Chung, "Debating Democracy Assistance"; and Hearns, *Foreign Aid, Democratization, and Civil Society in Africa.* For a very thorough general discussion, see White, "Foreign Aid, Taxes, and Public Investment."

3. For generally negative portrayals of civil society in Africa, see Ottaway and Chung, "Debating Democracy Assistance"; and Monga, "Eight Problems with African Politics."

4. In addition to being a student of and researcher on civil society and democratic development in Africa, I head the Ghana Center for Democratic Development—an Accra-based independent trusteeship–type research nongovernmental organization focusing on African/Ghanaian democratic development funded through external grants and contract research.

5. As used in this chapter, "civil society" refers to the realm between the household and the state, populated by voluntary groups and associations, sharing common interests, and largely autonomous from the state. Lying at the core of the concept are intermediate institutions and private groups such as voluntary associations, charities, choral groups, religious organizations, social clubs, professional associations, and trade unions. It also includes the media, especially the nonstate media.

6. For accounts of the role played by voluntary associations and youth groups in the anticolonial movement in Africa in the 1950s, see Hodgkin, *Nationalism in Colonial Africa;* and Coleman, "Nationalism in Tropical Africa."

7. On the centralized authoritarian state in Africa, see Wunsch and Olowu, *The Failure of the Centralized State;* and O'Brien, "Modernization."

8. See, for example, Bayart, "Civil Society in Africa." Bayart credits civil society for wittingly and unwittingly helping to forestall the "totalization" of power by the state. See also Azarya, "Civil Society and Disengagement"; Bratton, "Beyond the State"; and Gyimah-Boadi, "Associational Life."

9. Diamond, "Rethinking Civil Society"; and Diamond, *Developing Democracy.*

10. For a detailed account of the impressive contribution made by independent domestic observers in the Nigerian election of 1999, see Nwanko, "Monitoring Nigeria's Elections." See also Agyeman-Duah, *Elections in Emerging Democracies.*

11. Aili Tripp discusses the political progress of women in Africa in her article "New Political Activism in Africa."

12. See Lancaster, *Aid to Africa.*

13. On the role of civil society and the development of social capital for Asian economic and social development, see Fukuyama, *Trust;* for Italy, see Putnam, *Making Democracy Work;* and Putnam, "Bowling Alone."

14. For details, see Hill, *The Migrant Cocoa Farmers.*

15. See Landell-Mills, "Governance, Cultural Change, and Empowerment"; Lancaster, *Aid to Africa;* Carothers, *Aiding Democracy Abroad;* and Hearns, *Foreign Aid, Democratization, and Civil Society in Africa.*

16. Excellent discussions of the underdevelopment of the private sector in Africa are found in Kennedy, *African Capitalism;* Young, *Ideology and Development;* and Bates, *Markets and States.*

17. For highly informative discussions of the "informalization" of African economies in the 1980s, see MacGaffey, *The Real Economy of Zaire;* and Chazan, "Patterns."

18. Julie Hearns, in *Foreign Political Aid, Democratization, and Civil Society in Ghana,* contends that national consensus over neoliberal economic reform in Ghana may no longer prove so elusive as a result of donor support to civil society.

19. See Ottaway and Chung, "Debating Democracy Assistance."

20. I attempt to rebut some of these arguments in my article "Debating Democracy Assistance." Hearns's research on selected civil society organizations in South Africa, Uganda, and Ghana appears to corroborate my position. See Hearns, *Foreign Political Aid, Democratization, and Civil Society in Ghana;* and Hearns, *Foreign Aid, Democratization, and Civil Society in Africa.*

21. See *The Economist,* January 29, 2000, p. 25.

22. Reported in *The Sowetan,* December 16, 1997.

23. Saad Ibrahim states his case eloquently in "A Reply to my Accusers."

24. The term is associated with prominent antiapartheid campaigner Reverend Allan Boesak. He reportedly cited this as part of his court defense against a charge and conviction for embezzling donor funds originally intended to support anti-apartheid work.

25. See Bratton, "Civil Society and Political Transitions"; and Fowler, "Non-Governmental Organizations."

26. These figures are reported in Zangor, *The Non-Profit Sector.*

27. See Mekenkamp, van Tongeren, and van de Veen, *Searching for Peace in Africa.*

28. See Pinto-Duschinsky, "The Rise of Political Aid"; and Carothers, *Aiding Democracy Abroad.* Hearns discusses the cases of South Africa, Uganda, and Ghana in *Foreign Aid, Democratization, and Civil Society in Africa.*

29. See Diamond, *Developing Democracy;* Bratton, "Beyond the State"; Bratton, "Civil Society and Political Transitions"; and, for general discussions, Putnam, *Making Democracy Work;* and Shils, "The Virtue of Civil Society."

30. The moral economy of patron clientelist politics in postcolonial Africa is memorably portrayed in classic African novels such as *Man of the People* (by Chinua Achebe) and *The Beautiful Ones Are Not Yet Born* (by Ayikwei Armah).

31. For details, see Gyimah-Boadi, Oquaye, and Drah, *Civil Society Organizations;* and Gyimah-Boadi, "Associational Life, Civil Society, and Democratization."

32. See especially Post, "State, Civil Society, and Democracy." See also Gyimah-Boadi, "Civil Society in Africa."

33. Gyimah-Boadi, "Associational Life, Civil Society, and Democratization"; Gyimah-Boadi and Essuman-Johnson, "PNDC and Organized Labor."

34. Exclusivist and nonliberal elements of African social structures and civil societies are highlighted in Post, "State, Civil Society, and Democracy"; Ekeh, "Colonialism and the Two Publics in Africa"; Ekeh, "The Constitution of Civil Society"; Ekeh, "Historical and Cross-Cultural Contexts of Civil Society"; and Mamdani, *Citizen and Subject.*

35. See a perceptive analysis of the Rwandan case in Lemarchand, "Uncivil States and Civil Societies."

36. On forms of social capital and their potential to generate productive social outcomes, see Putnam, *Bowling Alone,* pp. 24–26.

5

Corruption and Corruption Control

Sahr J. Kpundeh

That corruption adversely impedes development is no longer an issue of debate. Cross-country empirical work has confirmed its negative impact on institutions, growth and productivity, policy processes, property rights, and consequently, development.[1] In several African countries, the effects of corruption have translated into political instability, frequent regime changes, and unstable economic investment environment. These factors have resulted in slowing the consolidation of participatory governance in the region. Therefore, controlling corruption is one of the greatest challenges to the establishment and consolidation of democratic systems and a propoor governance environment in African countries. Until recently, citizens and donors, particularly bilateral and multilateral donors, have rarely held African governments accountable. But the globalization of markets dramatically highlights developmental inequities and citizens appear to demand economic and political reforms, thereby renewing interest in democratic forms of governance. Domestic stakeholders and the international community are insisting on transparency and accountability, creating a big dilemma for those leaders who are averse to inclusive and participatory forms of rule. The demand for increased transparency, accountability, integrity, political and economic competition, and the involvement of civil society in the broader governance of the country has helped to place corruption at the center of these changes.

Nonetheless, controlling corruption is one of the greatest challenges to the establishment and consolidation of democracy systems in Africa. The centralized nature of African governments, the personalization of power at the top and at all levels of authority, as well as the lack of transparency and accountability (both horizontal and vertical accountability) contribute significantly to the exacerbation of poverty and inequality in Africa. The capacity of widespread corruption to erode the legitimacy of regimes and pose a profound threat not only to democratic systems but to all systems of government is closely linked to the fact that corruption is antidevelopmental: it diverts resources and efforts away from productive activities into rent-seeking, fosters negative incentives for investment, consolidates patronage networks as a principal form of influence on state economic management, and suppresses civil society and civil liberties. The ineffectiveness of past and current political leaders of Africa to build political institutions, mobilize democratic participation, and manage dissent and opposition with democratic grace has contributed to the erosion of democratic legitimacy. It has in turn delayed, distorted, and diverted economic development and fostered glaring inequities.[2]

Theoretically, democratic institutions offer the potential for citizens, nongovernmental organization (NGOs), the private sector, independent media, and other stakeholders to carefully scrutinize the actions of politicians and government officials. However, some scholars have argued that corruption actually increases during the transition to more democratic forms of governance and that democratic political systems provide incentives and opportunities for corrupt practices. They also contend that newly elected leaders are under the same pressures as the former ones, particularly with respect to financing elections, which in almost all cases involve some level of corruption.[3] But democracies benefit from an underlying consensus on rules, independent law enforcement bodies, news media, and political opposition and on voters' ability to throw out the government without threatening the constitutional regime.[4] Moreover, there is growing consensus among policymakers and academics that anticorruption reforms can only be sustained if a wide range of stakeholders—government, civil society, NGOs, the private sector, as well as the international community—are involved. This is best done within the context of democratic governance.

The chapter begins with an investigation into the causes of corruption and the consequences for democracy and development. Second, it analyses the current academic and policy debate on reform strategies, highlighting policies designed to control, deter, and punish, and discusses potentially effective initiatives. Third, it explores the institutional and political requirements for a serious assault on corruption, focusing on the significance of political will and the necessary elements for designing and empowering anticorruption agencies and building effective judicial systems to enforce anticorruption laws and regulations. Fourth, it analyzes the need for an integrated strategy and examines the roles of civil society (independent NGOs and the mass media), the private sector, and community-based organizations in the process. The chapter concludes with a look at the international community and how international institutions and foreign governments cooperate with and strengthen the efforts of African states and societies to control corruption.

Causes of Corruption in Africa

While there is widespread agreement among academics, policymakers, and the informed public that corruption essentially involves the use of a public office for private gain, there is no consensus on the causes of corruption. An array of explanations includes centralization of power; lack of ethical leadership, morality, accountability, and transparency; greed; excessive or overcentralized economic and political power; and inefficiency. The variety of causes explains the often morally charged and ethnically grounded debate on this contentious issue.[5] However, for Africa, there can be no argument that the problem of corruption derives largely from general lack of accountability. Using Andreas Schedler's two-dimensional definition of accountability—that it involves *answerability,* the obligation of public officials to inform about and to explain what they are doing, and *enforcement,* the capacity of accounting agencies to impose sanctions on power builders who have violated their public duties[6]—this section attempts to make the case that the lack of accountability as it relates to both answerability and enforcement has contributed to deepening the problem of corruption in Africa. The two-dimensional meaning of the concept is inclusive of terms such as *surveillance, monitoring, oversight, control, checks, restraint, public exposure,* and *punishment*—terms that are used to describe efforts to ensure the exercise of power in a rule of law environment.[7]

The notion of answerability refers to the ability to ensure that officials in government are answerable for their actions. It therefore affirms the obligation of rulers to the ruled, public officials to the public, and government to the citizens. This is crucial for inducing governmental effectiveness and responsiveness and ultimately generating legitimacy. More broadly, it involves the right of citizens to receive information and the corresponding obligation of office holders to release all necessary details as well as explain and justify their conduct. In other words, ensuring accountable governance requires the creation and sustenance of a variety of crosscutting institutions and processes: free, fair, and regularly scheduled elections in which incumbents face a real possibility of losing; an independent judiciary; an independent election authority; effective parliamentary oversight; an effective public accounts committee of parliament; an independent audit body; an independent ombudsman; and an independent media strong in investigative reporting.[8]

In the context of Africa, it can be argued that the frequent and recurrent refusal of public office holders to follow the fundamental tenets of participatory governance and to account for their actions and expenditures is a major reason why corruption has lingered and even grown. The structures and processes of monitoring and oversight that could have ensured some

degree of accountability are weak and consequently ineffective. For example, the mobilization of civil society and effective institutional reforms are
crucial for combating corruption. But in most African countries, both civil
society and institutional reforms are controlled by the political and economic elites, who are interested in protecting the status quo. Thus, anticorruption reform efforts—legal and otherwise—are seldom initiated by the
elites. And civil society's role in participatory governance is sporadic
because of deliberate exclusion by government. More important, various
groups and interests in civil society are fragile and unable to act as a potent
force for reforms. In most cases, they lack the opportunity and protection to
improve the quality of governance in their societies.

Institutions such as elected legislatures, parliamentary oversight committees, and watchdog groups are present in nearly every African country.
But their effectiveness remains questionable. In many African countries, the
ruling party or the executive branch of government controls the legislature
and influences decisions and recommendations in parliamentary committees. The notions of strict separation of powers and real checks and balances are not entrenched in these countries. Consequently, the nominally
autonomous agents of horizontal accountability (which should have provided oversight) are incapable of demanding answers from the other agencies (which are immensely more powerful on all accounts). In any event,
these formal agencies of accountability hardly have the ability to demand
accountability and play a meaningful role in the fight against corruption.

Additionally, this lack of horizontal accountability can also be explained primarily as a form of capture of state and other governmental institutions by ruling elites.[9] State capture leads to systemic corruption because
political leaders and other powerful forces are not constrained by society's
institutions. National resources are monopolized, patronage and political
cronyism are rampant, and the government dominates all facets of the economy. Such domination creates a climate conducive to systematic exploitation of illegal income and rent-seeking opportunities by public officials.
Recent empirical evidence suggests that corruption thrives where the state
is unable to protect property and contractual rights or to provide institutions that support the rule of law.[10] Such governments repress citizens and
NGOs and muzzle the independent press in their advocacy for improved
governance. In such contexts, anticorruption agencies lack the independence to be effective; political competition is stifled, and a vocal opposition
is marginalized, preventing it from making valuable contributions to the
country's governance. Such actions undermine political development and
stability and threaten the democratic experiment and ultimately national
development.

Lack of decentralization is also a key problem. Governments have not
only centralized political and economic power in the urban areas, particularly

the capital cities, but also marginalized rural areas as well as vulnerable groups in society. Some countries have attempted to decentralize, but often-times with "strings" attached. Often political elites select their cronies or party sympathizers as their rural operatives, safeguarding their interests as opposed to encouraging genuine citizen participation and representation. Rural areas are unable to mobilize funds or taxes to develop their communities and have remained poor. In those circumstances where they are able to levy taxes, the proceeds are controlled and the priorities are determined by central-level government elites. This inability of marginalized groups to genuinely participate and make governance decisions in their communities has been a major contributor to entrenched corruption and the abject poverty in most rural areas in African countries.

The failure to develop a participative and inclusive approach to the design and implementation of anticorruption strategies is part of a general breakdown in accountability. Governments that ignore the voice of citizens (by discounting their views on corruption and other governance-related issues), either through empirical data evidence or the findings of investigative media, breach a fundamental tenet of participatory governance. It is this desire to depoliticize the corruption debate, focus on concrete areas for reform, and encourage a participatory process that mobilizes civil society and other stakeholders to fight against corruption that has prompted the utilization of diagnostic surveys of households, public officials, and business enterprises in countries such as Benin, Ethiopia, Sierra Leone, Nigeria, Zambia, Guinea, Malawi, and a few other African countries.

Weaknesses in the second dimension of accountability—enforcement or lack thereof (that is, rewarding good and punishing bad behavior)—also constitute a major contributing factor to the deepening of corruption in Africa. For rules to be effective, they must be accompanied by mechanisms of monitoring that ensure that violations of rules are detected (the informational function of accountability). But they must also be complemented with mechanisms of enforcement that "get the incentives right" by keeping acts of cheating from going unpunished (the enforcement dimension of accountability).[11] In quite a few African countries, enforcement has tended to focus on selected targets, especially the "small fry," while the "big fish" or top public officials are left alone. But until corruption is made a high-risk, low-profit activity—when public officials perceive a substantial risk that if they engage in corrupt conduct, they will lose their offices, forfeit illegally acquired wealth, and even go to prison—engaging in corruption will continue to be seen as a high-profit, low-risk activity, hence the deepening of the problem.[12]

Another challenging area in the fight against corruption in Africa is how to get the incentives right, especially by paying a living wage and establishing an adequate and progressively fair pay structure. Present salaries in most African countries appear to lock public service employees into detrimental patterns of behavior and offset efforts to improve discipline, promote ethical conduct, and adhere to conflict-of-interest guidelines.[13] Most unskilled workers and clerical staff are not paid a living wage in countries such as Uganda, Sierra Leone, Nigeria, and Benin (to name a few); the middle and upper income levels are perhaps sufficient for family survival but well below market value.

However, corruption would not necessarily be reduced by raising salaries alone. Susan Rose-Ackerman, for example, argues that high pay only marginally reduces the amount of extra funds resulting from bribery.[14] Therefore, reform efforts must include incentives such as pensions and other retirement benefits that are generous enough to deter civil servants from accepting payoffs. Moreover, as Larry Diamond argues, implementing sanctions against corruption requires an institutional framework to control corruption. A single institution or instrument, such as an anticorruption commission, will not do. Effective and durable corruption control requires multiple reinforcement and overlapping institutions of accountability.[15]

Multiple instruments and institutions for fighting corruption must be backed up by strong political will. But the will to fight corruption in most African countries is questionable. In some cases, the factor of political will is simply absent, thereby contributing to the ubiquity of corruption.[16] Senior government officials rarely translate into action their numerous pronouncements about reform programs.

Due to a variety of constraints, including legal and financial, the capacity of the established institutions to punish, which also forms an integral part of accountability, is ineffective in most African countries. For example, in quite a few African countries with established bodies to fight corruption, such as Tanzania, Ghana, and Malawi, the anticorruption instruments do not have powers to prosecute citizens for corruption unless and until they get approval from the director of public prosecutions or the attorney general. But in practice, top-level government officials are hardly prosecuted because prosecutorial authority is vested not in the independent anticorruption agencies but in agencies controlled by the ruling party and appointed by the partisan executive branch. Thus, for example, the former Kenya Anticorruption Authority (KACA) was declared an illegal operation by a constitutional court in December 2000 on the grounds that the law under which KACA was established clashed with Section 26 of the constitution—which says that only the attorney general can prosecute criminal offenses. The judges declared that "the existence of KACA undermines the powers and authority of the Attorney-General and the Commissioner of Police as conferred on them by the Constitution. Consequently, we find that the provisions establishing KACA are in conflict and inconsistent with the Constitution."[17] However, some countries, notably Uganda, have introduced positive reforms in this area. The Ugandan inspector general of government has been given the power to prosecute following a 1995 constitutional change. Anticorruption agencies in Tanzania, Malawi, and Ghana are also seeking the independent authority to prosecute and impose sanctions on offending officials.

The role of macroeconomic policy in deepening the problem of corruption, especially in nonreforming countries, is also worth mentioning.[18] The distortions caused by policies pushed by international financial institutions and bilateral donors have contributed to the undermining of economic stability in almost every African country. According to Marina Ottaway, "The international community seeks to increase the impact of the limited resources it provides to Africa by imposing an avalanche of demands and conditionalities that supposedly ensure that resources will not be squandered. But this avalanche makes it impossible for any African government to develop a coherent policy of its own."[19] In other words, donors have not discriminated effectively among different countries and different phases of the reform process. They have tended to provide the same package of assistance everywhere with the "one size fits all" approach, which contributes to deepening corruption primarily because it involves passing large amounts of aid to nonreforming countries with authoritarian leaders and military dictators, which also sends the wrong signals and contributes to sustaining bad leaders and their bad policies.

Failure to be fully inclusive and a tendency to depend on the good nature and good intentions of particular leaders constitute yet another contributor to the persistence of corruption and intractability of reforms. Collective action to fight corruption is particularly valuable because society supports a reform project that removes control from individuals and popularizes the mandate for accountability with effective citizen involvement. But more important, broadening political participation enhances the array of tools and strategies that can be utilized to deal with a wider range of needs, priorities, and objectives in civil society and the political system.[20] Recent African history is replete with examples of well-intentioned reformers who, unable to mobilize supportive constituencies, faltered because they could not neutralize resistance—such as Nigeria under the short-lived administration of Muhammad Buhari from December 1983 to August 1985, Ghana under Jerry Rawlings in 1979, and Liberia under Samuel Doe in 1980. Tanzanian president Benjamin Mkapa's anticorruption initiatives have been largely ineffective, at least in part because he has failed to adopt an inclusive and participative approach. Instead, his anticorruption reforms have inadvertently painted a picture of a "one-man show" and given the impression that he has inadequate understanding of the systemic nature of the problem and the political dynamics and complexities involved in addressing it. He also appears to have failed to adequately appreciate the value of building coalitions with other stakeholders.

Reform Strategies

The previous section has outlined some of the reasons for the persistence of corruption in Africa, its deleterious effects on development, and why reducing the debilitating effects of corruption has become a priority in a majority of African countries. Corruption is very much a part of the so-called "coming anarchy" scenario in Africa, with crimes and social crises as some of its leading characteristics. One dimension of this scenario, consistent with Robert Kaplan's analysis, is that of dissident or rebel groups organized into armed cliques, ready to overthrow an alleged corrupt government.[21] Three events in Africa appear to have given significant visibility to this new phenomenon: the overthrow of Mobutu in Zaire; the overthrow of Joseph Momoh in 1992 and Ahmed Tejan Kabba in 1997 in the Sierra Leonean government; and Charles Taylor's long fight in Liberia to oust Samuel Doe, a fight that not only plunged the country into a bloody civil war but also resulted in Taylor being forced to resign as president and go into exile.

Table 5.1 summarizes the variety of approaches adopted by African countries to tackle the problem of corruption. They range from violence, including kangaroo trials and extrajudicial punitive actions; to national campaigns (utilizing inquiries, training, capacity building, and anticorruption agencies); to local or citizen campaigns emphasizing community oversight, investigative media reporting, and civil society/private sector efforts (which may include local chapters of Transparency International); to populist initiatives, including military coups, moral campaigns, and civil servant purges; to interventions by external agencies such as the World Bank, the International Monetary Fund, Transparency International, and other bilateral donors. This section reviews and critiques these approaches and strategies.

National Efforts

National anticorruption programs have been fundamentally government-driven with scanty nonstate and other stakeholder involvement. With different levels of authority and powers, public institutions (such as the inspector general of government of Uganda, the Kenya Anticorruption Authority, the Prevention of Corruption Bureau of Tanzania, the Commission on Human Rights and Administrative Justice and the Serious Frauds Office of Ghana, and the Anticorruption Bureau of Malawi) have been recently established to attack corruption. But their effectiveness has often been hampered by vulnerability to regime changes, lack of sufficient autonomy, lack of support from the political leadership, and in most cases and most important, lack of resources. Moreover, they tend to do little to involve other stakeholders in their work.

Table 5.1 Types of Anticorruption Strategies

National Efforts	Corruption inquiries; training within state and public institutions; "islands of integrity"; legal approaches; anticorruption agencies; auditor-general and parliamentary oversight committees; police and interagency cooperation; capacity building; codes of conduct for public officials; declaration of assets.
Local or Citizen Efforts	Community oversight, media, coalitions with stakeholders, ombudsman—complaints and redress; local chapters of Transparency International promoting "pillars of integrity"; decentralization and deregulation; protection against arbitrary nature of the state; service delivery surveys on public services; business enterprise surveys on corruption.
Populist Initiatives	Military coups d'etat; moralization campaigns; civil servant purges; public humiliations and executions; quasi-official tribunals; property seizure, heavy fines, and imprisonment.
International Efforts	World Bank and IMF policies; OECD efforts to criminalize transnational bribery; Transparency International interventions; bilateral donor efforts.

Source: Compiled by the author drawing from, among other sources, Stephen Riley, "The Political Economy of Anti-Corruption Strategies in Africa," in Mark Robinson, ed., *Corruption and Development* (London: Frank Cass, 1998).

Parliamentary oversight committees have had little, if any, impact. Legislative committees have been utilized with partial effectiveness only in a handful of cases (Uganda, Kenya, and Ghana). The Ugandan Public Accounts Committee has vigorously demanded proper accounting of government expenditures from ministries. Its work has resulted in the prosecution and/or dismissal of government agencies and senior officials. It has helped to expose malfeasance in all areas of the Ugandan government, forcing corrupt ministers out of office and censuring others. Arguably poor institutional arrangements and ruling-party dominance in parliament largely account for the ineffectiveness of legislative oversight in the other countries (such as Sierra Leone, Nigeria, and Tanzania). In Tanzania, for example, members of the Public Accounts Committee are often rotated, prohibiting continuity in policies and procedures.

Codes of conduct for senior government officials and civil servants have been introduced in Tanzania, Uganda, Mali, and Malawi. Top government officials and high-level civil servants are required to adhere to a leadership code of conduct, which in most cases includes a declaration of assets, income, and liabilities. While these procedures can be productive, they often suffer from weak enforcement. Schedler argues that only public accountability can achieve the aim of curbing power and that confidential accountability, exercised behind closed doors, tends to be perceived as a farce and amounts to a caricature of accountability.[22] But in many cases, inadequate attention is given to the monitoring of declarations, thereby drastically reducing its potential to prevent illicit enrichment. Ineffectiveness also derives from the lack of capacity and political will on the part of leaders and the institutions they set up to verify declarations. In Uganda, Tanzania, and Ghana, public officials declare their assets behind closed doors to the inspector general of government, the commissioner of ethics, and the auditor general respectively. Typically, the declarations are not public documents, and where there are provisions for public access, as in the case of Tanzania, the procedures are so ambiguous that such access is difficult, if not impossible, for citizens to exercise.

Local or Citizen Efforts

The influence of Transparency International has raised the stakes in the political economy of addressing corruption. Several countries, including Ghana, Uganda, Tanzania, Kenya, Nigeria, Zambia, and Zimbabwe, have established local chapters. Between 1996 and 1999, Transparency International in partnership with the World Bank Institute organized national integrity workshops in Tanzania, Malawi, Uganda, and several other African countries. Additionally, this collaboration conducted training for investigative journalists—aimed at improving skills and confidence, and cultivating a renewed commitment to reform. A recent initiative has seen coalitions formed in several countries—with the assistance of and under the World Bank Institute's Core Course Program on Anticorruption. Good examples of this initiative are the anticorruption coalitions of Ghana and Uganda, which involve a variety of stakeholders (public, private, and civil society bodies) working closely together to evolve a national anticorruption plan. Similarly, civil society, media, and private sector representatives have formed the Tanzania Civic Monitor to observe the implementation of the country's national anticorruption action plan.

Civil society involvement is central to the successful exercise of the oversight function. It represents a homegrown strategy, which demonstrates ownership and improves chances for sustainability. A strong civil society is essential for the kind of structured political competition that can remedy some of the problems inherent in systems where civil liberties, political freedoms, and other constructive incentives are lacking. More important, it can reinforce the political will needed for reform.[23] However, traditionally, civil society in African countries has been weak and divided. Consequently, its contributions to governance improvements have also been sporadic. In the early 1990s, Africa's prodemocracy movements drew large numbers of people into political debate and organization. However, this momentum was not always built on, especially in the face of repressive laws (see Chapter 4).

Ironically, the actions and omissions of governments appear to have done more to undermine local and national anticorruption efforts. Official hostility and lack of support for civil society initiatives have been detrimental. And institutions such as Malawi's ombudsman body, Ghana's Commission on Human Rights and Administrative Justice, Nigeria's Public Complaints Commission, and similar agencies elsewhere on the continent are typically in constant conflict with government officials. Although many are constitutionally established, most governments have tended to view them as adversaries and attempted to stifle their progress through intimidation as well as control of their personnel and budgets. In Ghana, Tanzania, Uganda, and quite a few other countries, budgetary constraints have forced official anticorruption agencies to rely on bilateral donors to support their operations, thereby raising credibility questions for the institutions.

Populist Initiatives

Populist initiatives such as civil servant purges, arrests, detention, and public humiliation of senior government officials have been prevalent in the aftermath of military coups d'etat. In such heady contexts, allegedly corrupt officials are given draconian punishments. Ghana's Flight Lieutenant Jerry Rawlings and Liberia's Head of State Samuel Doe sanctioned the execution of corrupt officials in 1979 and 1980 respectively. Military governments characteristically institute commissions of inquiry to investigate embezzlement and mismanagement of government funds by deposed officials.

Corruption and other crimes are based upon motive, opportunity, and means, as well as how these elements are built into the relationship between private citizens and government agents. Military governments have tended to focus their anticorruption efforts on individuals—thanks largely to general lack of understanding and appreciation of the systemic nature of corruption. However, quick-fix anticorruption measures such as purges and moralization campaigns instituted by military regimes to deal with corruption have been hardly successful or sustainable. This confirms Dele Olowu's contention that "the existence of political will to genuinely tackle corruption must not be assumed on the basis of policy pronouncements by political leaders. Those most vocal often turn out to be the ones who aid and abet corruption most."[24]

International Efforts

Anticorruption efforts at the international level highlight the need to address official malfeasance as integral to the new development agenda to reduce poverty. This new agenda emphasizes sustaining reform efforts in developing and transitioning countries to enable market economies and liberal democratic political systems to grow. Additionally, these efforts are designed to prioritize the interests of the poor and marginalized within the context of higher ethical standards among donors and in an enabling state.[25] Based on this agenda, international organizations such as the World Bank, the International Monetary Fund (IMF), the United Nations Development Programme (UNDP), the Organization for Economic Cooperation and Development (OECD), and bilateral donors have developed new policies to demonstrate intolerance for corruption and push African governments to institute measures to control this malaise. Through technical and other forms of assistance, multilateral and bilateral donors have sought to encourage African governments to implement measures that reduce opportunities for corruption, build capacity, reform the public sector, and improve the quality of governance.

However, international and regional initiatives to address corruption are not always supported by and coordinated with domestic efforts.[26] Switzerland, for example, has discouraged money laundering by agreeing to freeze and return stolen wealth deposited in its banks. In 1997, U.S. President Bill Clinton and some European governments also agreed to support such efforts. In 2000, at the request of Nigeria's President Olusegun Obasanjo, about U.S.$650 million was frozen in 140 Swiss accounts that belonged to former head of state Sani Abacha.[27] In April 1997, Swiss authorities returned U.S.$2.2 million to Mali as repatriated funds of former president Moussa Traoré, and in May of that year, Switzerland froze the assets of former Zairean president Mobutu Sese Seko. Authorities subsequently identified U.S.$3.4 million in bank accounts belonging to Mobutu and his relatives.[28]

This concerted international effort to deal with corruption is a far cry from the Cold War days, when despots like Mobutu often had the backing of Western capitals. Because kleptocrats like Mobutu resisted communism, the developed world condoned their get-rich-fast schemes that plundered national treasuries. The battle against corruption is quickly becoming a priority for Western powers trying to bring stability and prosperity to global markets. In the United States, for example, at least three pieces of legislation were proposed to make the handling of corrupt money a crime. Between 1996 and 1999 the Treasury Department under the Clinton administration also announced a proposal to give the government more power to battle money laundering of all types.[29]

The above discussion clearly demonstrates there is no silver bullet to deal with corruption. The forms and causes vary from country to country, and consequently, attempts to confront it also vary to fit each country's realities. However, the lessons that have emerged from successful reform efforts clearly illustrate that strong political will at all levels of government is pivotal.

The Significance of Political Will

Reform is oftentimes unsuccessful due to a combined influence of inadequate strategies, political resistance, poor participative approach, failure to develop sustainable efforts, and inability to construct appropriate tools to establish systemic change. Political will is another critical component for sustainable and effective anticorruption strategies and programs. Without it, governmental efforts designed to improve civil service, strengthen transparency and accountability, and reinvent the relationship between government and private industry will prove to be ineffective.[30] However, neither its presence nor absence can be presumed in any single initiative. Political will is evident by the level of participation that is built into reform initiatives, incorporating a range of political actors and civil society. Unwavering determination to fight corruption is not just a problem for leaders and bureaucratic reformers. The private sector, too, may lack the will to overcome corrupt systems. Citizens face the problems of mobilizing for collective action and turning their convictions into changes in public administration.

The desire to change the culture of corruption can reside in many locations. Numerous examples illustrate reform efforts that have arisen from each branch of government, the political opposition, civil society, international organizations, and private sector institutions. Each group has different motives and goals and consequently defines success differently. But political will neither originates nor manifests in a vacuum. Rather, it is the reflection of complex circumstances that incorporate the aspirations of individual leaders, a calculation of the benefits that can be derived from changes in rules and behaviors, and a belief in the ability to muster adequate support to overcome resistance to reforms.[31]

While these reformist opportunities represent platforms for change, they often do not incorporate comprehensive strategies for sustainable change. In many cases, anticorruption campaigns are political, rather than ideological, in motivation, scope, and objectives.[32] As such, they are political instruments employed to delegitimize the previous regime, purge the opposition, or legitimate the current regime by temporarily decreasing corruption. Alternatively, they may be a tactical response to challenges from a counterelite, popular discontent arising from socioeconomic conditions, or adverse publicity or investigations. Even when the anticorruption campaigns are not just political instruments, the strategies may be too broadbased to have any impact or may create disequilibria by overfortifying the powers of the head of state or, instead, undermining his effectiveness.[33]

Michael Johnston describes political will as being that nexus "where the analytical and practical aspects of the corruption issue meet, recognizing that active political processes and strong leadership are necessary parts of any effective response to malfeasance."[34] But what has been lacking in several African countries is the demonstration of a credible intent by political leaders to attack the perceived causes and effects of corruption at a systemic level—translating policy pronouncements and rhetoric into sustainable actions.

In several countries, the leadership has taken steps to demonstrate a commitment to reform by disclosing their assets and seeking aid and technical assistance from international and bilateral donors. In Tanzania, for example, President Mkapa disclosed his assets and those of his wife after he assumed the presidency in 1995. In Ghana, Benin, Nigeria, Zambia, and Malawi, the various heads of state have requested assistance directly from the World Bank to help with corruption. With the assistance of the World Bank Institute, diagnostic surveys are either under way or are in advanced planning stages as first steps to understanding the causes and consequences of corruption prior to developing reform strategies.

It is important to stress that remedies should be country-specific based on sound analytical work that delineates vulnerable areas and reasons for the lack of progress. "One size fits all" suggestions are ineffectual. Initially, several political and institutional requirements must be established—divided into governmental actions and civil society programs. The former category comprises a variety of legal, administrative, and organizational responses executed by a system of incentives; the latter category comprises initiatives to engage the forces and interests of society in anticorruption efforts, thereby providing sustainable support. Neither strategy is likely to be sufficient alone. Both government and civil society programs work best in partnership, where public opinion and social interests support reform and anticorruption efforts in civil society enjoy the protection and encouragement that only government can provide.[35]

Government actions fall into four broad areas: legal reforms, public administration and regulation, financial management and control, and intra-governmental accountability and oversight. All countries have laws against fraud and corruption, and rather than create more laws, it is important to review and, if necessary, strengthen existing legislation. Modernizing the penal code to increase the costs of corruption includes efforts to criminalize bribery and strengthen laws against illicit enrichment, protect whistleblowers, require financial disclosure, promote freedom of legislation, and enlist watchdog agencies, supreme audit institutions, and financial management systems. Aggressive enforcement of existing laws in African countries remains one of the missing links in supporting reform.

Some countries have chosen to create special agencies that have the primary responsibility for change. For example, the inspector general of government of Uganda, the Kenya Anticorruption Authority, the Prevention of Corruption Bureau of Tanzania, the Commission on Human Rights and Administrative Justice and the Serious Frauds Office in Ghana, the Anticorruption Bureau of Malawi, the Directorate for Control of Economic

Crimes of Botswana, and the Anticorruption Bureau of Zambia were all created to lead their countries' reform efforts. Most have been modeled on the successful operations of the Independent Commission Against Corruption (ICAC) in Hong Kong. Despite their duplication, the agencies fail to produce similar results. Unfortunately, the Hong Kong model cannot easily be transferred to African countries.

Aside from its abundant resources and highly qualified staff, neither of which is always available in African countries, the ICAC operates within a relatively well-regulated administrative culture, alongside a well-equipped police force, within a supportive political and legal framework.[36] This is extremely critical, as there is usually the suggestion that anticorruption agencies can only be successful when they report to parliament. Hong Kong, Singapore, and to some extent Botswana are evidence of such: in these three countries, respectively, the ICAC reports to the governor (now chief executive); the director of the Corrupt Practices Investigation Bureau is appointed directly by, and reports to, the president; and the director general reports to the president. What all these examples demonstrate is that to whom the anticorruption agency reports is less important in an environment where the legal framework, enforcement and oversight mechanisms, whistle-blower protection laws, lack of genuine political competition, and the institutional structures that introduce a checks and balances schematic are absent or weak.

In Tanzania for example, the director general of the Prevention of Corruption Bureau reports to the president, but to whom the director general reports is less important than the kinds of legislation and resources the bureau needs to perform daily operations. This is especially the case in countries where the head of state has the political will to effect change. If legislation were passed to make bureau report to parliament, the current parliamentary oversight mechanisms (budget, finance, and public accounts committees), with their lack of resources and trained personnel, would be ineffective. The Chama Cha Mapinduzi political party dominates parliament. Consequently, reports and policies from the executive have the rubber stamp of approval. Instead, the current operational laws of the bureau should be examined to ensure that it has the power to investigate and prosecute, and it is not subject to veto from the director of public prosecutions (as is the case currently in Malawi). It must also have adequate resources to attract and recruit a competent and dedicated staff.

I do not wish to imply in the preceding argument that anticorruption bureaus should not report to parliament or be provided autonomy. Reporting to parliament is a way of insulating the agency from political interference. But the more critical issue is that a system of checks and balances ought to be present and functioning. Measures to improve the competence of the executive, judiciary, and legislature need to be introduced. The judiciary cannot play a significant role if it is not autonomous. A checks and balances schematic that introduces multiple chances of veto can prevent government from acting without the consent of the institutions organized along different interests and representing various constituencies.[37] As Larry Diamond has argued, where corruption is endemic, these institutions need to have three kinds of accountability: horizontal, vertical, and external. Or, as he has further suggested in the case of Nigeria, a whole new layer of insulation needs to be constructed, in the form of a state council appointed from civil society and academia and other independent bodies that would appoint and supervise critical agencies of horizontal accountability such as the counter-corruption commission.[38]

A serious assault against corruption is difficult in an environment where political will is absent. Additionally, the fight against corruption has to be part of an ongoing reform process. Similarly, any anticorruption strategy has to be a major component of an overall public sector reform that addresses civil service issues, financial management systems, supreme audit institutions, strengthened watchdog and oversight mechanisms, judicial and legal reforms, strengthened incentives, and the like. This is not to imply that without political will, the reform process is doomed. Political will can be nurtured by involving a variety of stakeholders in the reform process—building a constituency that recognizes the value of reform and dedicates itself to monitoring and defending a reform strategy. Such a constituency, its interests not always aligned with the political leadership, can serve as an effective check on political actors' abuse of power by challenging the nonresponsiveness of the status quo. Additionally, an independent media, a balance of power between state and society and between economic and political power, and periodic service delivery surveys that give consumers a voice and a means of conveying strong messages to service providers are all ways to help strengthen and institutionalize political will.

A participatory approach to governance—where locals are involved in designing and implementing programs—means that the people participate in establishing priorities. In some African countries, the government has ignored the "voice" of the rural areas. However, the desire to improve governance has introduced new "actors" seeking to defend and further their interests in the policy process. Politicians who have practiced the policy of exclusion by monopolizing the benefits of state resources find it more difficult now to appropriate the benefits of governance for their own private interests. Decentralization of power can be tricky, particularly if there is no real delegation of authority, including the authority to generate and reserve a portion of local revenues. The African Development Foundation and the World Bank are currently supporting participatory development projects that give group members not only control over the design and implementation of their project but also the resources needed to implement it. This simply means that all the individuals in the group are able to participate in the decisionmaking process, including identification of the problem, project design, implementation, distribution of benefits, and evaluation of impact.

This example demonstrates that a participative and inclusive approach helps to generate local ownership, put people in the driver's seat, harness their capabilities, and, inevitably, improve development. The fight against corruption should be seen from this perspective. Strategies should be home-grown. Even when they are locally developed, they should not be driven by central government, as this creates a dependency syndrome. When people own reform programs, it helps to prevent social exclusion and the capture of the programs by both politicians in the center and elites in the urban areas.

The Role of the International Community

International donors have taken several steps to address corruption both within their various organizations and in their policies for granting loans and assistance to developing countries. Multilateral institutions such as the World Bank, the International Monetary Fund, and the UNDP, and several bilateral donors, have all instituted new policies to prevent corruption in their projects and support international anticorruption efforts, such as the OECD convention that seeks the criminalization of bribery in international business transactions. However, international efforts, especially from multi-lateral and bilateral donors, have to support and complement domestic strategies, but if a particular country does not have ongoing public sector reforms as part of its broader governance policy process, international remedies will most likely be ineffective.

Donors can continue to support the domestic agenda in countries genuinely struggling with reform. First, they may want to consider putting additional pressure on countries with invasive persistent fraud and mis-management by insisting that they demonstrate their commitment in their country budgets through an increase in the resources allocated to anticor-ruption efforts. Additionally, matching anticorruption funds from donors could also be a useful tool to put pressure on governments to demonstrate their commitment.

Second, bilateral donors should ensure that political corruption is a priority in their policy agenda, especially since the mandates of multilaterals such as the World Bank limit this activity. Political corruption is a funda-mental problem that needs to be addressed—campaign financing, checks and balances, civil liberties, structured competition in both political and economic realms, and so forth, are all important factors in the fight against corruption. It might also be quite useful if donors were to increase cooper-ation with African countries to help return wealth acquired illicitly by their leaders, as is currently the case with Nigeria and the wealth acquired by its former head of state Sani Abacha.

Third, donors may want to encourage and provide support for collective action to deal with corruption and, more important, target additional support for programs that promote such action among various stakeholders in developing and implementing anticorruption reforms. Having an inclusive and participatory approach (involving all stakeholders—government, civil society, the private sector, media, etc.) to designing and implementing anticorruption reforms helps to sustain the process of reform and energizes the necessary political will.

Finally, and most important, donors should provide support to nurture political will in countries where it is either weak or totally lacking. The success of anticorruption reforms depends upon achieving short-term solutions to build political will, such as sequencing reforms and identifying short-, medium-, and long-term tasks and publicly distinguishing their respective goals. In the short term, the tasks are to identify anticorruption "champions" and provide the occasions, and possibly the protection, they need to begin to act. This includes creating opportunities for political will to emerge as well as including anticorruption views on the political and development agendas. An intermediary challenge donors can also support is the development of pivotal systems and incentives that provide reformers with political and economic support—in other words, providing aid and possibly debt relief to support countries that formulate broader political, bureaucratic, and economic processes and incentive systems that will create alternatives to corruption and encourage personal and societal changes. If the short- and medium-term goals are achieved, donors can then support reforming countries in shifting their emphasis to long-term targets—programs that institutionalize anticorruption forces and incentives in the political and economic arenas. In other words, support countries to build anticorruption policies into the daily procedures that regulate the economic and political systems. Consequently, when commitment and action become the rule rather than the exception, then political will to act against corruption will be sustained by lasting support.

Notes

1. Rose-Ackerman, *Corruption and Government;* Kaufmann, "Corruption: The Facts"; Kaufmann, "Corruption in Transition Economies"; Mauro, "The Effects of Corruption"; Wei, "How Taxing Is Corruption?" and Knack and Keefer, "Institutions and Economic Performance."

2. Diamond, "Introduction: Roots of Failure, Seeds of Hope," p. 21.

3. Médard, "The Crisis of Neo-Patrimonial State."

4. Przeworski and Limongi, "Political Regimes," pp. 51–69.

5. Riley, "The Political Economy"; Johnston, "Political Will and Corruption"; Kaufmann, Kraay, and Zoido-Lobaton, "Governance Matters"; Kpundeh, *Politics and Corruption in Africa;* Olowu, "Roots and Remedies"; Hope and Chikulo, *Corruption and Development in Africa.*

6. Schedler, "Conceptualizing Accountability," pp. 13–28.

7. Ibid.

8. Gyimah-Boadi, "Good Governance."

9. I am grateful to Daniel Kaufmann for emphasizing this point.

10. Hellman, Jones, and Kaufmann, "Seize the State, Seize the Day."

11. Schedler, "Conceptualizing Accountability," p. 16.

12. Diamond, "Fostering Institutions."

13. World Bank, *Recommendations.*

14. Rose-Ackerman, "The Political Economy of Corruption."

15. Diamond, "Fostering Institutions."

16. Kpundeh, "Political Will."

17. "Major Blow for KACA," pp. 1–2.

18. See Chapter 2 in this volume for a more detailed analysis of this point.

19. Ottaway, "Less Is Better," p. 4.

20. Kpundeh, "Political Will."

21. Kaplan, "The Coming Anarchy"; Kaplan, "Was Democracy Just a Moment?"

22. Schedler, "Conceptualizing Accountability," p. 21.

23. Johnston, 1998; Kpundeh, "Political Will."

24. Olowu, 1993. p. 231.

25. Riley, "The Political Economy."

26. Johnston, "Fighting Systemic Corruption."

27. Masland and Bartholet, "The Lost Billions."

28. Ernest Harsch, quoted in Hope, "Accumulators and Democrats."

29. Masland and Bartholet, "The Lost Billions."

30. Kpundeh, "Political Will."

31. Ibid.

32. Gillespie and Okruhlik, "The Political Dimensions of Corruption Cleanups"; Riley, "The Political Economy of Anti-Corruption Strategies."

33. Gillespie and Okruhlik, "The Political Dimensions of Corruption Cleanups."

34. Johnston, "Fighting Systemic Corruption," pp. 85–102.

35. Kpundeh, Johnston, and Leiken, *Combating Corruption;* Dininio, Kpundeh, and Leiken, *USAID Handbook for Fighting Corruption.*

36. Kpundeh, Johnston and Leiken, *Combating Corruption.*

37. Rose-Ackerman, "The Political Economy of Corruption."

38. Diamond, "Fostering Institutions"; Diamond, "Nigeria's Perennial Struggle."

Conflict in Africa

Stephen John Stedman and Terrence Lyons

Africa has been the site of many of the world's deadliest wars. The Nigerian civil war (1967–1970) killed more than 1 million people, civil war and state collapse led to more than half a million deaths in Uganda in the early 1980s, and in Sudan a war begun in 1984 rages on; it is estimated that as many as 1.5 million people have died as a result.[1] Between 1991 and 1993, 240,000 Somalis died from war-induced famine.[2] In little over two months in 1994, nearly 1 million Rwandans fell victim to genocide. In October 1993 approximately 30,000–50,000 people lost their lives in Burundi during a one-month eruption of ethnic violence; in the ensuing civil war an additional 100,000 people have died.[3] When Angola's civil war resumed in late 1992, the death toll reached 1,000 people a day.[4] Seven years of civil war killed 150,000 people in Liberia.[5] Armed conflicts in sub-Saharan Africa now account for more than half of armed conflicts in the world.

Although many analysts took notice of Africa's wars only in the 1990s, political instability and violence have plagued the continent since most of its countries became independent in the 1960s. As Figure 6.1 shows, eleven civil wars erupted in Africa in the 1960s. In the 1970s the number of new civil wars dipped to five but rose back to eleven in the 1980s. In the 1990s eight more civil wars broke out in Africa, fewer than in the 1960s or 1980s. But since fighting continued in nine wars that had begun prior to 1990, an observer of the continent in the 1990s might at a given time have seen as many as seventeen countries (about 30 percent of all the countries in sub-Saharan Africa) at war.

Figure 6.1 reveals several interesting trends and patterns. From 1960 to 2000 there were thirty-five civil wars in Africa, but many of those wars took place in repeat-offender states. Four countries (Chad, Burundi, Uganda, and Zaire) account for fifteen (about 40 percent) of the total. Although there have been thirty-five separate wars, only nineteen African countries have actually suffered civil wars. Of those nineteen, 100 percent

Figure 6.1 Civil Wars in Sub-Saharan Africa, 1960–1999

	1960s	1970s	1980s	1990s
			Angola ──────────────────────────────▶	
	Burundi I	Burundi II	Burundi III	Burundi IV
	Chad I	Chad II	Chad III	Chad V
			Chad IV	
				Congo-Brazza
	Ethiopia I ──]			
			Ethiopia II ───────────────]	
				Guinea-Bissau
				Liberia
		Mozambique ───────────────────────────]		
	Namibia ───────────────────────────────]			
	Nigeria			
	Rwanda I			Rwanda II
			Senegal ──────────────▶	
				Sierra Leone
			Somalia I	
			Somalia II ──────────────────────▶	
	South Africa ──]			
	Sudan I ───────────]		Sudan II ──────────────▶	
	Uganda I		Uganda II	
			Uganda III ──────────────▶	
	Zaire I	Zaire II		Zaire III
	Zimbabwe I ───────────]		Zimbabwe II	
Wars begun	11	5	11	8
Wars under way at any given time	11	10	16	17

of the Belgian colonies (Zaire, Burundi, and Rwanda) and 100 percent of the Portuguese colonies on the continent (Angola, Mozambique, and Guinea-Bissau) are represented.[6] Whatever else one wants to say about Belgian and Portuguese colonialism in Africa, its legacy for its colonies is repeated and protracted war. At the beginning of 2000, ten major civil conflicts continued in Africa: Sierra Leone, Sudan, the Democratic Republic of Congo (DRC), Angola, Rwanda, Uganda, Burundi, Congo-Brazzaville, Senegal (Casamance), and Somalia. In addition, a major war between two states, Ethiopia and Eritrea, erupted in May 1998 and resulted in nearly 100,000 deaths before an agreement was signed in Algiers in December 2000.

Another pattern that can be seen from Figure 6.1 is a geographic shift in conflict over the past forty years. In the 1960s, 1970s, and 1980s, most of the conflicts on the continent were concentrated in southern Africa, where wars associated with late and contested decolonization raged in the Shaba region of Zaire, Zimbabwe, Mozambique, Angola, Namibia, and South Africa. By the 1990s, all of these except Angola were settled. In contrast, West Africa saw increased conflict in the 1980s and 1990s. With the exception of the brutal Biafran civil war in Nigeria and the endemic violence in Chad, West Africa saw fewer wars until the crises in Senegal in the 1980s and particularly the upsurge of violence in Liberia, Sierra Leone, and Guinea-Bissau in the 1990s. In the 2000s, this pattern continues, with interlinked conflicts a regionalized zone of conflict.

Figure 6.1 fails to capture a critical dimension of conflict in Africa. Wars in Africa are increasingly becoming regionalized and the distinction between civil war and international war less meaningful. An interconnected war centered on the Democratic Republic of Congo (the former Zaire) now runs from Angola and the Congo Republic (Brazzaville) in the west through the DRC, Burundi, Uganda, and Rwanda in the center of the continent all the way to Sudan in the northeast. This constellation of conflict includes a series of civil wars and internal conflicts—in Angola, Congo-Brazzaville, the DRC, Rwanda, Burundi, Uganda, and Sudan—and a series of cross-border military interventions by neighbors, particularly within the DRC. Conflict resolution has been hindered by the nested nature of each of these conflicts and the multiple agendas of intervening powers that have their own security, prestige, and, not least, economic agendas in play.

Under Mobutu, Zaire aided and provided sanctuary to the Union for the Total Independence of Angola (UNITA) in its war against the Angolan government; it also provided arms and support to the Rwandan government of Juvenal Habyirimana in its war against the Rwandan Patriotic Front (RPF). After factions close to the Rwandan government committed genocide in an attempt to prevent implementation of the Arusha peace agreement that would have curtailed their power, and were subsequently militarily defeated, Mobutu Sese Seko provided weapons, military equipment, and sanctuary to allow the *genocidaires* to regroup and restart the war with the RPF in Rwanda. Hutu rebels in Burundi and Rwanda have both used Zaire as a staging ground for attacks into Burundi, Rwanda, and Uganda. Believing Mobutu to be a cancer on the region, the governments of Rwanda and Uganda organized a rebellion in Zaire, which along with military intervention by the armies of those countries and Angola toppled Mobutu in eight short months. When Laurent Kabila, the leader of what was renamed the Democratic Republic of Congo, proved unable or unwilling to establish control over eastern Zaire and eliminate the Hutu rebels who used the region as their base, Uganda and Rwanda again militarily intervened and again assisted Congolese rebels disgruntled by Kabila's authoritarian ways. This time, however, Angola, Zimbabwe, Namibia, and Chad intervened to protect Kabila and turn back the revolt. In addition, Angola intervened in the Republic of Congo (Brazzaville) to help rebels overturn the elected government of Pascal Lissouba, who supported UNITA. Finally, Sudan and Uganda have engaged in mutual undermining of each other: Uganda has long supported the Sudan People's Liberation Army (SPLA) in southern

Sudan; in retaliation, Sudan is the principal external patron of the Lord's Resistance Army in northern Uganda.

A similar regionalized zone of conflict is developing in the West African subregion—notably conflicts in Liberia, Sierra Leone, Guinea, and Côte d'Ivoire, conflict in Casamance echoing in Guinea-Bissau, and continuing strife in Nigeria (both in the Niger Delta and in northern Nigeria) threatening conflict in the late 1990s and continuing into the early 2000s. The civil war in Liberia contributed to the conflict in Sierra Leone. Former factional leader Charles Taylor supported the insurgent Revolutionary United Front (RUF) in Sierra Leone and maintained these ties, and the links to lucrative diamond and gun networks, since ascending to the presidency in Monrovia in 1997. Conflict has spread to Guinea, where a massive humanitarian disaster developed in 2001, and there are reports that Taylor has established links to General Robert Guie, the deposed military leader in Côte d'Ivoire. The relationship between Senegalese intervention in Guinea-Bissau and connections with insurgents in the Casamance region points to the regionalization of conflict in that zone as well.

In the Horn of Africa, conflict has long been regionalized, as Ethiopia supported insurgents in Sudan and Somalia while each of these two states responded in kind with support for Eritrean and other opposition groups in the 1970s and 1980s.[7] In the 1990s, Ethiopia, Eritrea, and Uganda formed a set of "Frontline States" with encouragement from the United States to contain the National Islamic Front regime in Sudan and in support of the insurgent SPLA. Sudan responded by supporting Eritrean and Ugandan opposition groups. The border war between Ethiopia and Eritrea in 1998 cooled their support for insurgent groups within Sudan, but both sides began to engage in war by proxy in Somalia. After the Algiers Accord created a cease-fire along the Ethiopia-Eritrea border, Ethiopia became more involved in conflict within Somalia.

Regionalization of conflict and the blurring of distinctions between civil war and interstate war are furthered by a growing willingness to intervene in a neighboring state. As indicated in the Horn of Africa, such intervention is not new on the continent. Southern African states had supported national liberation movements as the frontier of self-rule moved south through the region from Angola and Mozambique through Zimbabwe to Namibia and finally South Africa. Moroccan and other African troops intervened during the 1977 and 1978 Shaba crises in Zaire, Tanzania intervened in Uganda in 1979, and Zimbabwe sent troops to protect vital transportation corridors threatened by guerrillas of the Mozambique National Resistance (Renamo). Roy May and Arnold Hughes counted thirty instances where African militaries deployed in a neighboring state between 1960 and 1985, generally to shore up a regime threatened by military mutiny or popular unrest.[8] But in the 1990s the norm against interference in a neighbor's internal affairs, which had limited or at least kept covert such assistance in the past, lay in tatters. As one analyst wrote in 1998, "Africa's hallowed doctrine of non-interference in the affairs of sovereign states has been abandoned. Borders are no longer sacrosanct."[9]

Three factors associated with state building explain much of Africa's history of war. First, general aspects of state formation in Africa—artificial borders, quasi-states, low human capital, underdeveloped economies with low tax bases, weak governing institutions with minimal capacity, a statist model of political and economic development—created a continent ripe for violence. Contrary to past international practice, Africa's newly independent states received recognition by fiat rather than by earning it through a process of consolidation.[10] Second, a more particular aspect of the African state formation process generated immediate violence in a number of states that continues to haunt the afflicted: the rapid, unplanned, turbulent transfer of power at independence, where little attempt was made to create the conditions for an orderly decolonization. This subgroup of African states reads like a "who's who" of the worst atrocity-filled wars of recent memory: Angola, Mozambique, Zaire, Rwanda and Burundi, and the Sudan. Third, the historically late decolonization of southern Africa, a process not finished until the 1990s, produced three interlocking conflicts: wars for independence in Angola, Mozambique, Namibia, and Zimbabwe; the attempt by South Africa's National Party to maintain white supremacy in South Africa; and South Africa's destabilization of its neighbors in the 1980s, which was a direct extension of its own civil war. From 1980 to 1988, between 1.2 and 1.9 million people were killed in war in Angola and Mozambique.[11]

Colonial powers established borders that corresponded little to African political, cultural, and economic life. Colonial governments were primarily policing and taxing organizations with few representative functions and emphasized the export of primary products to their respective metropoles. Strategies of colonial control manipulated ethnic division and exacerbated group conflicts over political and economic resources. The first generation of African independence leaders accepted colonial borders and eschewed the arduous and politically volatile task of redrawing them. The charter of the Organization of African Unity (OAU) placed great emphasis on the permanence of existing borders and the principle of territorial integrity. Although many analysts attribute Africa's lack of interstate wars to this commitment, it guaranteed that internal instability would be rife throughout Africa.[12]

If Africa's borders generated intense domestic conflicts over political identity, the lack of domestic economic capital ensured that states would become the object of intense distribution conflicts. As Larry Diamond observes, the state structures established by the colonial powers dwarfed in wealth and power both existing social institutions and various new fragments of modern organization.[13] At independence, Africa's new elites sought to harness the power of their states to drive their economies. Regulatory and other state-sponsored bodies and widespread nationalization of foreign industries provided income opportunities for state officials. The state soon became the largest employer in these new countries; for example, 47.2 percent of Senegal's budget in 1964–1965 was spent on administrative salaries, and 81 percent of the budget in the Central African Republic went to the civil service.[14]

Africa's new leaders consolidated their rule through access to state coffers. Some leaders, fearing potential ethnic conflicts, created inclusive coalitions that provided rewards for many societal groups.[15] In other cases, one ethnic group succeeded in capturing the state and shutting other groups out. In still other cases, political leaders chose to ignore ethnicity and insist on establishment of a national identity as a unifying principle for the country. As the state became the main source of employment and capital in the new countries of Africa, a pattern of patrimonial politics soon crystallized. Groups organized to ensure access to state largesse—the only way to accumulate wealth. Office holders expropriated state resources to consolidate their power bases and reward their networks of clients. National interests were subordinated to the interests of politicians and their supporters, who viewed public office as private property.[16]

Challenges in the 1990s

Africa's generally weak patrimonial states underwent far-reaching transformations in the 1990s, marking a significant watershed. As Christopher Clapham stated, "The post-colonial era in Africa is now, and only now, coming to an end; and the problem confronting the continent, and those who seek to understand it, is to discern what is taking place."[17] The Cold War and apartheid ended and their departure removed two issues that shaped international interest in the continent. Domestically, continued economic crisis, the collapse of the neopatrimonial postcolonial state, and, in response, a surge in pressure for reform shifted political calculations. These international and domestic transformations altered the topography of power and institutional arrangements across the continent and hence the context in which elites made decisions relating to peace and conflict. In some cases, African leaders responded with difficult and still fragile efforts to reform their economies and political systems while in others the pressures led to violence or state collapse. Many states fell somewhere in between these two extremes, with the future still in the balance.

The Cold War never explained the sources of conflict on the continent, but the willingness of the two superpowers to provide assistance to states regarded as important to their global strategies allowed a number of African patrimonial leaders to hold on to power and insurgents to believe they could win the struggle on the battlefield. International financial institutions similarly bolstered the prospects of many neopatrimonial regimes on the continent. In some cases, once Cold War patronage stopped, client regimes soon fell. It is notable, for example, that among the six top recipients of U.S. aid during the Cold War, five (Ethiopia, Liberia, Somalia, Sudan, and Zaire) suffered from severe conflict during the 1990s, while the sixth (Kenya) has seen violent ethnic clashes.[18] The loss of patronage and diplomatic support from the Soviet Union altered the prospects for governments in Ethiopia, Angola, and Mozambique and the strategies of liberation forces in Namibia and South Africa. At the same time the International Monetary Fund and the World Bank imposed structural adjustment policies on African states weakened by debt, economic decay, and corruption.

These combined pressures led to the collapse of a number of states in Africa. State collapse is not a wholly new occurrence either, as demonstrated by Uganda and Chad in an earlier era. In the 1990s, however, as a result of the changing global geopolitical landscape, states collapsed in Mozambique, Somalia, Liberia, Sierra Leone, Burundi, and the DRC, and a number of other states lost control over large parts of their territory, as in Sudan and Angola.

As the state collapses, and political space and economic space retract, the center no longer has authority and power withers away.[19] As the old institutions give way, political entrepreneurs create alternative institutions based on violence, fear, and predation to accumulate power and resources. Institutions of war, such as militia organizations, black market networks, and chauvinistic identity groups, develop and even thrive in this context.[20]

Patterns of Response

As Africa entered the 1990s, many regimes found themselves in a crisis of state legitimacy, to which African leaders responded in five ways. In the first category were countries such as Liberia and Somalia, where dictators refused to give up political power in the face of armed challenges. When no quick victory was forthcoming, the armed factions splintered into smaller camps. The result was state collapse and the proliferation of armed warlords who controlled small pieces of territory and who sustained themselves through plunder.

In the second category were countries such as Cameroon, Kenya, Nigeria, Togo, and Zaire, where despots initially conceded to demands for democratic participation but then manipulated the process to retain power through corruption, coercion, ethnic mobilization, and other divisive tactics. Others in this category include states that saw a reversal to military rule following elections, as in Niger, Burundi, the Gambia, Congo-Brazzaville, and Côte d'Ivoire. Given diminishing resources to buy internal support, leaders in these countries focused their patronage on smaller segments of society and politicized ethnicity as a means of maintaining their hold on power.

A third category saw an insurgent force defeat an incumbent regime and begin to rebuild the state following a period of protracted conflict. In Uganda in the 1980s and then Ethiopia, Eritrea, and Rwanda in the 1990s, insurgent forces with both a highly developed capacity to fight and an ability to administer liberated territory during the armed struggle emerged victorious and initiated the process of rebuilding the institutions of governance.[21] Each of these regimes came to power through military force; each also initiated a process of democratization to legitimize its rule. In the states in this category, military rulers carefully controlled the political opening and managed elections to ensure they would remain in power.[22]

In the fourth category, several states engaged in a process of using a negotiated peace agreement to both end an internal war and initiate a period of democratization. In Namibia, South Africa, and Mozambique, the process of implementing agreements provided a mechanism for war termination and democratization. In Liberia, however, postconflict elections resulted in Charles Taylor, the factional leader who had initiated and pursued the brutal conflict, winning the presidency with worrisome implications for long-term peace and democracy. In Angola, an even more vicious round of fighting erupted when UNITA sought to win on the battlefield what it had lost at the ballot box. An agreement to end a civil war and begin democratization failed in Sierra Leone as well.

In the fifth and final category were countries such as Benin, Malawi, Mali, Zambia (in 1992 but not 1996), Senegal, and Ghana, where incumbent leaders ceded power to democratically elected forces. In these countries, civil society, emboldened by democratic successes in Eastern Europe and elsewhere in Africa, asserted itself. This led to multiparty elections and political freedoms. In these cases, former dictators did not have private sources of wealth that could be used to manipulate elections. Instead, they faced united opposition, which rendered the politics of ethnic hatred ineffective.

Only states in the latter category, along with the successful postconflict cases in the fourth category, have weathered the crisis. They remain, however, precariously balanced, attempting to establish multiparty political processes and implement tough economic reforms at the same time. Where dictators manipulated democratic processes to retain power, the potential for violence remains high. War finally engulfed Zaire in 1996 and led to its collapse. Cameroon, Kenya, and Nigeria all experienced intermittent ethnic fighting in the 1990s. The death of strongman Sani Abacha in Nigeria created an opening for a return to democratic politics, but violence continues in the north and in the Niger Delta.

The Challenge of Peace Implementation

Conflict resolution in Africa in the 1990s had a mixed record. Several long-standing wars—in Ethiopia-Eritrea, Namibia, South Africa, Mozambique, and (much more tentatively) Liberia—were brought to an end. Peaceful transitions through the ballot box in Zambia, Malawi, Benin, Mali, and elsewhere provided hopeful models of political change. On the deficit side, peace agreements in Angola, Rwanda, and Sierra Leone failed in implementation, with horrific results. Elections in Kenya and Burundi were marked by violence, and military coups continued to depose elected leaders in places like the Gambia and Niger. The United Nations intervened in Somalia but withdrew following attacks on U.S. and UN peacekeepers, leaving Somalia in much the same condition as when the intervention began. Regional intervention in Liberia prolonged the war there, and regional mediation in Sierra Leone led to one failed agreement. The 1990s also saw civil conflicts erupt in Burundi and Guinea-Bissau, and war continued to rage in Sudan and sputter in Senegal. The war in Ethiopia seemed to end in 1991 with the defeat of Mengistu Haile Mariam and the accession to power of the Eritrean People's Liberation Front in Asmara and the Ethiopian People's Revolutionary Democratic Front in Addis Ababa. A border conflict marked by intense trench warfare, however, broke out in May 1998.

Three themes that have received considerable attention relating to conflict resolution in Africa will be considered below. The first is the question of international support for peace implementation. The second is the role of regional organizations and the potential for "African solutions to African problems" as a means to resolve conflicts. The final theme is the set of complex relationships between conflict resolution and democratization.

Peace Implementation

Recent research on the implementation of peace agreements yields sobering results for Africa. A project between the Center for International Security and Cooperation (CISAC) at Stanford and the International Peace Academy (IPA) argues that countries emerging from civil war differ in the degrees of difficulty for implementing peace.[23] The seven factors most associated with implementation difficulty are the presence of (1) more than two warring parties, (2) easily marketable valuable commodities such as gems or timber, (3) likely spoilers—leaders or factions who threaten to use violence to undermine the agreement, (4) a coerced peace agreement, (5) neighboring states that oppose peace, (6) a collapsed state, and (7) more than 50,000 soldiers to be demobilized. Of these factors, the most important in determining implementation failure are spoilers, hostile neighbors, and lootable goods (spoils).

These factors do not doom implementation to failure; they can be overcome by financial and monetary resources. The problem for Africa, however, is that the most important factor in determining levels of money and commitment of troops by international actors is whether a major or regional power perceives that it has a security interest in the case. When cases are deemed to be humanitarian, as opposed to security interests, the rhetorical commitment of the major powers is high, but the commitment of money and military force is lacking.

This essentially means a divided world when it comes to implementing peace agreements. From 1995 to 2000, Bosnia received over U.S.$17 billion in military and economic resources to aid implementation of the Dayton Accords. Cambodia received nearly U.S.$2 billion from 1991 to 1993. Angola, on the other hand, received U.S.$175 million from 1991 to 1993; Rwanda received approximately U.S.$35 million between October 1993 and April 1994 to implement the Arusha Accords. A final example suffices to make the point: the North Atlantic Treaty Organization had 40,000 troops in Kosovo in 1999 in an attempt to enforce a tenuous peace there. By comparison, the major powers have committed a little over 5,000 troops to date to a proposed peace operation in the DRC, which would rank as the most difficult in the world; it is over 230 times the size of the Kosovo peace operation.

The lack of political will by major powers in African conflicts was demonstrated by the withdrawal from Somalia after suffering casualties; the willingness to remain on the sidelines when the Economic Community of West African States Cease-Fire Monitoring Group (ECOMOG), led by Nigeria, intervened in Liberia and later Sierra Leone; the abandonment of Rwandans to their fate during the 1994 genocide; and the unwillingness to prevent *genocidaires* from using camps in eastern Zaire to attack Rwanda. The U.S. government made its policy plain in Presidential Decision Directive 25, which noted, "It is not U.S. policy to seek to expand either the number of U.N. peace operations or U.S. involvement in such operations."[24]

Peace implementation is a complex set of tasks because it incorporates a wide variety of subgoals that generally do not move forward at the same speed. Many advocacy groups point to specific goals and measure the success or failure of implementation against only one or two of the multiple goals. For example, some criticize peace implementation for failing to hold accountable those who perpetrated human rights abuses during the conflict, while others emphasize refugee repatriation, elections, economic reconstruction, disarmament, or demobilization. The multitude of goals, combined with the lack of resources, often undermines the transitional process, especially in Africa. A demand for some combatants to be tried as war criminals, for example, makes sense—indeed is only feasible—if implementers are willing to employ a robust coercive strategy.

The CISAC-IPA project concluded that priority should be focused on demilitarizing politics: the demobilization of soldiers and their reintegration into civilian life and the transformation of armies and militias into political parties.[25] For demobilization to succeed, international implementers need to develop robust monitoring and verification of demobilization and support effective interim governments that can build confidence that groups can be secure while they make the difficult transition from war to peace. Other subgoals, such as disarmament, democratization, human rights, and refugee repatriation, are premised on successful demobilization and should not be pursued to the detriment of war termination and the demilitarization of politics. In addition, programs to build civilian security through police force reform and laying the foundation for the long-term development of civil society organizations should receive higher priority for successful peacebuilding.[26]

Regional Organizations

In the 1990s policymakers explored the potential of African regional organizations to fill the gap as instruments of conflict resolution and peacemaking. The OAU, which had played an important role in promulgating and legitimizing norms against interstate conflict and interference in internal affairs, created a mechanism for preventing, managing, and resolving conflicts in Africa in 1993. This mechanism, however, remained minimally funded, and the OAU never had a sufficient consensus to operate robustly in the face of internal conflicts. The African Leadership Forum, under the leadership of Olusegun Obasanjo, held a series of discussions that produced the Kampala Document and called for a conference on security, stability, development, and cooperation in Africa (often described as a "Helsinki process" for the continent), but African leaders who feared the scrutiny sidelined the proposal in the early 1990s.[27]

More significant have been the actions of subregional organizations. The Economic Community of West African States organized a military observer group (ECOMOG) to intervene in the Liberian civil war in 1990. Nigeria dominated ECOMOG and the operation quickly found itself engaged in a protracted war against Charles Taylor's National Liberation Front. The West African force succeeded in denying Taylor military victory but had greater difficulty in imposing a long-term political solution and served to lengthen and expand the conflict. The intervention transformed a war that probably would have ended in a quick victory for Taylor into a protracted struggle; increased casualties; caused a splintering of political movements, making conflict management more difficult; and expanded the conflict into neighboring Sierra Leone. In 1997, Nigeria and Taylor reached an accommodation, and a set of quick elections distorted by the fear of seven years of war resulted in Taylor assuming the Liberian presidency.[28]

Regional organizations struggled to promote peace elsewhere on the continent. The Inter-Governmental Authority on Development (IGAD) took up the challenge of mediating an end to the brutal Sudanese civil war and developed an important declaration of principles.[29] Divisions within the organization, however, and lack of leverage over the principal parties, led the talks into stalemate as the war continued. In southern Africa, the Southern African Development Community (SADC) discussed the establishment of an organ on politics, defense, and security with a mandate to manage conflicts and played a role in intervening in Lesotho following a coup. The SADC, however, faced its own rivalries between South Africa and Zimbabwe and proved powerless when confronted with major conflicts in Angola and Congo and the threat of instability in Zimbabwe. In general, weak states create weak regional organizations without the capacity to manage deeply rooted conflicts.

The United States under the Clinton administration supported several African-led peace initiatives, including the ECOMOG-managed Abuja process in Liberia and Lomé in negotiations for Sierra Leone, the Nyerere- and later Mandela-led Arusha process for Burundi, the IGAD initiative for Sudan, and the Africa-led Lusaka process for the Congo. These "African solutions for African problems" have been weak, highly flawed, and prone to breakdown. None has generated a durable, coherent accord. In order to support African peacekeeping, Washington pursued the African Crisis Response Initiative, which provided military training to potential African peacekeeping forces. The initiative, however, like similar programs sponsored by France and Great Britain, lacked a coherent framework for initiating and legitimatizing an intervention and emphasized traditional peacekeeping when much more vigorous peace enforcement was needed to staunch African conflicts. A U.S. State Department official noted the disjuncture and stated that "90 percent of the scenarios in Africa are those like Brazzaville (Congo) or Freetown (Sierra Leone), where an intervention force would have to impose peace."[30]

Conflict and Democracy

Democracy and elections have played multiple roles with relation to conflict and conflict management in Africa. Elections have served as a means to legitimate new political authority in the absence of a comprehensive peace agreement, as in Sierra Leone (1996). In other cases, elections consolidated the military victory of one party, as in Ethiopia (1992, 1995, 2000), Uganda (1989, 1996), and Rwanda (local elections in 1999). In Algeria

(1991) and Burundi (1993), elections sparked or reignited conflict as the military intervened to prevent the elected government from taking office. Electoral campaigns often have served as the context for heightened communal violence and political assassinations, as in Kenya (1993) and Zimbabwe (2000).

In nearly all recent cases following civil war in Africa and in other war-torn states, reconstruction of political order has involved elections. Such elections have become the principal means to legitimate the new leadership and institutional structures that emerge from a peace process. Western policymakers as well as parties to the conflict often regard elections as "the only alternative on the table."[31] Elections are one of the very few mechanisms available to provide internal and external legitimacy to a new government.

Following civil war, elections serve as important opportunities for institution (re)building as well as competition for political power. The legacy of institutions that developed during the war and an expanded and often unaccountable state security apparatus will structure the transition process. Recent studies of the political economy of humanitarian emergencies have pointed out how alternative structures based on the use of violence to accumulate assets and sustain political power arise, and demonstrate how institutions and leaders based in war economics and politics, rather than anarchy and chaos, characterize internal conflict.[32] The nature of the interim regime that manages peace implementation is critical because it will create the institutional setting that bridges the structures of wartime and the structures needed to support peace, state building, and democracy.

An examination of recent cases indicates that postconflict elections sometimes have provided a mechanism for selecting new political leadership and institutions capable of preserving the peace and serving as the first step in a process of democratization, thereby promoting peacebuilding and state reconstruction over time. This was the result in Mozambique (and outside of Africa, in El Salvador and arguably Cambodia). In other cases, elections precipitated renewed and even more violent conflict, as in Angola, thereby furthering the collapse of the state. In a third set of cases, including Liberia (and Bosnia-Herzegovina and Tajikistan), elections served more as a mechanism of war termination with only a limited (and perhaps negative) relationship to democratization.

The record is mixed in part because postconflict elections relate to multiple, often contradictory goals. They often are designated in the peace agreement as a primary instrument of implementation and therefore play critical roles in relation to war termination. At the same time, they are designed to promote a process of democratization and to serve as "breakthrough" elections that initiate a new set of rules and institutions for competitive, multiparty politics. However, in cases where victorious military parties organize elections, they serve to consolidate the power of the winning party with less reference to either war termination (which has been settled by victory on the battlefield) or democracy.

In addition to these goals relating to political reconstruction of the state, postconflict elections are important for a separate set of reasons to the broader international community. International peacekeeping missions need clear "exit strategies" in order to win the support of important states. A good example is when the West African peacekeeping force in Liberia demanded quick elections as part of its withdrawal strategy. In addition to peacekeeping, international support for economic reconstruction often requires elections. International financial institutions such as the World Bank and International Monetary Fund, and important bilateral donors, need a recognized government in order to begin disbursing money for critical development programs. Success with relation to one goal, such as war termination, does not necessarily mark success with relation to another, such as democratization. Similarly, success with relation to international peacekeeping strategy may not coincide with success in relation to local political dynamics.[33]

Voters in postconflict elections often choose to use the limited power of their franchise either to appease the most powerful faction in the hope that this will prevent a return to war or to select the most nationalistic and chauvinistic candidate who pledges to protect the voter's community. Outside observers often regard these leaders as warlords or war criminals, but to vulnerable voters they are seen as powerful protectors capable of defending them from rival military forces. In other cases, giving former military leaders political office may be perceived as the best chance for achieving peace through appeasement. Civilian candidates and those who do not have a convincing answer to the issue of postelection security are unlikely to prevail.

In Liberia, for example, memories of the brutal conflict and the consequent fear clearly shaped how many voters viewed the July 1997 election and the choices available to them.[34] As one observer put it, the voters "were intimidated not by thugs at the polling stations but by the trauma of the last seven years of war."[35] Many Liberians believed that if the powerful factional leader Charles Taylor lost the election, then the country would return to war. Taylor's rivals pointed to his violent past during the campaign but could not propose credible actions to contain him if he refused to accept the results. Many Liberians made a calculated choice that they hoped would more likely promote peace and stability and used their franchise to appease the powerful former militia leader. During the campaign young Taylor supporters frightened voters by chanting, "He killed my Pa, He killed my Ma, I'll vote for him."[36] In the end the elections ratified and institutionalized the political topography and imbalance of power created by seven years of war. An organization and leader that amassed great power during the conflict through violence and intimidation converted that influence into positions of authority under the constitution through elections. This result, understandable in the fearful context of Liberia in 1997, did little to advance democratization and and continues to raise considerable concerns regarding long-term stability and peacebuilding in the country.

Similar patterns of voters in postconflict elections supporting the party that offered security in a context distorted by fear are evident in other cases. In Uganda, the ruling National Resistance Movement of Yoweri Museveni charged that its opponent in the 1996 national election was a proxy for the forces of former president Milton Obote, who had ruled over a period of devastating violence. In Ethiopia, fear and memories of the authoritarian rule of the old regime of Mengistu Haile Mariam led many voters to acquiesce to the power of the ruling Ethiopian People's Revolutionary Democratic Front. As one Oromo farmer explained his vote for the ruling party, "I was afraid. The Government said I should vote so I voted. What could I do?"[37]

In Angola, many observers expected Jonas Savimbi's UNITA party to do well in the elections. UNITA had successfully used force to compel the ruling party, the Movement for the Liberation of Angola (MPLA), to hold elections, had a strong ethnic base among the Ovimbundu people, and was led by the charismatic (if demagogic) Jonas Savimbi. The period of the MPLA's rule under José Eduardo dos Santos had seen unrelenting conflict, economic hardship, and corruption. During the campaign, however, Savimbi used threatening language that heightened fears and persuaded many that continuing to live with the MPLA was better than the uncertain and potentially violent future promised by UNITA. The election results were quite close, with the MPLA winning a thin majority in the parliament and dos Santos holding just below 50 percent in the presidential race. In a context in which both parties had fought to a stalemate prior to the peace agreement, Angolan voters split in their perceptions of which party could best deliver peace and security to their communities.[38] In the end, the elections did not bring peace but sparked an escalation of the war as Savimbi rejected the outcome and returned to the battlefield.

For a transition to put in place new political leadership and institutions capable of preserving the peace and serving as the first step in a process of democratization, politics must be "demilitarized." To demilitarize politics entails building norms and institutions that bridge the structures of wartime, based on violence, insecurity, and fear (such as militias, black markets, and chauvinistic identity groups), and structures based on security and trust that can sustain peace and democracy (such as political parties and civil society). The powerful actors that developed and that were sustained during a protracted civil war following state collapse cannot be wished away. Neither can the enabling environment for peaceful political competition be proclaimed into existence. To the extent that politics is demilitarized during the transitional period, postconflict elections are more likely to result in a new political order that can sustain peace and democracy.

In Mozambique, successful processes to demilitarize politics reduced the legacy of fear and put in place institutions that could better sustain peace and democracy. Relatively strong interim regimes, consultative processes to manage the challenges of implementation and electoral administration, and successful programs to transform militias into political parties established a new institutional context that served to bridge the conditions of war and those of peace and democratization. Joint decisionmaking bodies such as the Supervisory and Monitoring Commission (CSC) and the Cease-Fire Commission (CCF) brought together the major political actors with the major donors in a consultative process chaired by a resourceful Special Representative of the UN Secretary-General, Aldo Ajello. Other specialized joint commissions dealt with reintegration of former combatants, reform of the Mozambican defense forces, and preparations for the election. These interim institutions created the context for overcoming some of the legacies of the civil war and thereby promoted the demilitarizing politics.[39]

Mozambique demonstrates that the manner by which disputes relating to electoral administration are managed during peace implementation can provide the context for building new institutions and norms that promote the demilitarization of politics. The Rome peace accords left many issues relating to the elections vague and subject to decisions made by the parties through the CSC. A series of controversies between Renamo and the Front for the Liberation of Mozambique (Frelimo) over the composition of the National Elections Commission (CNE) threatened to derail the peace process and forced the postponement of the election. Both parties used the issue of the CNE to test each other's commitment and intentions and to see if the interim institutions could protect their most important interests.

After a series of discussions and with the active involvement of the UN Special Representative, the parties reached an agreement on the composition of the CNE. Frelimo received ten seats, Renamo seven, and other political parties three. The partisan balance made efficient decisionmaking difficult but increased the confidence of each party in the process. Over time and under the leadership of its independent chair Brazão Mazula (who contributes Chapter 8 of this book), the CNE developed a reputation for nonpartisan decisionmaking. Unlike the Cease-Fire Commission and other commissions that included international actors along with representatives of the parties, the CNE was an independent and wholly Mozambican organization. The presence of UN technical advisers working within the Technical Secretariat, however, provided the parties with additional confidence in the process.

An additional component of the successful demilitarization of politics in Mozambique was the transformation of Renamo from an insurgent organization into a viable political party.[40] Renamo insisted that there could be "no democracy without money" and UN Special Representative Aldo Ajello agreed: "Democracy has a cost and we must pay that cost."[41] After initial concerns from donors reluctant to fund a party with a particularly brutal reputation, a U.S.$19 million fund was established to help Renamo transform itself into a political party. In addition to financial inducements, the international community worked to "socialize Renamo into the rules of democratic competition, and to make its legitimacy contingent on fulfilling its commitment to peace."[42]

The results in these recent cases suggest that postconflict elections may best be characterized as referendums on peace in contexts where the legacies of fear dominate voters' concerns, unless politics has been demilitarized. For elections to be fully meaningful, however, they must give voters a significant choice. In many of these cases, voters understood their choice to be either war or peace in the hands of a nationalistic, military leader, an unenviable range of options. However, if the transitional period of peace implementation prior to the elections can succeed to demilitarize politics and build confidence that a return to war is minimal, as in Mozambique, then a greater range of choice and elections that can better promote democracy are possible.

Notes

1. Bercovitch and Jackson, *International Conflict.*
2. Sommer, *Hope Restored?*
3. Human Rights Watch, *Burundi.*
4. Anstee, *Orphan of the Cold War.*
5. Alao, *The Burden of Collective Goodwill.*
6. Burundi and Rwanda had been German colonies until World War I and Congo had been the personal property of the Belgian king during a particularly tragic period of history. Portuguese colonials of São Tomé and Principe and Cape Verde are not included in this data set.
7. Lyons, "The Horn of Africa Regional Politics."
8. May and Hughes, "Armies on Loan."
9. "Big Men, Big Countries, Big Hopes."
10. Jackson, *Quasi-States.*
11. Ohlson and Stedman, *The New Is Not Yet Born.*
12. Herbst, "Responding to State Failure."
13. Diamond, "Class Formation."
14. Ibid., p. 574.
15. Rothchild, "Ethnic Bargaining."
16. Callaghy, *The State-Society Struggle;* Joseph, *Democracy and Prebendal Politics;* Diamond, "Class Formation"; Bayart, *The State in Africa.*

17. Clapham, "Discerning the New Africa," p. 263.

18. Clough, *Free at Last,* p. 77.

19. Zartman, "Posing the Problem of State Collapse."

20. Berdal and Malone, *Greed and Grievance.*

21. Clapham, *African Guerrillas,* provides case studies of these movements.

22. On the Ethiopian case, see Lyons, "Closing the Transition."

23. Stedman, Rothchild, and Cousens, *Ending Civil Wars.*

24. U.S. Department of State Publication no. 10161. Released by the Bureau of International Organization Affairs, May 1994.

25. Spear, "Demobilization and Disarmament"; Lyons, "Implementing Peace and Building Democracy."

26. Call and Stanley, "A Sacrifice for Peace?"; Prendergast and Plumb, "Civil Society Organizations."

27. See Obasanjo, "A Balance Sheet."

28. Stedman, "Conflict and Conciliation," p. 149; Howe, *International Security;* Lyons, *Voting for Peace.*

29. Deng, "Mediating the Sudanese Conflict."

30. Rupert, "U.S. Troops Teach Peacekeeping to Africans," p. A16.

31. Sisk, "Elections and Conflict Management in Africa," p. 146. See also Clapham, "Rwanda," p. 195.

32. Berdal and Malone, *Greed and Grievance.*

33. Lyons, "Implementing Peace and Building Democracy."

34. Lyons, *Voting for Peace.*

35. Tanner, "Liberia," p. 140.

36. Ellis, *The Mask of Anarchy,* p. 109.

37. Quoted in Buckley, "Ethiopia Takes New Ethnic Tack," p. A21.

38. Ottaway, "Angola's Failed Elections"; Anstee, *Orphan of the Cold War.*

39. Turner, Nelson, and Mahling-Clark, "Mozambique's Vote for Democratic Governance"; Synge, *Mozambique,* p. 52.

40. Manning, "Constructing Opposition in Mozambique."

41. Vines, *Renamo,* p. 146; "Mozambique: Funding for Peace," p. 4.

42. Stedman, "Spoiler Problems in Peace Processes," p. 41.

Botswana:
The Path to Democracy
and Development

Patrick Molutsi

Conceptually and practically, the link between democracy as a political system and economic development is complex and unclear. Many scholars have attempted to define the link between a political system and its capacity to create the environment for economic development.[1] But the ability of autocratic, totalitarian, and other less participatory regimes—such as the former Soviet Union, China, and more recently, several regimes in Southeast Asia—to economically outperform some of the major democracies such as India and others in Africa and Latin America has complicated any attempt to make ipso facto claims on behalf of the democratic system as a superior agency in the creation of a developmental environment.

The complexity and long debate notwithstanding, evidence from the last two decades of the twentieth century demonstrated a number of weaknesses in the capacity of nondemocratic regimes for development. First, the nondemocratic regimes tended to lack the capacity to sustain economic growth. The former Soviet Union and most of the East European socialist regimes, as well as one-party states in Africa, showed this weakness in the late 1980s. Second, nondemocratic regimes have failed to create an economic base relatively autonomous from the state. This has resulted in high levels of dependency on the state by all economic actors. Third, in contrast to their basic ideological premise, these regimes have generally failed to achieve the goal of equitable distribution of income, and this has been a major factor in their undoing.

Democratic regimes, on the other hand, have in general succeeded in creating conditions for relatively autonomous economic base. This has also reduced dependence of the population on state-provided services. Instead, private initiatives have provided alternative services for those who could afford them.[2] Democratic regimes have perhaps performed just as poorly on matters of both sustainable economic growth and income distribution. However, they have shown better resilience in recovering from economic crises than less politically open regimes. Thus superiority of democratic regimes comes from their adaptive capacity to deal with economic crisis and therefore their ability to deal with the critical issue of system maintenance at the political and economic levels.

This chapter focuses on the link between democracy and development in Botswana, which in the past three decades has become one of the few of Africa's showcases. At independence in 1966, Botswana was a rural society with up to 90 percent of the population living in conditions of abject poverty. Economically the country was backward, and political viability was questionable. Formerly Bechuanaland Protectorate, Botswana had suffered benign neglect under British colonial government, the "protecting power" for over seventy years. Yet in a short space of three decades, the country has achieved one of the highest rates of economic growth in developing countries. The per capita income is among the highest in sub-Saharan Africa. More important, Botswana has developed an elaborate social welfare program hardly known in the developing countries. As a result, in the mid-1980s Botswana graduated from the World Bank/International Monetary Fund's classification as a low-income country to a middle-income classification.

How has Botswana managed all this impressive development, and what does this experience mean for other developing countries? What role if any did the political system play in this case? These are the key questions addressed in this chapter. I seek to provide a critical analysis and interpretation of the factors underlying Botswana's democracy and development experience. Many scholars and journalists, among others, have written about some of these factors in the past. With the passage of time, however, new evidence has made it necessary to critically review some of the past analyses. For my analysis, I address five interrelated factors: history, ethnocultural context, politics, leadership, and the economic system. I also discuss the link between democracy and development by comparing Botswana to four other countries: Lesotho, Mauritius, Namibia, and Swaziland. These are small countries that share history and other common characteristics with Botswana, and yet some are performing worse than Botswana while others are performing much better. In conclusion, I present lessons learned, with a particular focus on the question of leadership.

History and Culture: The Contextual Factors

In the case of Botswana, the factors of history and ethnocultural context deserve a careful review in order to understand the country's relative political and economic success in the past three and a half decades. These factors interact in a complex way to explain both the success of democratic politics and the high levels of development in this southern African state. This section examines the contribution of each to the evolution of modern Botswana.

The Historical Context

Each country and society has its own history, which though not static remains both specific and determinant to the core values and ideals of its social formation. In this sense, Botswana is not an exception. Rather, the exception comes from its specific organization and experience. As a political entity, Botswana did not exist until three chiefs of some of the influential linguistic communities on advisement from locally based British missionaries traveled in 1885 to London to request British protection against the encroachment of both the Germans from the west and the Afrikaner "filibusters" from the south and east.[3] The British government took its time and it was only in 1891 that a small army under Charles Warren was sent to declare the country a British protectorate. Before then, several Tswana linguistic communities lived autonomously under their various chiefs. Hence the declaration of protectorate over the whole territory was seen as a threat to autonomy by those chiefs who were not party to the "mission to London."

The lack of a central authority in what became Bechuanaland Protectorate after 1891 had three important effects on the political history of the country. First, it meant that the protection was a negotiated political settlement between the individual chiefs and the British government. That settlement was indeed consummated in the territorial parceling of the country into eight "native/tribal reserves," white settler "blocks," and crown land between 1899 and 1933. By the end of this process, 48 percent of the country was portioned "tribal land," 5 percent freehold land, and 47 percent crown land. Effectively this process left the eight main chiefs in complete control of both the land in their "reserves" and their subjects. Within each reserve there was a large community of people who traced their descent and identity to their ruling families, but there was also a large community of people who had over time migrated as refugees from wars and other situations of insecurity into these tribal kingdoms. Others were indigenous minorities of Khoisan origins. Second, the declaration of a protectorate meant that a new political entity separate from South Africa was established for the first time. This entity had the effect of linking all the tribal/community leaders, thereby creating a central authority unknown before. And third, the nature of voluntary protection gave British rulers justification to neglect the country's development and yet continue to enjoy friendly relations with its rulers.

Over time, three direct political outcomes resulted. The first was that tribal-based territorial identities entrenched the separation of groups and

races. As will be shown below, even the postcolonial state has not been successful in dismantling the traditional tribal reserves. Instead they were
joined together. The small Barolong farms, too, were brought under the
Bangweketse reserve in a new southern district. Yet in each territory/reserve
the chief ruled as autocrat. Women, minority groups, and even enlightened
tribesmen were subjected to different forms of discrimination and systematic
exclusion. The "Kgotla democracy" was made up of male tribal elders from
senior tribesmen. However, this political foundation of tribal identity by
which the independence constitution was designed remains highly contested.
Despite several incidents of human rights abuse by chiefs and their tribesmen throughout the protectorate period, the essential elements of "reserve
identity" and their implied control by the chief remained and continue to
remain the cornerstone of Botswana's politics today.[4]

The second political outcome of the protectorate declaration was the
creation of a peaceful though unequal coexistence between races. Particularly, the Africans and Europeans in Bechuanaland lived separate lives
defined by territorial belonging. Political accommodation was limited and
at independence the settler community felt an insecurity comparable to that
of their counterparts in Kenya, Zimbabwe, and many other newly independent states of the 1960s. It therefore took skill and leadership to create a
sense of belonging to the new state. Adherence to the rule of law and the
constitutional guarantees to property rights were important factors in ensuring equal citizenship for the settler community in the new country.

The third outcome was that Bechuanaland became a satellite political
entity with no development of its own but with a strong link to South Africa
through communication infrastructure, markets, and labor migration. This
created both opportunities and constraints for the postindependence political economy of Botswana.

Ethnocultural Context

Botswana is not a nation-state, but in its ethnic structure it bears close
resemblance to one. It is estimated that 80–90 percent of the population
speaks the same language. There are small dialectic differences between the
groups. The common culture traditionally revolved around livestock-
rearing (cattle) and limited arable agricultural production. The traditional
mode of governance, with the chief at the center organizing ethnic/tribal
affairs around the Kgotla system of governance, is the same throughout the
country. Traditional primary institutions relating to education, health, religion, and family/marriage vary only marginally. The combination of a
common language and culture, the strong historical grip of the chiefs over
their subjects, and limited economic opportunities has meant that a fairly
conservative traditional rural society remains. Of course, relative ethnic and

cultural homogeneity is not peculiar to Botswana. As will be shown in the country comparison, several societies in southern Africa with comparable levels of development and organizational and ethnic structures have not always been able to keep political stability comparable to Botswana. Take the kingdom of Lesotho, for instance, which has a central monarchy, strong chieftaincy tradition, and homogeneous ethnic structure, but which stands out as one of the most internally divided and unstable states in southern Africa since 1970. There must therefore be several other factors of importance to consider in this analysis. As is evident, relative ethnic homogeneity is an asset but not a guarantee for political stability.

A number of negative trends not too conducive to democracy and political stability are also prevalent in this environment of ethnocultural dominance. Within the framework of relative cultural homogeneity and territorial identities, minority groups are suffering the most. They cannot have chiefs of their own other than subordinates who derive their power and authority from paramount chiefs of the "reserves" (now districts). Their languages, some of which are very different from the dominant Tswana language, can only be used up to the third grade in schools and at home, and their cultural practices are similarly discouraged at an early age. All government business operates in Setswana and English. This process of social and cultural marginalization of minorities remains one of the most contested aspects of Botswana's democracy today. Although political marginalization of minority groups has not been as overt as in other spheres, the main minorities in the northeastern and northwestern parts of the country have tended to seek political refuge in voting for opposition parties. There has also been a land issue among the minority San in the Kalahari, and less so with the majority groups in the districts.

The above scenario underlines the limitations of a blanket application of simple plurality/majority principles of democracy. It also shows that democracy can easily undermine the same values and principles that it seeks to promote when it ignores the cultural rights of minorities. As is evident, the rights of people to their culture, language, land, and other resources, even when these people are minorities, cannot be justifiably compromised for the sake of national unity and nation building. Fortunately, this dent in Botswana's democracy is now being widely recognized and corrected.[5]

The Evolution of the Democratic State: "Getting the Politics Right"

The democratic character of the Botswana state is best discussed in terms of its evolution. There are three periods, each representing both a change in the head of state but also, and more important, qualitative changes in policy direction. The first period, dating roughly from 1965 to 1980, shall be called the Khama period, after the first president of Botswana, the late Sir Seretse Khama. The second period, named after Sir Ketumile Masire, spans from 1980 to 1998. And the third and current period—the Festus Mogae period—began in March 1997. As is evident, there were overlaps between the periods. Furthermore, aspects of one period may be the outcomes of earlier policy decisions. This is particularly so because the regime itself has remained the same from independence to the present, with each successor bound by both the footsteps of his predecessor and the broad ideology of a fairly stable party and leadership. This said, however, in broad terms these periods represent the times of insecurity, consolidation, and transformation in the character of the Botswana state respectively. Each of the periods is characterized by new forms of state-society relations, innovations in both the politics and the economy, as well as progress and regress in some development aspects.

The Khama Period (1965–1980): The Weak and Insecure State

At independence in 1966, Botswana's leaders inherited a poor, weak, and insecure state. Three sources of insecurity could be identified: poverty, internal opposition, and regional hostility. The country was poor because it had no identifiable resource base. The only possible source of economic sustenance was the livestock subsector, which at the time had been decimated by one of the harshest droughts in the country's history. Until fiscal year 1971/1972 the government relied on grant-in-aid from the British government to balance its meager budget. The labor force was small and dominated at the top by former colonial officers and white settlers whose loyalty to the new state was often in doubt.[6] The government's budget was largely focused on the social sector.[7] From the onset the emphasis was on building schools, health facilities, and water provisions as the basis for economic development. Where resources were devoted to the productive sector, they were slated to the less reliable livestock sector. It appeared on the whole that Botswana had embarked on a slow and painful path to development.[8]

The economic insecurity was worsened by several threats at the political level, which can be categorized into internal and external enemies of the young state. Internally, the traditional chiefs were threatening to destabilize the state, whose program of democratization posed a threat to their power base. As noted above, under the protectorate administration the chiefs had enjoyed relative autonomy. They were allowed to manage their territories and communities with limited interference as long as they were loyal to the protectorate administration. They collected taxes and imposed different types of levies on their people and were direct and indirect beneficiaries to whatever taxes their people paid. Thus during the protectorate period the chiefs became one of the wealthiest groups of Tswana society.[9] The attainment of independence under the leadership of the "new elite" constituted a threat to the hegemony and continued rule of the chiefs. Since the 1930s a new element (a product of Christian liberal education) had begun to emerge across various communities in the country. This element, constituting the new elite, was critical of the governance style of the chiefs from the start.[10] For close to two decades prior to independence, this new element manifested its distaste of the administration of the chiefs by forming modern associations of workers, teachers, civic groups, and ultimately political parties in the late 1950s.

Apart from the chiefs, the other main threat to the young state was the settler community. Scattered in far-apart places of Ghanzi in the extreme west, Francistown in the northeast, Tuli block in the east, and Gaborone, Lobatse, and Molopo blocks in the southeast and southwest, the settler community in Botswana, though small in size when compared to neighboring countries, had nevertheless kept its political identity and presence internationally known. During the early days of the establishment of the Union of South Africa (1910–1939), the European settlers in this country wanted Bechuanaland to become a territory of South Africa.[11] Although the tensions that developed between Britain and the Afrikaner-led government of South Africa, first under Hertzog (1921–1933) and later under Malan and Voerwood (1948–1961), made this possibility increasingly remote, the settlers were very openly opposed to Botswana's independence under "black" leadership.[12] The settler community thus constituted a political threat to the new state.

Externally, the Botswana state was surrounded by militarily and politically hostile white settler regimes in South Africa and Southern Rhodesia.[13] Interestingly, the South African regime regarded the "multiracial democratic experiment" in Botswana as a direct challenge to its proclaimed apartheid program. Henceforth all manner of pressures were put on the Botswana state to weaken it. The settlers' insistence on joining South Africa was thus in some ways perceived by the Botswana state as an act of incitement from the external enemy. The Rhodesian regime under Ian Smith also perceived Botswana as a hostile neighbor harboring nationalist fighters. Indeed, the period between 1965 and 1978 was characterized by intermittent localized military confrontations between the Rhodesian armed forces and Botswana's mobile police unit, the largest of which sometimes resulted in police fatalities.

As is evident, this was a state faced with a number of contradictions in character and program. On the one hand, it had to face the challenge of laying down the foundation for democratic governance necessary to distinguish itself from both the colonial regime and the traditional autocracy of the individual chiefs. On the other hand, it had to keep strong control over the society in order to establish its own legitimacy and ensure security against perceived and real external enemies. As a result, its democracy was both driven from above and accompanied by strong tendencies toward centralization.[14] However, the statecraft of Seretse Khama came from his ability to co-opt moderate chiefs and white settler leaders and mold them together with the less radical element of the new elite under the liberal-democratic ideology of the Botswana Democratic Party (BDP). His skills and authority, partially derived from his royal birth of the Bangwato chieftaincy, were reinforced by two other important factors. First, like Nelson Mandela, he was a classic victim and ultimate victor in the struggle against racism and racial segregation. His multiracial marriage to a British woman in the mid-1940s had caused a furor that reverberated among both his tribal leaders and the white regimes in Rhodesia, South Africa. Even the British government turned against him. Second, the Seretse government was clean of corruption. This gave it the credibility necessary to attract to foreign aid.

Nevertheless the centralizing tendencies of the state limited the powers of the local government, trade unions, and nongovernmental organizations. These institutions were encouraged and their development was facilitated, yet restrictive legislation was instituted and crafted in such a way to keep them out of politics and to ensure that they remained under the strong hand of the state.[15] Over time, this approach of the Botswana state led to development of a tradition of paternalistic governance that restricted the activities of the other social partners, particularly the labor movement. This tradition became so deeply entrenched that even after liberalization legislation in 1990, the trade unions in particular still find it difficult to muster the strength required to participate with other social partners as equals.

On the economic front, however, the Khama administration received a considerable material and moral boost in the early 1970s from two important but unrelated developments. The first was the discovery and exploitation of large diamond deposits in the small remote settlement of Orapa/Letlhakane in the Central district and another slightly later in Jwaneng settlement in the Southern district. The exploitation of diamonds immediately brought about a fiscal revolution in the coffers of the state. The second was the positive response by donor countries to the appeals of Botswana's leaders for development assistance. The Botswana government received one of the highest levels of per capita aid from the 1970s through to the mid-1980s among all foreign aid country recipients.[16] This period thus witnessed major policy initiatives in rural development, land reform, income, education, and manpower training and localization, as well as important programs such as accelerated rural development,[17] the self-help housing, and many others. By the time of Khama's death in 1980, the foundations of the

Botswana state as a dominant development agency in its own right had been established.

Politically, the earlier internal and external tensions had receded. There had been three successful general elections, all returning Khama's Botswana Democratic Party with overwhelming majorities (see Table 7.1). In contrast, the chiefs had been weakened. A substantial number succumbed to incorporation programs at the local government level and became salaried servants of the new state. Those who would not embrace the latter arrangement had opted to join politics on the opposition side.[18] And others were given specific assignments in government and outside the country as ambassadors.[19] The year 1980 was also the year of Zimbabwe's independence, and the victory of the Zimbabwe African National Union Patriotic Front brought to power a government friendly to Botswana. The next period can justifiably be characterized as the period of both political and economical consolidation.

The Masire Period (1980–1998): Political and Economic Consolidation

By 1980, Botswana could be counted as one of the fastest-growing economies in the world. According to the seventh national development plan (NDP) of 1991, the average annual rate of growth was 11 percent and in some years as high as 21 percent. Government revenues trebled with the opening of the Jwaneng diamond mine in about 1982, and the infrastructural and social development program was accelerated. Formal sector employment also grew rapidly, from about 25,000 employees in the early 1970s, to 176,000 in late 1980, to 234,000 in the 1990s, to 287,000 in 2002. The government became the largest employer of labor, enlisting over 40 percent of the work force. Through a concerted program of construction, schools, health facilities, roads, and dams were built, boosting both the

Table 7.1 Number of Seats by Political Party, 1965–1999

	1965	1969	1974	1979	1984	1989	1994	1999
Botswana Democratic Party (BDP)	28	24	27	29	28	31	31	37
Botswana National Front (BNF)	—	3	2	2	5	3	13	6
Botswana People's Party (BPP)	3	3	2	1	1	0	0	0
Others[a]	0	1	1	0	0	0	0	1
Total	31	31	32	32	34	34	44	44

Source: Various reports of the Elections Office, Gaborone.

Note: a. In 1969 and 1974 the one member of parliament belonged to the Botswana Independence Party. In 1999, the one member of parliament belonged to the Botswana Congress Party, a breakaway party from the BNF.

private and the local government sectors, which became increasingly dependent on the central government as their main client. It was during this period that the more economically and politically relaxed and confident Botswana state emerged—with new policies and programs supporting private sector initiatives, relaxed wages, income and price control policies, and substantially reduced personal and company taxes; a number of restrictive labor laws were removed as well.[20]

On the democratic front too the Masire administration made a number of reforms. Since the early 1980s the opposition parties had begun to raise critical questions on two substantive areas of elections. First, they wanted the elections to be administered not by the government but by an autonomous body. They claimed that there was some rigging in elections supervised by civil servants. Second, presuming that their support came mainly from the young voters, the opposition parties urged the government to change the voting age from twenty-one to eighteen. Two other areas of contention—voting by proxy, or as it was called in Botswana, "postal voting," and limiting the term of office of the president—were raised. Although initially opposed to them, the ruling BDP found itself eventually conceding to all four opposition party demands.

The reforms could be understood as resulting from a combination of factors. First, the ruling party performed relatively badly in the 1994 elections. It lost ten seats to the opposition and its popular vote dropped from 67 percent in 1989 to 55 percent in 1994. Meanwhile, the main opposition party, the Botswana National Front (BNF), gained ten new seats and its popular vote rose from 27 percent in 1989 to 37 percent in 1994. Civil society, particularly through women's and environmental lobby groups and human rights organizations, also made strong demands on the state for the reform of laws discriminating against women, the granting of land rights (to some minority groups), and the introduction of better environmental policies and programs. The pressure from the opposition parties and civil society was given impetus by concurrent developments taking place in the region, but especially in newly independent states of Namibia and majority-ruled South Africa. In these two countries far-reaching democratic programs relating to election law, the role of local government, labor laws, gender equality, and minority rights were being implemented. In response to this enormous pressure, the Masire administration undertook a program of rapid political reform between 1995 and 1998.

An independent electoral body was established following a referendum. The voting age was lowered from twenty-one to eighteen. Postal voting was introduced. The term of office of the president was limited to two periods of five years each. Extensive legal reform was undertaken in the areas of gender and labor. By the 1999 election not only had the BDP reformed the state, but it had also mended its relations with civil society, reformed its leadership, and reconciled, at least temporarily, its internal factions. Coupled by divisions in the main opposition party—the BNF—this environment could only ensure sound victory for the BDP. Indeed, in the 1999 elections the BDP won back five of the thirteen seats previously held by the BNF and increased its share of the popular vote from 55 percent to 57 percent.[21]

The Mogae Period (1997–current): The Era of Transformation

The current period, marked in Botswana's planning cycle as that of the eighth national development plan, covering 1997 to 2003, has new challenges. During the seventh NDP (1991–1997) the economic growth rate dropped from an average of 11 percent to 4.8 percent. Public sector employment growth was even slower, at 1.1 percent. Poverty in rural areas persisted as agriculture failed. Shortage of training opportunities for young people coupled with a reduction in migrant labor and a slump in the construction industry put a major political dent in the electoral performance of the BDP in the 1994 elections.

The retirement of President Masire, the ascendance to the helm of political leadership by his former vice president, Mogae, and subsequent major policy reforms in the areas of gender, labor, economy, and poverty alleviation, among others, marked a new period of reform and transformation. Since the 1990s, the government seems to have become more serious about "corporate governance." In 1997 it introduced an informal structure, chaired by the president, called a "high-level consultative structure." It consists of senior government officers, the private sector, and limited labor and civil society representation. A system of tripartism, though still weak and largely consultative, has been introduced. Civil society organizations in particular have found more accommodation with the government with the implementation of programs delegated to them.

A national vision strategy has been produced. Two new programs, one on privatization and the other on poverty reduction, have been introduced. They are meant to reduce state involvement in the economy and at the same time to provide targeted assistance to the poor. Two new institutions—an anticorruption body (1996) and an ombudsman office (1997)—have also been introduced. A major review of the education system was undertaken as well, resulting in the introduction of a more comprehensive program targeted to the needs of a modern economy.

The Mogae period is still unfolding. However, new challenges are evident. A major issue in the democracy agenda involves a demand that the constitution's clause on "eight major tribes" be eliminated. This would ensure major restructuring of local tribal administration and would have direct implication on territorial control at the district level. A related demand concerns greater devolution of real power to local government. Local authorities are pushing for constitutional provisions that would entrench them as legitimate governing bodies. At present, local authorities are created through acts of parliament. On both demands the government set up presidential commissions to collect public opinions and make recommendations. However, on the first issue, recommendations to rename districts in a tribally neutral manner were not successful. For example, instead of calling a district "Kgatleng" after the Bakgatla tribe/reserve, the presidential commission recommended a name like "East-Central." A related matter was a recommendation to increase the membership of the House of Chiefs, through which minority groups will elect their representatives. Both recommendations, initially accepted by the government, had to be withdrawn following a nationwide protest from so-called major tribes. The commission established to address the local structure of government also produced radical recommendations on the status quo. However, political parties are continuing their demands for review of the electoral system, hoping to replace its "first-past-the-post" nature with some kind of proportional representation.

Summary of the Democratic Process

From the foregoing discussion, several important elements of Botswana's democratic process can be discerned. First, it has been influenced by the very specific historical, ethnocultural, and geopolitical context of the country. Second, it has been, from the start, sensitive to and considerate of the broad interests of the population—even though in practice it did not treat them equally. Third, it has been based on a comprehensive institutional setting uniquely weaving together the traditional and modern institution of governance. Fourth, it has been dynamic and receptive to societal pressures and demands. Fifth, it has delivered the basic needs of the majority of citizens through a conscious program of social and economic development. Notwithstanding all the above elements, major problems of economic development, poverty, unemployment, and disease remain. An analysis of the economic sector helps explain why some of these problems persist.

The Economic Strategy

The Botswana government has been successful in its pursuit of the principal goals of its economic program, which sought to achieve rapid economic growth, sustainability, and diversification. These developments were in turn expected to result in economic independence. The approach was that of a mixed economy with a strong role for the private sector. This program was premised on the economic realities at independence, when the growth rate was very low, the economy was dependent on one or two hardly sustainable sectors, and there was a heavy dependence on British government grant-in-aid, donor support, and South African trade and communication links.

The country has since experienced rapid economic growth and relative political and industrial stability, enabling significant capital accumulation by the state, which is particularly dependent on the foreign-exploited mineral industry and the small capitalist class. Currently, capital from mining constitutes about 37 percent of gross domestic product (GDP) and over 55 percent of government revenue.[22] Diamond mining since 1972 has brought a fiscal revolution in the economy of Botswana. From a small economy characterized by budget deficit at independence in 1966, Botswana has developed one of the strongest economies in sub-Saharan Africa and in the world through a combination of diamond and beef exports (only two similarly small economies, those of Mauritius and Seychelles, have surpassed Botswana's).[23]

However, there are problems too. Revenue from agriculture, which constituted 42.5 percent of GDP at independence in 1966, currently constitutes less than 5 percent.[24] This represents both a relative and an absolute decline in the sector, which has had negative impact on employment in agriculture as well as on the general incomes of the rural population. The high rural-urban migration[25] and the persistence of rural poverty (47 percent of the country's population, or 38 percent of the country's total households)[26] are directly related to this decline in the agricultural sector. And as would be expected, the rural population has suffered most from poverty and unemployment. Yet efforts to diversify the economy and move it away from the enclave-based mining sector have been slow and generally unsuccessful. Revenue from the manufacturing and services sectors together constitutes less than 40 percent of GDP. The manufacturing sector in particular is underdeveloped, comprising only three subsectors—beef production, beer brewing, and lately a fragile motor vehicle industry.

The Development Strategy

The unique feature of Botswana's development strategy is its strong adherence to the national development plan. Although many postcolonial states started the same way, many have since dropped the use of NDPs. First adopted in 1966 in the context of scarce resources, the NDP has become a powerful gate-keeping tool for the government. It is not so much a "national development plan" as a schedule of government development programs over a period of five years. It defines government priorities and spells out new policies, approaches, and targets. It suggests the changing roles and functions of business and labor from the perspective of government. The plan has been adhered to with considerable fidelity, and projects not originally covered in the plan have generally not been well received in the course of the implementation period of the plan.

Thus, in spite of Botswana's proclaimed commitment to a free market economy and increasing evidence pointing toward a more liberalized economy,[27] the country has insisted on using the plan as a tool for resource allocation. Through the NDP a relatively centralized tradition of development planning has emerged. So far it appears to have served the country very well in terms of economic growth. Through the NDP it has been possible to set development priorities and define the roles of different actors. Botswana's major policy instruments and a broader development framework are therefore to be found in the various incarnations of its NDP, from the transitional NDP (1966–1969) to the current and ninth NDP (2003/2004–2008/2009).

The Social Welfare Program

The overall impact of economic growth on social development in the past three decades since independence has been significant. Three areas of success are discussed here: employment, rural development, and education and health.

Employment. The highest growth in employment took place between 1970 and 1990. Between 1985 and 1989, for instance, formal sector employment grew by almost 50 percent, from 117,100 to 176,300 jobs, or 12.4 percent per annum over the four years.[28] During this period the leading sectors in employment growth were construction (106 percent growth), manufacturing (79 percent growth), finance (71 percent growth), and agriculture (65 percent growth). Between 1991 and 1997, however, an average growth of 4.8 percent in GDP was matched by only 1.1 percent growth in public sector employment.[29] Encouragingly, from March 1997 to March 1998, it is estimated that formal sector employment rose by 5.4 percent, of which 57 percent was attributed to public sector employment.[30] Increased employment significantly improved incomes in both urban and rural areas. Many households had at least one member working in the wage sector. Other social and economic mechanisms linking the urban and rural populations further ensured that rural households in particular benefited from the employment boom.

However, since about 1990 Botswana's economy has generally displayed characteristics of jobless growth. Unemployment increased significantly. The major victims of unemployment and associated poverty have been women, youth, and unskilled laborers. In 1991 the national population and housing census estimated the national unemployment rate at 14 percent.

When disaggregated by gender and age, the rate of unemployment was highest among women (22 percent) and youth (30 percent). In the late 1980s, different labor surveys further showed that women constituted only 37 percent of those employed in the formal sector in Botswana.[31] Similarly, young people in general found it more difficult to break into the labor market and secure stable and better-paying jobs for themselves.

Exacerbating unemployment within the country at the time was a decline in external employment opportunities for unskilled laborers. In the mid-1980s many Botswana who had been working as migrant laborers outside the country started experiencing difficulties finding work in South African mines, farms, and industry. Many of those already in the system were retrenched. Between 1976 and 1996, for instance, the number of migrant mine laborers working outside Botswana fell from 27,000 to 8,000 men.[32]

The high rates of unemployment in Botswana have thus resulted from three factors. First, there was a decline in the traditional migrant labor system, which had been providing a window of opportunity for unskilled men and women since the 1920s. No new recruits were enlisted, while those already in the system were retrenched in large numbers. Second, due to regular droughts, among other factors, the subsistence agriculture sector, which historically absorbed large numbers of unskilled workers, experienced major declines in both output and employment opportunities. Third, cutbacks in government expending on social infrastructure—schools, health facilities, and roads after the sixth NDP (1985–1991)—directly affected the construction industry and led to considerable layoffs of workers in the early 1990s. Unemployment in the context of a rapidly growing population—3.5 percent per annum since 1981—could only contribute to persistent poverty.

Rural development. From the beginning the government realized that the success of its development lay in improving the quality of life of the majority of people living in rural areas under conditions of extreme poverty. A multisectoral development strategy was adopted to bring about this improvement. First, a number of new policies and programs targeted at land reform and increased productivity were introduced. For instance, the now notorious and failed Tribal Grazing Land Policy of 1975, the Rural Development Policy of 1972, the Tribal Land Act of 1968, and a number of programs were introduced. The emphasis was on better management of land resources, increased productivity, and improved incomes. Most of these programs, as already discussed, achieved significant progress in the areas of increasing water provisions and improving rural infrastructure, but much less in the main areas of better managing resources and improving rural incomes. Thus the symptoms of rural underdevelopment, in the form of low incomes, high levels of unemployment, rural-urban migration, low productivity, and persistent poverty, remain daunting challenges for the government.

Close to 40 percent of the rural household are estimated to live in poverty, and inequality of incomes is high, with the Gini coefficient of over 50 percent.[33]

Education and health. The greatest progress in development has occurred in the social sector. There has been a transformation for the better in both health and education. Over the past twenty years the government has spent close to 40 percent of its annual budget on social development.[34] The result of this massive investment was already evident by the 1990s. Table 7.2 indicates high and sustained growth in both education and health provisions, from a very low base in 1966, resulting in a significant rise in life expectancy and a commensurate decline in the death rate. Since then educational development has continued. By the mid-1990s, 83 percent of primary school–aged children were attending school. Some 35 percent were attending junior secondary school and about 25 percent senior secondary school. Also in the mid-1990s, with regard to health, some 85 percent of the population was estimated to be within a fifteen-kilometer walking distance from the nearest health facility. Over 55 percent had access to clean drinking water and 40 percent had access to a sanitary waste disposal facility.[35] However, when disaggregated into regions and districts, education and health services differ significantly. In 1991, 90 percent of primary school–aged children in urban areas and 80 percent in rural areas were attending school. In some faraway western districts, however, up to 35 percent of these children were not attending school. These districts happened to be those outside the "traditional reserves" and also had poor access to health service, water, and sanitary means of waste disposal.

But by far the most problematic feature of Botswana's social sector at the present time is the challenge of HIV/AIDS. Botswana ranks first, followed by

Table 7.2 Social Indicators in Botswana, Selected Years

	1966	1975	1981	1991	2001
Total Population	541,000	597,000	941,000	1334,000	1,680,900
Life Expectancy at Birth	48.0	55.8	56.3	60.2	55.7
Death Rate (per 1,000 live births)	n/a	14.5	13.9	11.5	12.4
Primary School Enrollment	72,000	116,000	234,000	293,000	332,000
Secondary School Enrollment	2,000	12,000	32,000	55,000	161,000
Teacher Training Colleges	293	489	1,188	1,356	2,908
University Health	22	n/a	1,022	3,133	6,364
Doctors per 100,000 Population	5	11	16	17	n/a
Nurses per 100,000 Population	6	86	143	179	n/a

Source: Adapted from the eighth, ninth, and tenth national development plans (1991, 1997, and 2003 respectively).

Note: n/a = not available.

South Africa and Zimbabwe, in HIV/AIDS prevalence. The effects are dec-imating. In 1997 the World Health Organization estimated that life expectancy at birth had dropped from sixty-seven to fifty years. The 2001 national population and housing census confirmed an eleven-year drop in life expectancy, from sixty-seven to fifty-six years. Projections show that unless a credible solution to this pandemic is found soon, life expectancy in Botswana will continue to drop.

Summary of the Economic Strategy

Botswana boasts, on the one hand, a stable economic base of about U.S.$5 billion (1997) rising to about U.S.$6 billion (1999) in foreign reserves and an admirable GDP per capita of over U.S.$3,500; a stable democratic sys-tem; and a relatively peaceful industrial climate. On the other hand, it has high unemployment, estimated at 21.5 percent according to the most recent labor force survey (1995–1996); high levels of poverty, affecting over 40 percent of households; and a highly unequal income distribution. These fac-tors pose a serious threat to the development of a harmonious democratic society.

Democracy and Development: What Is the Link?

On the surface, Botswana's democratic governance appears to have been central to its successful economic performance. However, as pointed out at the beginning of the chapter, this relationship is complex and symbiotic in nature. It is not evident whether politics brought about success in the econ-omy or whether the prosperous diamond revenue brought about political stability. This notwithstanding, the private sector, especially in the mining industry, has relied on both stability and policy predictability to continue its investment in the country. Regular free and fair elections, minimal corrup-tion, transparent management of public resources, and policy sensitivity to the plight of the poor were certainly helpful to the implementation of growth-promoting policies. Adherence to the priorities of the national development plan has also been important. Nevertheless, it is necessary to examine the country's performance in relation to what the citizens them-selves think and say.

Citizen opinion on the government's performance is reflected in the large support for the BDP at the polls. Although the BDP's popular vote dropped by close to 25 percent between 1965 and 1999 (from 80 percent to 57 percent), the party still enjoys widespread popular support, especially in the rural areas. In 1997 the Helen Suzman Foundation of South Africa con-ducted a survey of public opinion in a number of countries in the southern

African region. Table 7.3 presents the results of the survey for four comparable countries. The table reflects answers to three important questions linking democracy and development. The first was whether citizens felt that
their lives had become better or worse in the preceding five years. The second was whether or not they felt that the government had fulfilled its promises. And the third was how secure they felt living next to someone who
held political views different from their own.

Questions may be raised about the reliability of the results of this survey on grounds of currency, varying sample size, and selection of respondents. However, taken as indicative, the results pertaining to the perception
of government fulfilling promises tell an interesting story (see Table 7.3).
Botswana emerged as comparatively better off economically and socially
than Lesotho and Swaziland, but worse off than Namibia. In general, voters
in Namibia felt they were much better off (34 percent), that the government
had done very well in fulfilling its promises (72 percent), and that they
were fairly comfortable holding an opinion different from that of a neighbor (68 percent). The positive rating for the Namibian government may be
partly explained in terms of its newness (with the South West African People's Organization coming to power only in 1990 from exile). Botswana's
moderate ratings, on the other hand, show the period of difficult years for
government. As discussed above, during the period of the survey, employment opportunities were limited, poverty was persistent, and there was pressure for a number of political reforms. This said, though, it is clear that
Botswana citizens do not feel very free to hold opinions different from those
of their neighbors. In fact, citizens felt more comfortable to do so in Lesotho
than in all the other countries, with Botswana and Swaziland being the
poorer performers. It is not clear how the respondents were distributed in
this survey. However, the paternalistic authority of the chiefs and government
functionaries is still evidently felt in the rural areas of Botswana.

**Table 7.3 Public Surveys on Government Performance and Freedom of Opinion,
Selected Countries, 1997**

	Sample Size	All People Better Off (%)	All People Worse Off (%)	Government Promises Completely or Partly Fulfilled (%)	Few or No Government Promises Fulfilled (%)	Free to Hold Differing Opinion (%)
Botswana	704	20	34	41	57	48
Lesotho	880	20	70	21	78	69
Namibia	679	34	44	72	26	68
Swaziland	422	38	33	21	76	56

Source: Adapted from R. W. Johnson, *The Condition of Democracy in Southern Africa*
(Johannesburg: Helen Suzman Foundation, 2000).

Another way of determining Botswana's democratic and development success is to compare it with countries of related population and economy. Table 7.4 compares Botswana to four such countries—Lesotho, Mauritius, Namibia, and Swaziland—using key democracy and development measures. By and large, Botswana comes out second best in this group. Its per capita income, political freedom, and competitiveness indices are good by comparison. Only Mauritius outperforms Botswana on the human development index (HDI), per capita income, freedom, and competitiveness indices. However, in the areas of life expectancy and gender equality, Botswana is not performing that impressively.

On the basis of these analyses, it appears evident that there is a close link between Botswana's democracy on the one hand and its development progress on the other. On the whole, despite serious problems of poverty and unemployment, Botswana is a successful development case. The most encouraging thing is evidence of a government that is responsive to public opinion, committed to accountability, and engaged in assisting the needy.

Conclusion

This chapter has put Botswana's experience with democracy and development into a very specific context. It has dealt at length with issues of history, ethnic relations, and culture in order to underscore their relevance to the sustenance of democracy. The subject of a rich mineral economy has been downplayed here simply because it was an important but certainly not the key factor in Botswana's success. Cases abound in which potentially rich countries with diamonds, oil, and agricultural resources have performed poorly compared to Botswana. In Africa, many states with organizational and stability problems, with the exception of a few like Somalia and Eritrea, are the ones with large deposits of different minerals and other wealth.

This brings us to one key factor in Botswana's experience that requires much more systematic research and analysis—the question of visionary leadership and the difference it makes. The discussion here has implied some foresightedness and vision on the part of Botswana's leaders. But discussion of individual leaders and their skills has the danger of conflating the structure of leadership. Sometimes such discussion falls into the trap of personality cult. However, it is increasingly evident that the missing link in politics not only in Africa but in other parts of the world is visionary leadership. Self-proclaimed African visionary leaders of the 1960s committed several mistakes, but most were clear on what it was they wanted to achieve.[36] The fact that many if not all failed is indisputable. While visionary leadership may have been present, functioning democratic structures and respect for rules were missing. The Botswana experience becomes relevant here. Granted that the country has yet to experience a change of

Table 7.4 Performance on Basic Democracy and Development Indicators, Selected Countries

	Life Expectancy at Birth, 2001	GDP per Capita (U.S.$), 2001	HDI Rank (out of 175), 2001	Gender Empowerment Measures Rank (out of 70), 2003	Gini Coefficient,[a] 2003	Rate of Investment Competitiveness[b]	Freedom House Ranking, 2000[b]
Botswana	44.7	3,066	125	31	63.0	20	2
Lesotho	38.6	386	137	—	56.0	18	4
Mauritius	71.6	3,750	62	—	—	22	1
Namibia	47.4	1,730	124	29	70.7	16	2
Swaziland	38.2	1,175	133	—	60.9	19	6

Sources: UNDP, *Human Development Report: Millennium Development Goals: A Compact Among Nations to End Human Poverty* (New York: Oxford University Press, 2003), tab. 1, 12, 13, and 23.

Notes: a. For gini coefficient, a value of 0 represents perfect equality, and a value of 100 perfect inequality.

b. For the competitiveness rating a higher score indicates that a country is more competitive, whereas for the Freedom House index a lower score indicates better performance.

power from one party to another, its leaders have over the years developed a commitment to democratic governance. In fact, leaders in recent years have developed an informal structure, the All-Party Conference, which meets from time to time to discuss issues of common concern. This conference discussed and recommended most of the reforms of the 1990s discussed in this chapter.

Leadership displays itself at different levels, but its presence at the policy level is most important. It is at this level, too, that Botswana's leaders have shown a high degree of sensitivity combined with sound principles. For instance, the government has on several occasions in the past successfully resisted the pressure for wage increases, tax concessions, spending hikes, and many other such interests.[37] Several other factors, including history, geopolitical imperatives, resource constraints, and more important, personal skills and experience, explain Botswana's prudent management and democracy. But it is clear that the leadership of Botswana's first president, who had himself been a victim of racial discrimination, was exceptional. His successors have not found it easy to emulate him.[38]

Botswana's success with both democracy and development has derived from a combination of elements. Some were unique to the country, while others were more general. Key to them all seems to be an ability to accommodate differences and adapt to changing conditions. The story of Botswana is still unfolding and merits continuous observation.

Notes

1. See Bhagwati's earlier and most recent writings among others. See, for example, "Democracy and Development."

2. Of course, democratic regimes also differ substantially in experience and extent in this regard. The Scandinavian experience is, for example, substantially different from both the continental European and the UK and U.S. experiences.

3. See Fawcus, *Botswana*.

4. See, for instance, the findings of the Tuggart Commission, which investigated the conditions of the Bushmen among the Bangwato Reserve in the 1930s.

5. The new education policy recommended that government integrate the teaching and use of minority languages in public institutions. There have also been several motions passed in parliament seeking to remove the constitutional clauses 77 and 78, which refer to "eight major tribes."

6. See an elaborate discussion of this problem in Colclough and McCarthy, *The Political Economy of Botswana*.

7. Ibid. (1980).

8. Hence many critics doubted the viability of the country's independence. See a 1970 speech delivered by Khama in Sweden, in Carter, *From the Frontline*.

9. See Parsons, "The Economic History of Khama's Country."

10. Isaac Schapera in his different works on Botswana during the 1930s and 1940s captures this issue very well. See, for instance, "Circa 1938–1940."

11. See an elaborate discussion of this issue in Cohen and Parson, "Politics and Society in Botswana."

12. See ibid.

13. Carter et al., *From the Frontline.*

14. Different writers on the Botswana state have described it as "paternalistic," "administrative," and so forth. See, for instance, Duncan, Jefferis, and Molutsi, *Social Development in Botswana.*

15. See Mogalakwe, Molutsi, and Mufune, "The State Legislation and Trade Unions in Botswana"; and Mogalakwe, *The State and Organized Labour in Botswana.*

16. Molutsi and Holm, "Developing Democracy When Civil Society Is Weak."

17. Botswana Central Statistics Office (CSO), Ministry of Finance and Development Planning, *National Development Plans I–V.*

18. The most vocal chief, Bathoen II, did so in 1969 and brought to the opposition Botswana National Front a solid support base, which remains to date.

19. Chief Linchwe, another substantial skeptic, was assigned ambassadorship of Botswana in the United States. Incidentally, the present government has repeated this strategy this year when it assigned Chief Seepapitso IV, its widely recognized critic, to the same post in the United States in 2001.

20. Mogalakwe, *The State and Organized Labour.*

21. See the Botswana Election Body's report of the 1999 general elections.

22. A detailed analysis of sectoral contributions to GDP can be found in the different national development plans and Bank of Botswana annual reports.

23. See 1999 quarterly reports of the Economic Intelligence Unit.

24. See Botswana CSO, Ministry of Finance and Development Planning, *National Development Plan VIII.*

25. In the early 1980s the population of Gaborone, the capital city of Botswana, was growing at an average of 12 percent per annum. Botswana CSO, Ministry of Finance and Development Planning, *National Development Plans I–V.*

26. A reanalysis of the results of previous income and expenditure survey, conducted in 1998 by the Botswana Institute for Development Policy Analysis, showed that the level of poverty might have dropped from 45 percent to 38 percent of the households between 1975 and 1989. See Botswana Institute for Development Policy Analysis, Ministry of Finance and Development Planning, *Study of Poverty Alleviation.*

27. Both the eighth NDP and the reports of the commissions on privatization (1999) and salaries (1999) underscored this policy direction.

28. Botswana CSO, Ministry of Finance and Development Planning, *National Development Plan VII*, p. 42.

29. Botswana CSO, Ministry of Finance and Development Planning, *National Development Plan VIII*, p. xxi.

30. World Bank, *Botswana.*

31. Botswana CSO, Ministry of Finance and Development Planning, *Labour Surveys 1983, 1985.*

32. Botswana CSO, *Population and Housing Census Report 1991.*

33. See, for instance, Botswana CSO, Ministry of Finance and Development Planning, *Household Income and Expenditure Surveys 1975, 1986.*

34. See the calculation of the budget over the past twenty years in Botswana CSO, *Planning for the People.*

35. Ibid.

36. Thandika Mkandawire presents an elaborate and interesting discussion of the vision of nation building and development as the agenda of most of these leaders. See Mkandawire, "Shifting Commitments."

37. For a detailed documentation of worker strikes and student demands in 1970s and 1980s, see Molutsi, "Inequality in Botswana"; and Mogalakwe, *The State and Organized Labour in Botswana.*

38. Parsons et al., *Seretse Khama,* has full detail of Seretse's leadership skills. Also see Fawcus, *Botswana.*

Mozambique:
The Challenge of Democratization

Brazão Mazula

In this study of the process of pacification and democratization in Mozambique, I analyze the factors that facilitated and/or impeded peacebuilding and democratization in the country and examine the proposition that there is a positive correlation between democracy and peace and among democracy, peace, and development. The central argument of the chapter is that the construction of a stable democratic society, the rule of law, and sustained economic development are largely functions of the mobilization and engagement of civil society, the private sector, and political society. In a multicultural society such as Mozambique's, these capacities require the establishment of a political order that places a premium on respect for human rights and inclusive participation.[1]

A key concept in the chapter is civil society, which is used here in Harbemas's sense to refer to more or less autonomous associations, not state owned, that capture the private concerns of social forces and condense and transmit them to the public sphere of politics.[2] In this regard, democracy is defined not only in terms of "separation of powers," but also in terms of interdependence among the various centers of power.[3] Democracy is greatly strengthened by the existence of a critical and responsible opposition, functioning in an environment of political freedom.[4]

In the context of Mozambique, is the relationship between civil society and the state a top-down process (descending from the state to the political system and then to civil society) or a bottom-up process from civil society to the political system and from there to the state, without depriving the state or the political system of autonomy?[5] Addressing this question, in this study of peace and democracy in Mozambique I take account not only of the proliferation of movements, organizations, associations, and ethnocultural identities, but also, and above all, of the nature of the emerging relationship involving the state, political forces, and civil society.

General Background

Mozambique is located in southern Africa, adjacent to the Indian Ocean, with 2,515 kilometers of coastline. It borders Tanzania to the north, Malawi, Zambia, and Zimbabwe to the west, and South Africa and Swaziland to the south. Its surface encompasses 799,380 square kilometers.

Mozambique has attracted the desire of kings and marine Portuguese at least since the Portuguese sailor Vasco da Gama navigated around it in 1498.[6] Effective Portuguese occupation of the colony took place in the twentieth century, after successive fights against the Arabs in the sixteenth and seventeenth centuries and wars of resistance by local authorities from the eighteen century onward, as well as political and military frictions with the British crown. Under Laws 1005 and 1022, of August 7 and August 20, 1920, the Portuguese overseas territories began to be called colonies, with a formal fiscal and administrative relationship to the metropolis.[7]

Effective occupation of the territory by Portugal did not prevent bouts of nationalist resistance from Mozambicans. On the contrary, they grew in direct proportion to the duration and cruelty of the colonial regime. For example, in 1933 the Associative Center for Blacks of Mozambique was formed as a result of the growth of nationalist movements—the African Association and the Negro Institute. On June 25, 1962, the Front for the Liberation of Mozambique (Frelimo) was formed in Dar es Salaam (Tanzania) as a merger of three nationalist organizations operating outside the country, each of which had been seeking ways to fight the Portuguese colonial regime: the National Democratic Union of Mozambique, the National Union for the Independence of Mozambique, and the National African Union of Mozambique.

On June 25, 1964, Eduardo Chivambo Mondlane, the first president of Frelimo, declared the beginning of the Mozambican armed struggle. This struggle lasted ten years and ended with the Lusaka Accord, signed on September 7, 1974, by Samora Moisés Machel, president of Frelimo after the death of Eduardo Mondlane in 1969. Melo Antunes, then minister without portfolio and member of the Portuguese armed forces, signed the agreement on behalf of the Portuguese government in the presence of key Portuguese officials and personalities such as Mário Soares, António de Almeida Santos, and Victor Crespo. After a transition period of about nine months, the independence of Mozambique was proclaimed on June 25, 1975.

In 1976, barely one year after the accord, the Rhodesian regime led by Ian Smith began military attacks on Mozambique, especially in the provinces in the central parts of the country—with the excuse that Mozambique was providing support for the Zimbabwean liberation struggle. This military aggression continued until the 1979 Lancaster House Accord, which ended the war in so-called Southern Rhodesia and ushered in the independence of Zimbabwe.

However, the independence of Zimbabwe in April 1980 did not necessarily bring peace for Mozambique. A civil war had broken out in 1976 between the government of Frelimo and the Mozambique National Resistance (Renamo), a rebel movement led by Andre Matsangaíssa and later by Alfonso Dhlakama. This civil war lasted approximately sixteen years and ended with a general peace accord signed in Rome in 1992 by the president of the republic, Joaquin Alberto Chissano, and by the president of Renamo, Alfonso Dhlakama.

Economic Conditions

Mozambique has always been one of the poorest countries in the world. The total value of foreign reserves in gold and foreign currency transferred to the Bank of Mozambique from the Overseas National Bank (the Central Bank of Mozambique during the colonial period and with headquarters in Lisbon) on the day of independence was only 39.7 million escudos (approximately U.S.$1 million).[8] According to official data, the gross national product at 1980 constant prices was 71.1 billion escudos in 1975. This slipped to 55.6 billion escudos in 1984, reflecting a decline in all sectors of the economy—agriculture, industry, construction, transport, commerce, and others.[9]

With regard to the global balance of trade, imports increased from 10.7 billion escudos in 1975 to 22.9 billion escudos in 1984, having reached 31.6 billion escudos in 1982; while exports decreased from 5.1 billion escudos in 1975 to 4.0 billion escudos in 1984, the years that registered the highest volume of exports were 1980 and 1981, having oscillated between 9.1 and 9.9 billion escudos respectively.[10]

The average annual population growth rate rose from 1.5 percent in 1975 to 2.6 percent in 1985.[11] According to World Bank statistics, this figure has declined slightly in recent years and stabilized at around 2.0 percent between 2000 and 2002. Life expectancy at birth in the period of 1975–1980 was 43.6 years of age (42.1 for men, 45.0 for women).[12] This figure slightly worsened to 41 years by 2002. Also, between 1975 and 1980, the infant mortality rate was of 159 per 1,000 live births.[13] In 2001 the infant mortality rate fell to 125 per 1,000 live births, as indicated by World Bank statistics. Thanks to an intense literacy campaign initiated soon after independence, levels of illiteracy for Mozambicans aged seven and above decreased from 93 percent in 1975 to 73 percent in 1979[14] and to 72 percent in 1980.[15] For Mozambicans aged fifteen and above, the illiteracy rate was 54 percent in 2002.

In both comparative and absolute terms, the level of human development in Mozambique has remained low. Life expectancy is just a over 42 years, compared to an average of 48.9 years in sub-Saharan Africa. The country's index of human poverty, at 59 percent, is the highest in the Southern African Development Community.[16]

In spite of this weak economic situation, Mozambique has achieved international respectability for overcoming conflict; by putting an end to its sixteen-year civil war, the country raised hopes that it could reconstruct itself economically and democratically. The economic performance of the country after the first general and multiparty elections of 1994 redoubled that hope. A country that registered an inflation rate of 54 percent in the beginning of 1995 reduced the inflation rate to single digits, 5.8 percent, in 1997.[17] The per capita gross domestic product at current prices increased from U.S.$93.90 in 1996 to U.S.$126.90 in 1997.[18] With the economy growing at 11 percent between 1994 and 1998 and a commensurate human development index rating, it was concluded that the economic development of Mozambique was showing "a positive trend."[19] Democracy almost certainly had something to do with this positive performance: it activated the participation of the citizens in the reconstruction of the country.

Nonetheless, the country continues to face high levels of poverty. Two-thirds of the population (69.4 percent of the total population), representing some 10.9 million people, lived in situations of extreme poverty in 1996–1997.[20] Flooding in two consecutive years, 2000 and 2001, the deaths of a dozen citizens in the city of Montepuez in the north of the country on November 9, 2000 (resulting from the political demonstrations by Renamo), and the barbaric murder of journalist Carlos Cardoso in Maputo on November 22, 2000, had a negative impact on the economy, raising the inflation rate to about 30 percent.

The Cultural Context

In reality, apart from short spells of tranquillity, Mozambique lived a war situation for twenty-six years. However, an analysis of the country's prospects for reconstruction and democratization of the state and society must look not only at the effects of the war on the economy and infrastructure but also the cultural factors that affect the functioning of the society. It is important to include them if we recognize that ethnic and linguistic diversity can serve as a catalyst or as a constraining element of democracy in culturally heterogeneous societies.

The indigenous populations of the country were largely excluded from the process of governance and organization of the state in colonial Mozambique. Indeed, the Portuguese colonial practices were tantamount to "ethnocide." In a sense, they represented an attempt to destroy civilizations. Out of 5.7 million inhabitants registered in the 1950 census, only 92,000 whites, coloreds, and Indians were identified as "nonindigenous." The largest groups—Makwa-Llomwe (representing 40 percent of the total population), Tsonga, Shona, Chopi (Tonga), Nyanja and Chewa, Makonde, Yao, Barore, and Ngoni—were blacks.[21]

Prime Minister António Salazar of Portugal defined the relations between colonialism and the Portuguese nation in 1954 in the following terms:

> Colonialism essentially demands the unevenness of the races and the cultures, an objective of economic exploitation served by the political domination, which generally reflects the differentiation between the citizen and the subordinate. There is no colonialism where no strategic or financial benefit is taken. . . . It is not possible to conceive a colonial situation in which people enjoy the same standard of living, identical cultures. . . . There can be no colonialism where the people are an integral part of the Nation, where the citizens collaborate actively in the running of the state on equal terms with all others, where all the people can occupy public offices and move and work together in the territories. And this is not a new situation, established or legislated in a hurry, but it has evolved over the centuries, we can almost say it has always been so.[22]

Similarly, Marcelo Caetano, who came to replace Salazar as prime minister, also contended that blacks in Africa were "indispensable as assistants," but that they had to be led and made fit by Europeans.[23]

Seen against this background, colonialism was an "act of destruction of civilization."[24] Regarding them only as being "indispensable for economic exploitation," the colonial regime rejected any possibility of integrating the "indigenous" or blacks into the running of the state. Thus we cannot speak of democracy in the colonial period, since colonial relations were based on "the different levels of races and cultures" and exclusion of some members of the society from the construction of the state.

But how have cultural factors in general and the country's ethnic and linguistic diversity been handled in postcolonial Mozambique? In its constitution and mode of operation, Frelimo was confronted with the dilemma of how to deal with the cultural diversity of a complex society. Recognizing the heterogeneous composition of Mozambican society, Eduardo Mondlane called in 1967 for the mobilization of all segments of Mozambican society, "making use of the talents of each one of the national tribes" and uniting "for the good of the struggle." He also believed that the national liberation struggle was in itself a process of creating a new reality for Mozambique, united and free.[25] Of course, unity was needed to win the war for independence, but it was also expected that this consciousness of cultural heterogeneity would be positively reflected in the independence constitution and lead to the establishment of a pluralistic democratic order.

Unfortunately, however, cultural diversity was not always seen as positive, particularly in moments of national crisis. It came to be suspected as a factor that the "enemy" could exploit to break the unity of Frelimo. It was also seen as an obstacle to the formation of the "revolutionary popular state." Indeed, Frelimo's ideological concept of the national unit implicitly regarded the demise of tribalism as a necessary condition for the emergence of the nation.[26] To Frelimo, the revolutionary state, based on the "true personality . . . of the people," demanded uniformity in behavior and habits: "For the formation of the true personality of our people, it is necessary to create conditions that will unify the habits, customs and traditions, giving to them a revolutionary dimension."[27]

This conception of unification of "habits, customs and traditions" translated itself into a vision of national unity as cultural uniformity and behavior. At the same time, it implied the exclusion of other cultures in favor of a culture considered superior. A version of the conception of uniformity as national unity saw a dance from the southern region—*makwayela*—imposed on all the schools of the country and administrative posts in the provinces and districts filled with cadres from the ethnic groups in the south. What appeared to the Frelimo hierarchy as a way to promote national unity and constitute a solid base for democracy was perceived by others as an attempt to put southern ethnic groups in a position of dominance over the rest of the country, which generated strong feelings of unhappiness.

For largely ideological reasons, the 1980 national census chose to exclude items on the ethnic makeup of the country. Refusing to accept the cultural reality of ethnicity and even fighting it, Frelimo sought to assert its political hegemony over the entire national territory. But the 1997 census, conducted in the context of the new democratic system, classified the citizens by their ethnic origin, identifying five large linguistics groups—Emakhwa, Xichangana, Elomwe, Cisena, and Echwabo—and added "other Mozambican languages" and "other foreign languages."[28] The Portuguese language remains the official language. Other studies mention about twenty languages, the majority coming from the Bantu group, and distribute them by regions: Emakhwua, Ciyao, Cinyanja, Shimakondi, Elomwe, and Echwabo to the north; Cinyanja and Cisenga to the northwest; Cisena and Sishona to the central zone; and Xitswa, Xichangana, Xironga, and Gitonga to the South.[29]

At the fourth congress in 1983, Frelimo proclaimed recognition of the complexity of Mozambican society. It also rejected "a simplistic tendency to deny the diversity as a way to consolidate the unity" and the consideration of diversity as "a negative element of creation of national unity," and promised to correct the mistake in thinking that national unity meant uniformity.[30] At the same congress and from that time onward, Frelimo came to give recognition to Mozambican languages—leading to the creation of a "specialized structure" dedicated to its study.[31] Eventually, the University

Eduardo Mondlane became the nucleus of a Mozambican language studies program. Today, in the context of the new democratic system, ethnic and cultural diversity are taken into consideration in the appointment of people to leadership positions in local and central government.

The multiplicity of religions in Mozambique is an additional and complex challenge to the democratic project of the country. A recent study by Obede Baloi, commissioned by the Ministry of Justice, concluded that all main religious denominations are represented in all parts of the country, but the distribution is uneven across the provinces. Catholics have a more even spread in the country, but they are highly concentrated in the provinces of Zambezia (38.6 percent) and Tete (22.7 percent), while the Church of Siao, also known as Zion, has more of its followers in the provinces of Manica (26.4 percent), Sofala (17.7 percent), Inhambane (34.0 percent), Gaza (37.2 percent), and Maputo (48.9 percent, with 38.7 percent in Maputo city). Islam is more concentrated in the northern provinces of Niassa (63.5 percent), Cabo Delgado (54.8 percent), and Nampula (39.1 percent). Other Mozambicans, representing 27 percent of the population, were identified as "without religion"—a designation that could mean those individuals who do not practice any religion or those who practice traditional or animistic religions.

For a long time and for ideological reasons, religion was regarded as inimical to the advancement of Mozambique's liberation struggle. For the same reasons, traditional authorities were also denigrated as feudal structures and obscurantist and, above all, a threat to the power of Frelimo. Frelimo maintained this position of antireligious and antitraditional rule after independence. This position is also reflected in the 1977 constitution.

In the prevailing ideology, religion was considered obscurantist and therefore incompatible with the creation of the "new man" or the "socialist man."[32] This explains why Christian and Islamic educational establishments and health posts were included in the Mozambican political structure after nationalization—declared on July 24, 1975, one month after the proclamation of independence. The first national seminar of education, organized in Beira in January 1975, also decided to remove from the educational curricula everything that contradicted the ideology of Frelimo.[33] Religion was deemed to be an enemy of the state.

Frelimo was forced to enter into dialogue with representatives of different church denominations in the country in December 1982 under the slogan "let's consolidate what unites us."[34] This decision by Frelimo to enter into dialogue with its so-called ideological enemies was driven largely by the harsh conditions of the civil war economy, which was in turn aggravated by drought and famine. The decision was also driven by strong pressure on the regime from Christian churches.[35] Was Frelimo recognizing the social role of the churches by removing the label of obscurantism? Was it rethinking its position and accepting cultural and ideological diversity, which would need to be accommodated in order to achieve real social stability in Mozambican society itself? At this stage in the civil war, Frelimo, which was leading a war against external aggression, apartheid South Africa, and Renamo, found it expedient to appeal to the various religious denominations for support and unity. It was a strategic and instrumental appropriation of the religious denominations. The December 1982 meeting did not speak openly of the establishment of a national church. But the meeting resulted in the creation of a Department of Religious Affairs within the Ministry of Justice to resolve conflicts between the state and the churches. Similar initiatives were developed by other religious denominations who organized themselves into associations such as the Islamic Council, the Islamic Congress, the Evangelical Association, the Association of Independent Churches, and the Mozambique Christian Council.[36]

The revised constitution of 1998 reaffirms the secular nature of the state, provides for a strict separation of religious institutions and the state, and mandates that all religious activities must conform to the laws of the state. Provisions in Article 25 of the constitution prohibit discrimination on the basis of religion. They also enjoin religious institutions to ensure that their actions do not "jeopardize social harmony" or "create divisions or situations of privilege."

A key lesson to be drawn from official hostility to religion and attempts to exclude religious denominations from the processes of social and political development in Mozambique is not only that this effort was antidemocratic, but also that it generated social conflicts. For religion as a belief in ancestor spirits and in God[37] is an integral part of the African culture. Another lesson to be drawn is that social tranquillity must not be equated with the mere absence of war. Social stability is best secured when the living forces of society, including religious bodies and traditional authorities, are involved in national development and governance processes. Indeed, the attempt to exclude civil society from the process of social and political development of Mozambique may well have been a contributory factor in the weakening of the Frelimo regime.

From Popular Democracy and
Militarism to Multiparty Democracy

With independence, the people of Mozambique proved their ability to resist dogged efforts by Portuguese colonialists to occupy their territory by military force—beginning with Mouzinho de Albuquerque, Oliveira Martins, and Antonio Enes as architects of colonial policies dating from the nineteenth century.[38] The break from the yoke of colonialism brought great pride and joy to the people and raised popular expectations for a bright future. This euphoria was well captured in the various political speeches made in the period between the Lusaka Accord in 1974 and the third congress of Frelimo in 1977, notwithstanding consciousness of the challenges ahead.[39]

From the third congress onward, Frelimo presented itself as the custodian of popular democracy and assumed the role of leading the state and the society with a program aimed at moving Mozambique toward a socialist stage of development.[40] A key feature of the Frelimo brand of popular democracy was that party leaders and government officials claimed to speak on behalf of the people and claimed that their actions were legitimate because they represented the will of the people. This was done within a framework of democratic centralism combined with a central planning model of economic development. As Norman Barry shows, this type of democracy is based on a superstructure of power that is directed from the top to the bottom of society.[41] The state was an instrument of Frelimo. On the cultural front, popular democracy translated into attempts at the integration of Mozambicans of the different ethnic, racial, and religious groups.

However, almost from the beginning, this model of democracy proved to have several weaknesses. Based on a sort of dictatorship of the proletariat, and oriented toward imposition of Frelimo and state preferences, it could hardly accommodate individual freedoms and engage in dialogue. In fact, Frelimo became more and more oblivious to the weaknesses in its model of governance and the rising popularity of Renamo. A wide gap developed between the official (Frelimo) reading of the political, economic, and social reality and that of the public. In addition to the civil war, Mozambique was confronted with natural calamities such as flooding in 1978 and drought and famine 1982–1984. The economy was also affected by the Cold War (until 1989) and it felt the consequences of worldwide recession, provoking a fall of 11 percent in the average price of exports from 1981 to 1982, which aggravated the fiscal crisis.[42] The model of a centrally planned economy and popular democracy proved grossly incapable of resolving the war and other problems of Mozambique.

Extremely weakened by the war, the economy was experiencing an inflation rate of 70.2 percent by the eve of the first elections in 1994.[43] The manifest inefficiency of the model of a centrally planned economy compelled Frelimo to agree to liberalize the economy and introduce an economic recovery program in 1987.[44] But did this sudden change in economic direction represent the embarkment on a path of liberal democracy and a break with popular democracy? In fact, the change in economic direction did not go all that far. It coexisted with the "war economy"—which was deeply rooted in central planning. It created an unstable situation of one nation with two incompatible systems: a war economy on the one hand, and a tentative neoliberal economy on the other.

Another weakness resided in the relationships among the citizen, civil society, and the state. The Frelimo system placed emphasis on the collective and not the individual—although it recognized the individualist dimension of the human being. The individual was often treated as a "subject" incapable of *speaking and acting* and incapable of interacting freely with the state and its leadership in decisionmaking.[45] Nor was he or she regarded as an actor with the capacity to participate in the modification of his or her environment and freely change his or her views in the light of experience. Thus the individual was reduced to an instrument of the collective, or of Frelimo and the state. The involvement of mass organizations in Frelimo and the attempt at political openness did not necessarily produce a democratic order and a culture in which the governors and the governed could freely exchange ideas and interrelate on an equal basis. Thus the state was indirectly deprived of the "intercommunicative power" that is so important for the engagement of citizens in development activities as well as for social stability.

In the end, Frelimo lost much of its popularity and credibility. It proved incapable of carrying out its political and economic project to institute a new social and economic order of scientific socialism. Drought and the changing of the geopolitical situation of the subregion—the independence of Zimbabwe, the end of the apartheid regime in South Africa, and peaceful democratic transition in Malawi—forced Renamo, too, to rethink its position. The same factors also undermined the validity of Renamo's claim that it was fighting a war to bring about democracy in Mozambique.

Eventually, both Frelimo and Renamo came to the realization that the civil war was not one of the important choices facing the country and that the real choices to be made were whether to democratize or not to democratize the political order; whether to adopt the centrally planned model of socialist economic development or the model of neoliberal economic development. It thus became imperative for Frelimo and Renamo to agree to enter into negotiations to end the war.

The Peace Accord

The war demanded a realistic solution. This, in turn, required political will and mutual trust as basic conditions for the negotiation. It also implied willingness to accept that far-reaching political, structural, and economic changes were needed in the country.

Negotiations between the Frelimo government and Renamo began in Rome on July 8, 1990. They were mediated by the Catholic archbishop of Mozambique, D. Jaime Gonçalves; Mario Rafaelli (member of the Italian House of Representatives), representing the Italian government; and Andrea

Ricardi and Don Matteo Zuppi (two members of the community of Santo Egidio). Characterized by an atmosphere of tension and deep mutual mistrust, the peace negotiations lasted about twenty-seven months. The mutual commitment of Frelimo and Renamo to the peace process was placed in doubt, and the expectations of the people of Mozambique and the international community for peace were threatened many times, especially when complications appeared two days before the signing of the general peace accord on October 4, 1992.

The conditions for cease-fire, peace, and political stability imposed under the accord included the taking of political power through the ballot box, universal suffrage, adoption of a more open and participatory approach to development, the mechanisms of governance that conform to internationally accepted democratic rules, effective participation of citizens in the life of the nation,[46] and integration of military units of the government and Renamo into a 30,000-member unified armed force (24,000 in the army, 4,000 in the air force, 2, 000 in the navy).[47] The two parties were also made to commit to cooperation and the use of dialogue as the means to resolve conflict and achieve lasting peace.[48]

The negotiations were a long process of patience, construction of mutual trust and consensus, and search for understanding.[49] In short, they were part of the learning process toward adopting a new democratic system, moving beyond entrenched partisan ideological positions, recognizing each other as compatriots in the same country, and accepting that differences in political opinions do not constitute a barrier to social cohesion. The discovery that it was possible to coexist with each other in spite of mutual differences was perhaps the greatest development in this new era.

Of course, the mediators played a crucial role in the processes of political reconciliation. By understanding the historical context of the negotiations between the two leaders and by being sensitive to the prevailing cultural and psychological conditions, the mediators facilitated the building of mutual trust and confidence for future peace.[50] The role of mediators in the Mozambican peace process also confirms the thesis that successful mediation of conflicts cannot be reduced to the perfect application of techniques. Peace cannot be imposed from outside by mediators or by those who fund the negotiations. Sustainable peace can only emerge from a condition of mutual understanding between those previously engaged in conflict. It was the mediators' ability and patience in searching for convergences and removing divergences that prevented the possibility for Frelimo and Renamo to return to war, in spite of mutual provocations.

A second conclusion is that a successful process of peacebuilding must not be a closed shop—confined only to experts and intellectuals and excluding ordinary people. It must include civil society. Without doubt, it was the pressure and determination of the people opposed to the fratricidal war and their demand for peaceful coexistence and dialogue that helped to bring an end to the war. Thus the people embraced democracy not necessarily because of its intrinsic value, but because they saw it as a means to maintain peace and to prevent a new war. This is the background against which people turned out massively to vote in the first multiparty general elections (presidential and legislative), held in 1994. Out of 6.4 million registered voters, about 81 percent voted.[50] There was a similarly high voter turnout in the second presidential and legislative elections, held in 1999, in which 84 percent of registered voters voted, making nonsense of pessimistic predictions of mass abstentions similar to the municipal elections of 1998, which suffered 85 percent abstentions.

Unlike the Nkomati Accord (signed between the government and the apartheid regime of South Africa in 1984 to contain the civil war), the Mozambican general peace accord brought significant changes in internal social relations and the rules of the political game, resulting essentially in the introduction of democratic space. It inaugurated a new era of economic and social relations tolerant of market economy democratization of society.

In spite of the stability being experienced in the country, it is clear that the pacification process is incomplete. It requires a continuous capacity to monitor developments, identify conflict spots, and develop preventive interventions. The internal conflicts of today turn on the distribution of economic and social opportunities. The consolidation of peace depends upon the degree to which the distrust between citizens and the state and regional asymmetries are reduced and is built among different agents of development. Learning to accept setbacks as normal is part of the process of democracy.

Democratic Expressions of Civil Society

Multiparty democracy presented new challenges to Mozambique. It has been faced with the challenge of establishing new relationships between the state and the citizen and between the state and civil society, within the context of the rule of law. Popular democracy was based on a vertical relationship between the state and civil society. Citizens and the society at large had to adjust to the rules of coexistence unilaterally defined by the party-state. Until 1990, only a few mass and professional organizations were accorded recognition as expressions of popular democracy by the ruling party. They included the Organization of Mozambican Women, the Organization of Mozambican Workers, the Organization of Mozambican Youth, the National Organization of Teachers, the Organization of Young Adult Mozambicans, and the Dynamizing Groups.[51] The main mission of these organizations was to mobilize citizens and society according to rules defined by the party-state. Citizenship was defined largely in terms of compliance with rules and fondness for the party-state. But today, these organizations have transformed themselves into nongovernmental organizations (NGOs) or trade unions. Multiparty democracy brought a change in direction: the state and political parties have had to adjust to the social and economic norms defined by the market and the dynamics of the civil society.

The new political order has brought a multiparty parliament, unified army, an independent media, and multiple political parties. Above all, it has brought a proliferation of NGOs. More than 400 organizations, associations, and movements have been formed in the past decade or so, and the majority of them are not affiliated with Frelimo. The directory of NGOs produced by LINK in November 2000 recorded 427 national nongovernmental organizations. Twenty-four of these cater to gender, two cater to human rights, twenty-one deal with issues related to children, and fifty bring together friends or sympathizers of a province, city, or locality.[52] It is important to remember that the general peace accord gives recognition to the right to form associations to defend local, sectional, and narrow interests of a social group or a specific class of citizens—so long as such associations distance themselves from the political parties.[53]

The NGOs come out of an awareness of the right of citizens to participate actively and independently in the processes of national reconstruction and development.[54] They insist on their right to be independent from the state while demanding assistance from external donors and the government. It has not been an easy relationship. The very presence of these civil society bodies imposes a limitation on the power of the state. They insist on their right to demand an equal share of economic and social resources.[55] This is the essence of the battle being waged on the floor of parliament between the former civil war combatants—Frelimo and Renamo.

Many political parties have been formed during this period. In a majority of cases, such groups are formed and led by former military leaders of Frelimo who claim to have defected from the party. Examples include the Democratic Party of Mozambique (led by Wehia Ripua), the Social-Liberal and Democratic Party (led by Casimiro Nhamitambo), the Independent Party of Mozambique (led by Ya' kub Sibindy), the Democratic Congress Party (led by Vasco Campira), the Party for the Progress of the Mozambican People (led by Padimbe Kamati), the National Union of Mozambique (led by Carlos Reis), and the Party of the Democratic Union (an electoral coalition party), among others. In addition to Frelimo and Renamo, the following parties also participated in the elections: the Labor Party, Domingos Arouca's United Front of Mozambique/Democratic Convergence Party, the Democratic Renewal Party, Lutero Simango's National Convention Party, and the Patriotic Alliance coalition. All of them contested in the first general and multiparty elections, in 1994, bringing the total number of competing parties to seventeen. Today there are more than twenty political parties.[56]

The Political Parties Law, enacted in 1991, governs the formation and official recognition of political parties in Mozambique.[57] It establishes the legal framework for their formation and operation and, in Article 3, enjoins political parties to defend the national interest, promote the spirit of patriotism, and support nation building. It also prohibits the formation of political parties based on region, ethnicity, tribe, race, and religion. This prohibition is also reinforced in Article 16 of the constitution. Moreover, a party is obliged to obtain a minimum of 100 signatures in each one of the ten provinces of Mozambique and in the city of Maputo to be recognized as a nationally representative political party. It is instructive to note that this law enjoyed the endorsement of all the political parties then in existence. And significantly, Renamo too accepted the law after the general peace accord.

The growth of an independent mass media is another excellent and relevant expression of democracy in Mozambique. Up to 1992, only three newspapers, one radio station, and two progovernment television channels existed. Today there are four privately and publicly owned radio stations and over a dozen daily newspapers, weeklies, and periodicals.[58] Recently, an increasing number of community radios have been subsidized by the United Nations Educational, Scientific, and Cultural Organization. In addition to the independent media, other nonstate and civic organs have also emerged, including the Center for the Study of Democracy and Development, the Movement of Women for Peace, the Movement for Peace and Citizenship, and youth clubs to promote a culture of peace.

In the meantime, traditional authorities, long ago alienated by Frelimo, are demanding official recognition of their space and a role for themselves in the democratic dispensation. They are challenging the Dynamizing Groups and other structures created by Frelimo immediately after independence to countervail or supplant the power of traditional authorities in the various ethnic groups. Various revisions in the constitution appear to have failed to resolve this conflict between the modern state and traditional authority.

Conclusion

A number of questions have been raised in this chapter. Is there any democracy in Mozambique and, if so, what is the state of this democracy today? How stable is the country, given the experience with peace agreements in Angola and Burundi? Is it different from other African countries? What is the future for peace and democracy in Mozambique? Taking the economic situation into account, can we say that peace and democracy are here to stay, as Frelimo and Renamo politicians would have us believe? Would their claims convince investors to invest in the development of the country?

At this stage, it is only possible to talk of democracy in Mozambique in terms of the establishment of democratic institutions such as an elected president of the republic, parliament, and some municipal governments. But this is not to say that democracy has been institutionalized in those institutions. The goal established in the general peace agreement of 1992 "to allow complete political freedom in accordance with democratic principles recognized at the international level" has yet to be reached.[59]

It will certainly take a long time for a culture of democracy to be entrenched in Mozambique.[60] Democracy itself will only become real in Mozambique when such a culture emerges to complement the democratic structures that have already been established. Cultural diversity and other social complexities will need to be institutionalized. The party in power (Frelimo) and the opposition (Renamo and other parties), the different ethnic, religious, and racial groups, as well as the regions of the north, center, and south, must collaborate on the project of building unity and developing their nation—as equal partners. Power symmetry is a necessary condition for overcoming social, economic, and political exclusion based on race, ethnicity, and religion. Mozambican democracy must learn to see these differences not as obstacles to social and political harmony. Rather, they must be seen as opportunities for promoting dialogue,[61] the rule of law, and good governance. Such a transformation in the relations among the divergent political, economic, and social groups in the country would induce mutual collaboration.[62] But given this complex configuration, the transformation of Mozambique is bound to be a very difficult process.

Democracy has helped to end the long civil war and has facilitated mutual tolerance. In spite of ideological differences, the political forces (notably Frelimo and Renamo) have remained committed to the understanding contained in the general peace agreement. They have behaved as if they are convinced that dialogue is the best way for solving conflicts. This is what has stabilized the country to date.

Democracy has helped to promote mutual tolerance and helped to prevent actions that could provoke another war. But there is another reality at work. The two parties and their leaderships, once engaged in war against each other, remain dominant in the politics of the country. They may have disarmed their respective armed forces and established a unified army as mandated by the general peace agreement,[63] but their leaders have not undertaken a corresponding demilitarization of mentality. Thus, while their practice of democracy is strictly limited to mutual tolerance and avoidance of provocation, it has yet to extend to positive cooperation and collaboration. Frelimo and Renamo tolerate each other, but they do not collaborate to solve the problems of the country.

The incident in Montepuez in November 2000 in which over 100 people were killed, in connection with Renamo demonstrations against perceived electoral fraud, offers a good illustration of this point. A double-digit inflation was one of the direct negative economic consequences of the demonstration. Inadequate participation and unequal access to social and economical opportunities continue to fuel internal conflicts and constitute an impediment to political and social stability.

It is true that globalization has brought a development model based on a globalized economy and market. It has been imposing a "global culture," molding "global citizens," and evolving a "global nation" with no borders. But Mozambique must confront the challenge of rethinking its model of democracy and development in the same manner that it was able to find a formula for peace. And it should be a model of democracy and development that is fully participatory and inclusive.

Notes

1. Jürgen Habermas, *Direito e democracia entre facticidade e validade* [Between facts and norms], p. 85, emphasis in the original.
2. Ibid., p. 99.
3. Alain Touraine, *O que é a democracia?* [What is democracy?].
4. Ibid., p. 77.
5. Ibid., p. 64.
6. Malyn Newitt, *A History of Mozambique*, pp. 13–30.
7. Pedro Ramos de Almeida, *Historia do colonialismo português em África* [A history of Portuguese colonialism in Africa], p. 144.
8. Conselho Nacional do Plano [National Planning Council], *Informação económica* [Economic information], p. 22.
9. Direcção Nacional de Estatística [National Directorate for Statistics] (DNE), *Informação estatística 1975–1984* [Statistical information, 1975–1984], p. 38.
10. Ibid., p. 68.
11. Ministério de Educação e Cultura [Ministry of Education and Culture], *Atlas geográfico* [Geographic atlas], p. 6.
12. Ibid., p.76.
13. DNE, *Informação estatística 1985* [Statistical information, 1985], p. 22.
14. Ibid., p. 25.
15. Ibid.
16. United Nations Development Programme (UNDP), *Moçambique: crescimento económico e desenvolvimento humano: progresso, obstaculos e desafios* [Mozambique: economic growth and human development: progress, obstacles and challenges], pp. 15–16 (Relatório nacional do desenvolvimento humano [National human development report]).
17. Conselho de Ministros [Council of Ministers], *Linhas de acção para eradicação da pobreza absoluta* [Action steps for the eradication of absolute poverty], pp. 9, 18.
18. Ibid., p. 9.
19. United Nations Development Programme, *Moçambique: relatório nacional de desenvolvimento humano, 1998. Paz e crescimento económico: oportunidades*

para desenvolvimento humano [Mozambique national human development report, 1998. Peace and economic growth: opportunities for human development], p. 11.

20. Conselho de Ministros [Council of Ministers], *Linhas de acção*, p. iii.

21. Pedro Ramos de Almeida, *Historia do colonialismo português*, pp. 292–293.

22. Ibid., p. 317.

23. Ibid., p. 307.

24. R. Jaulin, *La decivilisation: politique et pratique de l'ethnocide* [Decivilisation: the politics and practice of ethnocide], p. 9.

25. Eduardo Mondlane, "Tribos ou grupos étnicos moçambicanos (seu significado na luta de liberatação nacional)" [Mozambican tribes or ethnic groups: their significance in the struggle for national liberation], p. 79.

26. In Samora Machel's well-known slogan, "The tribe must die, so that the nation may be born" (see his *Educar o homem novo para vencer a guerra* [Educate the new man to win the war]), p. 4.

27. This position was taken by the Party's First National Plenary (Primeiro Plenário Nacional) meeting in Mocuba city, Zambézia Province in 1975. See Reis and Muiuane, *Datas e documentos*, p. 308.

28. Instituto Nacional de Estatística [National Statistical Institute], *II Recenseamento geral da população e habitação, 1997: resultados definitivos* [2nd general population and housing census, 1997: final results], p. 50, tables 22–24.

29. Antonio Romão and others, *Moçambique: um país do futuro* [Mozambique: a country of the future], p. 10.

30. Partido Frelimo [Frelimo Party], *Relatório do Comité Central ao IV Congresso* [Report of the Central Committee to the 4th Congress], pp. 78–79.

31. Ibid., p. 59.

32. Frelimo, *Relatório do Comité Central ao III Congresso* [Report of the Central Committee to the 3rd Congress], p. 94.

33. Ministério de Educação e Cultura [Ministry of Education and Culture], *Sistema de educação de Moçambique* [The education system in Mozambique], p. 40.

34. Renamo has been fighting against the Frelimo government's policy since 1976.

35. In Brazão Mazula, *A construção da democracia em África: o caso moçambicano* [Building democracy in Africa: the Mozambican case], p. 128.

36. Obede Baloi and others, eds., *Estudos específicos* [Specific studies], p. 40.

37. Cf. the studies by Placide Tempels, *La philosophie bantoue* [English edition published as *Bantu philosophy*]; and P. E. A. Elungu, *L'éveil philosophique africain* [The African philosophical awakening].

38. Pedro Ramos de Almeida, *Historia do colonialismo português*, p. 144.

39. These speeches may be read in Reis and Muiuane, *Datas e documentos*, pp. 194–195, 199–228, 245–259, 431–448, 451–463, and 477–486.

40. Samora Moisés Machel, *O Partido e as classes trabalhadoras moçambicanas* [The Party and the Mozambican working class], p. 72.

41. See Norman P. Barry, *An Introduction to Modern Political Theory*, p. 270.

42. See Florentino Dick Kassotche, *Globalização* [*Globalization*], pp. 93–94.

43. Conselho de Ministros, *Linhas de acção*, p. 9.

44. Frelimo, *Construímos o futuro com as nossas maos* [Let's build the future with our own hands].

45. Jürgen Habermas, *Pensamento pós-metafísico* [*Postmetaphysical thinking*], p. 70.

46. Protocol II of the General Peace Agreement (GPA).

47. Protocol IV of the General Peace Agreement (GPA), no. 2.

48. Protocol I of the General Peace Agreement (GPA).

49. Brazão Mazula, *Eleições, democracia e desenvolvimento* [*Elections, democracy and development*], pp. 61–65.

50. Comissão Nacional de Eleições [National Electoral Commission], *Relatório final* [Final report], pp. 33, 70.

51. Today they have changed themselves into trade unions and nongovernmental organizations, maintaining strong links with the party in power.

52. Link Forum de ONGs [Link NGO Forum], *Directório de ONGs, Novembro de 2000* [NGO directory, November 2000] (Maputo, 2000).

53. Protocol II of the GPA, paragraph (a).

54. Brazão Mazula, *A construção da democracia*, p. 116.

55. Alain Touraine, *O que é a democracia?* p. 62.

56. Link Forum de ONGs.

57. Assembleia da República [Assembly of the Republic], *Regulamentos para a formação e actividades dos partidos políticos. Lei no. 7/91 de 23 de Janeiro, e Diploma Ministerial no. 11/91 de 13 de Fevereiro* [Regulations governing the formation and activities of political parties. Law no. 7/91 of 23 January and Ministerial Regulation no. 11/91 of 13 February] (Maputo, Imprensa Nacional, 1991).

58. See Mazula, *A construção da democracia*, p. 255.

59. Acordo Geral de Paz, Declaração conjunta [General Peace Agreement, Joint Declaration], paragraph I.

60. According to Kant's philosophy of conscience, individuals become citizens when they become aware that they are subjects and claim this status in society. Habermas, *Pensamento pós-metafísico*, p. 70.

61. Protocol I of the General Peace Agreement (GPA).

62. Ibid.

63. Protocol IV of the General Peace Agreement (GPA).

Nigeria:
Prospects for the Fourth Republic

Adigun Agbaje

It is disheartening that despite the metaphorical inclination towards a democratic civilian government, what is experienced everyday . . . is an ugly reminder of the past. . . . Indeed, the only difference between the present and the past is that soldiers are no longer in government. . . . But the people of these shores are expectant and forward-looking in spite of their present travails.
—Godwin Onyeacholem, "A Collapsible Entity," p. 3

Perhaps nothing captures the extent to which Nigeria astounds and confuses its well-wishers at home and abroad more than a tale of the first four anniversaries of its final transition from military to elected civil rule and the inauguration of its Fourth Republic on May 29, 1999.

Consider Scene One: The first anniversary caps a year characterized by instability, uncertainty, elite bickering, a state of gridlock between the National Assembly and the presidency at the center, as well as a sense of immobilism at the political, economic, and social levels. A few days after that anniversary is marked on May 29, 2000, the country is plunged into a nationwide strike reminiscent of the dark days of the regime of General Sani Abacha. The strike, called by the powerful central labor organization to protest the government's announcement of a 50 percent hike in the price of petrol, literally leads to a shutdown of the polity for several days, until the government announces a reduction in the hike acceptable to labor.

Scene Two: The second anniversary is held in a context in which government-owned universities and hospitals nationwide are shut down by strikes, electricity and potable water supplies remain erratic, general insecurity holds sway in the form of rising waves of assassination, communal clashes and armed robbery take place across the land, and intergovernmental as well as intragovernmental relations remain fractious, characterized by bickerings over the sharing of public revenue, responsibilities, and power, among other things.

Scene Three: It is May 29, 2002. There is lingering tension and apprehension over the failure of the federal government to resolve the brutal assassination in December 2001 of the federal attorney general, Chief Bola Ige. Nigerians are asking: If the country's chief law officer could be so easily killed in his bedroom, then who is safe? There is also a major crisis brewing between the presidency and the National Assembly over the country's privatization program and unpaid entitlements to assembly members. Added to this is uncertainty and bickering over the tenure of local governments.

Scene Four: The fourth anniversary, coinciding with the inauguration of the second set of elected office holders in the republic's thirty-six states and the center, is held against the backcloth of disagreements over election results, with parties opposed to the ruling party at the center challenging the reelection of President Olusegun Obasanjo and calling for "mass action" even as some local and international observers raise critical questions about the results. Universities remain shut due to a strike stretching back to 2002, and organized labor threatens to violently resist any attempt by government to increase the pump price of petrol, although by the middle of June it reportedly tones down its rhetoric and gives conditional approval for the hike. Political and criminal violence recur at an unacceptable rate. Ige's murder remains unsolved. There is a heightened state of insecurity following the appearance of Nigeria on a "hit list" of "infidel countries" purportedly released by Osama bin Laden in the post–September 11, 2001, world.

Given all this, it is not surprising that as Nigerian federalism moves beyond the first four years of the first set of elected civilian governments in the Fourth Republic, little has been done in the area of seeking to construct and consolidate the republic's nascent democracy, reinvigorate and turn its economy into a productive one, and satisfy the people's yearning for a better life. Of course, the point is not lost on Nigerians that the current parlous state of democracy and development is due in part to the many years of undemocratic rule (military *and* civil) to which their country has been exposed. These events have weakened the structures and processes of constitutionalism, defined not simply as government under a constitution but as the observance of due process and the rule of law in the running of politics, the economy, and social (including private) life. In the same vein, it is also conceded that the current crop of leadership in the Fourth Republic, along with the mass of the people themselves, have not had significant experience with democracy and its management. The nature of the transition to the Fourth Republic neither prepared the emerging leadership for responsible behavior nor allowed for the full negotiation and renegotiation of the construction and revalorization of strong ramparts for democracy and development in the emerging republic.[1]

Despite all this, as the prefatory note above clearly indicates, Nigerians still identify with the democratic experiment, but it is a matter for conjecture how long they will continue to do so if democracy does not deliver dividends in the areas of peace, freedoms, equity, security, and development. The old Nigerian adage that no condition is permanent is fast becoming a constant warning to the Nigerian political elite. For what historical and comparative evidence underscores is that any form of governance, dictatorial or democratic, that fails at the level of economic and social performance can only be provisional in the medium to long term.

The main task of this chapter is to capture the primary challenges to the reconstruction and consolidation of democracy and development in this deeply troubled country, and how the two phenomena of democracy and development interact and complement, or fail to interact or complement, each other and to what effect. The goal is to explore the causal roots of Nigeria's troubled and limited experience with democracy as well as its developmental problems. Questions that arise in this regard, to which this chapter seeks to provide answers, include the following: What is the central challenge, or nexus of challenges, for democracy and development in Nigeria? Why have things gone so wrong? And what must change if Nigeria is ever to be able to sustain democracy and develop economically? The rest of the chapter seeks to provide empirical answers and insights to these issues against a background of a theoretical/analytical argument about the causal roots of the Nigerian dilemma and matters arising from the questions listed above.

Democracy and Development: Contested Aspirations, the Dearth of Reality, and Other Tragedies

It is generally agreed in informed quarters that Nigeria is an unfinished state of uncertainty.[2] A much troubled state since it was put together by British colonialists through the famous amalgamation of imperial northern and southern possessions in 1914, it has swung erratically and without rhythm from colonial rule to versions of a civil democratic order (1960–1966) in the First Republic and then from one military government to the other (1966, 1975, 1985) with a short interregnum of elected civil rule (1979–1983) and an unelected interim government (August–November 1993) punctuated by the return of the military (1993–1999). While it has witnessed two completed transitions from military to elected civil rule (in 1979 and 1999) leading to the Second and Fourth Republics, as well as a truncated one now described as the aborted Third Republic under General Ibrahim Babangida, the country has witnessed neither a successful and sustained constitutional transfer of power nor a consolidation of any type of rule, military or civil, undemocratic or democratic.

In effect, Nigeria remains a state of aspirations unmatched by reality. While the balance of aspirations has historically been in favor of a federal system of government, which was in fact officially adopted by the country in 1954 while still under colonial rule, Nigeria has in practice actually operated a more or less unitary system with a strong center for much of the postindependence era following the collapse of the First Republic (1960–1966). This is not surprising, since effective federalism can be practiced only in a democratic context.[3] In addition, while the balance of aspirations is generally identified as being antagonistic to the consolidation of undemocratic rule, Nigerians have experienced a meaningful experimentation with democracy for only a few years (1960–1962 in the First Republic and 1979–1982 in the Second, the truncated Third Republic having played itself out under the military regime of General Babangida between the late 1980s and the early 1990s) since the 1914 amalgamation. And by no means least important, popular and officially declared commitments to development expressed regularly in well-crafted national development plans as well as micro-level community action have not meaningfully transformed the Nigerian economy from one obsessed with consumption, rent-seeking, and neopatrimonial practice to one concerned with production and capacity building for long-term development.

Essentially, therefore, as Nigeria moves to reconstruct and consolidate democracy in the Fourth Republic, it is faced with an experience deficit in those core areas that are traditionally held up as defining its aspirations and raison d'être and guaranteeing its future as well as its assumed status as a regional power. These core areas can be described as democracy, development, and federalism, and this lack of experience poses the primary challenge to Nigerians and their leaders. The challenge is made all the more daunting by the complex interconnectedness of democracy, development, and federalism for a resource-rich country of such big size and diversity as Nigeria.

Nigeria is by far the most populous country in Africa, with a population of about 120 million made up of ethnic nationalities and linguistic groups estimated at between 250 and 400. Of these, the major groups (in alphabetical order) include the Edo, Efik, Fula (Fulani), Gbagyi (Gwari), Hausa, Ibibio, Idoma, Igala, Igbo (Ibo), Ijaw, Itsekiri, Kanuri, Nupe, Tiv, Urhobio, and Yoruba, among others. It is an equally diverse country in religious terms. The three major religions include the indigenous forms (themselves as diverse as the country itself), Christianity (with Catholics, Pentecostals, and Protestants forming the majority) and Islam (with the Quadriyya, Ahmadists, Tijaniyya, Wahabbiyya, and the Syncretics, among others).

The country occupies a total land area of 923,773 square kilometers (356,669 square miles) that traverses several ecological zones from the swamp region of the coast to the Sahel savanna of the northernmost parts. It is thus richly blessed in resources. Major minerals include crude oil, the mainstay of its economy, natural gas, bitumen, tin/columbite, coal, limestone, and uranium. Major export crops include cocoa, hides and skin, cotton, oil palm, groundnuts, and rubber.

The occasional coincidence of the boundaries of geopolitical, regional, ethnic, religious, and major resource considerations, as well as popular perceptions or reinterpretations of the limits of these identities, have further complicated the Nigerian landscape against the backdrop of its largely undemocratic tradition of governance. In addition to a tendency to emphasize exclusionary practices, this impedes the development and adoption of strategies for positive, inclusive, integrative, accountable, and transparent management of differences and heightens combative identities, particularly in the context of resource generation and distribution.[4] On the positive side, the expectation would be that the collective memory of the events that led to the thirty-month civil war (1967–1970) that pitched Eastern Nigeria (which renamed itself the Republic of Biafra) against the rest of Nigeria in a secession bid would stand the country in good stead in grappling with these problems.

For Nigeria, all this creates a particular set of challenges and opportunities in the current context:

- The challenge of managing ethnic, regional, and religious tension against a backdrop of the tendency of the authoritarian past and its persisting elements in the post-1999 order to accentuate such tension. This challenge should also be considered in the light of the potential for democratization to generate its own set of destabilizing effects in such countries as big and complex as Nigeria where democratization has not been preceded or accompanied by widespread elite and non-elite consensus as to intent and content. The problem is exarcebated where there is strong and occasionally violent expression of group rights, often without the required sense of responsibility or respect for due process or appropriate institutional vehicles and channels. Restructuring the federal arrangement and addressing the differing visions of what Nigeria should be are imperatives here.
- The related challenge of turning Nigeria's size, resource endowment, and diversity into strong ramparts for genuinely federal democracy and economic development. In terms of economic possibilities, the range of policy options available to Nigeria as a result of its size is replicable only in a few other African countries, such as South Africa. The challenge, therefore, would be to manage the "downside" to Nigeria's size in the political realm to enable the country to derive full economic benefits from its size.
- The challenge of addressing corrupt and rent-seeking practices in order to create appropriate foundations for viable economic growth and a coherent social order.

In comparative perspective, the Nigerian case poses the question of what happens to the nexus of democracy and development in countries emerging from long periods of dictatorship and its attendant corruption with very little or no experience (among the elite and nonelite) in the democratic governance of the political and economic realms and the democratic management of differences and dissent.

If Nigeria has anything to show for having passed through many years of undemocratic rule, it is the validation of the iron law, namely, *no constitutional order, no democracy; no democracy, no development*. It is for this reason that a symbiotic line can be traced linking democracy, constitutionalism, and development in the Nigerian context. If Nigeria has had this long experience (a minimum of twenty-nine out of forty-three years of independence) with dictatorial and unconstitutional rule, resulting in the distressed state in which it finds itself today, what better evidence could there be for the point that undemocratic rule does not pay? This, of course, is an argument by default, and one specific to the Nigerian case. It is not to suggest, for instance, that the more democratic a polity becomes, the more developed it will become. Rather, it is to emphasize the lessons of the Nigerian past, written largely by despots and their fellow travelers. In the second sense, it is not being argued that there are no other cases in which undemocratic rule has presided over a developmental regime.

At the comparative level, this point on the Nigerian case nonetheless poses a challenge to the position that proposes the nondemocratic path to good governance and development. For one, such an argument is not very sensitive to the fact that, shorn of its core defining characteristic, the concept and practice labeled "authoritarian" is not a constant, but that its "form, manifestation and consequences vary from country to country."[5] More specifically, there is growing evidence that it is only through the consolidation of democratic governance that practices conducive to efficiency, economic well-being, and social justice such as respect for individual and group rights as well as a shift from distributive logic to productive logic can emerge. In other words, it is becoming increasingly clear that the conditions required for lasting democracy, including the observance of rules and rights, are the same as those required for the creation of an efficient, developmental regime and social peace and for ensuring that when conflicts do occur, they do not degenerate into unmanageable proportions.[6]

Implicit in the argument so far is the point that undemocratic rule can only lead in the long run to poor performance. The search for constitutional governance, therefore, is by definition a search for or revalidation of democracy and development. While governance is a feature of all social systems,[7] it is difficult, in light of Nigeria's experience, to subscribe to the notion that undemocratic and unconstitutional practice can provide development and good governance in a sustained manner without unraveling and transforming itself into a more democratic and constitutional dispensation. Evidence of this abounds in Asia. In the same manner, it appears that the more authoritarian a regime is, and the more it lacks constitutional authority, the more it can only provide poor governance and underdevelopment in the very long run.

It is important to underscore the emphasis on a constitutional order in this formulation, rather than merely identifying the presence of a constitution as the foundational basis for democracy. For, "while Nigeria has produced many constitutions, it has yet to entrench constitutionalism."[8] The country witnessed ten written constitutions between 1922 and 1999 (specifically, the 1922, 1946, 1951, 1954, 1960, 1963, 1979, 1989, 1995, and 1999 constitutions). In effect, much attention has gone into the making of constitutions, but little success has been achieved in ensuring that "governments govern according to the constitution and that the rule of law is enforced in place of capricious governance."[9] None of these constitutions were initiated and drafted under a genuinely democratic environment, and virtually all were conceived as gifts from autocrats to a besotted people.

The implications of this for the nature of the Nigerian state as it has evolved since it was founded under British colonial rule in 1914 are ominous, if clear. If it is agreed that Nigeria has been more or less in permanent transition since amalgamation in 1914,[10] then it is obvious that such a transition has not fully succeeded in "domesticating" and democratizing the Nigerian state and its institutions. Literally imposed from outside by colonial fiat and sustained thereafter by a largely undemocratic local elite (military and civil), the Nigerian state remains "unfinished,"[11] hence uncertain and incoherent, lacking the required dosage of legitimacy and popular acceptance for transforming it from a weak and unstable contraption of force into a strong, restrained, and effective system of contractual rule.[12] Under colonial rule, Nigerian constitutions "were not designed to build a Nigerian state; rather, they were measures of administrative strategies for better administration of the colonial state, although occasionally they bent to the realities of increased political consciousness among the colonial elite."[13] In the period leading to independence in 1960 and thereafter, the emerging local political elite manipulated ethnic, religious, and other sectional symbols to their advantage, in the process ensuring that Nigerians would continue to "hold different views about limits on the state" and be "(mostly) unwilling to defend those limits,"[14] thus creating fertile ground for unconstitutional rule in which "the sovereign can violate these limits and retain sufficient support to survive."[15] Given this lack of trust and common views on such limits, the net result has been a largely unrestrained state that, for this reason, chips away at the sources of its own strength, eroding its legitimacy and confirming yet again Joel Migdal's assertion about the paradox of elusive power.[16] In essence, therefore, constitutionalism in the form of the triumph of the rule of law and due process in public and private life should provide the solid foundation for good governance and development within a democratic dispensation in Nigeria's Fourth Republic.

Travails of the Fourth Republic

The point has been made elsewhere that the thirteen-year transition that led to the Fourth Republic in 1999 actually increased Nigerians' exposure to the harsher forms of military rule and dictatorship while officially and publicly committing the unelected rulers of the period to democratization.[17] The transition period witnessed three transition programs announced in turn by the governments of General Ibrahim Babangida (1985–1993), General Sani Abacha (1993–1998), and General Abdulsalami Abubakar (1998–1999).

The announced terminal dates for the programs were in several instances changed, a presidential election was annulled in 1993, polarizing the country into north and south, while the regime of General Abacha (a northern general like the other two) brought the country close to disintegration and anarchy. This flirtation with anarchy stemmed from Abacha's penchant for exploiting the country's deep ethnic divisions to wage war against all forms of opposition, but especially the western part of the country, home base of Chief M. K. O. Abiola, winner of the 1993 presidential election annulled by his predecessor, General Babangida. Abacha in November 1993 sacked an unelected interim government put in place by Babangida before relinquishing power in August 1993 and clamped Abiola into detention in 1994 for daring to declare himself president-elect. Abacha died in office in June 1998 shortly before a scheduled election programmed to ensure his transformation from unelected military ruler to elected president. Abiola himself died in detention barely a month later, paving the way for the new military ruler, Abubakar, to preside over the last phase of the political transition to the Fourth Republic and the inauguration of General Obasanjo as the elected president of the republic on May 29, 1999.

For much of the 1990s, therefore, emphasis was on political chicanery, with the economy suffering not only from neglect or lack of sustained and rational policy focus but also from the regime of sanctions imposed on Nigeria by the leading players in the international community, including the United States, the European Union, the UN system, and the Commonwealth, among others. In effect, from Babangida to Abacha (1986–1998), Nigeria for the first time witnessed military administrations that, in the guise of democratization, "focused resources and energy on weakening the structures for national government, accountability and democratic participation even as they . . . moved to strengthen the institutions for arbitrary, oppressive and insensitive personal rule."[18]

The major focus of the Abubakar administration was to organize, in less than a year, the full transition to elected civil rule. It therefore did not impact positively on the legacy eventually bequeathed to the Fourth Republic. It was a flawed legacy lacking the required base, experience, resources, and dispositions for democratic governance and its ingredients. The net result has been that the leaders and institutions of the Fourth Republic, especially in the executive and legislative arms at all levels of government (central, state and local), as well as the mass of the people, generally lack significant experience with democracy and its management for social progress and economic development.[19] In looking at the travails of the Fourth Republic, including openings, opportunities, challenges, and dilemmas as they have unfolded since May 1999, I group these in the rest of this section under constitutional and legal imperatives, the political terrain, sociocultural dimensions, and economic issues.

Constitutional and Legal Matters

There is a respected body of opinion that believes that the 1999 constitution of the Fourth Republic is fundamentally flawed.[20] Even the presidency as well as the first National Assembly of the Fourth Republic set up parallel commissions to collate views on areas of the constitution that needed to be reviewed. An even farther-reaching step was taken by the Citizens Forum for Constitutional Reform (CFCR), a nationwide network of civil society organizations, to review the same constitution.[21] It has been pointed out, for instance, that the constitution's prefatory statement, alluding to the role of the Nigerian people in its making, is fraudulent, given the fact that the final version of the document was authored by a few military officers in the countdown to the Fourth Republic.

Beyond this, several provisions of the constitution have been widely criticized.[22] For instance, although it is nominally a federal constitution, it gives too much power to the federal government in relation to state governments while leaving the third tier of government (i.e., local government) literally at the mercy of state governments.[23] The principles of separation of powers and checks and balances have also not been well observed, with the president being given wide, including legislative, powers, especially through subsisting transitional provisions in Section 315 of the constitution. In addition, the short period of the constitution's operation has witnessed the calling into question of one of its major tenets, namely, the secularity of the Nigerian state, in the wake of controversies, allegations, and counterallegations that have followed the decision of some state governments to legislate on matters of Islamic law for their states.

Another vital constitutional issue concerns resource management. The provisions of the constitution in relation to the powers to raise taxation appear for now to favor the federal government over states and local governments, providing the material bases for a centralizing or, worse still, a unitaristic framework for the country's putative federal framework.

In addition, existing provisions remain unsatisfactory to mineral-producing, especially oil-bearing, parts of the country, and this has led to crises in such areas. A scheme needs to be put in place to increase the level of resources flowing into such areas, which are often coterminous with the territories of politically marginalized ethnic minorities. For instance, it should be possible to ensure that a significant proportion of mining rents, royalties, and taxes on other exploited resources is allocated to a state in which such activity is carried out. This problem touches on a fundamental problem in governance relating to the extent to which local communities should benefit from resources extracted from their areas, especially when such resources are largely unreplenishable and destructive of other resources in the community.[24]

The centralizing drift in constitutional design (or its abrogation under military rule) can be traced through chronological analysis of government allocations from the immediate years before independence onward. Following the 1954 constitution, which regionalized control over major foreign exchange earners as well as personal income, the regions were allocated 50.4 percent and the central government 49.6 percent of public revenue in the 1959–1960 fiscal year. After the 1966 coups the central government assumed more tax powers and took over or subsidized the functions of state governments; in the 1980s it established and managed special accounts (such as a stabilization fund, dedicated accounts, and a petroleum trust fund). Following the reports of the Aboyade and Okigbo Commissions in the late 1970s and early 1980s, the federal government began to get a greater share of revenue. For much of the 1990s, over 45 percent of revenue allocated went to the federal government on average, compared to about 24 percent to all states and 20 percent to all local governments. As little as 3 percent of revenue was specially shared among oil-producing states for the development of their areas. Since the founding of the Fourth Republic, it has been constitutionally mandatory that not less than 13 percent of revenue accruing to the Federation Account from any natural resources shall be allocated to the area from which such resources are extracted (as provided for in Section 162[2]). The oil-producing areas are asking for more, however, often in a manner that antagonizes other areas, as was witnessed when virtually all northern members of the Nigerian House of Representatives voted down a bill for resource control for oil-bearing areas in 2001. In addition, issues so relating to resource control with regard to oil and control of territorial waters became a subject of litigation at the Supreme Court in 2001, which subsequently confirmed the federal government's preeminence on this issue.

The task of redesigning the constitution for better governance can be facilitated only when the appropriate level of consensus has been reached among the various fractions of the Nigerian political class. Unfortunately, however, and in contrast with the South African experience in which the transition to postapartheid democracy was preceded by the conscious negotiation of pacts and consensus building, the posttransition period in Nigeria has been marked by a lack of consensus among the Nigeria political elite on what to do. This has been the case on virtually every important and not-so-important issue of the day, thereby turning governance into a perpetually contentious enterprise.

In specific terms, the CFCR document recommends the need to make the process of remaking the constitution more inclusive, participatory, transparent, autonomous of government, accountable, and therefore more legitimate in the eyes of the people through a referendum to test the popularity of the new draft constitution when completed. It calls for a more gender-sensitive constitution in language and content and for more autonomy for such commissions as those in charge of elections, the judiciary, anti-corruption, human rights, mass media, gender and social justice, the office of the public defender, national orientation and mobilization, and the national census. Some of these commissions (such as those for gender and social justice, mass media, the office of the public defender, human rights, and national orientation) either are currently not constitutional creatures or do not exist at all. The CFCR document seeks to abridge the powers of the electoral commission.

On citizenship, the CFCR document recommends that Nigerians who have lived in and performed their duties in a given state for five years should be entitled to all the rights and privileges enjoyed by indigenes of the state. The rights of minorities and the disabled should also be protected. The CFCR document calls for a less centrist federal system as well as fiscal federalism that would enable federating units to exercise control and ownership of the resources in their areas while paying taxes on same to the federal government.

In its own reports, the Presidential Committee lists contentious issues in the 1999 constitution as including the following:[25]

- The constitution's preamble lies in claiming that the document was put together by the Nigerian people.
- Nigeria's federal system is federal only in name but is unitary in content.
- The constitution does not establish clearly and without contradictions the secularity of the Nigerian state.
- Federal control of judicial institutions and personnel in the states is excessive.

- The constitution has not fully addressed the principle of derivation in revenue allocation—to the effect that areas from which resources providing public revenue for the federation are derived receive a special percentage from the Federation Account for that reason.
- The constitution not only is gender-insensitive but also contains no affirmative clauses to address historical injustices and discriminations against women.
- The National Human Rights Commission should have been enshrined in the constitution and empowered further to handle socioeconomic and cultural rights.
- The constitution upholds the language rights of major ethnic groups without granting equal status to other languages.
- The constitution should, given Nigeria's experience, draw lessons from South Africa, Ghana, and Uganda on how to contain and control the military.
- In state-federal relations, the center has too much power.
- The constitution does not have a clear definition of social indigeneship that guarantees full rights to Nigerians in any part of the country.
- There are no institutions built into the constitution to enhance constitutionalism; in other words, there are no institutions to make the constitution a living document accessible to all Nigerians.
- There is disagreement as to whether or not to empower the states to establish their own police services in addition to the existing federal police force.
- The federal government has too much control over the formation and registration of parties, and existing provisions negate the right to form small parties exclusively for local politics.
- Existing provisions for constitutional amendments can only frustrate the process because they are cumbersome, expensive, and unrealistic.
- The Land Use Decree, which vests land in the federal government, is undemocratic in a federal system.
- Local government has not been accorded due status.

On the basis of all these issues, the committee proceeded to make specific recommendations. Of interest here is the level of agreement between the constitution and the CFCR document as well as the extent to which the 1999 constitution is considered unsuitable for the reconstruction and consolidation of a democratic order in Nigeria in the search for peaceful development. In fact, much of the other matters arising as outlined below partly derive from these constitutional issues.

It is therefore appropriate at this stage to further contextualize, albeit briefly, three of these constitutional concerns, namely those on secularity, decentralization, and citizenship. Before the 1999 constitution, states wishing to do so were allowed to set up a (Muslim) *sharia* legal system to adjudicate matters of civil personal law, and not only was the *sharia* court system inferior to courts of record (the State High Court, the Federal High Court, the Court of Appeal—also federal—and the Supreme Court of the Federation), but it was also barred in law from adjudicating matters in which at least one party was a Christian. The ambiguities in the 1999 constitution have led some state governments in the north to pass legislation that in effect extends the application of *sharia* law to criminal law, with some taking the extra step of literally turning their states into Islamic states with prescriptions on mode of dressing and banning of sale of alcohol not only for Muslims but for Christians and other adherents residing in their states.

Given Christians' long-standing suspicion and conspiracy thesis arising from the dominance of Muslims in the military administrations preceding 1999, as well as the history of religious upheavals and the controversies that had always trailed attempts to broaden the scope of *sharia* in previous constitution-making exercises, it did not take long before it was widely held in the Fourth Republic that the ambiguities in the 1999 constitution had been smuggled into the document at the last minute by such Muslim generals.

In October 1999 the stakes were raised when Governor Ahmed Sani Yerima of Zamfara, a largely Muslim state, formally fixed January 2000 as the date for the adoption of the broader *sharia* legal system. Several other states in the north subsequently announced plans to follow suit. The attempt in February 2000 by the Kaduna House of Assembly to pass similar legislation, despite the predominance of Christians in southern Kaduna, led to massacres and arson on both sides, with allegations that foreigners had been brought in to strengthen the hands of one group as well as reports of splits in the security forces on how the mayhem should be handled.

The Kaduna killings, which also had ethnic and regional colorations, with southerners and people of middle-belt stock becoming targets of attacks from Muslim elements, led to retaliatory killings in several cities in the south, especially in the Igbo east. One or two states in the south (specifically Cross River) also threatened to established a canonical (Christian) legal system while the Abia state governor went on air and threatened to organize retaliatory killing of northerners in his state.

President Obasanjo's initial stance was to threaten tough federal sanction against such states as Zamfara, but it soon became clear that even his own administration was divided over how to respond to this development. Subsequently, rather than seek judicial interpretation, the president and his attorney general adopted a new position to the effect that the *sharia* initiative was basically a political fad that would soon fade away or collapse in the face of its own contradictions. For the president and his associates, this was a politically expedient position to take in order not to alienate a significant mass of northern Muslims who were showing support for this version of *sharia* and often seizing the initiative from their governors in this regard. It must be pointed out here that the idea of the secular state is coming under increasing siege globally, and even more so in Nigeria—from not only Muslim but also Christian fundamentalists and revivalists.

On the issue of decentralization, the Nigerian context has been interestingly different from that of neighboring Ghana. Decentralization preceded democratization in Ghana, and the institutional and cultural requirements for meaningful decentralization had become fully routinized and were perceived to be working well from the 1980s onward in that country. On the other hand, much emphasis was placed in the Nigerian case on a democratic transition that turned out to lack content, and decentralization was perceived more or less as a process of creating more states and local governments, more often as a way of dispensing favors and patronage, with the end product being the progressive reduction in size, influence, and affluence of the federating units in relation to the center.

On indigeneity as a basis for full citizenship of the federating states in Nigeria, it is important to note that it is only since the 1979 constitution that this practice has assumed constitutional status.[26] As a result, two constitutional categories of citizenship for Nigerians were introduced: national citizenship, which was largely unproblematic; and, state citizenship or indigeneity. Segun Osoba and Yusuf Bala Usman (who were members of the committee whose 1976 draft report was amended to become the 1979 constitution) described the second category in their dissenting *Minority Report* as

> state citizenship (i.e. indigeneity) [which] is even more stringent and biologically determined than national citizenship in the sense that it does not make on state citizenship comparable provisions to those on national citizenship by registration or naturalization . . . no matter how long a Nigerian has resided in a state of Nigeria of which none of his parents is an indigene, such a Nigerian cannot enjoy the right to participate fully in the public life of that state.[27]

Obviously, a vital step toward addressing the persistent problems of ethnicity and regional chauvinism will have been taken when the indigeneity qualification for full citizenship of the federating units (states, local government areas, even communities) is gradually and sensitively replaced by liberal residency clauses. The interests that have grown around the principle of indigeneity are entrenched and countrywide, touching as they do on such vital issues as ancestral land, access to resources, and other preferments. Wide consultations and a process of consensus building would therefore be required to meaningfully tackle this problem. On the other hand, since the practice is not restricted to a part of the country, the task should not be too daunting, more so since the benefits from prosecuting the task are immense. In the words of a group of Nigerians from all parts of the country who took part in a democracy audit of the Fourth Republic: "There is a need to redefine citizenship on the basis of residency to redress sexual, ethnic and gender identities, to redefine the federal character to de-emphasize ethnicity, or reconcile ethnicity, citizenship and indigeneity."[28]

The Political Terrain

The Fourth Republic was born in 1999 in the context of apparently increasing ungovernability of the Nigerian polity at the political level, among other factors. A major challenge thereafter, which has remained largely unattended to successfully, is that of turning the choppy waters and unpredictability of the political terrain into a stable platform for national rebirth without overturning the ship of state or losing any of its crew and passengers. Issues that must be examined here include the quality of political leadership, the institutional framework for governance and attendant consequences for intergovernmental relations, the increasing salience of violence as an instrument of politicking, and the nature of the evolving civil-military relations.

The republic started off on a wrong footing with its founding elections being perceived as having been widely rigged and the legitimacy of the regime in contention. However, the overriding need to get the military out of governance ensured popular acceptance of the outcome of the elections, regardless of shortcomings. A similar shadow of doubt was cast over the outcome of the 2003 elections, with key losers in the presidential election going as far as to call for "mass action" against the ruling party's alleged victory. It did appear, however, that the ruling party's saving grace remained the determination of Nigerians to hold on to democracy, no matter how flawed. Nonetheless, a huge question mark continues to be attached to the quality of persons elected and appointed to high office in the republic. Many are either retired military officers unable to distance their regimented and high-handed past from the requirements of democratic governance, young and inexperienced persons, or others with known shady pasts linked to such practices as fraud and obtaining unmerited privileges and resources through false claims (known in Nigeria as "419 scam people") or linked to the drug trade. The elections that ushered in the republic were held under a shadow of doubt as to the commitment of the military to hand over power to elected civilians, and understandably many qualified and competent Nigerians opted out of the fray.

To be sure, the republic cannot be said to count among its managers only people of low character, but evidence of shortsightedness, arbitrariness, selfishness, intolerance of opposition, opportunism, and crass ignorance of the requirements of a democratic dispensation abound among those chosen to preside over the affairs of the country.[29] This problem was highlighted by heightened maneuverings among former military president Ibrahim Babangida and retired military officers and civilians who had served under his unpopular government and that of the late general Sani Abacha. The fact that the 2003 presidential election was essentially a contest between two retired army generals—incumbent president Olusegun Obasanjo of the People's Democratic Party (PDP) and General Muhammadu Buhari of the All Nigeria People's Party (ANPP), both of them former military heads of state, with retired major-general Ike Nwachukwu and former Biafran warlord Emeka Ojukwu also featured—underscored the extent to which the retired military had become entrenched in the republic's political life.

To compound the problem, the institutional bases for governance of the political realm are also weak and require strengthening. Such institutions as the legislatures at the federal and state levels as well as the political parties, which are crucial to ensuring accountability and effective governance, are weak and shallow. With little experience in constitutional governance, some of their operatives perceive their role essentially as that of supervisor and/ or opposition to the executive. Others are unable to clearly separate their functions from those of the executive branch and thereby try to usurp executive functions while neglecting their own constitutional roles. The most serious altercation in this regard almost led to the impeachment of President Obasanjo in the second half of 2002 over allegations that were neither grave nor very clear.

On the other hand, the president and many of the governors heading the executive branch appear to have thoroughly imbibed a militaristic culture intolerant of institutions and procedures of restraint. This intolerance manifests itself in their dealings with the legislature, occasionally in the manner in which they or their agents respond or fail to respond to judicial pronouncements, and also in the peremptory manner in which they deal with lower tiers of government.

The various scandals and crises in which prominent operatives of the Fourth Republic have been embroiled since shortly after its inauguration can only have negatively impacted on the process of institutionalization and capacity building for the proper governance of the political realm. A good example would include the scandal that led to the resignation and prosecution of the first speaker of the House of Representatives, the removal of the founding Senate president and his successor, as well as the impeachment of several speakers of state assemblies and quarrels between several governors and their deputies. In addition, leading operatives of legislative houses at the federal and state levels often interpret the principle of separation of powers in a maximalist sense to mean an absence of extralegislative, specifically executive, checks on their actions.

Effectively, therefore, key institutions for ensuring recruitment, political restraint, and vertical accountability (people to government) as well as horizontal accountability (intragovernment),[30] such as the electoral commission, the legislature, and the Code of Conduct Bureau, are not strong enough or willing to discharge their functions objectively and effectively. The Independent National Electoral Commission has not been able to demonstrate adequate autonomy from the federal government and the PDP, the party in power at the center. Its position is often too close to that of the PDP, as in the controversy in 2001 over whether the commission should register new parties to join the existing ones—the PDP, the All People's Party (APP), and the Alliance for Democracy (AD).

For its own part, the judiciary emerged from military rule with some of its previously enviable image tainted by disdain for court rulings, questionable appointments to the higher bench, and tales of corruption and inadequate resources, especially in states.[31] To stem the problem of irregular salaries and dearth of resources for the judiciary at the state level, a National Judicial Service Commission, through which resources to courts of record in the states are channeled and which also plays a role in appointment and removal of state judicial officers, has now been created. Critics say that this violates federalism, but state judges appear to prefer the system. Overall, the judiciary, as epitomized by courts of record at the state and federal levels and especially by the apex judicial body, the Supreme Court, has gradually won over many Nigerians with the quality of judgments it has delivered on such matters as the tenure of local governments, resource control, and the constitutionality of federal legislation, among others. It has emerged as a stabilizing and deadlock-breaking factor in the polity.

Generally, if unaddressed, institutional erosion could gradually substitute electoralism and democratism for a properly functioning electoral and democratic process, a replacement of substance with appearance. Left unchecked, the republic will end up with elections that are highly inadequate and a democratic process emptied of much of its democratic content and credentials. The controversy that followed the 2003 elections, real or manufactured, shows clearly that this problem is intractable and alive and well in the perception of Nigerians. The challenge, therefore, is to effectively institutionalize practices that are conducive to good governance and democracy. This will ensure not only that democracy is maintained but also that it is effectively attained in substance and consolidated nationally as literally the only game in town.[32]

Simultaneously, cause and effect of a low level of institutionalization and routinization of the political process is the rising profile of violence or the threat of violence as a means of venting grievance, attracting attention, forcing negotiation, or seeking advantage in the political arena. Key political figures, including local government chairpersons, councilors, party officials at all levels (national, state, and local), state commissioners and advisers, as well as political/rights activists have been attacked, kidnapped, assassinated, and harassed in states as diverse as Lagos, Ondo, Oyo, Anambra, Abia, Rivers, Bayelsa, Enugu, Kano, Plateau, Osun, Kaduna, Nassarawa, Akwa Ibom, and Taraba, among others. Factions in virtually all the political parties (from three in 1999 to thirty by late 2002) have been susceptible to serious internal conflicts symptomatic of a lack of coherence and have had recourse to violence to pursue their interests or enforce their rights.

Ethnic and regional groups and their militias have equally become a major part of the political landscape, often inflicting or threatening to inflict violence for political advantage. Such groups as the Oodua People's Congress (OPC) in the Yoruba west, the Movement for the Actualization of the Sovereign State of Biafra (MASSOB) in the Igbo east, the Arewa People's Congress (APC), the militant wing of the Arewa Consultative Forum (ACF) in the north, and the Egbesu among the Ijaw of the Niger Delta, among others, assert their own version of the interests of their nationalities/regions in Nigerian politics, occasionally with violent means or threats thereof. The OPC, MASSOB, and the Egbesu clearly pursue an agenda against perceived marginalization and for self-determination that is often difficult to separate from an agenda of secession for the groups they claim to represent, and for this and other reasons they are constantly under security surveillance. Ganiyu Adams, the barely educated leader of the more militant faction of the OPC (Frederick Fasheun is leader of the other faction) was declared wanted by the police for over a year. The MASSOB leader, Ralph Uwazurike, has been in and out of prisons and police cells constantly since 1999, with his latest detention experience covering the period March 29–June 6, 2003.[33] Initially, MASSOB was not known for violent acts.[34] One of its first actions was to petition the United Nations and to issue what it called the "Biafra Bill of Rights." Uwazurike's travails in the hands of the police are due partly to the images of Biafra constantly deployed by him and his movement. In his petition to the UN, he announced that "the said Biafra are currently struggling to gain independence from Nigeria. We, therefore, under the present circumstance, humbly apply to be admitted, registered or treated, as the case may be, as an unrepresented nation in any of the organs of the United Nations, having renounced our Nigerian nationality."[35] By 2000 and 2001, MASSOB had started singing the old Biafran anthem and planting the Biafran flag in Igbo cities, threatening to "invade" Lagos and allegedly forcing Biafran currencies on traders in parts of Abia state, and engaging in strong-arm tactics against perceived opponents, among other acts.

The Egbesu "boys" constitute the more militant arm of the more broad-based Supreme Egbesu Assembly, itself part of the Niger Delta Consultative Assembly, which was initiated to prosecute the agenda and provide a common front for all the diverse (often warring and divided) ethnic groups in the oil-bearing Niger Delta, stretching from Rivers, Bayelsa, Cross River, and

Akwa Ibom to Delta and Edo states. Shortly after it was formed, the Niger Delta Consultative Assembly impaneled a group to prepare a draft constitution for the Delta people by April 2000 that would form a basis for their renegotiation of the Delta's future relations with the rest of Nigeria, backing this up with the threat that "if they will not hasten, we will compel Nigerians to listen. Nigerians cannot be forced to live together."[36]

As indicated earlier, the Egbesu "boys" are an Ijaw militant group.[37] Renegades from this group have been accused of going beyond political action into such criminal activities as piracy, armed robbery, and extortion.[38] Of interest here, however, is the series of political events that led President Obasanjo to order the military sacking of Odi, an Ijaw town in the Kolokuma/Opukoma council area of Bayelsa state. Apparently in line with the exhortation in the Ijaw Nation's Kaiama Declaration in December 1998 that Nigeria's security forces, in their deployment to protect oil operations in Ijaw territory, be viewed "as an enemy of the Ijaw people,"[39] Ijaw youths in Odi on November 4 and November 8, 1999, attacked and killed policemen stationed in their area as well as those sent on a surveillance mission to Odi "following security reports received by the state police command that the Ijaw Youths [had] procured more sophisticated weapons."[40] As a result, the government sacked the entire town. This remains a dark spot in the Obasanjo administration's rights record to date.

The Arewa People's Congress was formed partly in reaction to what was perceived as the role of OPC in communal clashes involving Yoruba communities and their "Hausa" (read "northern") settler or trading communities in Lagos, Ogun, and Oyo states, among others. These clashes predate 1999 but have since intensified. The APC constantly threatens to avenge further killings of northerners in the south, a threat that has subsequently been endorsed and appropriated by the mainstream ACF and the regular meeting of the governors of the nineteen northern states. Much of July and August 2001 witnessed threats by the OPC to march on Ilorin and install a Yoruba *oba* (traditional ruler or king) there. Ilorin is a major city of the Yoruba that, because it is the capital of Kwara, a state traditionally considered as belonging to northern Nigeria, as well as for historical reasons, has in modern times had a Fulani emir as its traditional ruler. The APC equally threatened to meet force with force in its determination to defend and protect the status quo, with reports of APC mobilization of youths from several northern states for the coming battle of Ilorin.

These and similar altercations persist amid official fears about an increase in the illegal importation of small arms into the country by various groups and from literally all entry points into Nigeria—coastal (southern), western, eastern, and northern (by land). Ranking officials, including President Obasanjo, Theophilus Danjuma, the defense minister from 1999 to May 2003, Admiral Ibrahim Ogohi, the chief of defense staff from 1999–June

2003, and General Alexander Ogomudia, the new chief of defense staff, have publicly voiced concerns over this phenomenon. It has also reportedly been receiving policy attention.

On the brighter side is the consensus that one dividend that Nigerians have enjoyed from the inauguration and operation of the Fourth Republic is an expansion of the political space for democratic politics and the observance and enjoyment of basic freedoms and rights. A human rights violation investigation panel under retired Supreme Court justice Chukwudifu Oputa held public sittings over human rights abuses since 1966 and helped to bring into the open the bestialities of the past, especially the recent past. Its findings and recommendations should further help to make rights abuses more unattractive and consolidate the improving human rights situation in Nigeria. Abuses still linger under the current regime, however, in such areas as the observance and enforcement of the death penalty, extrajudicial killings by agents of the state and private militias and vigilante groups, assassinations, ritual and other killings, disappearances, avoidable disasters, arbitrary arrest and detention, torture and other inhuman or degrading treatment, state failure in the provision of basic services and infrastructures, and conditions in the country's prisons, as richly reported by the Committee for the Defence of Human Rights.[41]

Sociocultural Dimensions

An enduring legacy of the many years of undemocratic rule (colonial, military, *and* civil) to which Nigeria and Nigerians have been exposed is a deep-rooted militarization of the sociocultural landscape. In the very appropriate words of Jibrin Ibrahim:

> Military rule has strongly impacted the country's culture and institutions [and] negatively on society by generalizing its authoritarian values which are in essence anti-social and destructive of politics . . . understood as the art of negotiating conflicts related to the exercise of power. Military regimes have succeeded in permeating civil society with their values—both the formal military values of centralization and authoritarianism and the informal lumpen values associated with "barrack culture" and brutality that were derived from the colonial army.[42]

Effectively, this legacy has bestowed on the Fourth Republic a deeply felt erosion of the social infrastructure for democratic governance of private and community life and of the public sphere. Although it has been demonstrated that the Nigerian sociocultural firmament has generally not been supportive of sustained dictatorship,[43] this has not translated automatically into mass democratic culture. As has been stated elsewhere, "To argue that mass political culture in Nigeria has tended to be anti-authoritarian is not to suggest that it has, therefore, also tended to be pro-democratic."[44] Indeed, there persists in the post-1999 order a virtual absence of a political culture of trust and restraint among the leaders and the led alike,[45] as well as "a strong undercurrent of anti-democratic ethos in civil society outlined by a pervasive lack of tolerance as well as some measure of authoritarianism and gerontocratic tendencies at all levels of society and in day-to-day existence beyond the assemblage of politicians."[46]

The erosion in the capacity and values of public bureaucracies, the attendant recourse to task forces, the privatization of channels for conducting government business through the creation and empowerment by leaders of government and party affairs of centers of power ("mafias" in local parlance) outside of the official bureaucracy, all of which were observed in the pre-1999 regime, persist in the posttransition order. These realities have been complemented by increased ehtnicization and regionalization of political competition, as well as the penchant for aggrieved groups (occupational, trade union, professional, social, cultural) to vent their grievances through episodic, confrontational, and noninstitutional platforms. The result for the Fourth Republic has been a harvest of communal, criminal, and religious violence.

As indicated earlier, the incidence of communal violence predates the Fourth Republic, but the relatively more liberal environment of the republic appears to have ironically "popularized" violence as a means of seeking redress, settling old scores, or "negotiating" with neighboring communities. Examples of this abound and are spread throughout the country like a rash of malignant spots. In the short life of the republic, violent communal clashes have been recorded among Yoruba agriculturists and Fulani pastoralists in the northern part of Oyo state, the Ife Yoruba and the Modakeke Yoruba, the Yoruba and "Hausa" (more accurately, "northern") settlers in Sagamu, the Ilaje Yoruba and settler Ijaw groups in Ondo state, Yoruba and "Hausa" traders in Bodija and Shasha markets in Ibadan, and between Yoruba elements and Ijaw, Urhobo, "Hausa," and Igbo elements at various times in Lagos—all in western Nigeria.

In the Niger Delta area, such community clashes have been recorded between the Ijaw and Itsekiri, Akwa Ibom and Cross River states over ownership of Bakassi; the Ijaw and oil companies; and the Urhobo and the Itsekiri. In the north, the long-running schisms between the Kuteh and the Jukun as well as the schism between the Jukun and the Tiv people persist, along with matters arising from the sacking of the Bassa from Toto local government in 1998 as well as various flashpoints in southern Kaduna arising from the imposition of emirs over non-Muslim populations. A recent eruption was in Nassarawa state, between Tiv and the local Hausa community. In the Igbo east, there are constant intercommunity and intracommunity clashes over land and boundary issues, the most celebrated being that between the Umuleri and Aguleri communities.[47]

The reasons for these conflicts are diverse, and include arbitrary creation of local governments or relocation of their headquarters, land hunger, environmental degradation, competing use of land between sedentary communities and migratory pastoralists, historical animosities, political competition, chieftaincy disputes, cultural differences, and tension arising from the dynamics of everyday life between indigenes and "settlers" or strangers. The deployment of sophisticated weapons and military strategy by combatants has compounded this problem, which the managers of the Fourth Republic have found difficult to handle. In a sense, an elected government has a peculiar handicap in this area, namely, a fear of electoral backlash that could arise from choices built into the taking of decisive steps. The result has been a pattern of vacillation among those who govern.

Criminal violence has equally been on the rise not only in the cities but increasingly also in peri-urban and rural settlings.[48] Given the danger this poses to economic progress, social peace, and general security, the federal government has taken such steps as reorganizing and decentralizing its police force, equipping it with more sophisticated military-style weapons, and organizing special workshops and training programs for police officers. In addition, it has approved the co-option of the military into crime fighting in notorious areas like Lagos and has pledged to increase the size of the police force.

For their part, several state governments in the east secured the services of a private vigilante group called the Bakassi Boys in crime fighting. Anambra state under former governor Chinwoke Mbadinuju (May 1999–May 2003) took the extra step of passing legislation to give this enterprise legal backing. The "boys" did engage in extrajudicial executions,[49] although they are quite popular with the masses over initial successes they recorded in Onitsha, which had previously been subdued by criminal gangs. By mid-2001, the Lagos state government also flew a kite over the possible use of the OPC to fight crime, a suggestion rejected immediately by the ACF, the APC, the federal police force, and the federal government, which has all along condemned the use of ethnic militias and vigilante groups by state governments to fight crime. It is also in this context that the debate over whether state governments should set up their own police forces to complement the federal police force, the only police force in the country at this time, has raged. The federal government is opposed to such a move, which in any case would require constitutional amendments.

The most serious religious conflicts in the life of the Fourth Republic were the ones recorded in February and May 2000 in Kaduna as well as the subsequent revenge killings of northerners in Aba and Owerri by their hosts over the news that many of those killed in the February violence in Kaduna were southerners, especially Igbo.

In the face of these fissiparous tendencies, a public discourse on the need for a national conference (labeled by some as a "sovereign conference" and others as "national dialogue") has run through the republic. There is a popular perception that the south is very much in favor of a conference whose mandate would include a full discussion of the terms of the Nigerian union, while the north, the National Assembly, and the presidency are opposed to it. But the reality is much more complex than that. In fact, virtually all the major stakeholders (be they governments, ethnic associations, or regional blocs) agree on the need for some form of dialogue. The bone of contention, however, is how such a dialogue would be held, and under what platform, with the first National Assembly (1999–2003) for instance insisting that it was competent to conduct such a conference.[50]

Finally, there is the difficult task of how to effectively ensure civilian control of the military on a more or less permanent basis in a socially and culturally rooted manner. Although much of the military officer corps that has occupied political office in the past has been disengaged from service, the fact still remains that the military constitutes a sword of Damocles, as it were, a huge question mark on the future of the democratic experiment and sustenance of good governance in Nigeria. The fear is that the increasing feeling of instability occasioned by violent crimes, ethnic clashes, bickering between various arms of government, and secession threats could yet serve as excuse for the adventurous wing of the military to move to truncate the Fourth Republic. With foreign assistance, especially from the United States and the United Kingdom, the Obasanjo government has embarked on steps to retrain and reprofessionalize the military to facilitate its subordination to civil authority. It has also commissioned a new defense policy to address these and other issues. Attention has to be paid also to democratic policing for an effective police institution so that the constant recourse to the military for internal security operations will be minimized, if not stopped.[51]

Economic Issues

Elements of ungovernability that characterize the political and sociocultural realms equally manifest in the economic sphere. They revolve around deepening poverty and corruption, the role of government and the private sector in the economy, and the implications for the economy of the nature of civil society and inadequacies in basic infrastructure.

The 1990s witnessed an increase in poverty and corruption. In the Abacha years, there was massive looting of the treasury, the dimension of which is still the subject of an international inquiry. Estimates put the amount looted by the Abacha family alone at over U.S.$4 billion. Between 1992 and 1998 the number of Nigerians below the poverty line is estimated to have jumped from 41 percent to 80 percent. The views of two lawyers on this issue, given their comparatively advantaged position compared to other groups in Nigeria as indeed in any other country, are revealing and graphic.

Interviewed in May 2001, one of these individuals, described as a senior lawyer resident in Abeokuta, President Obasanjo's hometown, lamented thus: "I have not gained anything from this democracy. . . . Before this administration, life was better. Today, I cannot afford a decent car. . . . People are dying everyday as a result of frustration. The naira is so bad and people cannot afford to buy common drugs to maintain their health. What manner of democracy is this?"[52] The second lawyer, based in Lagos, noted that "we were hopeful when Obasanjo came to power, but now we are tempted to say there is no light at the end of the tunnel."[53]

By May 1999 the Nigerian economy had been brought literally to its knees and the social contract between the state and its citizens had been seriously dented. In most instances, there were gross inadequacies in the supply of energy and the provision of infrastructure vital to economic and social life.[54] The Obasanjo regime immediately initiated a poverty alleviation program involving the creation of about 200,000 temporary jobs in the public sector for the skilled unemployed with a budget of approximately U.S.$72 million, though this scheme was literally hijacked at the federal, state, and local government levels by the president's political party, the PDP. And in May 2000 the government raised the national minimum wage by about 50 percent—although this was far less than the increase demanded by organized labor.

The government also moved quickly to retrieve money corruptly diverted by erstwhile military rulers into private hands and foreign bank accounts. It has not secured the full cooperation of the international community on this move, nor has it escaped accusations of focusing on the Abacha family and its associates in the anticorruption crusade, which received legal backing on June 13, 2000, with the signing into law of an anticorruption act by the president.[55] The act provides for an anticorruption commission to investigate allegations of corruption in the public and private sectors and recommend prosecution by designated judges in state and federal courts. In late 2002 the leadership of the first National Assembly, under investigation by the commission, fought back and, in 2003, presided over the abrogation by the assembly of the original act setting up the commission. In its place, the National Assembly passed another piece of legislation considered less stringent, to the consternation of members of the public and the presidency, with the latter indicating it would not assent to the new legislation. However, the new National Assembly, inaugurated in June 2003, has indicated it will uphold the old act, partly to assuage public opinion and also because the new legislation has been invalidated by a federal High Court.

Equally important has been the government's program of privatization of key public utilities and divestment of government shares in the banking, oil, and industrial sectors of the economy. This has proceeded at a slow pace, often with allegations that key government officials had been using fronts to buy up such privatized establishments. A typical case involved the sale of government shares in African Petroleum that had to be canceled and readvertised.

On the whole, President Obasanjo's economic measures failed to resolve the fundamental problems facing the Nigerian economy. There has been no credible effort to energize the agricultural sector in order to reduce Nigeria's monocultural dependence on oil, create an atmosphere to increase capacity utilization by industries, and attract local and foreign investors. All this needs to be accompanied by a far-reaching program of economic and political liberalization and decentralization that further reduces the role of the state in the economy, reduces the salience of the federal government, and devolves more power, responsibilities, and resources onto the state and local governments. Not much has been done to reduce administrative bottle-necks; upgrade physical infrastructure for transportation, telecommunications, and water and electricity supply; reduce persistent corruption and lack of transparency; and reverse the worsening security situation throughout the country arising from violent crimes, communal clashes, and religious schisms. In addition, the organized private sector has scarcely been encouraged to develop its capacity for autonomous action and to mobilize its resources for a more effective role in the determination of economic policy.

Civil society remains weak, divided, and therefore largely incapable of extracting vertical accountability and transparency from those in charge of government affairs.[56] In addition, the social terrain remains a highly fragile one, wracked by mounting religious tension and communal clashes. There is urgent need for innovative action to provide a more effective and crosscutting basis for managing Nigeria's diversity. Cries of neglect and marginalization, of course, provide tinder for the explosive situation, and better regime performance in the delivery of scarce material resources, leading to enhancement of the feeling of individual and group worth, will go a long way in dousing the ember of hatred.

The following is a list of what civil society organizations could do to facilitate both governmental decisionmaking and the unfolding democratic experiment:[57]

1. Strengthen themselves. Before seeking a developmental and prodemocratic role in governmental decisionmaking, civil society organizations need the following:
   • A change in attitude in line with unfolding changes at the political level so that elements in the community do not continue to see themselves as the self-righteous, partisan opposition to government. For too long, civil society organizations, under military dictatorship, had no choice but to perform the role of refuge of last

resort for the partisan, the opposition, and the persecuted in general—a role usually identified with political parties. While the ban on parties lasted, this was a welcome burden, and credit for the new experiment in democracy goes to those organizations that bore the burden and the subsequent backlash of state repression. They now need to engage government as partners, cautiously but not ab initio in a combative and adversarial manner.

- The fashioning of more democratic and effective systems of internal self-governance.
- A restatement of goals and methods to make them less maximalist, less uncompromising, and less undemocratic.
- Better organizational institutionalization, including networking (to enhance autonomy, adaptability, coherence, and complexity).

2. Contribute to the strengthening of the institutions of governance in the legislature, the judiciary, the executive, and the public bureaucracies.
3. Help to address what Cameroonian economist Celestin Monga calls "civic deficit." In a 1995 commentary on civil society and democratization in francophone Africa, he makes the point, equally valid for Nigeria of today, that "years of authoritarian rule have forged a concept of indiscipline as a method of popular resistance. In order to survive and resist laws and rules judged to be antiquated, people have had to resort to the treasury of their imagination. Given that life is one long fight against the state, the collective imagination has gradually conspired to craftily defy everything that symbolizes public authority."[58]
4. Link the elite to the people. To paraphrase noted scholar of civil society and democracy Larry Diamond, the elite may be preeminent, but they are not the whole story. The mass public also matters in the sense that it plays a pivotal role not only in democratic transition but also in the unending quest to deepen democracy beyond its formal structures.[59]
5. Assist in creating multiple avenues for people to express preferences, influence decisions of government, and scrutinize and check state power between elections.
6. Facilitate the generation of political pressure for accountability, transparency, stability, and orderly reform (political, economic, and social) as required.
7. Assist in upgrading the quality and quantity of mass thinking and consultation that precede governmental decisionmaking on such matters as the provision of public infrastructure, the delivery of social facilities, and broad economic policy.
8. Work to ensure that the public is not misled, misused, or abused by government and private forces alike. The goal, therefore, does not end with mobilizing the people for active engagement in public life.

Beyond this, nongovernmental organizations (NGOs) need to perform the equally important task of ensuring that those mobilized are
also equipped and organized for *democratic* ends and for activities
that sustain, rather than subvert, the democratic experiment and economic progress.

The challenges for good governance, development, and democratic consolidation at the national level are therefore threefold.[60] First is the challenge
of regime performance at the economic level and at the political level (providing freedom in the context of order). Second is the challenge of political
institutionalization involving, among other things, the strengthening of the
state and of the institutions of representation, accountability, rule of law, and
governance such as political parties, legislatures, the electoral body, and the
judiciary, and the professionalization of the military, the police, and the
security services. Third is the challenge of deepening democracy through
effective decentralization of power, resources, and responsibility to state and
local governments; proper management of civil-military relations and ethnic
conflicts; and the strengthening of civil society to enable it perform the task
of interest representation and monitoring of the state.

The preceding discussion has focused on what government has done in
the economic and other spheres. For civil society, it is appropriate here to
state that its organizations are beginning to network, as the very successful
CFCR experiment has shown. In addition, NGOs have started to engage
government meaningfully and productively, as has been the case with such
NGOs as the Society for Reproductive Health, which collaborates with
heath ministries at federal and state levels, and the Constitutional Rights
Project, which has a track record of working hand-in-hand with the federal
police, the prison system, and the judiciary. Several NGOs and their networks have successfully worked with state legislatures to push through certain legislation on negative widowhood practices and female genital muti-
lations (as in Enugu state). More of such collaborations are ongoing,
including that between Human Rights Law Service and other NGOs with
the National Assembly on the review of the electoral law.

Evidence of cooperation between the organized private sector and the
development community (including academia) on the one hand and government on the other can be found in the federal government's April 2000
economic blueprint.[61] However, the final document has been widely criticized by the private sector as being too optimistic in its growth forecast and
lacking detail as well as a general organizational framework or guiding philosophy. According to the document:

> Improvement in the well-being of Nigerians is the ultimate objective of
> this Administration, whose economic policy thrust is to make accessible to
> every Nigerian the basic needs of life. Significant reduction of poverty by

at least 50% from the current level must be achieved by the policy and
this poverty reduction shall be the true indicator for measuring well-being,
as would be demonstrated by:

• Food on Every Table;
• unemployment reduction; and
• provision of rural infrastructure including potable water, electricity,
  basic education and health, roads, telecommunications and housing.[62]

The document goes on to note:

> At the very foundation of the above national objective is the pursuit of a
> *strong, virile and broad-based economy* with adequate capacity to absorb
> externally generated shocks. A *buoyant economy with a high level of pro-*
> *ductivity of the factors of production* (land, labor and capital), is the goal
> of the Obasanjo Administration. The Administration aims, altogether, at
> *establishing one of the leading economies in Africa:* an economy that
> experiences *rapid and sustained growth of not less than 6–10% per annum*
> *at the end of the present Administration's tenure,* is the target. The creation
> of a national economy that is *highly competitive, responsive to incentives,*
> *private sector-led, broad-based, diversified, market-oriented and open,*
> *but based on internal momentum for its growth, is the aim.*[63]

In terms of overall strategy, the blueprint lists a mix of private sector–led
economic growth strategy, with poverty alleviation as a major priority,
backed by fiscal, monetary, income, trade, and debt policies that are nondis-
tortionary, ensure the prevalence of the right macroeconomic environment
for sustained economic development, and are efficient, in addition to measures to broaden the productive base of the economy.[64]

As suggested above, there is a yawning gap between declaration and
performance. In August 2001 the International Monetary Fund criticized the
state's management of the economy, accusing the federal, state, and local
governments of extrabudgetary spending, the hallmark of the preceding
period of military rule. The fund "stressed the urgent need for strong action
by the government to restore macroeconomic stability by containing government spending, and to ensure its quality through implementation of the
due process tests"[65]

In the area of employment and poverty, which has witnessed the federal government's earlier and largely poorly executed poverty alleviation
program transformed into a new national poverty eradication program, a
group that called itself the Movement for the Unemployed and the Destitute
warned that efforts by government to revamp the economy would come to
nought if what it called government's "unserious" handling of unemployment persisted. Noting that it had wrongly assumed that unemployment-
inducing policies were "a unique feature of the military regimes," the group
cautioned: "We believe that poverty is not to be tackled from the angles of

huge budgetary expenditure, rather the problems of poverty should be tackled from the root cause of social economic domination by the minority citizens who privately sit down on our collective social wealth and progress."[66]

These economic issues in the governance of postmilitary Nigeria have their international dimensions, and four will be briefly highlighted here. First, if corruption is not to become the bane and gravedigger of the republic, Nigeria requires the services of key institutions and countries in the international system not only for restitution against past corruption but also as check against corrupt practices in the present dispensation and as a deterrent in the future. Second, Nigeria requires external support for its nascent democracy in such diverse areas as training of key personnel and provision of logistical support for such tasks as elections and censuses. Third, the country's debt overhang vis-à-vis its gross national product is intolerably high, and international assistance is required in the areas of debt management and search for further debt relief.

In this regard, the formal transformation in 2001 of the Organization of African Unity into the African Union currently attempts to refocus the attention of the Economic Community of West African States away from its unplanned emphasis on politics and peacebuilding and toward its original priority of subregional economic integration. In addition, the joint initiative involving Nigeria, South Africa, and Algeria in providing a self-imposed leadership for the Millennium African Recovery Program, as well as the New Partnership for African Development, with Nigeria as a key player, to facilitate an African renaissance, and perhaps along the way a Nigerian renaissance, provides opportunities from which Nigeria can derive economic benefits at the regional and subregional levels, given the relative size of its economy.

Fourth, emerging international conventional wisdom occasionally encourages, perhaps inadvertently, the kind of grandstanding in regard to the manipulation of symbols of particularism for advantage, including self-determination, especially for those perceived as "underdogs." This turns rebellion into "a way of life in a culture of violence," and violence into habit, thus diminishing the capacity for conflict resolution and the consolidation of an environment of peace and freedom germane to the sustenance of democracy and development.[67]

Conclusion

This chapter has highlighted some of the issues that are crucial to the reconstruction and consolidation of democracy and development in Nigeria. The Fourth Republic rose literally out of the ashes of discredited authoritarian rule. The public rage that made this long-expected transition possible is still there, simmering. Should constitutional governance and the development project fail again in the current dispensation, there are no guarantees that the earlier rage against authoritarian rule would not then turn against all forms of authority, including the democratic. It is therefore imperative that the factors that hinder development and the effectiveness of the democratic experiment outlined above be addressed, quickly, in order to provide the right atmosphere for the consolidation and deepening of constitutional governance, development, and democracy.

In the wake of the Fourth Republic's "second" set of elections for state and federal offices in April and May 2003, Nigeria obviously needs to move quickly out of its authoritarian past if it aspires to enjoy the developmental fruits of its labor and keep the forces of dictatorship at bay. Steps to be taken in this regard include appropriate constitutional review to provide for effective decentralization and the strengthening of critical institutions of political, economic, and social governance. In addition, an arrangement needs to be worked out that brings together the state, civil society, organized labor, and local communities in a social pact for democratic consolidation and economic development, which needs to be cemented by better networking and information sharing and conducive to consensus building and the peaceful and innovative management of differences.[68] Bearing in mind the good news that the conditions for democratic consolidation are precisely the same as those required for economic development,[69] the country's citizens and their foreign friends need to move quickly to facilitate the emergence and deepening of these conditions through respect for human rights and the needs of minorities and other marginalized groups. Such efforts should equally include sensitive management of scarce resources, the development of a culture of moderation, trust, and restraint, and finding the right balance between the democratic carrot and the stick for conformists and dissenters alike.

Notes

I wish to thank E. Gyimah-Boadi and Larry Diamond for inviting me to contribute to this project, for their very useful comments on an earlier draft of this chapter, and above all, for their patience. The facilitative role of the Calouste Gulbenkian Foundation, Lisbon, is also deeply appreciated, along with comments from participants at the June 2000 conference in Lisbon that led to this volume. M. A. Emmanuel provided excellent secretarial assistance when it was most needed.

1. Agbaje, "Party Systems and Civil Society," p. 362; Diamond, "Preventive Diplomacy for Nigeria," pp. 18–20; Beckett and Young, *Dilemmas of Democracy in Nigeria;* Diamond, Kirk-Greene, and Oyediran, *Transition Without End;* and Suberu, "Can Nigeria's New Democracy Survive?" pp. 207–212.

2. On this, see Diamond, *Class, Ethnicity, and Democracy;* Diamond, "Nigeria"; Dudley, *Instability and Political Order;* Joseph, *Democracy and Prebendal*

Politics; Joseph, Taylor, and Agbaje, "Nigeria"; Whitaker, "The Unfinished State of Nigeria," p. 6; Diamond, Kirk-Greene, and Oyediran, *Transition Without End;* Beckett and Young, *Dilemmas of Democracy in Nigeria;* Oyediran and Agbaje, *Nigeria;* Lewis, "Nigeria"; and Suberu, "Can Nigeria's New Democracy Survive?"

3. See Suberu and Agbaje "The Future," pp. 335–349; Stepan, "Towards a New Comparative Analysis," p. 4; Linz, "Democracy," pp. 7–8; Watts, "Federalism."

4. On this, see the very useful Jega, *Identity Transformation;* Diamond, *Class, Ethnicity, and Democracy;* Bach, "Indigeneity, Ethnicity, and Regionalism"; Falola, "Christian Radicalism and Nigerian Politics"; Bako, "Muslims, State, and the Struggle for Democratic Transition"; and Paden, "Nigerian Unity and the Tensions of Democracy."

5. Agbaje, "Africa Demos," p. 15; and Remmer, "Exclusionary Democracy," pp. 64–68.

6. Olson, "Dictatorship, Democracy, and Development," pp. 567–576; Padgen, "The Genesis of Governance"; Stoker, "Governance as Theory."

7. Hyden, "Governance and the Study of Politics."

8. Joseph, Taylor, and Agbaje, "Nigeria," p. 307.

9. Kirk-Greene, "The Remedial Imperatives," pp. 31–53; Joseph, Taylor, and Agbaje, "Nigeria," p. 307.

10. Beckett and Young, *Dilemmas of Democracy in Nigeria;* Diamond, Kirk-Greene, and Oyediran, *Transition Without End;* Lewis, "Nigeria."

11. See endnote 3.

12. Schedler, Diamond, and Plattner, *The Self-Restraining State.*

13. Federal Republic of Nigeria, *Report of the Political Bureau,* p. 21.

14. Aborisade and Mundt, *Politics in Nigeria,* p. 259.

15. Weingast, "The Political Foundations," p. 258.

16. On being a largely unrestrained state, see endnote 3. On Migdal's assertion, see Migdal, *Strong Societies and Weak States.*

17. See discussion earlier in the chapter, and endnote 1.

18. Oyediran and Agbaje, *Nigeria,* p. 312. See also Diamond, "Preventive Diplomacy," pp. 18–20.

19. Suberu, "Can Nigeria's New Democracy Survive?" pp. 207–212.

20. See Federal Republic of Nigeria, "Constitution."

21. The CFCR is a network of over 100 nongovernmental organizations drawn from Lagos, Maiduguri, Makurdi, Port-Harcourt, Kano, Enugu, Owerri, Okigwe, Lokoja, Kaduna, Ibadan, Jos, Uyo, Lafia, Sokoto, and Calabar, among others. It has its coordinating office in Ilupeju, Lagos.

22. The civil society network and the Presidential Committee in 2001 published draft proposals on the review of the constitution. By June 2, 2003, when its term ended and it was dissolved to pave way for the inauguration of a new National Assembly, the committee set up by the Fourth Republic's first National Assembly had yet to complete its own assignment. See CFCR, *The Position of the Citizens' Forum,* pp. 1–40. See also, Federal Republic of Nigeria, *Report of the Presidential Committee,* vols. 1–2.

23. Agbaje, *A Century of "Power Sharing,"* pp. 1–49.

24. On all this, see Agbaje, "Love's Labor Lost?," pp. 1–13; Mbanefoh and Egwaikhide, "Revenue Allocation in Nigeria," pp. 213–231; Adesina, "Revenue Allocation Commissions," pp. 232–246; Olowononi, "Revenue Allocation," pp. 247–260; Obi, "The Impact of Oil," pp. 261–275; Phillips, "Managing Fiscal Federalism," p. 109; Osayimwese and Iyare, "The Economics of Nigerian Federalism," p. 91; Odion et al., "How Do Oil Governors Spend Their Money?," pp. 10–12; Onimode, "How Twenty-three Nations Control Their Resources," pp. 9, 11, 16; Sagay,

"Nigeria," pt. 1 (p. 4), pt. 2 (pp. 8–9), and pt. 3; "South-South Empowerment Front," pp. 23, 25; and "Governors Insist on New Revenue Formula," pp. 1, 2, 6. In the course of 2001, President Olusegun Obasanjo, Vice President Atiku Abubakar, and the Revenue Mobilization Allocation and Fiscal Commission, established by Section 153(1) of the constitution to, among other things, oversee revenue allocation among the tiers of government, announced that a new revenue allocation formula that would give more to states and local governments was being planned.

25. Federal Republic of Nigeria, *Report of the Presidential Committee,* vol. 1, pp. 4–5.

26. On this, see Bach, "Indigeneity, Ethnicity, and Federalism," pp. 333–349.

27. Quoted in ibid., p. 339.

28. International Institute for Democracy and Electoral Assistance (International IDEA), *Democracy in Nigeria,* p. 42.

29. As captured by the media. See a random selection of newspapers and news magazines for the period. Characteristic headlines and cover stories include: "North Set for War," "Arms Build Up," "The Fall of (Former Senate President) Okadigbo: How He Stole Himself Out of Office," "'I'm Ready to Fight Another War!' Brigadier Adekunle," "AD Crisis Deepens," "'Nobody Can Probe Me: I Won't Allow It!' Ghali Na' Abba (Speaker, Federal House of Representatives," "The North Prepares to Fight," "Tension Escalates . . . over Secession Threats," "Battle for Anambra: Mbadinuju, Offor Fight to Finish," "The Battle for Nigeria: Governors Set Southern Agenda," and "2003: The High Tension States—Bombs Waiting to Explode."

30. Introduction to Schedler, Diamond, and Plattner, *The Self-Restraining State,* pp. 1–10.

31. On corruption, see Adegbamigbe, "Tainted Judges," pp. 14–23.

32. Joseph, "A Democratic Nigeria," p. 4.

33. Iwenjora, "Agonies of Freed MASSOB Leader," pp. 13, 15.

34. Chukwumba, "Tension in the Land," p. 17.

35. Ibid.

36. Ibid.

37. Other groups in the multiethnic Niger Delta include the Ibibio, the Edo, the Efik, the Itsekiri, and the Urhobo, some having developed their own ethnic militias in the context of intra–Niger Delta communal conflicts discussed later in the chapter.

38. Abubakar, "No Way for Hoodlums," pp. 18–19.

39. Chukwumba, "Tension in the Land," p. 17. See also International IDEA, *Democracy in Nigeria,* pp. 237–260.

40. Abubakar, "No Way for Hoodlums," p. 18.

41. Committee for the Defence of Human Rights, *2000 Annual Report.*

42. Ibrahim, "Obstacles," pp. 160–161. See also International IDEA, "Building a Culture," pp. 45–65; and Agbaje, "Mobilizing," pp. 143–167.

43. Diamond, "Nigeria's Search," p. 70; Agbaje, "Mobilizing," pp. 160–161.

44. Agbaje, "Mobilizing," p. 161.

45. On the concepts of trust and restraint, see Putnam, *Making Democracy Work;* Putnam, "Bowling Alone," pp. 664–683; Cohen and Arato, *Civil Society;* and Schedler, Diamond, and Plattner, *The Self-Restraining State.*

46. Agbaje, "Mobilizing," p. 158.

47. On this, see chaps. 4 and 11–13 in International IDEA, *Democracy in Nigeria.* See also Soremekun and Agbaje, "Developing Conflict Management Capabilities," pp. 131–155.

48. See these cover stories for instance: Agekameh, "Robbing and Killing," pp. 30–41; Agekameh, "Raiders," pp. 34–45; Agekameh, "Guns, Guns Everywhere," pp.

30–36; Adekanmbi, "Robbers' Terror," pp. 16–23; Adegbamigbe, "Robbers in Police Uniform," pp. 14–23; Owoeye-Wyse, "The Face of Shame," pp. 24–29; Omenuwa, "At the Mercy of Armed Robbers," pp. 16–24; and Adegbamigbe and Aham, "The Robbers' Revenge," pp. 16–21.

49. See, for instance, Owoeye-Wise and Omenuwa, "End of Road for Derico," pp. 14–21.

50. Agbaje and Adebanwi, "Informal National Conference," pp. 1–20.

51. For details of government effort and what else can be done in this regard, see, for instance, International IDEA, *Democracy in Nigeria*, pp. 173–197; Adegbamigbe, "Coup No More Possible," pp. 15–18; Agekameh, "Burden of the Men in Black," pp. 12–19; Agekameh, "Malu," pp. 26–31; Offi, "Governors Would Use State Police," pp. 32–34; Adebajo, "Descent to the Abyss," pp. 26–27; and Agekameh, "Dangers Ahead," pp. 28–34.

52. Owoeye-Wise, "Dashed Hopes," p. 15.

53. Ibid. For graphic description of people's reactions to their fortunes so far in the Fourth Republic, see ibid., pp. 14–21; and Fiakpa, "Hard Times Are Here," pp. 32–40. Very early in his administration, President Obasanjo himself acknowledged aspirations about democracy and development. See Obasanjo "Democracy and Development," pp. 173–186."

54. See Central Bank of Nigeria, *Annual Report,* pp. 53–72, 127–129, 131–132.

55. See Federal Republic of Nigeria, *The Corrupt Practices and Other Related Offences Act,* pp. 2–76. For the extent of corruption and the limits of some of the actions taken by the federal government on this, see, for instance, Niboro, "Lawmakers on the Rampage," pp. 14–23; Agekameh, "The Case Against Okadigbo," pp. 12–21; Oche, "Budget Scandal," pp. 14–23; Agekameh, "A Senate and Its Scandals," pp. 16–22; Uwugiaren, "Stinking Senate," pp. 14–19; Osifo-Whiskey et al., "My Conscience Is Clear," pp. 20–29; Semenitari, "Paying for Civil Rule," pp. 24–28; and Elesho, "Mr. Integrity," pp. 16–20.

56. On divided civil society, see Lewis, Robinson, and Rubin, *Stabilizing Nigeria;* and Walker, "Civil Society."

57. This draws largely from Diamond, *Developing Democracy,* pp. 218–260.

58. Monga, "Civil Society," p. 363.

59. Diamond, *Developing Democracy,* p. 219.

60. Diamond, "Consolidating Democracy," pp. 18–19.

61. Federal Republic of Nigeria, *Obasanjo's Economic Direction,* pp. 1–87.

62. Ibid., p. 8. Emphasis in original.

63. Ibid., pp. 8–9. Emphasis in original.

64. Ibid., pp. 9–13.

65. Obidigbo, "IMF Scores Government Low," p. 1.

66. Ogidan, "Group Faults Obasanjo," p. 33.

67. On conflict resolution, see Zartman, "Dynamics," p. 10. See also International Peace Academy, *Civil Society,*" p. 6; Etzioni, "The Evils," pp. 21–35; Connor, "Nation-Building," pp. 119–135; and Soremekun and Agbaje, "Developing Conflict Management Capabilities," p. 141.

68. On a social pact, see International IDEA, *Democracy in Nigeria,* pp. 9–11.

69. Olson, "Dictatorship, Democracy, and Development."

South Africa:
Building Democracy After Apartheid

Steven Friedman

At first glance, ten years after its establishment, South African democracy is in surprisingly robust health. Two general elections and two rounds of local elections, accepted as free and fair by the participants, have passed. Civil liberties remain intact, as do the institutions created by the 1993 and 1996 constitutions, widely seen as exemplars of liberal democracy. After a history of polarization, violent political conflict, and antidemocratic tendencies on both sides of the racial divide, democratic performance seems to have far surpassed expectations.

While South African media and commentators often tend to take the post-1994 order's democratic features for granted, the fact that civil liberties (for citizens rather than undocumented migrants)[1] remain entirely intact, that court decisions that frustrate government intentions are accepted, and that regular competitive elections—of which the most recent were the December 2000 local government poll—are now part of political routine, is remarkable. Political debate is, to be sure, robust and often conflict-ridden; during 2000, race became a more visible divide than at any time since 1994. But while sections of the white-led opposition regularly bemoan "subtle" curbs on their freedom of speech, the fact that they often do this on a national platform tends to undermine the credibility of their assertions. It may well be that, as some black opponents of the governing African National Congress (ANC) suggest, it would quickly lose its enthusiasm for pluralism if its hold on power were threatened by a credible electoral rival. But that remains largely hypothetical: if the ANC does remain in power for a generation under democratic conditions, democratic practice may become so deeply embedded that it will prove irreversible.

Yet threats to the democratic project lurk beneath the surface, including some that are immediately apparent, such as the reracialization of politics in the 1999 election campaign and its outcome and the threat to accountability and responsiveness posed by the currently unassailable electoral

235

majority of the ANC. This threat is exemplified by the 1999 ballot, which eroded countervailing power within the system by reducing the key levers of opposition influence, control of two subnational governments, and the ability to block governing party constitutional initiatives in the national legislature.

It should be noted here that, while statutory race discrimination has ended, race remains a key divide in the society and this has inevitable effects on the practice of democracy. Race is the key determinant of party affiliation and electoral choice.[2] And while its impact is mitigated by bargaining by elites across the racial divide and by important strains of pluralism within the racial blocs, it also does much to shape social and political attitudes: enthusiasm for the new order is far more likely to be expressed by blacks, misgivings are far more often the preserve of whites. The importance of racial identity ensures three related facts. First the ANC is overwhelmingly supported by black Africans and the opposition Democratic Alliance is supported mainly by whites as well as substantial sections of the other racial minorities. Second, only a predominantly black party can assemble an electoral majority, making it impossible for the existing opposition ever to take the seat of government. Third, public debate is often polarized, as whites seem to search for ways of finding fault while government politicians seek to dismiss all criticism as an expression of racism. While the immediate post-1994 period was marked by a degree of pluralism within racial camps, this narrowed substantially as the Inkatha Freedom Party (IFP), the largest black party besides the ANC, moved into a coalition with the governing party in one province and in the national cabinet, and the white-led opposition coalesced.[3]

These trends have been analyzed elsewhere and are country-specific and thus of limited value to a cross-country exploration of democracy.[4] Suffice it to say that they are hardly propitious for democracy—both because the governing party is insulated from electoral challenge for the foreseeable future, which reduces pressures for accountable government, and because the pressures for politics to become a ritualized acting out of racial divides is great. And yet a complex political history and culture that I have tried to analyze elsewhere has ensured that, at least among the urban middle class and the organized working class, democratic politics not only survives in form, but is remarkably vigorous.[5]

The chapter will focus on a less evident but perhaps more foreboding threat to democratic health: the strengthening after the 1999 election of assumptions that reduce the quality of democracy to, at best, a secondary issue behind enhancing government effectiveness, promoting economic growth, and delivering services. The prevailing view among much of the elite—in government, business, and the media—assumes that the key challenge facing the postapartheid order is "getting things done," showing that a majority-ruled South Africa can dispel the myth that African governments are incapable of managerial efficiency and at the same time addressing a perceived demand among the electorate for "delivery" of goods and services. That democracy might be deepened and broadened is, by implication, a luxury next to the technical imperatives posed by this challenge. While this implication is unlikely to result in any formal abridgments of democracy or erosions of human rights (at least at present), it closes off opportunities to enhance the quality of a democratic system still in its infancy and in need of nurturing. The rush to "get things done," ironically, impairs prospects for effective delivery, as it tends to ignore overwhelming evidence that government programs are ineffective when they fail to understand or respond to the preferences of beneficiaries or are based on misconceptions about grassroots social and economic behavior, weaknesses that can best be overcome by stronger democratic institutions.

The chapter contends that this paradigm has emerged in response to two, mutually reinforcing dynamics. Developments in domestic politics unfavorable to a concerted quest for democratic quality have meshed with a prevailing paradigm among international opinion-formers and development agencies to produce a consensus on formal democracy as a means to material ends (which may, presumably, be dispensable if superior means present themselves). Thus, while local political considerations play an important role in producing the prevailing view, donor governments, as well as international financial institutions, are not only complicit in, but also often enthusiastic proponents of, an agenda that relegates democracy to, at best, a means to material ends. South African developments are thus not only of interest in themselves, but also illustrate important international trends. Such trends are expressed in intellectual interchange and practical policy choices—and may threaten democracy as much as the more obvious dangers of authoritarian recidivism.

From Nation Builders to Managers: Origins of the Current Paradigm

Concerns about the health of South African democracy are often linked to the retirement of Nelson Mandela in 1999 and his replacement as president by Thabo Mbeki. This explains, but also obscures, much. The explanatory power lies not only in the reality that the two leaders do indeed have different personalities and approaches to politics, but also in the reality that Mbeki's ascendance marks the dominance within the ANC of the exile faction. This brings a particular approach to politics that helps explain the current shift in emphasis.

For those unfamiliar with South African political history, the ANC is the world's oldest "liberation movement." It was formed in 1912 in response to legislation that denied the black African majority the right to own land in much of the country and operated until 1960 as a legal, albeit often repressed, political organization. In that year, together with its rival, the Pan-Africanist Congress, it was banned and forced into exile.[6] Those of its leaders who had not been imprisoned left the country and continued to wage war against apartheid until the banning of the ANC was lifted in 1990 as a precursor to negotiations that ultimately produced a nonracial, democratic constitution. Domestic resistance, however, was revived during this period, first by the reemergence of a black trade union movement that during the 1980s provided an organizational nexus for resistance activity, and then, from 1983, by the United Democratic Front (UDF), an alliance of domestic resistance organizations and activists that owed symbolic loyalty to the ANC but was relatively autonomous from it.[7] After the ANC was legalized, however, the UDF disbanded and was in effect absorbed into the ANC.

This ensured the emergence within the ANC of several political cultures, of which the most dominant is the divide between exiles and those who were engaged in domestic resistance. Mandela himself is part of an intermediary category since, like some other key ANC leaders of the 1950s, he was jailed before 1960 and was thus never in exile. The political culture of which he was the most prominent product shared with the internal resistance an experience of conducting politics in the domestic context. But ANC activity during the 1950s had a distinctly patrician flavor, in contrast to the grassroots focus of the 1980s, giving him and his imprisoned colleagues a link to the exile faction too.

A crude distinction between exile and domestic resistance cultures can do some violence to reality, both because some individuals who were in exile have tended to ally themselves with the veterans of domestic resistance and because the divide is complicated by the fact that some key political figures have experience of both contexts (since some resistance figures from the 1970s onward reacted to repression by choosing exile). Furthermore, a simple distinction between conspiratorial, authoritarian, exile politics and democratic, mass-based, resistance activity is in part a caricature. Nevertheless, while domestic resistance often failed to practice the responsiveness to the grassroots and commitment to act only on popular mandates that it preached,[8] the logic of attempting to mobilize domestic constituencies demands a respect, at least in theory, for mandates and responsiveness. In contrast, the exigencies of exile political life would not have fostered respect for such values. The fact that internal resistance leaders, whether they were trade unionists or civic activists, were compelled by the logic of their position or the balance of power to negotiate with business or the authorities at the time instilled a familiarity with the politics of compromise and open contest that is pivotal to democracy. The demands of exile, by contrast, engendered suspicion and a penchant for conspiracy (since exile movements were routinely penetrated by government agents). The fact that waging guerrilla war was a component of exile activity also ensured that military discipline and the accompanying style of politics met the needs of the situation. Democratic politics was not possible among leaders separated from their constituents; nor, given the background sketched here, was it a preference.

Mbeki spent his adult life in exile, which does much to explain his political style. Most of his strongest allies are also former exiles. This ascendancy of the exile faction is responsible for a trend that began at at the time when Mandela began to hand over control to his successor. It is manifested chiefly in a diminution of democratic practice within the ANC, whose symptoms include a propensity to discourage competitive elections within the organization,[9] an insistence prior to the 1999 election that candidates for provincial premierships be appointed by the national leadership rather than elected by provincial branches,[10] and the centralized appointment of mayoral candidates in the December 2000 local elections.[11]

Events within the ANC are important to democratic prospects. Multiparty competition is a necessary condition of democracy, but is hardly sufficient, least of all in South Africa, where the electoral dominance of the majority party seems set to endure for some time and in which much opposition is deligitimized by the fact that it represents racial minorities, particularly whites who were privileged by apartheid.[12] In this context, the degree to which the diverse interests and values that compose the ANC can find expression within the movement is crucial, although, worryingly, the trend has been to reduce this sharply. It is of some importance that, particularly in the choice of provincial and local leaders, the stated rationale is that the administrative competence of persons "deployed" by the center is superior to that of "populist" leaders thrown up by unpredictable local and provincial elections.[13] The concern for managerial ability ahead of popular support reinforces a desire by the leadership to allocate posts through central patronage, not internal election.

Important as the political cultures produced by the exile-internal dynamic are, however, they do not explain everything. Factors that could have produced a relegation of concern for inclusion and democratic strengthening existed before Mbeki's accession ensured exile dominance. The first is that the balance of power that produced the compromise of 1993 did not endure much beyond it. Even by the time the bargain was struck, the notion that the postapartheid polity would be founded on a relatively equal bargain between the majority and minority elites had begun to fray; the National Party, which governed under apartheid, failed to achieve its key goal of an elite pact in which the minority would retain a veto over decisions.[14] Not long after the Government of National Unity assumed office in 1994, it became apparent that the chief vehicle for bargaining between the majority and minority would not be interaction between political parties, but instead would be between the ANC and key white constituencies organized outside parliament.[15] This meant that the power balance did not need to express itself in a strengthening of democratic institutions to accommodate minorities: this could be achieved, if necessary, through elite bargaining outside the formal political process.

This became relevant once the ANC concluded that the need to avert right-wing white subversion of the new order had passed. Analyses by senior figures in government indicated that the initial post-1994 period had been seen as one of consolidation, in which consultation and negotiation had been required to defuse overt threats to the system. Once it became clear that no such threats existed, the need to include was said to have passed too, to be replaced by the need to govern. Inclusion was not seen as an end in itself, an essential component of a common citizenship, but as a temporary expedient.

This, in turn, was important because key aspects of the constitution that introduced potential checks and balances into the system had been inserted primarily because the ANC had seen them as concessions to minorities whose potential power exceeded their numbers. Prime among these was the provincial system: while it has promise as a source of subnational opposition power and a vehicle for the expression of regional diversity within the ANC, later events suggest that it was seen largely as a means of allaying minority fears, not only among whites but also in the Inkatha Freedom Party, whose prime concern had been to retain its ethnic and regional power base through strong powers for its KwaZulu-Natal stronghold. When it became evident that these fears would not overtly threaten the constitutional order, and negotiating between the IFP and ANC leadership proved sufficient to avert this threat, the incentive to take seriously the strengthening of provincial government abated.

The ANC's disinclination to see bargained compromises or autonomous provincial government as a strength had its roots deep in the society's divided past, which instilled within the leading resistance movement a deep suspicion of difference. Whereas democratic theory sees difference as a source of potential strength to be accommodated, a strong strain of ANC thinking sees it as a threat. This is hardly surprising. Not only did apartheid deny the majority rights and dignity by stressing difference as a virtue, it also carved up the country into—in theory—hermetically sealed geographic units designed as vehicles for difference. The leitmotif of resistance politics was thus an emphasis on sameness. As an expression of South Africans' common humanity during the period of racial oligarchy, it was a powerful statement; yet placed in the context of a need to build vibrant democratic institutions, it is a severe obstacle.

Equally important, the pressure to "get things done" stems from the society's racial dynamics and their effects on attitudes toward governance.

Postapartheid politics have been underpinned by a theme that often is not stated overtly, but that is pervasive: whites expect a black government to fail and the leaders of that government know this.[16] It is therefore a key preoccupation of much of the new governing elite to demolish these assumptions by demonstrating that blacks can govern an industrialized society with a complex market economy. This, more than concern for democratic depth, is considered likely to show whites that assumptions of black inferiority are myths.

A further consequence is that, ironically, the government can only dispel the myths by demonstrating competence *on white terms:* How else to prove to the white skeptics that race is no guide to competence than to succeed at those endeavors that whites are considered to hold dear? And since whites are perceived to value technical and managerial efficiency above all else, it is to demonstrate this capacity that most government efforts are directed. Rather than stress South Africa's actual and potential contribution to conflict resolution through bargained compromises, or, as in the early period of the Mandela administration, its interest in entrenching human rights in an unlikely setting, emphasis increasingly falls on aspiring to techniques and outcomes that are assumed to characterize "winning societies"—without, in many cases, acknowledgment that resolving conflicts and respecting rights were in many cases preconditions to "winning," not an incidental by-product. In a paradox that would no doubt have intrigued Frantz Fanon, many in the new black elite believe that they can only demolish racial prejudice by embracing one of its cornerstones, the belief that there is a "white" and a "black" way of doing things and that the former is superior to the latter. Many assumptions about what whites value may be as stereotyped as suburban myths about what blacks prize, but myths and generalizations can shape actions.

One final nuance that flows, less obviously, from the preceding analysis is the new elite's obsession with showing that postapartheid South Africa is capable of "world-class standards." Whether the subject at hand is constitutional design, public management systems, or inventing new technologies, the new elite, regardless of race or political allegiance, is obsessed with "world-class" status. Again, the roots lie in racial dynamics.

Many whites, imbued with deep forebodings of the consequences of majority rule in Africa, are concerned to maintain the standards of Western Europe and North America, to which they were accustomed under apartheid. They therefore measure the new society's progress not against its capacity to include the once excluded, but against its ability to offer as amenable a home as the Northern countries to which whites with the will and resources emigrate. It is against these standards, therefore, that the black elite must measure itself if it wants to persuade these whites that they are as well off under a largely black government in Africa as under a largely white one in Australia, Canada, or the United States. The result, crucial for the argument of this chapter, is an enthusiastic willingness to imbibe fashionable theories of public and economic management from Western capitals, not because, as in some other parts of the South, the World Bank and the International Monetary Fund insist on it, but because domestic intergroup dynamics dictate it.

The final building block in this analysis is that these factors combine to produce a particular stereotype of the new South African voter to which the current governance agenda responds. In essence, it is assumed that the average voter is a utility-maximizing individual concerned only with material benefits rather than with participation as a value in itself—because the average Northern voter is assumed to be such a person. This was most evident in both the conduct of and the response to the 1999 election. Since it is a powerful explanatory paradigm, I now turn to this point in an attempt to show how these assumptions operate to foreclose democratic options—and the extent to which, whether applied in the North or Africa's southern tip, they fundamentally misread the motives of democratic citizens.

The 1999 Election and Its Consequences: Reinterpreting Democratic Rationality

While Philippe Schmitter and Terry Karl are correct to warn against the "fallacy of electoralism,"[17] the tendency to reduce democracy to the electoral process, elections retain an importance beyond ascertaining the relative public support of contending parties.[18] For many citizens, an election may be—and equally important, may be seen to be—the only occasion on which their choices are stamped on the political process. Voting is an act of giving voice and thus of asserting the political self, of expressing identity and autonomy; in the view of one analysis it is also a crucial act of commitment to democratic values, which include the capability to develop positive, democratic character traits such as community mindedness and political self-competence.[19] This is particularly important in South Africa, where citizen behavior in 1994 demonstrated that the vote takes on added meaning in a society in which a racial minority monopolizes the franchise.[20] Just as the denial of the vote was seen as a symbol of exclusion, its achievement became a sign of restored dignity.

While this may seem obvious, it was less so to ANC constitutional negotiators who urged special measures to induce many black South Africans to vote because the violence of the past few years was said to have made them fearful of taking the risk.[21] Understanding voting as an instrumental cost-benefit analysis in which citizens weigh the uncertain benefits of casting a ballot against the sure cost of doing so is a hallowed tenet of rational choice theory,[22] which has failed repeatedly to find empirical verification.[23] As later events were to show, its application in South Africa borders on the absurd.

This is so not only because the memory of a racial franchise is a compelling spur to electoral enthusiasm. ANC dominance at the polls, and the concomitant perception that the outcome of elections is hardly in doubt, would make voting irrational were it not spurred by factors other than cost-benefit calculations. Prime among these, as I have argued elsewhere,[24] is that South African parties are defined, and draw their support from, identities—race, language, and religion primary among them. Voting is not an instrumental calculation, but an expression of who a citizen is. In this context, it seems logical to assume that people will go to considerable lengths to express who they are. This may explain why the overwhelming majority of adults planned to vote in the second universal franchise elections (see below).

In principle, South Africans' enthusiasm for voting gives the new democracy an important resource not always available to embryonic democratic systems—a degree of citizen commitment to democracy. And, while some of the points made here about the 1994 election may seem obvious, they apply equally to the second ballot. If, for some scholars and commentators, second elections are less important than founding ballots, this is not necessarily the perception of African citizens. Thus a survey of fifteen African second elections reveals that seven—almost half—recorded higher levels of voter turnout than the founding election,[25] confirming that participatory impulses do not disappear the moment the first election ends.

Nevertheless, both the framing of the electoral rules and the conduct of the campaign reveal that the elite's pessimistic and instrumental perception of the value of elections—as well as of citizens' propensity to vote—has not changed fundamentally since 1993. On the first score, the ANC—which waged an eight-decade battle for majority rule—concluded early on that the putative benefits of a secure poll, achieved by the use of bar-coded identity documents, outweighed those of extending the franchise to as many eligible adults as possible. The choice was underpinned by precisely the assumption criticized here: that the chief purpose of the election was to produce a technically unassailable measure of citizen preferences (or, more accurately, of those citizens logistically able to express a preference) and that this merited, if necessary, curtailing the numbers able to enjoy the democratic opportunity that voting provides.

A similar lack of enthusiasm for extending participation as widely as possible is suggested by the approach of the Independent Electoral Commission (IEC) to eligibility. It adopted a U.S.-style approach that placed the burden of enrolling as a voter squarely on the shoulders of the citizen. It implied both that the vote was a right to be applied for rather than one automatically conferred, and that citizens enthusiastic about casting their ballot would also be willing to submit themselves to official strictures to do so.

The assumption that citizens must apply for the most basic democratic right is hardly self-evident—in the United States, stringent registration criteria are arguably as responsible for low voter turnout as political indifference or the instrumental calculations posited by rational choice theory.[26] It might also be argued that, precisely because voting is an act of democratic identification, the democratic state, if it wishes to ensure its continued survival in robust health, has a core responsibility to ensure that this opportunity is available to all who might wish to use it.[27]

However, if citizens are enthusiastic about voting, will they not be willing to register to claim that right? If impressionistic conclusions from queues at the offices of Department of Home Affairs are a guide, many were prepared to do just that. Nonetheless, not all could take advantage of these opportunities, despite some effort to lengthen office hours to accommodate citizens who wished to register. Furthermore, the assumption of the elite that anything published in the media is known to all citizens is flawed—a survey found that up to 12 percent of eligible adults did not know that they needed to register in order to vote.

Nor did the IEC do all it could to expand the corps of registered voters, even within the terms set by its own rules. Only three weekends were set aside for registration, the last of which was three months before the poll, which would have excluded many voters who may have learned of the registration requirements only as the campaign gathered pace. In addition, no sustained effort was made to seek out voters and persons who, because of IEC errors, registered but were not placed on the voters' roll. They were rather informed that it was their responsibility to inspect the roll.[28] The result was registration of some 75 percent of those eligible to vote, according to the IEC, but a figure that, allowing for its creative treatment of population figures, may have been as low as 70 percent.[29] Since even the most pessimistic survey data on voting intentions found that some 75 percent of those eligible planned to vote,[30] at least 5 percent of citizens who wished to exercise the franchise may have been unable to do so.

This level of exclusion is not nearly high enough to question the election's legitimacy. The loss was not in the diminished accuracy of the nose count—there is no reason to assume that it would have differed if everyone who wished to vote had. Instead, it lay in the denial of democratic participation with its potential for strengthening the new polity.

Politics as Calculus: The Two-Thirds Question

The elite's understanding of motives for democratic participation was confirmed by the election's central issue: whether the ANC would achieve two-thirds of the vote. Late in the campaign, the ANC was to claim that the "two-thirds bogey" was purely an opposition invention designed to scare minority voters. The claim was disingenuous, for while the Democratic

Party and New National Party indeed used the prospect of a two-thirds majority for precisely that end, it was the ANC that started the ball rolling by conjuring up images of the liberatory effects of the magic number.[31]

Why did the ANC and the opposition feel the need to use the size of the majority as a campaign theme, since the ANC showed little interest in constitutional changes—for which two-thirds of the seats in parliament were required? Because each believed that focusing on the size of the majority, in a context where the winner was not in doubt, was essential to get out its vote. Further confirmation of this fact lies with the response of a senior ANC official who exhorted a research organization not to publish an analysis that indicated that the ANC was likely to do far better in the election than was then predicted because "we will then not be able to motivate our people."[32] The two-thirds question reflected a community of interest between the governing party and opposition in manufacturing an issue that would encourage voters who firmly expected their party to either lose or win to turn up at the polls despite this. It was born of a common perception that, to a degree, the rational choice theory of voter behavior was accurate in the current conditions. By setting a much higher, less certain threshold for "deciding" the election, the parties sought to increase the degree to which voters perceived a concrete benefit from voting (helping to achieve or thwart a two-thirds majority) so that they would be more willing to incur its costs.

But do South African voters cast ballots on utility-maximizing criteria of this sort? For obvious reasons, the argument must remain hypothetical, since there is no usable counterfactual: South Africa has had no post-1994 national election in which the two-thirds question was not at issue. There is anecdotal evidence of voters who did register and vote because they wished to affect the "two-thirds" result, but it is hardly of a form that could support or refute the argument.

There is, however, a test of sorts of the degree to which the perceived benefit of influencing the result determined propensity to vote, namely the provincial percentage polls. If voters are indeed more likely to vote if they believe their choice will determine the result, we would expect higher turnout in provinces where the outcome was in doubt. The figures provide no support for this argument: not only is there a high degree of uniformity—the highest recorded poll was 89.76 percent, the lowest 85.19—but the highest polls were recorded in Northern Province and Free State, where the results were most lopsided, the lowest in Western Cape, where they were perceived to be close.

The test is hardly definitive—even instrumental voters may not care whether their ballot influences provincial outcomes if they regard only the national result as important—and rational choice theorists could protest, with justification, that it is entirely irrelevant to the theory.[33] But the purpose is to test, with the only data available, the proposition that South Africans vote on instrumental criteria: the only—tentative and crude—test available from the 1999 poll suggests that they do not.

The limited evidence available also suggests that voting behavior is influenced far more by democratic enthusiasm than the elites allow. Thus, in the two provinces where voters would be expected to have the lowest sense of political efficacy, because the majority are opposition voters, majorities of 67 percent (in KwaZulu-Natal, despite a recent history of political violence) and 64 percent (in Western Cape) insist that their vote does make a difference.[34]

Elite assumptions prior to both elections posited the notion of a citizenry far less attuned to democracy's benefits than their betters in the media, politics, academia, and the nongovernmental organization (NGO) movement: the perennial enthusiasm for "voter education" is an example.[35] Another proposition, partially canvassed above, is that voters are inherently apathetic. Among the minority, "apathy" is said to stem from disenchantment with majority rule, which prompts a preference for disengagement.[36] In this case, survey data are produced to substantiate the claims. Among the majority, apathy is said to stem from "disenchantment with delivery," a claim that appears to lack any empirical verification at all.

The turnout on election day 1999 contradicted both claims—and there is no evidence that participation among racial minorities, who are said to be disaffected with the new order, was lower. On the contrary, Indian voters, who in survey evidence are said to feel most alienated by the postapartheid polity,[37] are said to have turned out in particularly large numbers.[38] This does not mean that these citizens are *not* disenchanted—merely that, if they are, they choose to express their grievance at the polls. While the inconvenience to which voters were subjected in 1999 rarely paralleled the 1994 experience of standing in line for up to three days, the queues were mostly long enough to persuade anyone in them whose democratic commitment was tenuous to abandon their quest.

Also significant was the widely reported ethos at the polling stations. As in 1994, the 1999 experience of voting appeared to instill in South Africans a sense of camaraderie and mutual regard, expressed in some cases in acts of generosity not always evident between elections. And despite a bad-tempered and sometimes violent campaign, polling day violence was largely absent. While it would be unwise to romanticize the phenomenon, it does seem fair to suggest that many citizens derive sufficient satisfaction from voting, and enough of a sense of identification with the society, to induce an unusually high level of "civic" behavior.[39] The levels of participation may therefore confirm that the degree of citizen commitment to democracy is much higher than presumed by elites. But it may also say something important about the preconditions for effective governance.

It has become conventional wisdom to portray South Africa as an unruly society in which citizens resist meeting their side of the "social contract" with the democratic state. There is much evidence to support this, such as high crime and poor payment levels for public services. Nonetheless, the election should give some pause for reassessment of the assumption that South Africans are beyond the reach of the state unless it uses force or blandishment—a pattern that could perhaps be attributed to the majority's experience of a past in which it was irrational to obey the law and the minority's disenchantment with majority rule.

A significant minority of citizens were first prepared to stand at least twice in lengthy queues to claim their right to vote. A society in which many are prepared to comply with onerous official requirements to claim a civic right does not seem inherently ungovernable. This does not mean that the problem of creating a sense of civic obligation is illusory—there is much difference between, on the one hand, submitting to public authority to claim a right that bestows a sense of efficacy and an opportunity to express an identity, and on the other hand, doing the same for a more indirect public benefit that entails more obvious personal cost, such as paying electricity bills to ensure that the service is continued. But it may mean that the building blocks of an effective state-building enterprise are more available than many analyses have assumed. Nevertheless, that up to a third of citizens may not have voted and that the majority party's 66 percent share of the vote may translate into the express support of little over 40 percent of the adult population holds as many lessons for the democracy and governance challenges ahead as the democratic enthusiasm noted here.

The Election and Democracy's Prospects

If citizens are not moved to vote primarily by interest calculations, the tasks facing democracy may be very different from those now assumed by many in government. The dominant view is shaped by an ideology of delivery that translates as the need to induce citizens to endorse democratic norms and institutions. Given the apartheid legacy of material inequality, this can be achieved only by "delivering" goods and services to them. The implication is that, if some democratic intangibles, such as vigorous provincial representation, must be compromised in the process, the gains in citizen confidence will far outweigh any democratic losses. There are again strong elements of instrumentality in this assumption—citizens are believed to see democracy as a source of material benefit only and not to value self-expression.

The implied claim that there is a "tradeoff" between material improvement and democratic quality ignores data from developing countries indicating that democracy is not only compatible with growth and poverty reduction, but also may be indispensable to both.[40] It also misreads the South African citizenry and therefore the preconditions for democratic viability.

As implied in the preceding discussion, a society in which most citizens are inclined to participate in democratic politics, at least by casting their ballot, and do so in part because they see the vote as an expression of their identity, is one in which the task of "winning society for democracy" may be relatively less onerous. It is also one in which the delivery of material goods will not be sufficient.

To suggest that South African political affiliations are shaped by identities is deeply threatening to many politicians and intellectuals because it implies atavism and "irrationality" among the electorate. The claim that the black majority was incapable of rational political choices underpinned racist ideology throughout the continent and, despite the formal end of white and colonial domination, it still does. This may explain why elite perceptions of the electorate constantly resort to instrumental criteria: racism's opponents have a deep need to demonstrate that South African voters are "normal," rational, utility-maximizing citizens.

The response is understandable but crucially flawed because it assumes, uncritically, that there is something "normal" about the ideal type of the citizen who votes for his or her interests rather than identity. In reality, the utility-maximizing voter is itself an ideological creation. Not only do intangibles such as citizenship and democratic commitment influence voter behavior in all democratic societies: Why else would people regularly vote for candidates or parties which have no hope of winning? But identities are also important to democratic choices in even the most seemingly instrumental democracy. In Britain, does the fact that, for a century, some regions have returned Labour candidates, others Tories, mean that the majority make the same interest calculations every time or that their ballots have something to do with their identity? And is being a U.S. "conservative" or "liberal" purely an interest calculation, or might it have something to do with who people think they are? And what of the importance of religion in determining choices in Holland and Italy? Even in democracies assumed to be "normal" because voter choices are shaped by interest calculations, identity turns out to be important.

The importance of asserting the primacy of identity in determining political loyalties lies not in the use to which it is put by some scholars— to bemoan the failure of South African democracy to yield a "normal" outcome.[41] It is, rather, to assert an opportunity created by the electorate's willingness to see democracy, at least in part, as a "deliverer" of intangibles such as self-expression rather than as purely a source of material benefit. To name an example, there is no correlation between citizens' evaluation of local government and the resources municipalities have to "deliver": people are as dissatisfied in those localities that enjoy the funds and the power to "deliver" as they are in those rural councils that are not financially able to do so—their dissatisfaction centers on factors such as perceived remoteness to "what ordinary people think" and suspicions of corruption, not "lack of delivery."[42] Similarly, unlike many members of the political elite, voters appear to welcome the opportunity to elect provincial legislatures, despite the widespread perception that delivery by these governments has been poor: only 8 percent wanted provincial powers reduced in 1996.[43] In societies such as South Africa's, where material benefits are for many in short supply, voter concern for intangibles suggests a more optimistic prognosis for democracy than a purely instrumental analysis would yield. It also suggests a strategy for strengthening democracy very different from the strategy that dominates.

So most South African voters care about being heard—it may be of some significance that, despite the overwhelming vote for the government, between two-thirds and four-fifths (depending on the province) of its black African support base believe that the "complete freedom to criticise the government" is an important feature of democracy.[44] The challenge therefore lies not in "delivering" at the possible expense of political self-expression, but in deepening and broadening the latter by strengthening democratic participation and solidifying the relationship between legislators and citizens. It also requires, in the interests of economic growth and poverty reduction as well as democratic strengthening, a stress on difference as an asset, for only this can enable the new polity to accommodate differing identities in a common political space.

Despite the electoral enthusiasm described here, the task of encouraging citizens into the polity remains important and this too is a powerful argument against one aspect of the ideology of delivery. An implicit message of the election result is that citizens have overwhelmingly conferred a mandate on the majority party to implement its agenda. On that assumption, respect for difference may appear unnecessary, given that those who are different compose at most a third of the population. But if we consider that those who have explicitly endorsed the majority party at the polls constitute less than half the electorate, extending the reach of the democratic state remains as urgent a task as material "delivery," if not more so.

Nor is the election result the only evidence that democracy is an essential ingredient of any program seeking to address material deprivation. In the latter stages of the Mandela administration, the social policy debate was dominated by an obsession with numbers—how many houses were to be built, how many water connections installed. Despite the constant refrain that the government was way behind its (numerical) delivery targets, the number of housing subsidies awarded came close to the—largely rhetorical—target of 1 million set by the ANC prior to the 1994 election,[45] while over 3 million new water connections were provided. But research revealed that the houses delivered were widely rejected by beneficiaries, not because they were too small, as many in the housing debate claimed, but because recipients complained that they had not been offered a say on the type of shelter they were provided.[46] There is also growing evidence that the much-vaunted water projects are not being sustained, largely because the desire to "deliver" rapidly has caused a retreat from participatory approaches.[47] In the housing case, the problem is that the voices of beneficiaries are not heard; in water, it is the failure to secure their cooperation in maintaining the new schemes. In both, the antidote lies in deeper democracy, not in boosting the delivery numbers.

Indeed, while the first five years of postapartheid government is indicted by the delivery ideology for its preoccupation with talking rather than "getting things done," the evidence points in a contrary direction—social policy was obstructed because democracy was not deep enough, not because it substituted for delivery. Thus, in housing, policy was devised by a multistakeholder national housing forum: after 1994, it soon became apparent that the policy that emerged had been hammered out by every significant group—except the homeless, who, as noted above, insisted that they wished to be consulted but had not been.[48] This was, by implication, a strong argument for representative democracy, because it illustrated that the multistakeholder forums beloved by the first administration could not represent the poor, who lacked the resources to organize associations and whose only access to decisions was through elected public representatives.[49] Education, one of the poorest performers, was severely retarded by the ministry's failure to win the support of interest groups—or to give low-income, black parents a say in decisions.[50] Water, as noted above, is regarded as a star performer because it "got on" with delivery; proponents of the delivery "ideology" note that it did this after scrapping a policy that initially committed it to working with "communities" to supply water.[51] However, the Water Affairs Ministry, at least in theory, did not abandon democratic representation in principle, since its approach shifted to a stress on working with elected local governments.[52] It has been the failure to find appropriate partners that has ensured that delivery has been gained at the expense of sustainability. It may also be important to note that history may yet judge that the ministry's chief success was not the delivery "numbers" it achieved, but the fact that it was able to win suburban white consent for redistributive tariffs by presenting them as measures required by universal values such as conservation and fairness rather than retribution: securing the consent of the affluent is a key ingredient of "delivery" that can only be achieved by democratic politics.[53]

One reason for some of the false starts was the dynamic mentioned above in which the new government's politicians were anxious to show that they could meet the standards of "efficiency" that they believed to be expected of them. This prompted them to set arbitrary numerical targets and then to become obsessed with achieving them as the media and political opponents cited their elusiveness as evidence of failure. But the claim that democracy obstructed delivery in the first administration is a myth. Incomplete democracy led to inadequate delivery—to the extent that the latter is favored over the former, so will delivery itself founder as democracy atrophies.

Democratic prospects will therefore depend not primarily on improved public administration and enhanced "delivery," though they remain important, but on the degree to which the necessary fight against poverty and inequality is pursued in ways that broaden and deepen the channels for democratic self-expression of all of South Africa's varying identities—in a manner that recognizes that, even in postapartheid South Africa, democratic intangibles matter to citizens as much as material improvements.

International Trends and Local Choices

While the governmental choices described here stem from country-specific dynamics, they also mirror an important strain in current international thinking on development and governance to which they also, in part, respond.[54] The World Bank's 1997 *World Development Report* rehabilitated the role of the state as a catalyst to economic growth.[55] In principle, this opened the way for enhancing the value placed on democracy, since it is a potential antidote to the notion that the private sphere is the prime repository of freedom and development. While the relative autonomy of the private sphere is an important democratic principle, it is a complement to that other key democratic idea, the role of the state as a vehicle for deliberation on the public good: the state is an essential prerequisite for the realization of democratic values and aspirations. If evidence is needed, it can be supplied in the negative by reference to a work by British conservative William Rees-Mogg, which predicts, with undisguised enthusiasm, a future of rampant individualism in which the state becomes irrelevant because all its functions, from personal security through education, will become the preserve of the private realm.[56] His normative framework will be rejected by democrats—just as it leads him to reject democracy. But the book is largely accurate in its description of the likely world without the state: it is one in which the affluent live in guarded fortresses and much of the rest of humanity in abject misery, a world far more redolent of the one Hobbes believed the state had been created to transcend than a new golden age.

But the World Bank's change in perspective did not pay the same honor to democratic politics as it did to the state. The only reference to representative democracy is a half page in which its formal resurgence is noted without comment; the discussion then passes to a topic more familiar to development specialists—public participation techniques designed to simulate representative democracy.[57] More generally, democratic politics can be seen, in current development agency literature on economic adjustment, as an obstacle to appropriate policy, not its precondition.[58]

Part of the enthusiasm for participation techniques rather than competitive elections may stem from an intellectual current in which, on the left as well as among libertarians,[59] civil society is proposed as a realm of freedom and social progress rather than of inequality and partial interests, a development helped by the role that it played as a driving force in transitions from authoritarianism to democracy.[60] However, many of these writings were faithful to democratic theory in their insistence that civil society was a supplement (albeit an important one) to the democratic state, and indeed in some cases were concerned to propose ways of deepening representative democracy.[61] In contrast, development thinking appeared to see it as an alternative to democratic representation. Nonstate actors are seen as more efficient sources of material provision than the state: in Sri Lanka, a change in state policy from direct housing delivery to citizen provision is said to have increased output several fold;[62] in Bolivia, religious NGOs are reported to have achieved more effective schooling than state provision.[63] Similarly, associations, charities, and communal networks are seen as more effective means of addressing needs ranging from education and health through more intangible functions such as building and maintaining social trust and solidarity, imparting and enforcing mores, or enhancing self-esteem—an important theme in current "social capital" writing.[64]

Horizontal relations between citizens clearly are important preconditions for democracy and economic development. The proposition that they are a superior vehicle for citizen participation and for action against poverty than the state, however, ignores the important potential for "antisocial capital"[65]—for these relationships to be sites of perpetuated inequality and violence, which the democratic state seeks to regulate through free participation in decisions rather than fiat. Perhaps far more important is that this interpretation of "social capital" writing can form a justification for bypassing democratic government and politics. If citizens are "not ready for democracy" until their "social capital" has been built, concern for strengthening democratic institutions must give way to a focus on social networks. However, an important recent study of the Indian state of Kerala suggests precisely the reverse, namely that only active participation in the democratic state can rapidly build the "social capital" that development technicians seek to invent. This active participation must be assiduously encouraged by the governing party, and a crucial element of the "capital" so created is respect for the norms and institutions of democracy.[66]

It is perhaps no accident that enthusiasm for civil society as an implied alternative, rather than supplement, to the state, is applied primarily to countries where the state is weakest—bar the work of political philosophers,[67] which has little impact on the public policy debate. The suggestion that civil society is a better guarantor of liberty and equity than the state may therefore be more a despairing symptom of the malaise of many new democratic states than a pointer to a fresh democratic direction. It may also be worth noting here that, while intellectuals and donor agencies exalt civil society in the South, Robert Putnam's finding that associational activity in the United States has declined,[68] while it is hotly disputed, has claimed widespread attention. This does not imply that the state has somehow rendered civil society redundant, but it does provide further reason for skepticism about notions of civil society as an alternative to the democratic state.

More important, civil society, for all its importance in providing a realm of citizen participation in public life, is by definition the realm of the partial interest: unlike civil society associations, democratic states cannot explicitly reject the claims and concerns of any section of society. For those who believe that human interdependence and cooperation are as essential to the good society as individual liberty, the democratic state represents an aspiration, even if its reach requires limitation. Without the democratic state there is no cooperation, there are no common loyalties, there is no public deliberation and action.

It may be no accident that, in practice, the exaltation of civil society in many Southern contexts has produced patronage rather than development, clientelism rather than democracy.[69] Analyses that emphasize the effectiveness and representativeness of nonstate actors may thus hand control of resources to individuals and oligarchies who may limit democracy's reach and ensure that "development" becomes a source of patronage rather than equity. And this is possible because they remain beyond the political accountability that democratic states may not always guarantee, but that only they can offer because only they subject the allocation of resources and discussion of priorities to public contest between *all* of society's interests.

But reemphasizing the state is not enough. If, as some of the literature on the "developmental state" seems to imply, the state's role in triggering growth is essentially a matter of cementing relations with business, important interests and the majority of citizens are reduced to passive bystanders, with questions such as reducing poverty and inequality relegated to technical matters. If we put aside a sentimental attachment to idealized notions of democratic politics, why should that matter? Because current trends suggest that attempts to address inequality—and poverty—within this paradigm are not achieving results, even if they are measured in purely technical terms. An illustration can be found in current World Bank attempts to address poverty intellectually and in practical policy. The Bank's approach[70]—in broad outline—is to set a poverty level of U.S.$1 per person a day and to define all those below it as the "poor," all above it as the "nonpoor." It then posits an inherent conflict of interest between the two, criticizing measures that reach the "nonpoor" as diversions of resources from the needy. This almost inevitably excludes the possibility of democratic action against poverty, an outcome tacitly acknowledged by the Bank in early 1999, when it convened a meeting of scholars to advise it on why governments were not "propoor."

The effect is to separate off those at the bottom of the rung from the rest of society and to make poverty reduction purely a matter of technical concern. Because the poor are rarely able to organize themselves and are therefore forced to rely on alliances with other strata of society, egalitarian social policy tends to command political support in two circumstances. First, where its application is justified by criteria that elicit wide consensus—for example, the expressed need to cater for Civil War veterans ensured a generous social policy regime in the postbellum United States, despite that society's presumed resistance to social spending, because it tapped into and built on widespread public support for those who had defended the Union.[71] Second, where it is supported by a significant organized group—such as organized labor—which is able to forge alliances with other interests who also stand to benefit from action against inequality.[72]

Given these realities, a strategy and analysis that separates the poor from the rest of the society—and insists that their interests are in conflict with those of other groups—is certain to relegate their concerns to the peripheries, rendering democracies unable to address poverty or inequality. First, because by creating an antagonism between the poor and other strata, it excludes the possibility of consensus. Second and similarly, because it eliminates the prospect of alliances between the poor and other, more organized and influential groups. The only mystery attending the tendency of governments not to be "propoor" in these circumstances is that anyone should regard it as a mystery. If further evidence is needed, the hostility toward welfare recipients in the United States provides a useful illustration.[73] Once alliances and political action are removed from the equation, the only champions of equality and action against poverty are the scholars and policy advisers whose influence is hardly guaranteed and who, in any event, are as likely to oppose as to defend measures designed to address inequality. Ultimately, neither alliances nor political action can be effective without a vigorous and accessible democracy.

The World Bank's literature on poverty also highlights another anomaly in current attempts to exalt technique above democratic politics. Emphases on "public participation" often also tend to ignore or suppress one of the key assumptions of democratic politics—the acknowledgment of difference not only as an intractable reality but also as both a virtue that enriches society and an injunction to tolerance and engagement. Ironically, the same literature that divides society starkly into the "poor" and "nonpoor" also assumes that there is a homogeneous "public" whose participation can be sought. But if all have the same interests, why bother to invent institutions to express difference and mediate between contending positions? Since the inevitability of differences of interest and value is not only an empirical reality but also a normative precondition for democracy, the effect of such a stark division is to deny the need for politics and so to hand control of the public agenda to whichever interest is strong enough to dominate it. Whatever efficiencies it may yield, its result is unlikely to be greater freedom or equality. And the inequities and suppression of weaker interests it brings stem from its denial of democratic politics.[74]

Similarly, the current enthusiasm among international financial institutions and development specialists for "good governance," conceptualized as government without democratic politics, commits an error that, ironically, owes its provenance to Lenin: it reduces politics to administration.[75] Public management technique is presented as an alternative rather than a supplement to democratic politics, which often then appears as an obstacle to, rather than the raison d'être for, effective government.

If, then, new democracies are to strengthen their states, create wealth, and address inequality, they can do so only if democratic politics is strengthened. Since interest differences cannot be wished away by any amount of "good governance" or public participation techniques, the effect of substituting technique for democratic contest is to frustrate those goals that the architects of the new orthodoxy proclaim. A realistic prospect of progress depends not solely on generating more sophisticated proposals and techniques, but also on a recognition that only strengthening and enriching democratic institutions sufficiently to ensure that they are able to allow conflicts to be resolved through politics allows any prospect of permitting the freedom promised by democracy to translate also into greater social equity and human well-being.

These points are ignored by many in the South African elite. But they are also deeply embedded in the thinking and action of those with whom it interacts—key donor governments and their agencies. It should be no surprise, therefore, that the activities of donor governments in South Africa over the past couple few years have focused increasingly on governance technique rather than democratic strengthening, on civil society as "an instrument of delivery" rather than citizen participation in democratic institutions as a goal in itself. There are numerous examples, but two illustrate the point clearly. First, despite recommendations to that effect by policy analysts, few donor programs pay attention to the need to strengthen legislatures and legislators, their connection with their electorates, as well as their capacity to hold the executive to account on their behalf. There are important exceptions but, in the main, support for democratic government is narrowed to support for the executive—and in many cases the bureaucracy.[76] Second, the effect of the insistence of one major donor, the U.S.

Agency for International Development (USAID), on channeling funds to voluntary associations only if they are engaged in partnerships with the government[77]—is to mandate consensus, to deny the importance of pluralism.

It is therefore ironic that an agenda that, in South Africa, threatens prospects for a fuller, more robust, and resilient democracy is reinforced by some of the approaches and programs of the world's established democracies. Indeed, while donor governments may on occasion be responding to the preferences of their South African counterpart in an attempt to maintain a bilateral relationship, their governance assumptions often fit neatly with the current assumptions of South African decisionmaker. This ensures a mutually reinforcing set of ideas and approaches that militates against a vigorous attempt to nourish democratic institutions and practices.

Conclusion: The Limits of "Delivery"

The analysis presented here suggests a pessimistic prognosis for the quality of South African democracy. While the danger of authoritarian reversion remains slight, it suggests that the democratic project will remain incomplete: while democracy's form may well survive, its content may remain stunted by an emphasis on the ability of the enlightened technician to achieve a task for which democratic politics cannot be trusted.

But the die is not yet cast, for "delivery" is not achieving its own stated goals: the public goods and services hastily provided in an attempt to reach numerical targets are often not proving sustainable—cracks are literally appearing in the facade as houses fall apart or water projects run out of momentum.[78] A macroeconomic strategy based on the assumption that manipulating technical indices, rather than harnessing the energies and enthusiasm of economic actors, can produce growth and jobs, is failing to achieve enough of either.[79] An anticrime strategy based on coordinating state agencies rather than eliciting citizen cooperation has yet to demonstrate a capacity to reduce crime,[80] despite government claims that the number of arrests and prosecutions is rising.[81]

Events since June 1999, when the second administration took office, have provided convincing refutation of the delivery ideology. Thus Kader Asmal, who served as water minister in the first administration, earning the title "Mr. Delivery," took over education: he immediately unveiled an ambitious five-year plan, insisting that the time for negotiating with interest groups was over and the time for implementation had begun.[82] But the minister's insistence that the time for talk was over, while that for centrally directed action had arrived, produced the worst final secondary school examination results since 1994 and a lame ministerial excuse that, because they were only slightly worse than the previous year's, the slide to poorer results had been halted.[83] Management of action against crime—like education, one of the first administration's failures—followed a similar path. The new minister, the late Steve Tshwete, a close Mbeki ally, presided over a strategy in which cooperation between ministers and the formation of crack specialist units was meant to "deliver"—Tshwete also proposed more powers for the police,[84] and lambasted human rights activists for siding with villains rather than victims.[85] But constant official claims that the crime rate had decreased were contradicted by a careful analysis of official statistics,[86] which may well explain a decision by the ministry to no longer release them to the public.

More important for democracy's prospects, perhaps, attempts to steer delivery from government offices continue to run up against resistance from citizen groups. An approach to AIDS that has alienated medical specialists and NGO activists is proving a block to an effective response to the virus.[87] The macroeconomic strategy still faces resistance from trade unions and other interest groups,[88] while in education the initial insistence that policy debate was no longer necessary—and that government goals could be achieved by tough management—ran aground against the intractability of interest group activity, forcing a volte-face that produced significant policy changes and a renewed focus on intangibles such as common values.[89]

The ideology of delivery cannot produce an effective program of reform from the top. The current emphasis on centralized political direction and the substitution of technical solutions for public dialogue will not eliminate or subdue the diversity that remains one of the society's crucial strengths: at some point, then, the limits of this approach may become clear to opinion-makers and political leadership.

It may be, then, that South Africa's new democracy will reach its critical moment of choice. The response from the current leadership may be to conclude that the attempt to control and direct change through technique has not been pursued vigorously enough. In that case, democracy's prospects may be in even graver peril, for the temptation will be to rely even more heavily on control and to widen the gap between state and society. The possible consequences are depressingly familiar: political leaders insulated from society by admiring acolytes and self-justifying organograms relying increasingly but without noticeable success on control rather than inclusion and compromise.

But there is another choice. The president—who, for all the flaws of the current approach, remains among the most intelligent of currently serving heads of government—and his allies, could recognize that their strategy has failed not because democracy was given too much credence but because it was not allowed enough. In that case, delivery's discontents could produce a return to the stress on inclusion, participation, and pluralism that sustained the early period of transition. The limits of the attempt to afford priority to the technicians rather than democratic citizens could then prompt a new search for a fuller, richer, and more vigorous democracy.

Notes

1. "Illegal" immigrants are arguably the sole victims of human rights abuse in postapartheid society. See, for example, Reitzes, *Divided on the "Demon"*; and Dolan and Reitzes, *The Insider Story?*

2. Friedman, "Who We Are."

3. The Democratic Alliance, the official opposition, was the result of an alliance between the Democratic Party and the New National Party (NNP); while under apartheid, the former was a liberal party, and the National Party, from which the NNP emerged, was the architect of apartheid. The two have found common cause in a shared antipathy to the ANC. The alliance has since collapsed, with the NNP entering an alliance with the ANC.

4. See Friedman, "South Africa: Entering the Post Mandela Era."

5. Friedman, "South Africa: Divided in a Special Way."

6. For the most authoritative political history of this lengthy period, see Roux, *Time Longer Than Rope.*

7. See, for example, Rantete and Swilling, "Organization and Strategies."

8. For a critique, see Fine, "Civil Society Theory"; and Friedman, "Bonaparte at the Barricades."

9. During 1997 the leadership was repeatedly defeated in internal ANC elections for provincial leadership posts. This prompted a tendency to dissuade rival candidates from competing using appeals to loyalty to the movement. This trend reached a head at the ANC conference in December, when a concerted attempt was made to dissuade Mosiua Lekota, a prominent former UDF leader, from opposing the leadership's candidate, Steve Tshwete. Lekota insisted on competing and won in a landslide. Centre for Policy Studies (CPS), *Quarterly Trends,* January, 1998.

10. Rapoo, *Twist in the Tail?*

11. Given the points made above, the constant use of the military term "deploy," which is invoked to describe any shift of ANC figures from one public post to another, is revealing. CPS, *South Africa Update,* April 2000.

12. Friedman, "No Easy Stroll to Dominance."

13. CPS, *South Africa Update,* April 2000.

14. Atkinson, "Brokering a Miracle?"

15. Friedman, *Yesterday's Pact,* 1995.

16. The attitude is by no means restricted to South African whites. In a 1995 discussion, a (white) senior mining executive told of visiting fund managers in North America and Western Europe in an attempt to raise investment capital. His and his colleagues' pitch consisted largely of references to healthy economic fundamentals and progress in resolving conflicts. In many cases, the appeal was not persuasive. "But you have a black government," many of his audiences responded.

17. Schmitter and Karl, "What Democracy Is."

18. This section summarizes the argument presented in Friedman, "Who We Are."

19. Finkel, "The Effects of Participation."

20. See, for example, Friedman and Stack, "The Magic Moment."

21. Robertson, "Contesting the Contest."

22. Downs, *An Economic Theory.*

23. Green and Shapiro, *Pathologies.*

24. Friedman, "Agreeing to Differ."

25. Bratton, "A First Look."

26. Piven and Cloward, *Why Americans Don't Vote.*

27. Graeme Gotz, in *Buying In,* develops this argument relying heavily on the proposition that the democratic state is obliged to create a public realm accessible to all.

28. The IEC later retreated from this stricture by ruling that persons who arrived at the polls with proof that they had registered would be allowed to vote whether or not they appeared on the roll. Among those forced to take advantage of this "concession" was the leader of the Pan-Africanist Congress, Bishop Stanley Mogoba.

29. Mackay, "IEC's Sleight of Hand."

30. Both the Human Sciences Research Council and Opinion 99 polls, the most often cited, found 83 percent expressing a voting intention. Alence and O'Donovan, *If South Africa's Second Democratic Election Had Been Held in March 1999,* p. 7.

31. See, for example, comments by ANC general secretary Kgalema Mothlante in CPS, *Quarterly Trends,* June 1998.

32. The exchange occurred at a seminar in Bonn, Germany, in April 1998.

33. As noted above, the theory, in its "pure" form, insists that no one will vote unless they perceive that their ballot alone will prove decisive—see Green and Shapiro, *Pathologies.* While there was clearly a greater likelihood of this perception in the "close" provinces, the difference in perceived utility, given that even in close elections it may not be rational to assume that one's vote will be decisive, may not have been great enough to influence behavior.

34. Idasa Public Opinion Service (POS), *Building a Democratic Culture in the Western Cape,* p. ii; Idasa POS, *Building a Democratic Culture in KwaZulu-Natal,* p. ii.

35. The assumption that voters need to be "educated" holds either that they are unable to cast a ballot without elite aid, which was effectively refuted by behavior in both elections—see Friedman and Stack, "The Magic Moment"—or that they are unable to discern their own interests without similar assistance, which has also been empirically refuted—see, for example, Charney, *Voices.*

36. See, for example, the survey reported in CPS, *Quarterly Trends,* August 1998.

37. CPS, *Quarterly Trends,* January 1999.

38. South African Broadcasting Corporation, *Election Special,* June 2, 1999.

39. Understood in the sense it is used by Robert Putnam in *Making Democracy Work,* as an indicator of those attitudes of reciprocity and public education that are, in this view, at the core of a democratic culture.

40. Rodrik, *The New Global Economy.*

41. Important elements of this argument underpin, for example, the analysis of Hermann Giliomee and Charles Simkins in the conclusion to their book *The Awkward Embrace.*

42. Taylor and Mattes, *Public Evaluations,* pp. 5–6.

43. Idasa POS, *Provincial Politics,* p. 8.

44. Idasa POS, *Building a Democratic Culture in the Western Cape,* p. 8; Idasa POS, *Building a Democratic Culture in KwaZulu-Natal,* p. 6.

45. CPS, *Quarterly Trends,* April 1999.

46. Tomlinson, *From Institution-Building to House-Building.*

47. Schmitz, *Rethinking Delivery?;* Breslin, *Lessons from the Field.*

48. Tomlinson, *From Rejection to Resignation.*

49. For an elaboration of this argument and a critique of attempts to substitute forums for representative democracy in the first administration, see Friedman and Reitzes, *Democratic Selections?*

50. For one analysis of policy failure, see CPS, *Quarterly Trends,* January 1998.

51. Republic of South Africa, Department of Water Affairs and Forestry, *Water Supply and Sanitation Policy,* p. 8.

52. Stacey, *New Capacities for Old?*

53. The willingness of more affluent whites to accept redistributive water policies if they appeal to universals was established by Project Manzi in 1995.

54. See Friedman, *Democracy.*

55. World Bank, *The State.*

56. Davidson and Rees-Mogg, *The Sovereign Individual.*

57. For a discussion, in the South African context, of ways in which "participation" techniques substitute for, rather than supplement, representative democracy, see Friedman, "Bonaparte at the Barricades"; and Friedman, *The Elusive "Community."*

58. See, for example, Raczynski, *Strategies.*

59. On the views of the left, see Keane, *Democracy;* and Keane, *Civil Society.* On the views of libertarians, see Tanner, *The End of Welfare.*

60. O'Donnell and Schmitter, *Transitions;* Keane, *Democracy.*

61. Keane, *Democracy.*

62. Maqsood Ali and Sirivardana, "Towards a New Paradigm."

63. World Bank, *The State,* p. 90.

64. Putnam, *Making Democracy Work;* Fukayama, *Trust.*

65. Budlender and Dube, "Starting with What We Have."

66. Heller, "Social Capital."

67. Keane, *Democracy.* See also Barber, *A Place for Us.*

68. Putnam, "Bowling Alone."

69. In the African context, many shack settlements "began with an emphasis on participation and ended up with a shacklord." Mamdani, *Citizen and Subject,* p. 295. See also White, *Makhulu Padroni?*

70. See, for example, World Bank, *Poverty Reduction and the World Bank: Progress and Challenges in the 1990s;* and World Bank, *Poverty Reduction and the World Bank: Progress in Fiscal 1996 and 1997*

71. Skocpol and Katznelson, *Social Policy,* 1996.

72. Esping-Andersen, *The Three Worlds;* Przeworksi, *Capitalism.*

73. See, for example, Jencks, *Rethinking Social Policy.* Scholarly examples of the attack on welfare in the United States are provided in, among other sources, Murray, *Losing Ground;* and Tanner, *The End of Welfare.*

74. For a classic expression of politics's indispensability as a vehicle for the institutionalization of tolerance, see Crick, *In Defence.* For a critique of Marxism-Leninism's attempt to eliminate politics by asserting a putative proletarian interest as an alternative to political exchange and contest, see Polan, *Lenin.*

75. Polan, *Lenin,* pp. 58 ff.

76. These conclusions are based on a series of donor assessments conducted by the Centre for Policy Studies and on information gathered for the *Development Cooperation Report 2000,* commissioned by the South African Department of Finance, to which the author enjoys access.

77. Recent information suggests that this view might be changing. However, the assertion is based on extensive discussions between the author and USAID consultants during 1998, when this view was firmly held.

78. Presentation by Moshe More, South African National NGO Coalition, Centre for Policy Studies seminar, University of the Witwatersrand, Johannesburg, June 7, 2000.

79. Mangcu, "Why GEAR Is Not Delivering."

80. CPS, *South Africa Update,* April 2000.

81. Presentation by Robinson Ramaite, director-general, Public Service and Administration, Centre for Policy Studies, June 13, 2000.

82. CPS, *South Africa Update,* September, 1999, January 2000.

83. Ibid., January 2000.

84. CPS, *Quarterly Trends,* July 1999.

85. CPS, *South Africa Update,* January 2000.

86. Ibid., June 2000.

87. Friedman, "Society Must Be Brought On Board."

88. CPS, *South Africa Update,* January 2000.

89. Ibid., September 1999, January 2000, April 2000.

Promoting Real Reform in Africa

Larry Diamond

The statistics tell a grim story. Sub-Saharan Africa (which I will sub-sequently term "Africa") is trapped in the world's worst poverty and stagnation. As we see from Table 1.1 (see Chapter 1), most African countries had lower per capita incomes (in constant 1995 dollars) at the end of the twentieth century than they had in 1980. Improvements in life expectancy have stagnated over the last two decades, and in many countries the gains that have been made are rapidly eroding in the face of the HIV/AIDS pandemic. Progress in reducing illiteracy has been slow. As shown in Table 1.2, two in five Africans (and half of all African women) are illiterate; only South Asia has a worse rate. By comparison, only about one of every eight adults in East Asia or Latin America is illiterate. A clear reason why is because far fewer Africans are in school than are young people in other regions (see Table 11.1 for all the regional comparisons). Africa is the only region of the world where school enrollments have been declining at every level and the only region where life expectancy has been declining, falling in 2001 to just forty-seven years. It is also the only region where average life expectancy is less than sixty years of age. Because so many African infants and young children die (Africa also has the highest infant and child mortality rates), women have more children to ensure that some survive to adulthood. Low levels of female literacy and formal employment also are associated with higher fertility. As a result, Africa also has the highest population growth rate—higher than the next fastest growing region by half a percentage point.

Africa is the world's poorest region. Its average per capita national income, in purchasing power parity (PPP) dollars, is a third lower than the next poorest region, South Asia (which has little in the way of oil or other mineral resources). Its ratio of external debt to annual national income is the worst of any region (about two-thirds of national income, on average). With 13 percent of the world's population, Africa accounts for only 1.6 percent of

Table 11.1 Relative Development Performance of Africa

	Sub-Saharan Africa	East Asia/ Pacific	Latin America/ Caribbean	South Asia	Middle East/ North Africa	Eastern Europe FSU[a]
Per Capita Gross National Income, 2002, U.S.PPP$	1,620	4,160	6,750	2,390	5,410	7,070
Life Expectancy at Birth, 2001	46.5	69.5	70.3	62.8	66.0	69
Adult Literacy, 2001	62.4	87.1	89.2	56.3	60.8	97
Population Growth Rate, 1990–2001	2.6	1.2	1.6	1.9	2.1	0.2
Official Development Assistance: U.S.$ per Capita,						
2001	21	4	12	4	16	23
1998	21	4	9	4	18	14
1990	36	4	11	5	42	13
School Enrollment Ratio: Primary, Secondary, Tertiary Combined, 2000–2001	44	65	81	54	60[b]	79
Human Development Index, 2001	0.468	0.722	0.777	0.582	0.662	0.787
Percentage of Adults 15–49 Living with HIV/AIDS, 2001	9.00	0.20	0.60	0.50	0.40[b]	0.50
External Debt as Percentage of Gross National Income, 2001	68	30	42	45	34	54

Sources: World Bank, *World Development Report 2004: Making Services Work for Poor People* (New York: Oxford University Press, 2004) tab. 5, p. 261, and tab. 1, p. 253. UNDP, *Human Development Report: Millennium Development Goals: A Compact Among Nations to End Human Poverty* (New York, Oxford University Press, 2003), tab. 1, p. 240, and tab. 7, p. 261.
    Notes: a. Former Soviet Union.
    b. Refers to Arab states only.

global trade and less than 1 percent of global investment, and it is the only major region where per capita investment and savings have declined since 1970. Overall, Africa has by far the worst average "human development" score (0.468) of any region of the world. Indeed, the statistics suggest that Africa is virtually equivalent to the average "least-developed country" (0.448 average on the index). According to the United Nations Development Programme (UNDP), thirty of the thirty-four countries that rank lowest in human development are in sub-Saharan Africa, as are *all* of the bottom twenty-five.[1] These are also, for the most part, the countries where the majority of the population lives in absolute poverty, forced to survive on less than U.S.$2 per day, or as with half of all Africans, even less than U.S.$1 per day.[2]

Yet Africa is hardly ignored by the international community. Historically, it has received far more per capita in official "development assistance" than any other region of the world.[3] By the late 1990s, well over half of all African states were deriving at least 10 percent of their gross national product (GNP) from foreign aid, which was also accounting (in the first half of the decade) for "over 50 percent of African government revenues and 71 percent of their public investments. In many countries in the region, virtually the entire nonrecurrent component of the budget as well as large parts of the recurrent budget were financed by the donors."[4] During the 1990s, Africa's ratio of official development assistance to GNP (13.4 percent) was three times higher than the next most aid-dependent region (South Asia, 4.7 percent), and total aid (including aid to nongovernmental organizations [NGOs]) averaged almost 80 percent of government expenditures (half as high as South Asia and fifteen times that of Latin America).[5] Even though Africa's total net official development assistance has declined in recent years from a high of U.S.$17 billion to U.S.$12 billion, in 1999 this was still two-thirds higher than its foreign direct investment (most of which was in the oil sector).[6] David Leonard and Scott Straus calculate that many African countries receive more in development assistance than they collect in tax revenue. An estimated half of this aid has been going to finance repayment of the most crushing external debt burdens of any region of the world.[7] Africa's external debt is now two-thirds of its annual income, a ratio much higher than any other "developing" region, despite far-reaching debt forgiveness (amounting to U.S.$13 billion of bilateral debt between 1988 and 1995).[8]

Aid flows to Africa—and to the developing world in general—have been driven by a long-standing theoretical model that assumes the key missing ingredient for development is financing. If external donors could just provide enough foreign aid to fill the "financing gap" between a country's own savings and a determined necessary level of investment, economic growth would take place. International development economists and policymakers clung to this "financing gap" model even when it became apparent that it wasn't working, that more aid was not producing more economic growth, but often less, because the aid was not being used for productive investment and was not being accompanied by corresponding increases in a country's savings rate.[9]

The core problem obstructing economic development in Africa is not a lack of resources, though that is a serious constraint in many countries. Those African countries, such as Nigeria, Angola, Cameroon, and the Democratic Republic of Congo (former Zaire), that are rich in oil and other natural resources have largely squandered their natural wealth, achieving little in terms of development. They are just about as poor and miserable as their less bountiful neighbors. In fact, there is increasingly compelling evidence and logic showing that natural resource wealth (most notably oil) produced from economic enclaves generates incentive structures that undermine economic development.[10] Only one African country with mineral wealth (diamonds) has managed it effectively for development, Botswana. Only two African countries, Botswana and Mauritius, have achieved a relatively good development performance in the past three decades (see Table 1.1). Not coincidentally, these are the only two African countries that have been continuously democratic since independence.

It is difficult to make a case for the economic benefits of democracy by comparing only two small countries with the other forty-six in Africa. Still, the data not only show that Botswana and Mauritius have had dramatically better development performance than the rest, but they also suggest that the African countries that democratized during the 1990s made some development progress during the decade while the lingering semidemocracies and autocracies performed much more poorly as a group and in general, continued to slide backward (see Table 1.1). It is too soon to know if democracies will continue to outperform autocracies on the continent. Uganda has made significant development progress under a regime that has been only semidemocratic at best. And the HIV/AIDS pandemic is already beginning to register a staggering negative impact on life expectancy and other aspects of human development throughout southern Africa, which contains the continent's largest concentration of democracies, including Botswana and South Africa, which are being ravaged by the disease. Yet as E. Gyimah-Boadi trenchantly argues in Chapter 1, the HIV/AIDS crisis exposes in sharp relief the shortcomings of governance even in the formally democratic countries of Africa, while the crucial elements of democracy—openness, civic organization, political empowerment (particularly of women)—are proving to be vital tools for combating the plague.

Evidence on the link between democracy and development is not only coming from Africa. Richard Roll and John Talbott recently found that among the most significant factors in explaining variations in per capita national income during the 1990s were several different measures of freedom, including political rights, civil liberties, press freedom, and property rights, each of which "has an independent, strong, and positive influence on country income."[11] More striking, they found that there is clearly a causal effect of democracy on economic growth, as "democratic events" (transitions to democracy or increases in freedom) "have been followed by rather dramatic increases in GNIpc [gross national income per capita]," which tend to accelerate further over time if a country sustains the democratic trend, while antidemocratic events are followed by declines in economic growth.[12] Comparing the 176 most democratic leaders and the 179 most autocratic leaders since 1952, Bruce Bueno de Mesquita and his colleagues found that the average democratic leader produced a real annual economic growth rate of 3.04 percent, compared to 1.78 percent for the average autocrat.[13]

Within Africa, Benn Eifert finds "a large and robust relationship" between political openness and economic growth, both across African countries and over time. "The difference in political openness between the most democratic and the least democratic African state is associated with a growth gap of over 4.5 percentage points per year."[14] Globally, democracy has had a discernible effect over the past half century in reducing infant mortality, even when other developmental factors such as per capita income are controlling for.[15] And when broadening the analysis to consider a wider range of governance variables (including "voice and accountability" and rule of law), Daniel Kaufman and his colleagues in the World Bank find "a strong positive causal relationship from improved governance to better development outcomes."[16]

One reason why Africa continues to lag so far behind economically is that it lags well behind in governance as well. In the latest survey of perceptions of global corruption, only seventeen African countries are assessed, but twelve of these are among the most corrupt half of the world's states (the other five African states in the survey are all democracies, and relatively liberal ones at that).[17] Among the major regions of the world, only the Middle East is clearly worse in terms of democracy and freedom. Only about two in every five of African governments are accountable to their people through the most minimal instrument of free, fair, and competitive national elections. And of these nineteen or so democracies (at the end of 2003), only about five can be said to be liberal, in terms of allowing extensive civil and political freedom (see Table 11.2). Certainly, freedom has improved and democracy has expanded dramatically in Africa since 1990, but the promise of a "second liberation" across the continent has stalled, and where political freedom is most abused so are economic and social development as well.

There is no disputing the fact that a few autocracies, mainly in East Asia, have achieved rapid economic growth over the past few decades. But African countries lack the unique historical circumstances (greater cultural coherence, an ideological external threat) that facilitated the East Asian miracles under authoritarian rule. As several scholars have noted, autocracies have a much wider range of variation in development performance, from stunning growth to staggering disaster, including mass famine. Democracies do not have famines, and generally they avoid developmental disaster because when people are truly able to turn out their leaders in free and fair elections, leaders must perform to some extent or they will be held accountable.[18] When a Mobutu Sese Seko or Idi Amin or Sani Abacha can loot his country and murder his compatriots with abandon, there is no check on predation. Resources bleed out of the country and production withers. Conflict and instability grow, further weakening already porous and fragile states and making entire regions "no-go" zones for investment.

Table 11.2 Democracy and Freedom in Africa by Region, 2002

	Number of Countries	Number of Democracies (% of total)[a]		Number (%) of Liberal Democracies with Freedom House Score < 2.5		Average Freedom Score for Region	
						1974	2002
Western Europe and Anglophone States	28	28	(100)	28	(100)	1.58	1.04
Latin America and Caribbean	33	30	(91)	17	(52)	3.81	2.49
Eastern Europe and Former Soviet Union	27	18	(67)	11	(41)	6.50	3.39
Asia (East, Southeast, and South)	25	12	(48)	4	(16)	4.84	4.38
Pacific Islands	12	11	(91)	8	(67)	2.75	2.00
Africa (Sub-Saharan)	48	19	(40)	5	(10)	5.51	4.33
Middle East/North Africa	19	2	(11)	1	(5)	5.15	5.53
Total	192	120	(63)	74	(38)	4.39	3.38
Arab Countries	16	0		0		5.59	5.81
Predominantly Muslim Countries	43	7[b]		0		5.29	5.33

Source: Adrian Karatnycky, "The 2002 Freedom House Survey," *Journal of Democracy* 14, no. 1 (January 2003): 100–113.

Notes: a. The current number of democracies as classified by Freedom House, with the exception that Russia is classified as a nondemocracy.

b. Counted among this group are Bangladesh, Mali, Niger, Senegal, Indonesia, Turkey, and Albania.

The fundamental new insight that is reshaping the political economy of development is in fact a very old one. Governance matters. The nature and quality of governance, and the types of policies that governments choose, have a huge impact—apparently, the decisive one—in shaping how economies perform and whether and how rapidly people will escape from mass poverty. As William Easterly writes, "Bad governments . . . can kill growth."[19] And that is exactly what has happened in Africa. Growth requires that people reduce present consumption in return for greater income in the future. Where government policies and actions discourage investment in the future—through policies and practices that generate high inflation, high black market premiums, negative real interest rates, high budget deficits, restrictions on free trade, rotten public services, and massive corruption—investors and producers run for cover.[20] Indeed, Easterly has found that "Africa's higher government budget deficits, higher financial repression, and higher black market premiums explain about half of the growth difference between East Asia and Africa over the past three decades."[21] If Africa's economic policies had been as liberal on average as East Asia's, African per capita income on average would be about U.S.$2,000 higher (in 1989 dollars).[22]

The partial understanding that economic policies would have to change if investors and producers were to be given the right incentives led to the wave of economic stabilization and structural adjustment pressures on African states in the 1980s and 1990s. As Nicolas van de Walle shows in Chapter 2, under pressure from the donors the majority of African states did much to stabilize their economies over the past two decades, particularly in the 1990s. But this progress has been halting, uneven, tentative, and partial. At the same time, stabilization has also further squeezed public investment budgets, while public infrastructure has continued to decay. Some liberalization of prices and regulations has occurred, but African states have not had the will or ability to implement the sweeping transformation of economic structures and policies that is needed. Again, as van de Walle shows, much of the old racket remains, as the state still obstructs and intervenes in ways that privilege the few over the many. And invariably, the few who benefit are those in state office or those with some connection to it.[23]

Beyond the very partial implementation of economic reform lies the pervasive problem of corruption in Africa, which, as Sahr Kpundeh argues in Chapter 5, is profoundly antidevelopmental. Corruption can be dressed up analytically in a variety of terms, but it is basically a process whereby the powerful (those with control over or access to the state) use their power illicitly to accumulate wealth without generating much of anything for the society in return. This "urge to steal everything not bolted to the floor is the most obvious growth-killing incentive."[24] It discourages private investment, distorts resource allocations, deforms policies, proliferates regulations, swells budget deficits, enervates institutions, diverts resources from productive (wealth-generating) activity, and squanders large amounts of resources. Funds that could go to educate and inoculate children, pave roads, build markets, dig wells, generate electricity, and otherwise provide an overall enabling environment for growth instead wind up in overseas bank accounts and real estate, financing luxury purchases for already wealthy individuals. Worse still, officials often waste even more money purchasing weapons and building structures the country doesn't need (and likely will never use) in order to generate an opportunity for kickbacks. A 2002 report prepared for the African Union estimates that corruption costs the continent U.S.$148 billion annually.[25] That is well over a quarter of the continent's entire gross domestic product.

As van de Walle explains, politics in the typical African country still remains deeply stuck in the "logic of neopatrimonialism." State incumbents at all levels use their power and office to appropriate resources for themselves and their families, cronies, clients, and kin.[26] State offices are distributed with the expectation and understanding that their incumbents will use them to accumulate wealth.[27] Corrupt resources flow up and down chains of clientage in a vast cascading drain upon public wealth and honest effort. Corruption in these countries is not an aberration. It is the way the system works, the way people acquire power and wealth, and the way officials retain power and expand wealth. At its most extreme, locally or nationally, the state is little more than a criminal racket, and the police and organized crime may be one and the same.

For the several dozen African countries that are caught more or less in this corrupt, neopatrimonial logic, there is no commitment to the larger public good and no confidence in the future. Every actor is motivated by the desire to get what can be gotten now, by any possible means. Communities as well seek immediate government jobs and favors, in a zero-sum struggle over a stagnant and potentially fleeting stock of resources. Thus there is no respect for law and no rule of law. The judicial system is politicized and routinely suborned or so demoralized and starved of resources that it cannot prosecute corrupt conduct in public and private life with any kind of energy and regularity. Governmental decisions and transactions are deliberately opaque in order to hide their corrupt nature and evade embarrassing disclosures. Information about how government works and how contracts are awarded is simply unavailable. Exposure of corrupt deeds typically brings little more than embarrassment, because the rule of law does not function to constrain or punish the behavior of public officials. Power is heavily centralized and institutions of scrutiny and accountability function only on paper, or episodically, to punish the more marginal miscreants or the rivals of the truly powerful. Lacking a sense of public purpose, discipline, and esprit de corps, the civil service, police, customs, and other public institutions function poorly and corruptly. Salaries are meager because the country is poor, taxes are not collected, corruption is expected, and government payrolls are bloated with the ranks of political clients and fictitious workers. Corruption is rife at the bottom of the governance system because that is the climate that is set at the top, and because government workers cannot live on the salaries they are paid.

In fact, institutions in such a society are a facade. The police do not enforce the law. Judges do not decide the law. Customs officials do not inspect the goods. Manufacturers do not produce, bankers do not invest, borrowers do not repay, and contracts do not get enforced. Any actor with discretionary power is a rent-seeker. Every transaction is twisted to immediate advantage.

In such circumstances, state elites may be feared (and envied) for their sweeping and unaccountable power, but the state as an institution is weak and porous. By every one of Samuel Huntington's criteria of institutionalization—coherence, complexity, autonomy, and adaptability[28]—the African neopatriomonial state appears as a shallow, brittle, highly personalized set of structures, captured by narrow (and typically, ethnically exclusive) elites for their own ends, lacking a larger sense of autonomous purpose and mission.

This is why the worst instances of plunder and neopatrimonial rule collapse completely into state failure and civil war. Indeed, most of the thirty-five African civil wars that Stephen Stedman and Terrence Lyons chronicle in Chapter 6 took place in contexts of highly authoritarian and abusive governance. This includes all the recent "textbook" instances of state collapse—Somalia, Liberia, Sierra Leona, and the Democratic Republic of Congo (the former Zaire). All four of the "repeat offenders" in suffering civil wars—Burundi, Chad, Uganda, and Zaire—have been notable for their extreme lack of democracy, and no African civil war has broken out in a truly democratic political system. Indeed, as Stedman and Lyons note, the same predatory quest for control of resources that has been dragging down African states internally has also been contributing to regionalizing these conflicts of late, as corrupt governments seek the spoils of war in neighboring countries.

For a long time, Africa's leaders and official institutions blamed these woes and failures on the legacies of colonialism and the injustices of the international system. Increasingly, however, Africans are recognizing that the core of the problem now lies in the defects of their own institutions of governance and the distorted incentives they generate. The 2003 *African Development Report* is strikingly reflective of this new spirit of candor, and thus merits quoting at some length:

> More than four decades of independence for many countries should have been enough time to sort out the colonial legacies and move forward. Thus, Africa needs to look at itself—especially the nature of political power and governance institutions. In most African countries, the economy is still dominated by the state—with the state as major provider of formal employment, contracts, and patronage while parties are regionally and ethnically based. And politics in most of these countries is such that victor assumes a "winner-takes-all" form with respect to wealth and resources, patronage, and the prestige and prerogatives of office. If there is lack of transparency and accountability in governance, inadequate checks and balances, non-adherence to the rule of law, absence of credible and peaceful means to change or replace leadership, or lack of respect for human rights, political control becomes excessively important and the stakes dangerously high.[29]

These dynamics, the African Development Bank argues, have been a major factor behind the plethora of armed conflicts in Africa, which, in addition to claiming several million lives over the past decade, displaced 12 million people into refugee status by 2000, 40 percent of the world total.[30] If Africans are to achieve peace, progress, and human dignity, they must get better governance, with democracy and a rule of law. But transforming governance will also require fundamental changes in the way the external world relates to Africa.

The Continuing Aid Addiction

Corruption is the bane of development and democracy in Africa. Yet the donor agencies were slow to recognize it as a fundamental problem, and even when they began to do so in the 1990s, the money kept rolling in to fill the coffers of most corrupt, decadent, unaccountable African states. Particularly in the early 1990s, pressure for better, more accountable governance did heighten the financial squeeze on bankrupt African states and led to a number of transitions from authoritarian rule, beginning in Benin in 1990. A number of African countries, such as Sudan, Somalia, and Kenya (until its dramatic breakthrough to electoral democracy in December 2002), saw their aid receipts decline significantly during the 1990s. But for most African states, the money has kept rolling in. By 2000, development assistance had begun to gravitate somewhat more to the democracies of Africa, which averaged higher per capita aid receipts than the nondemocracies (see Table 11.3). But a number of highly authoritarian and corrupt governments, in countries such as Cameroon, Angola, Eritrea, Guinea, and Mauritania, received levels of aid equaling or even well exceeding the African average of U.S.$20 per capita. Almost all the authoritarian regimes, including those under international pressure for bad governance (such as Kenya and Zimbabwe), received aid well above the global average (U.S.$11 per capita) in 2000 for low- and middle-income countries. Even most of the democracies receiving aid have yet to overcome the neopatrimonial style of politics, as they still suffer from extensive corruption and a weak rule of law.[31]

Thus, aid has so far had only a very limited and tentative impact in improving governance. And it is not just the aid recipients that are addicted. It is the donors, too, who need to offer aid in order to justify being aid institutions; who evaluate and promote their aid officers on the basis of their ability to push allocated aid dollars out the door; and who believe that they have a humanitarian obligation to help all countries, even where it is clear that aid is doing no real good—or even more harm than good.

In fact, the overall structure of Africa's current aid dependence *is* doing more harm than good, for it facilitates and reproduces the patterns of corrupt, neopatrimonial governance that obstruct development. Venal, abusive rulers need a flow of resources from somewhere in order to pay off their networks of supporters and cronies, accumulate personal wealth, maintain at least minimal control over a coercive apparatus, and thus survive in power. They cannot get much of these resources from the tax revenues of their citizens, because they do not have the legitimacy and their decrepit states do not have the capacity to raise much revenue from taxation. If their countries (like Cameroon, Angola, and Nigeria) have oil, or other geographically concentrated mineral wealth (diamonds, gold, copper, and so on) that can be mined, they may derive the necessary income from mining rents (both the official taxes on corporate revenues and the unofficial bribes). As

Table 11.3 Official Aid Receipts and Levels of Freedom in Africa

	Official Development Assistance Received (U.S.$ per capita) 2001	Freedom House Average Score 2000	Score on Corruption Perceptions Index (rank out of 133) 2003
Democracies	32.7		
South Africa	10	1.5	4.4 (48)
Botswana	17	2.0	5.7 (30)
Benin	42	2.0	n/a
Ghana	33	2.5	3.3 (70)
Mali	32	2.5	3.0 (78)
Namibia	61	2.5	4.7 (41)
Madagascar	22	3.0	n/a
Malawi	38	3.0	2.8 (83)
Central African Republic	20	3.5	n/a
Mozambique	52	3.5	2.7 (86)
Senegal	43	3.5	n/a
Niger	22	4.0	n/a
Ambiguous Regimes	34.5 (45.7)[a]		
Nigeria	1	4.0	1.4 (132)
Tanzania	36	4.0	2.5 (92)
Sierra Leone	65	4.5	n/a
Zambia	36	4.5	n/a
Nondemocracies	28		
Lesotho	26	4.0	n/a
Congo (Brazzaville)	24	5.0	2.2 (113)
Ethiopia	16	5.0	2.5 (92)
Togo	10	5.0	n/a
Côte d'Ivoire	11	5.5	2.1 (118)
Uganda	34	5.5	2.2 (113)
Zimbabwe	12	5.5	n/a
Chad	23	5.5	n/a
Guinea	36	5.5	n/a
Kenya	15	5.5	1.9 (122)
Mauritania	95	5.5	n/a
Angola	20	6.0	1.8 (124)
Burundi	19	6.0	n/a
Eritrea	67	6.0	n/a
Cameroon	26	6.5	1.8 (124)
Congo (Kinshasa)	5	6.5	n/a
Rwanda	37	6.5	n/a

Sources: World Bank, *World Development Report 2004: Making Services Work for Poor People* (New York: Oxford University Press, 2004) tab. 5, pp.260-1; Freedom House, *Freedom in the World 2000–2001* (New York: Freedom House, 2001), p. 660; Transparency International, *Corruption Perceptions Index 2003*, Press Release, London 7 October, 2003.

Notes: a. Score without Nigeria.

n/a = not available (the country was not included in the survey).

Leonard and Straus note, agricultural production on large corporate estates can also generate a "rentier" economy that does not "depend on widespread productivity" and tax revenue.[32] Strikingly, foreign aid can play a functionally similar role, producing a kind of pseudo-enclave economy. Whether the money derives from mineral rents or foreign aid, ruling elites get autonomous sources of revenue that disrupt the bonds of accountability between the rulers and the ruled. In either case, the state does not have to function effectively or responsibly or transparently in order to get the lifeblood of its existence, revenue. In either case, state elites get "a steady stream of lucrative, easily cashed 'rents' (taxes and bribes) that can be quickly dispersed to clients and personal networks, . . . while doing nothing to build the institutions or incentives that would discourage" corruption and clientelism.[33] In either case, elites are freed from the need to build and maintain broader domestic bases of support, which would require better, more open, and public-spirited governance.

African political systems based on the corrupt distribution of patronage (which includes, to a lesser degree, even most of Africa's democracies) are thus addicted to aid (even several of the oil states, such as Cameroon and Angola, now heavily depend on it). And the donors are addicted to providing the aid—partly out of bureaucratic inertia, partly out of misplaced idealism and guilt, and partly out of the need to keep recycling unpayable African debts. Unless this mutual addiction is overcome, Africa will not move onto the path of sustainable development. For development will only happen when governance fundamentally improves—when African state officials at all levels become truly accountable to their publics, and when state resources come to be used to advance the overall welfare of the society, rather than that of a narrow clan of beneficiaries. Controlling corruption and generating accountability, participation, and a true rule of law are not simply one set among a number of diverse requirements for development in Africa. These conditions of good governance form the essential prerequisite for Africa's emergence out of its entrenched, degrading, seemingly intractable poverty. And they can be generated. The situation is far from hopeless, for as Michael Bratton and Robert Mattes show in Chapter 3, African people do understand and value democracy and oppose authoritarian alternatives. Moreover, as Gyimah-Boadi shows, African civil societies have been organizing and mobilizing—despite significant handicaps and obstacles—for freedom, democracy, and better governance.

If Africa is to attain better governance, the push for it will have to come from within. The popular and civil society aspirations for better governance are evident. But the problem now is that in most African states, the incentives for elites to yield to these pressures from below are weak, because African state elites depend so little on their own people for the resources they need to operate. Until the donors embrace and interact with popular demands for justice, accountability, and good governance, most elites (including those elected in superficially competitive contests) will not permit (much less actively construct) the kinds of independent and vigorous institutions of horizontal accountability that will foster better governance.

We know what these are—autonomous courts, prosecutors, and legal aid systems; countercorruption and audit agencies; ombudsmen and human rights commissions; central banks; and so on.[34] Increasingly, international donor agencies stand ready (and able) to assist in the construction and institutional development of these agencies of accountability. But the political will to get them up and effectively running is extremely weak. The core challenge for African development is this: How can the political will for fundamental governance reform be generated?

The Stalled African Renaissance

African leaders are keenly aware that their legitimacy has badly eroded at home and abroad. The more serious and public-spirited among them know that something must be done to improve governance if there is to be any hope of healing the continent's bleeding sores of poverty, disease, and violent conflict. Others at least concede that some gesture toward reform is needed. In this spirit of criticism and reflection, the Organization of African Unity (OAU) resolved in July 2001 to transform itself the following year into a new African Union (AU), which held its first summit in Durban, South Africa, one year later. The hope of many was that the AU would take a tougher, more direct approach to the problems of poverty, conflict, and bad governance on the continent than had the OAU, which was "hindered in its activities by internal conflict and self-serving heads of state."[35] Yet it is difficult to see how a new body, made up of the very same heads of state—and initially proposed by one of the worst dictators on the continent, Libya's Muammar Qaddafi (who has been plying his fellow African leaders with all sorts of personal "gifts")—can transcend the limits of the old structure. The AU intends to have a pan-African parliament, an African court of justice, new continental economic institutions, and harmonized policies. Its founding objectives included promoting not only peace and security on the continent, but also "democratic principles and institutions, popular participation and good governance."[36] Yet when the new organization faced its first test, in confronting the blatantly rigged 2002 presidential elections in Zimbabwe and the subsequent deepening political and humanitarian crisis in that country, it failed to act.

The hopes for an African "renaissance" (as South Africa's President Thabo Mbeki has termed it) now rest heavily with the New Partnership for African Development (NEPAD), which envisions fundamental reforms of policy and governance on the African side in exchange for significant new infusions of development assistance from the multilateral and bilateral donors. Initiated in 2001 (with Thabo Mbeki and Nigeria's President Olusegun Obasanjo playing prominent roles), NEPAD embodies an affirmation by African leaders and their governments that they have a duty to eradicate poverty and pursue sustainable development, and it establishes 7 percent annual economic growth as a target toward that end. In a break with the statism of the past, NEPAD recognizes that the private sector must be the engine of growth in Africa and that a major task of the government is therefore to stimulate the development of the private sector. It concedes that Africans must take ownership of their own future, and it identifies peace, democracy, and good governance as preconditions for reducing poverty. Under NEPAD, African leaders have agreed not only to broad economic and social development goals—revitalizing education and health care, maintaining macroeconomic stability, making financial markets transparent and orderly—but also to promoting and protecting democracy, human rights, and accountability. They further pledge to combat the proliferation of small arms, strengthen mechanisms for conflict resolution and prevention, and promote the provision of public goods such as water, transportation, energy, and other infrastructure within the region and the various subregions of Africa. Toward these ends, NEPAD promises to use official development assistance more transparently and effectively, in a partnership of mutual accountability between African states and aid donors. At their annual summit in 2002, the leaders of the Group of Eight (G8, industrialized democracies), meeting with representatives of the European Union and several prominent African leaders, welcomed and endorsed NEPAD and pledged to deepen their partnerships with African countries that are committed to implementing NEPAD. Subsequently, donors announced increases in development assistance to Africa for the first time in many years. Also in 2002, the United Nations formally endorsed NEPAD as the framework for international (including UN) engagement with Africa.

At the level of rhetoric and objectives, NEPAD is an important step forward. But its success will depend on implementation, and that is where postindependence Africa has repeatedly faltered in the past. To prevent a repeat of past failures, NEPAD provides for a new African Peer Review Mechanism (APRM), which will review the institutions and policies of individual African governments in order to identify strengths and weaknesses and propose strategies for overcoming the latter.

At the second assembly of the AU, in Mozambique in July 2003, Nigerian president Olusegun Obasanjo, chair of the NEPAD Heads of State and Government Implementation Committee, announced that fifteen African countries (out of fifty-three) had so far agreed to the peer review mechanism and that an initial panel of "eminent persons" had been appointed for the purpose of developing the mechanism. Peer reviews began in the second half of 2003.[37] The formal architecture is moving forward, but there is little in the recent or distant past to suggest that African leaders—most of whom themselves are drenched in the very problems of corrupt, neopatrimonial, patronage politics that NEPAD is supposed to combat—are prepared to allow blunt and probing evaluations of their own and their fellow governments' performance.

There are two major criticisms of NEPAD. One comes from the political and intellectual left in Africa, such as the Dakar-based think tank Codesria, which sees the initiative as abandoning previous development action plans, too accepting of the neoliberal economic framework, and too deferential to international capital, which they regard as an agent of a hostile international economic system.[38] In this view, which clings to the discredited statist approaches of the past, NEPAD is just another surrender to the neocolonial forces of globalization. The other critique, which comes from below, in civil society (and overlaps in some instances with the first), challenges NEPAD "for being elitist and top-down in its approach, having been drawn up by a few Heads of State, and virtually excluding civil society in its preparation."[39]

While it registers valid concerns about the plight of Africa and the lack of popular participation in these policy processes, the first critique, advancing the tired and discredited arguments of dependency theory, is a recipe for the continued marginalization and immiseration of Africa. However, the second line of criticism speaks to the biggest flaw in NEPAD, its detachment from the nongovernmental forces in Africa that have been the most prominent and consistent advocates for democratic and good-governance reforms. By mid-2003, Africans still did not know what the NEPAD peer review standards would be.[40] But civil society advocates for good governance are clear in insisting that evaluation committees must be composed not only of government appointees, but also of parliamentary representatives (including from the opposition), ombudsmen, officials of counter-corruption agencies, and representatives from NGOs, think tanks, and the private sector. Unless these broader societal forces are given a prominent role both in the policy direction of NEPAD and, in particular, in the peer review process, African governments will pat one another on the back and turn away from confronting the fundamental and deeply rooted perversions of governance that represent the core obstacle to achieving the NEPAD goals. Then, NEPAD will just degenerate into a sad iteration of the previous aid failures: African states will pretend to improve their governance and the donors will pretend to reward them for it.[41]

The donor countries say they want a new approach, and NEPAD's explicit concern to promote democratic good governance and assess performance is partly a response to donor pressure. But it does not go nearly far enough. The idea of linking development assistance to better governance is one whose time has finally arrived. African leaders and governments acknowledge in principle the need for it. Many African civil society organizations are demanding it. But if linkage is to be effective and meaningful, it must be more than an idea, and more than a mechanism that African leaders "enforce" upon themselves in a closed and collegial process.

Monitoring of performance must be broad and from multiple sources. The G8 and other donors must then really link aid levels to performance, independently assessed, and not allow misplaced guilt, idealism, or flowery rhetoric to substitute for acute analysis and clear standards. All of this brings us back to the fundamental question of how the political will for genuine—not cosmetic—governance reforms can be generated.

A New Deal for African Development

Africa needs a truly new bargain: debt relief for democracy and development for good governance. Under such a new deal for African development, African governments would not merely hold each other accountable; they would be monitored, evaluated, and held accountable by the international community and by their own people working closely in coordination with the donor agencies. The political will for fundamental governance reform will not come from "peer" review among African governments. The incentives to fudge and dissemble are simply too powerful. The political costs of ripping up entrenched clientelistic networks and closing off the channels and practices of corrupt patronage are just too great. The habit of covering for and excusing each other's failings is too ingrained. African leaders will embrace fundamental reform only when they have no choice—when the costs of bad governance become too great, because the international community denies bad rulers the external resources with which to govern and the international social and financial access with which to enjoy the good life. Generating the political will for reform requires manipulating the incentive structure that ruling elites confront.

"Political will" is the commitment of a country's rulers to undertake and see through to implementation a particular policy course. At its most resilient, political will here involves a broad consensus among ruling elites, across parties and sectors of government, in favor of democratic and good-governance reforms. But consensus is always imperfect, and will is most important at the top levels of government (among major political leaders and senior civil servants). There, political will must be robust and sincere. That is, reform leaders must be committed not only to undertake actions to achieve reform objectives, but also "to sustain the costs of those actions over time."[42]

Such political will is generated from three directions: from *below,* from *within,* and from *outside.* Organized pressure from below, in civil society, plays an essential role in persuading ruling elites of the need for institutional reforms to improve the quality of governance. There may also be some reform-minded elements within the government and the ruling party or coalition who, whether for pragmatic or normative reasons, have come to see the need for reform (but are reluctant to act in isolation). Finally, external actors in the international community often tip the balance through persuasive engagement with the rulers and the society and by extending tangible benefits for improved governance and penalties for recalcitrance.

International assistance can help to develop the first two forms of pressure, and in fact has done so in a number of countries in the past decade. When political will for systemic reform is clearly lacking, the principal thing that foreign assistance can do on the political front is to strengthen constituencies for reform in civil society, including NGOs, interest groups, think tanks, and the mass media. Assistance can enhance these actors' understanding of key reform issues, their knowledge of other countries' experiences, their coordination with one another, their capacity to analyze and advocate specific institutional and policy reforms, and their mobilization of support and understanding in society. Sometimes international donors must redirect their democratic governance assistance programs away from the central government when political will falls sharply. But then they must be prepared to resume engagement with state actors when political will revives with the election of a different ruling party or coalition or a change of heart or calculus on the part of existing leaders. Often political will appears more patchy and ambiguous. In that case, the best strategy is to work with those elements of the government in particular agencies or ministries that seem serious about improving governance, while seeking to enhance demand for reform within the society.

A key lesson from international efforts to stimulate governance reform is that fundamental reform is only sustainable when there is a "home-grown" initiative for it. If changes in policies and institutions are promised merely in response to international pressures, they will not be seriously and consistently implemented. "Imported or imposed initiative confronts the perennial problem of needing to build commitment and ownership; and there is always the question of whether espousals of willingness to pursue reform are genuine or not."[43] International engagement, therefore, does not succeed if it simply compels a government to sign on the dotted line of some package of dictated reforms, as has frequently been the case with International Monetary Fund assistance packages. Its goal must be deeper and more procedurally democratic: to generate public awareness and debate, and to induce government leaders to sit down with opposition and societal forces to fashion a package of reforms that is unique to and owned by the country.

The vigor and depth of the political will to reform can then be assessed by several additional criteria. First, to what extent have (self-proclaimed) reformers undertaken a rigorous analysis of the problem and used it "to design a technically adequate and politically feasible reform program" that rises to the scale of the challenge? Second, to what extent have reformers mobilized political and societal support for their initiatives broad enough to overcome the resistance of threatened interests (and how sustained are these efforts to rally support)? Third, to what extent are reformers seeking changes in laws and institutions and allocations of human and financial resources that hold promise of effecting real change? In the case of controlling corruption, this would include, for example, laws to monitor and punish corrupt conduct and an anticorruption agency with the authority and staff to enforce them. These issues must be assessed through review mechanisms that broadly include civil society and international observers, not just government-chosen elites. They must then periodically use the above criteria "to track the evolution of political will over time" and to feed that assessment back into the reform implementation process.[44]

Successful international engagement must shift from *conditionality* to *selectivity* in foreign assistance. Traditionally in international lending, for example, conditionality has been "*ex ante* in the sense that governments promise to change policies in return for aid." As a result, "reforms are 'owned' by the donors."[45] This is why they have failed, and why "conditionality" is now such a widely discredited concept. A better approach is to dispense aid selectively to reward and deepen, and thus preserve and consolidate, reforms that have already begun to be implemented by the country, according to its own design. Selectivity focuses aid on good performers—countries that have reasonably good policies and institutions—and on assisting reform movements that are seriously under way by governments and societies that have taken responsibility for the design of their own policies and institutions.[46] Where governance is bad, international assistance should focus on trying to strengthen civil society actors that are pressing for democratic and good-governance reforms, while delivering humanitarian and health assistance directly via donor action or through civil society, bypassing the corrupt state.

It takes patience, intelligence, coherence, consistency, and dexterity for external actors to help generate authentic, "homegrown" political will for improved governance. Toward this crucial end, the following principles should guide the development assistance policies and allocations of international development donors:[47]

1. *Overall levels of international development assistance must be linked more clearly to a country's development performance, and to demonstrations of political will for reform and good governance.*
2. *Good performers must be tangibly rewarded.* Africa needs more "carrots" to encourage reform by being predictably and meaningfully rewarded when reform has already occurred. When political leaders demonstrate respect for democratic procedures and freedoms, and a willingness to undertake and see through difficult political and

economic reforms, they should benefit with steady increases in official development assistance. In addition, good performers—principally democracies that are getting serious about controlling corruption and strengthening the rule of law—should be rewarded in other tangible ways: with debt relief, incentives for foreign investment (including publicity about their good governance), and trade liberalization.

3. *Rewards must be granted for demonstrated performance, not for promises that may be repeatedly made and broken.* The only way to exit from the chronic "cat and mouse" game of international conditionality is to make increases in development assistance and other economic rewards contingent on what governments actually do (and keep doing), not what they say they will do. As much as possible, rewards should be structured to lock into place the institutions and practices of democracy and good governance. For example, the European Union requires that democracy and respect for human rights be institutionalized *before* a country can be considered for admission. A similar standard should be adopted before African states receive the enhanced aid flows of the NEPAD process and before they are given free trade access to the markets of industrialized countries. And there should be clear and credible procedures for suspending countries that depart from this standard.

4. *Permanent debt relief for the highly indebted poor countries should also be linked to the quality of governance.* Comprehensive relief (retiring most or all of a country's external debt) should only be granted to countries that have demonstrated a basic commitment to good governance by allowing a free press and civil society, an independent judiciary, and a serious countercorruption commission. Even in these cases, the debt should not be relieved in one fell swoop. Rather, debt service payments should be suspended and the existing stock of debt retired incrementally (for example, at 10–20 percent per year). This would generate ongoing incentives for adhering to good governance. After five or ten years of good governance, the country would have permanently retired its external debt and the institutions of democracy and accountability would have begun to sink roots.

5. *In the absence of any political commitment to democratic and good governance reforms, international donors (bilateral and multilateral) should suspend most governmental assistance and work only with nongovernmental actors.* The only exceptions to this suspension should be humanitarian relief, regional infrastructure, and responses to global public health threats, and even in these areas reliance on the poorly performing state to deliver aid should be minimized. Development assistance to the chronic offenders among badly governed

countries should be administered through and to nongovernmental actors. And beyond humanitarian and public health assistance, aid to chronic poor performers should mainly aim to empower civil society in an effort to change the regime or otherwise dramatically improve governance. Corrupt and repressive rulers must learn that they will pay a heavy international price for their bad governance. They will forfeit material resources and become more isolated diplomatically. For this approach to be truly effective, it must have substantial consequences.

6. *The donor countries should also impose targeted sanctions on particularly corrupt, repressive, and irresponsible ruling elites, as well as their families and cronies.* Such ruling elites should be prevented from traveling to, investing in, or schooling their children in the donor countries (including the European Union, the United States, Canada, Japan, and Australia), and in any other countries that will cooperate in this quest for better governance. The banking systems and legal institutions of all countries that want to be recognized as respecting the rule of law globally should be required to cooperate vigorously in tracking down and recovering assets accumulated through corruption, bribery, and theft.

7. *The bilateral donors need to coordinate pressure on truly bad, recalcitrant governments.* Reductions in aid from one or two donors will not have much impact in changing the calculations of political leaders if their governments continue to receive levels of funding from the other donors. Witness the continuing high levels of aid to several francophone dictatorships, such as Togo and Cameroon. Leadership calculations will be most likely to change, and most likely to be translated into action, when those leaders perceive a relatively coherent message from the universe of international donors.

8. *A greater proportion of international development assistance should be devoted to developing the institutions of democracy and good governance.* In intractable cases, the most important thing donors can do to help aid development is to help generate the demand for democracy and better governance. This could be done by strengthening the analytical and service delivery capacity of NGOs, interest groups, religious bodies, social movements, mass media, universities, and think tanks in civil society. For in the absence of minimally decent governance, efforts to work with state institutions to improve health, education, or agricultural productivity will be enervated by corruption, waste, and incompetence. In struggling democracies, and more generally, improvements in governance enhance reform efforts, and investments in better governance are likely to yield more numerous, immediate, and powerful multiplier effects. Whatever progress

is made on governance will almost certainly have a positive impact on other sectors, enabling given levels of sectoral assistance to go further. Probably no other dimension of foreign assistance yields so many synergies and such good development value per dollar.

9. *Where committed reformers can be identified within the state, donors should work with them.* If pockets of political will for reform exist within the state, donors should identify those opportunities and try to strengthen the hand of reform-oriented ministers, agency heads, and provincial governors through specific democracy and governance assistance programs. "Assistance can be provided to reformers to help identify key winners and losers, develop coalition building and mobilization strategies, and design publicity campaigns."[48] Often, reform majorities or nodes of reformers can be found in some branches of the state outside the executive, such as the legislature, the judicial system, and other agencies of horizontal accountability that may be deprived of resources and authority. Even when reformers lack the power today to implement far-reaching change, enhancing their training and technical capacity may enable them to enlarge public constituencies for reform. Such assistance may also represent an investment in the future, when electoral alternation or some other political shift gives reformers real power.

10. *State capacity must be generally enhanced, but it makes no sense to try to strengthen the technical capacity and administrative ability of state structures that lack the political will to govern responsibly.* Building effective state structures—and hence the ability to deliver on heightened societal demands and expectations—must become a major strategic objective of development assistance, but it cannot be pursued until state leaders are serious about governance. Expensive investments to improve the infrastructure and strengthen the technical capacity of bureaucracies, judiciaries, and legislatures will be largely wasted if there is no political will to use enhanced capabilities for more honest, responsive, and accountable governance.

11. *The global private sector should be encouraged to accelerate its efforts to incorporate judgments about the quality and transparency of governance into its decisions on private capital flows.* Support for Transparency International and other global anticorruption efforts should be institutionalized to continue pressing this agenda. An important priority is improving the comparative measurement of the quality of governance and then widely publicizing the results, so that investors will be encouraged to invest in countries that are governing well and adopting promising institutional and policy reforms. Credible (independent) and publicly disseminated

measurement of governance is particularly important for smaller, more peripheral developing countries about which investors are slower to find reliable information. Donors might also accelerate private capital flows to better-governed countries through incentives to invest in such countries (for example, through the U.S. Overseas Private Investment Corporation and through the negotiation of free trade agreements).

12. *International donors must strengthen the global rule of law, particularly the capacity to track down and close off corrupt flows of money in the international banking system.* The donors must work to institutionalize rigorous global standards and procedures for the rapid identification and recovery of corruptly acquired assets. They should work vigorously to ensure enforcement of the new Organization for Economic Cooperation and Development (OECD) convention against bribery. The same anti-money-laundering tools that are being used to fight the wars on terrorism and drug trafficking can be enlarged into a broader war on international criminality and corruption.

13. *The advanced industrial countries should work vigorously to negotiate an end to agricultural subsidies that impede African access to their markets.* The estimated U.S.$300 billion that rich countries pay their farmers in subsidies constitutes one of the biggest obstacles to development in Africa. By stimulating overproduction and dumping many crops on world markets, rich countries prevent African (and other developing-country) farmers from competing fairly. For example, with U.S. cotton growers able to dump cotton cheaply on world markets due to subsidies of $3 billion per year from the U.S. government, four of Africa's poorest countries (Benin, Mali, Chad, and Burkina Faso) lose a quarter of a billion dollars annually in exports.[49] Negotiating an end to these subsidies, through a generous stance in the current round of the World Trade Organization negotiations, and then mobilizing the political will in rich countries to face down special interests and implement the policy is one way to benefit all of Africa (even the poorest and most poorly governed states) through market forces, by strengthening the returns to productive activity.[50]

All sorts of arguments can and have been levied against a governance-led strategy of development assistance. First, critics contend that it risks plunging badly governed countries over the abyss into chaos and state failure. But that is where these countries are headed with aid flowing in a business-as-usual fashion. Zimbabwe and Côte d'Ivoire are classic recent cases in point. Only a radically different approach can pull countries out of the gradual descent into deepening praetorianism, violence, and stagnation. The conservative approach—just back stability—condemns Africans to indefinite misery. A second, related critique sees the above strategy as hard-hearted, punishing African people for the sins of their governments. But the statistics tell a different story. Hundreds of billions of dollars of aid later, most Africans remain desperately poor. Only where aid has been received in a context of democracy and good governance has it made dramatic progress in reducing mass poverty. Only when there is some degree of transparency and responsibility in governance does the aid really reach the people. Tying active forms of developmental assistance—aid, debt relief, and special trade preferences (see below)—to better governance can help to transform the structure of incentives that shape politics and governance in Africa. At the same time, broadly removing unfair trade barriers within the rich countries can enable African producers to benefit from world markets, even in the absence of any targeted assistance.

A third criticism sees the above approach as, in one respect, not radical enough. Some would like to simply do away with aid altogether and force African states to depend on the taxes of their people and the assessments of international investors about which environments are market friendly. A more sympathetic and creative approach, proposed by David Leonard and Scott Straus, would dramatically reduce development assistance to Africa, while also writing off all (or most) of Africa's external debt burdens. Under their proposal, general budgetary support for African countries would end, but targeted assistance for humanitarian problems, such as health and refugees, would continue.[51] They criticize my appeal to link debt relief to democracy and good governance, arguing that conditionality has not been effective in Africa and that "both debt and aid force African elites to be accountable to the international system, not to domestic populations."[52] But selectivity is fundamentally different than conditionality. It rewards countries for what they are already doing, not for what they promise to do. And as proposed here, it would *precisely* compel African rulers to be accountable and responsive to their own people as a prerequisite for permanent and comprehensive debt relief, as well as most official development assistance.

In fact, involvement of the African people themselves is crucial to the success of this approach. Only in a context of openness, accountability, popular participation, and debate can genuinely indigenous ownership of the necessary policies and institutions emerge. World Bank and other donor policies (such as the debt relief program for highly indebted poor countries or the multidonor budget support for country poverty reduction strategies) have begun to articulate some of the above-mentioned kinds of governance-related standards and concerns. But the problem in these programs, governance, still tends to be treated as an adjunct concern—relevant, worth mentioning, but not fundamental to sustainable poverty reduction. And the broader society is not adequately involved in the search for a viable strategy for development. Development assistance strategies must emphasize governance processes at least as much as policy outcomes if they are to be effective.

Can It Be Done?

I believe it is possible to construct a truly new structure of incentives for African rulers. But this will require a "tough love" approach—tough in that it will deny most corrupt ruling elites (i.e., those who do not have access to substantial mineral wealth) the resources they need to operate their neopatrimonial systems, and compassionate in that it will provide rulers committed to democracy and accountability with the kinds of resources (for public infrastructure, health care, education, and improved agricultural productivity) that will yield highly tangible improvements in popular well-being. Rulers who opt for good governance will thus find a different set of rewards. They will win reelection because they "deliver the goods" for their people. When they leave power, they will be honored and respected by their own people, and by the international community, rather than treated as criminals, thieves, and pariahs. Their children and grandchildren will grow up in a country that is economically prosperous and at peace. Their political successors will not need an army of bodyguards in order to campaign for office and a fistful of cash for the electoral officer in order to win. They will be free to travel abroad, even welcomed when they do so, rather than having to worry about evading warrants from international courts.

To work, both parts of this strategy must be vigorously, and coherently, pursued by all the major donors acting in concert. Corrupt, abusive, recalcitrant dictators must be stigmatized, isolated, and pressured from all sides—including by their fellow African leaders. Democratic rulers who are serious about controlling corruption and governing responsibly must get the infusion of resources early on to develop the human and physical capital that will then attract investment capital.

In addition, the donors must reform themselves institutionally and operationally. The corruption that blights development in Africa is not only in the recipient governments and societies. It is also in the international corporations that pay the bribes and almost never face prosecution in their own countries (despite the OECD requirement that the paying of foreign bribes be made a criminal offense). And it can be found within the administration and contracting of the donor projects as well. Beyond gross corruption, and much more common among the principal donors, are other wasteful and counterproductive practices, such as the lavish spending on expatriate experts, and the tying of aid to the purchase of products and services from corporations based in the donor country.[53] Political leaders in the donor countries need to summon the political will to face down their own domestic actors that want to capture overseas aid dollars to advance their own corporate or bureaucratic interests. If the donors are serious about promoting development, they need to allow themselves to be monitored and held accountable. They need to invest much more in understanding the countries and contexts in which they operate and in being able to monitor and evaluate developmental performance. At the same time, while monitoring carefully to ensure that aid is spent *for* development, they need to give recipient states and societies more leeway in how to use the aid to advance development. One vehicle for doing so might be to channel some aid through national development funds that are administered by autonomous, respected trustees who are separated from patronage politics; that are focused on specific sectors (such as agriculture, health, and education); and that award various types of grants and loans by reviewing competitive proposals from both governments and civil societies.[54]

There are some promising bilateral donor reforms on the horizon. In 2002, President George W. Bush announced a new aid initiative, the Millennium Challenge Account (MCA), which would allocate a new pool of development assistance to a limited number of low- and lower-middle-income countries on the basis of three criteria: governing justly (which includes political freedom, control of corruption, and the rule of law), investing in people (through health and education), and encouraging economic freedom (in pursuing market friendly economic policies). The Bush administration has pledged to increase funding for the MCA to U.S.$5 billion within three years of its creation, which would represent a roughly 50 percent increase in U.S. development assistance and "a near doubling in the amount of aid that focuses strictly on development objectives."[55] The attraction of the MCA is not only that it will selectively reward and support countries with better governance and more developmental purpose, but also that its goals are developmental (poverty elimination and economic growth), its country selection process is transparent, and its method of aid distribution involves extensive country participation (both by governmental agencies and by civil society groups) in the design and implementation of funded projects and programs.[56]

There are serious problems and pitfalls with the MCA proposal: the potential for a bureaucratic turf war between the proposed autonomous Millennium Challenge Corporation and the existing U.S. Agency for International Development, the potential for the selection criteria to be politicized and manipulated to reward political clients of the United States, the envisioned expansion of the program by 2006 to middle-income countries (weakening the focus on the poor), and the possibility that the poorest countries could be disqualified by a rigid and formulaic application of the policy criteria. This is why some sympathetic observers have recommended that the MCA be administered by a multilateral institution like the World Bank or the African Development Bank, which would be less likely to skew country selection with nondevelopmental (geopolitical) considerations.[57] One can also question the very limited emphasis on good (accountable, honest, democratic) governance, which is only one of three criteria and which only requires countries to be above the median (for all eligible countries) on half of the six indicators (including control of corruption).[58] Still, these defects are correctable, and if the MCA is administered objectively and intelligently, it could represent precisely the shift toward selectivity that would begin to foster and reward better governance in Africa (and elsewhere around the world). "With clear criteria and substantial sums of money with enticing terms, the MCA could [create] incentives for governments to improve economic policies and governance, while helping strong performers sustain growth and improve investment climates."[59]

Even if the MCA fulfills its lofty potential and provides a new model for dispensing international development assistance, this will only be a start. A deeper and more thoroughgoing reform of aid will be needed, not only rewarding good performers but also cutting off bad ones and enhancing governance assistance to countries that come near to qualifying and appear ready for reform. Debt relief must be similarly linked to performance. And substantial reform is needed on the part of the industrialized countries in providing Africa market access, beyond just eliminating the most egregious obstacle, agricultural subsidies. An important initiative in this regard is the Africa Growth and Opportunity Act (AGOA), passed by the U.S. Congress in June 2000. In eliminating U.S. duties on textile imports from eligible African countries, AGOA has generated significant inflows of foreign investment and new jobs in the dozen or so African countries that qualified in the first two years, most notably Madagascar. Significantly, AGOA establishes conditions that African countries must meet in order to obtain preferential tariff treatment. These include having a market economy, political pluralism, and the rule of law; fighting corruption; having policies to reduce poverty; and protecting human and worker rights. Yet in December 2002, President Bush certified for eligibility a total of thirty-eight countries of sub-Saharan Africa, excluding only ten and including such blatantly repressive and corrupt governments as those in Cameroon, Chad, the Democratic Republic of Congo (the former Zaire), Mauritania, and Eritrea. Such certification makes a mockery of the standards and sets a poor precedent for the future. Another problem is that AGOA is set to expire in 2008, which could undermine the nascent progress toward labor-intensive industrialization of the participating African countries.

More recently, in June 2003, the Commission on Capital Flows to Africa, a private U.S.-based group, released a report recommending a ten-year strategy for increasing capital flows to Africa.[60] Its proposals included a ten-year extension of AGOA beyond its current expiration date in 2008; the negotiation of a free trade agreement with the Southern African Customs Union, followed by other subregional free trade agreements and culminating in ten years in a free trade agreement between the United States and all of Africa; a ten-year moratorium on taxation of repatriated earnings from new investments by U.S. companies in Africa; and the publication of "best practices" for African governments seeking to increase foreign direct investment. These are the kind of bold ideas that are needed to jump-start development in Africa, but boldness and generosity must be matched by tough standards, which are lacking in the proposal. Like increased aid and debt relief, the benefits of truly free trade should be reserved for those countries that demonstrate a serious commitment to free, open, and accountable governance.

We are at a formative moment in the long, sad relationship between Africa and the West. More African countries are governed democratically today than ever before. If most are still not governed well, public pressures and international expectations are at least moving in the right direction. Today there is a chance—a real chance—to generate an entirely new set of incentives for political actors in Africa to govern constitutionally, responsibly, and effectively. Today there is a real chance to win the kinds of institutional reforms that will truly empower parliaments, courts, and civil societies, control corruption, and strengthen states. But all of this depends on political leaders mustering the political will to embrace and permit enormously difficult governance reforms. That will not happen through an indiscriminate flow of new benefits to African states, good and bad. Generosity and compassion, in the absence of clear standards, will do Africa little good.

African civil societies and governments must join with one another and with the international community to monitor and enforce their governance obligations under NEPAD—and for that matter, under the Universal Declaration of Human Rights. Only if governance is really transformed will Africa emerge from its needlessly protracted rut of poverty, conflict, and despair.

Notes

This chapter has benefited from the research assistance of Benn Eifert and the very helpful comments of E. Gyimah-Boadi and Nicolas van de Walle.

1. The UNDP's Human Development Index, which ranges from a low of 0 to a high of 1, measures overall levels of human development in a country relative to other countries in the world, using three indicators: life expectancy at birth, knowledge (with adult literacy weighted two-thirds and the combined school enrollment ratios one-third), and gross domestic product per capita in purchasing power

parity dollars. See United Nations Development Programme, *Human Development Report 1997,* p. 341.

2. United Nations Development Programme, *Human Development Report 1997,* tab. 3, p. 247; African Development Bank, *African Development Report 2003,* p. 255.

3. Temporarily, Eastern Europe and Central Asia had higher average per capita foreign aid receipts in 2000 than Africa (U.S.$23 versus U.S.$20), but since independence Africa has received much more per capita foreign aid than any other region.

4. Van de Walle, *African Economies,* p. 220. In some countries, aid "reached staggering levels—for five African states, aid represented at least one-fifth of gross national product (GNP) at some point in the 1990s, and in one year it stood at 42 percent in Mozambique." Leonard and Straus, *Africa's Stalled Development,* p. 13.

5. Leonard and Straus, *Africa's Stalled Development,* p. 26, tab. 2.1.

6. See the relevant data in tabs. 1 and 4 of the appendix to the World Bank's *World Development Report 2002,* pp. 233, 239. Africa's ratio of official development assistance to foreign direct investment is 166 percent compared to 132 percent for South Asia, 41 percent for Eastern Europe, 7 percent for Latin America, and 365 percent for the Middle East and North Africa.

7. Leonard and Straus, *Africa's Stalled Development,* p. 26, tab. 2.1; World Bank, *World Development Report 2002,* p. 28.

8. Van de Walle, *African Economies,* p. 222.

9. Easterly, *The Elusive Quest,* pp. 22–44.

10. Karl, *The Paradox of Plenty;* Leonard and Straus, *Africa's Stalled Development.*

11. Roll and Talbott, "Political Freedom," p. 79.

12. Ibid., p. 82.

13. Bueno de Mesquita et al., "Political Competition," p. 65.

14. Eifert, "Political Equality," p. 2. The relationship was tested for African countries during the period 1972–1999.

15. Zweifel and Navia, "Democracy"; Navia and Zweifel, "Democracy."

16. Kaufmann, Kraay, and Zoido-Lobaton, "Governance Matters," p. 15. Each of their six governance dimensions has a large and significant positive effect on per capita incomes and a large, significant negative effect on infant mortality. For example, "a one standard deviation improvement in governance leads to between a 2.5 fold (in the case of voice and accountability) and a 4-fold (in the case of political stability and violence) increase in per capita income" (p. 15).

17. Transparency International, *Global Corruption Report 2003,* pp. 264–265.

18. Przeworski et al., *Democracy and Development.*

19. Easterly, *The Elusive Quest,* p. 217.

20. Ibid.

21. Ibid., p. 237.

22. Ibid.

23. For further documentation and analysis of these trends, see van de Walle, *African Economies.*

24. Easterly, *The Elusive Quest,* p. 241.

25. African Development Bank, *African Development Report 2003,* p. 42.

26. The recognition that state power in Africa has been the basis for class formation and personal wealth accumulation, thereby destabilizing and distorting politics and governance, is one of the most widely established in the literature on postcolonial African politics. See, for example, Sklar, "Nigerian Politics in Perspective"; Sklar,

Nigerian Political Parties; Diamond, Linz, and Lipset, *Democracy in Developing Countries;* and more recently on neopatrimonialism, Bratton and van de Walle, *Democratic Experiments.*

27. Joseph, *Democracy and Prebendal Politics.*

28. Huntington, *Political Order in Changing Societies,* pp. 12–24.

29. African Development Bank, *African Development Report 2003,* p. 38.

30. Ibid., p. 39.

31. This is suggested by the rankings on the Corruption Perceptions Index published by Transparency International, although it is an imprecise and only very suggestive instrument based on a number of subjective surveys. As we see in Table 11.3, even some of the African democracies rank well below the midpoint on the 0–10 scale and are lodged in the bottom third of all the countries rated (as are all the African nondemocracies). If more countries, such as Mozambique, Ethiopia, Togo, and Chad, had been rated, the overall pattern would be much more decisive. As it is, Uganda, an international aid darling under Yoweri Museveni, has effectively a one-party regime with rising levels of corruption; and even one of the most promising new democracies, Ghana, has a long way to go to control corruption.

32. Leonard and Straus, *Africa's Stalled Development,* p. 13.

33. Ibid., p. 17. For a similar style of argument, showing how political systems with narrow winning coalitions (like those that prevail generally in autocratic and closed regimes) generate incentives for the provision of private, not public, goods, see Bueno de Mesquita et al., "Political Competition."

34. Schedler, "Conceptualizing Accountability."

35. African Development Bank, *African Development Report 2003,* p. 249.

36. Ibid., p. 251.

37. *Progress Report of H. E. Olusegun Obasanjo, President of Nigeria and Chairperson of the NEPAD Heads of State and Government Implementation Committee, to the Second Ordinary Session of the Assembly of the Heads of State and Government of the African Union, Mozambique, July 10–12, 2003,* available at www.avmedia.at/cgi-script/csnews/news_upload/nepad_2dcore_2ddocuments_2edb. progressreportof.pdf.

38. See the "Declaration of Africa's Development Challenges" of the CODESRI-Third World Network/Africa Conference in Accra, April 23–26, 2002, available at www.radi-afrique.org/nepad/docs/codesria.pdf.

39. African Development Bank, *African Development Report 2003,* p. 255. For a selection of early civil society critiques, see www.web.net/~iccaf/debtsap/nepad. htm#ngo.

40. The African Development Bank (*African Development Report 2003,* p. 224) identifies an excellent set of good governance criteria, including government transparency, simplicity of procedures, serious anticorruption measures, accountability of offending officials, individual and press freedom, independence of the legal system, competitive procurement, and efficiency in public service delivery.

41. The latter phrase was suggested to me by Nicolas van de Walle in a private communication.

42. Brinkerhoff, "Identifying and Assessing Political Will," p. 3. See also Brinkerhoff, "Assessing Political Will," p. 242.

43. Brinkerhoff, "Identifying and Assessing Political Will," p. 3.

44. Brinkerhoff, "Assessing Political Will," p. 249.

45. Collier, "Learning from Failure," p. 322.

46. Collier also calls this conditionality "as an agency of restraint." Ibid., p. 327.

47. I have previously proposed these as principles to guide U.S. foreign aid. Most of these recommendations appear (in slightly different form) in U.S. Agency for International Development, *Foreign Aid in the National Interest,* chap. 1, and some of the above analysis is also reproduced from my chapter in that report.

48. Brinkerhoff, "Assessing Political Will," p. 249.

49. See http://news.bbc.co.uk/2/hi/business/3099596.stm.

50. As this book went to press, the latest round of global trade negotiations had broken down acrimoniously in Cancun, Mexico, since November 2003.

51. Leonard and Straus, *Africa's Stalled Development,* pp. 31–35.

52. Ibid., p. 128, n. 40.

53. The U.S. Agency for International Development is also hampered by extremely ponderous personnel and procurement regulations and a host of congressional stipulations "earmarking" funding for very specific purposes. Steven Radelet ("Bush and Foreign Aid") proposes that this "morass" of rules and regulations be eliminated wholesale and that the legal and administrative architecture of U.S. foreign assistance be completely redesigned.

54. This model has been proposed by Goran Hyden in "Aid and Developmentalism," pp. 202–204.

55. Radelet, "The Millennium Challenge Account," p. 1. Unfortunately, pressures on the U.S. federal budget, as a result of recession, tax cuts, and the war in Iraq, make it unlikely that the U.S.$5 billion increase will be realized within the three-year time frame originally envisioned, and at this writing it is not clear what, if any, funding the U.S. Congress will allocate for the 2004 fiscal year, when the program was to have been initiated.

56. Radelet, "The Millennium Challenge Account," p. 2.

57. Van de Walle, "A Comment on the MCA Proposal."

58. In fact, the very standard of simply being "above the median" can be quite weak, given that most low-income countries are very corrupt and poorly governed. Eventually, it could also become quite perverse, if a large number of countries are motivated to improve dramatically their governance and development policies. A better approach would be to require certain absolute institutional conditions, such as judicial independence and an autonomous corruption control apparatus of some kind, verified by an international commission of neutral experts. Moreover, as Radelet notes in "The Millennium Challenge Account," the statistical data on levels of corruption are too unreliable to serve as a decisive criterion. I also believe that no country that badly abuses human rights and press freedom should qualify, and this requires more than one measure in order to enhance the reliability and legitimacy of a potentially fateful judgment.

59. Brainard et al., *The Other Ward,* p. 4.

60. See www.uneca.org/eca_resources/press_releases/2003_pressreleases/media advisory0403.htm.

Acronyms

ABN	Association for a Better Nigeria
ACF	Arewa Consultative Forum
AD	Alliance for Democracy (Nigeria)
AGOA	Africa Growth and Opportunity Act
AIDS	acquired immunodeficiency syndrome
ANC	African National Congress
ANPP	All Nigeria People's Party
APC	Arewa People's Congress
APP	All People's Party (Nigeria)
APRM	African Peer Review Mechanism
ASDR	African Security Dialogue and Research
AU	African Union
BDP	Botswana Democratic Party
BNF	Botswana National Front
CCF	Cease-Fire Commission (Mozambique)
CDD	Center for Democratic Development (Ghana)
CEPA	Center for Policy Analysis (Ghana)
CFA	Communauté Financière Africaine
CFCR	Citizens Forum for Constitutional Reform (Nigeria)
CHRAJ	Commission on Human Rights and Administrative Justice (Ghana)
CISAC	Center for International Security and Cooperation
CNE	National Elections Commission (Mozambique)
CPS	Center for Policy Studies (South Africa)
CSC	Supervisory and Monitoring Commission (Mozambique)
DRC	Democratic Republic of Congo
DWM	31st December Women's Movement (Ghana)
ECOMOG	Economic Community of West African States Cease-Fire Monitoring Group

ECOWAS	Economic Community of West African States
ERP	economic recovery program
ESAP	economic structural adjustment program
FAO	Food and Agriculture Organization
FDI	foreign direct investment
FIDA	International Federation of Women Lawyers (Ghana)
Frelimo	Front for the Liberation of Mozambique
G8	Group of Eight
GDP	gross domestic product
GERDDES-Afrique	Groupe d'Étude et du Recherche sur la Démocratie et le Développement Économique et Sociale en Afrique
GNP	gross national product
HDI	human development index
HIV	human immunodeficiency virus
ICAC	Independent Commission Against Corruption (Hong Kong)
IDASA	Institute for Democracy in South Africa
IEA	Institute of Economic Affairs (Ghana; Kenya)
IEC	Independent Electoral Commission (South Africa)
IFI	international financial institution
IFP	Inkatha Freedom Party (South Africa)
IGAD	Inter-Governmental Authority on Development
IMF	International Monetary Fund
IPA	International Peace Academy
KACA	Kenya Anticorruption Authority
MASSOB	Movement for the Actualization of the Sovereign State of Biafra
MCA	Millennium Challenge Account
MPLA	Movement for the Liberation of Angola
NDP	national development plan
NEPAD	New Partnership for African Development
NGO	nongovernmental organization
NNP	New National Party (South Africa)
OAU	Organization of African Unity
OECD	Organization for Economic Cooperation and Development
OPC	Oodua People's Congress
PDP	People's Democratic Party (Nigeria)
PPP	purchasing power parity
Renamo	Mozambique National Resistance
RPF	Rwandan Patriotic Front

RUF	Revolutionary United Front (Sierra Leone)
SADC	Southern African Development Community
SAP	structural adjustment program
SPLA	Sudan People's Liberation Army
SWAPO	South West African People's Organization
TMG	Transitional Monitoring Group (Nigeria)
TUC	Trade Union Congress (Ghana)
UDF	United Democratic Front (South Africa)
UK	United Kingdom
UN	United Nations
UNDP	United Nations Development Programme
UNITA	Union for the Total Independence of Angola
USAID	U.S. Agency for International Development
YEAA	Youth Earnestly Asking for Abacha (Nigeria)
ZANU-PF	Zimbabwe African National Union Patriotic Front
ZCCM	Zambia Consolidated Copper Mines

Bibliography

Ablo, Emmanuel, and Ritva Reinikka. "Do Budgets Really Matter? Evidence from Public Spending on Education and Health in Uganda." World Bank Policy Research Paper. Washington, D.C.: World Bank, 1998.

Aborisade, O., and R. J. Mundt. *Politics in Nigeria.* London: Longman, 1999.

Abubakar, A. "No Way for Hoodlums." *Tell* (Lagos), November 22, 1999.

Adamolekun, Ladipo, ed. *Public Administration in Africa: Main Issues and Selected Country Studies.* Boulder, Colo.: Westview Press, 1999.

Adebajo, A. "Descent to the Abyss." *Tell* (Lagos), January 22, 2001.

Adegbamigbe, A. "Coup No More Possible." *The News* (Lagos), July 9, 2001.

———. "Robbers in Police Uniform." *The News,* April 16, 2001.

———. "Tainted Judges." *The News,* August 30, 1999.

Adegbamigbe, A., and U. Aham. "The Robbers' Revenge." *The News,* August 6, 2001.

Adekanmbi, D. "Robbers' Terror." *The News* (Lagos), November 26, 2000.

Adesina, O. C. "Revenue Allocation Commissions and the Contradictions in Nigeria's Federalism." In K. Amuwo et al., eds., *Federalism and Political Restructuring in Nigeria.* Ibadan: Spectrum and IFRA, 1998.

African Development Bank. *African Development Report 2003: Globalization and Africa's Development.* Oxford: Oxford University Press, 2003.

African Governors of the World Bank. *Partnership for Capacity Building in Africa: Strategy and Program of Action: A Report to Mr. James D. Wolfensohn, President of the World Bank Group.* Washington, D.C.: World Bank, September 1996.

Agbaje, Adigun. "Africa Demos: An Evaluation Essay." In R. Joseph, ed., *African Democratic Perspectives: Evaluative Essays on Africa Demos.* Atlanta: African State and Democracy Project, 1996.

———. *A Century of "Power Sharing": Nigeria in Theoretical and Comparative Perspective.* Ibadan: Development Policy Center, 1998.

———. "Love's Labor Lost? Okigbo and the Travails of Fiscal Federalism." Paper presented at the conference "Vision and Policy in Nigerian Economics: The Legacy of Pius Okigbo," Program of African Studies, Northwestern University, Evanston, Ill., June 8–9, 2001.

———. "Mobilizing for a New Political Culture." In Larry Diamond, Anthony Kirk-Greene, and Oyeleye Oyediran, eds., *Transition Without End: Nigerian*

Politics and Civil Society Under Babangida. Boulder, Colo.: Lynne Rienner, 1997.

———. "Party Systems and Civil Society." In Paul A. Beckett and Crawford Young, eds., *Dilemmas of Democracy in Nigeria.* Rochester: University of Rochester Press, 1997.

Agbaje, Adigun, and W. Adebanwi. "Informal National Conference: Memory, Restitution, and Reconciliation in Twenty-First-Century Nigeria." Paper presented at the Ethno-Net Africa conference "Africa at Crossroads: Complex Political Emergencies in the Twenty-First Century," Douala, Cameroon, May 19–24, 2001.

Agekameh, D. "Burden of the Men in Black." *Tell* (Lagos), February 28, 2000.

———. "The Case Against Okadigbo." *Tell,* May 15, 2000.

———. "Dangers Ahead." *Tell,* January 22, 2001.

———. "Guns, Guns Everywhere." *Tell,* August 6, 2001.

———. "Malu: More Heads to Roll." *Tell,* May 14, 2001.

———. "Raiders of the Cash Cows." *Tell,* July 16, 2001.

———. "Robbing and Killing with Style." *Tell,* June 25, 2001.

———. "A Senate and Its Scandals." *Tell,* May 7, 2001.

Agyeman-Duah, Baffour. "Civil Military Relations in Ghana's Fourth Republic." In *Critical Perspectives,* vol. 9. Accra: Center for Democratic Development, June 2002.

———. *Elections in Emerging Democracies: Ghana, Liberia, and Nigeria.* Accra: Center for Democratic Development, 2000.

Ake, Claude. *Democracy and Development in Africa.* Washington D.C.: Brookings Institution, 1996.

———. *Democratization of Disempowerment in Africa.* Lagos: Malthouse Press, 1994.

———. "Rethinking African Democracy." *Journal of Democracy* 2 (1991): 32–44.

Alao, Abiodun. *The Burden of Collective Goodwill: The International Involvement in the Liberian Civil War.* Aldershot, UK: Ashgate, April 1998.

Alence, Rod, and Michael O'Donovan. *If South Africa's Second Democratic Election Had Been Held in March 1999: A Simulation of Participation and Party Support Patterns.* Pretoria: Human Sciences Research Council, 1999. Mimeo.

Ali, Ali Abdel Gadir, and Erik Thorbecke. "The State of Rural Poverty, Income Distribution, and Rural Development in Sub-Saharan Africa." Paper prepared for the African Economic Research Consortium conference "Comparative Development Experiences in Asia and Africa," Johannesburg, November 6, 1997 (revised version April 1998).

Amuwo, K., et al., eds. *Federalism and Political Restructuring in Nigeria.* Ibadan: Spectrum and IFRA, 1998.

Anstee, Margaret Joan. *Orphan of the Cold War: The Inside Story of the Collapse of the Angolan Peace Process, 1992–3.* New York: St. Martin's Press, 1996.

Asmal, Kader, and Wilmot James. "AIDS: Losing 'The New Struggle'?" *Daedalus* 130, no. 1 (Winter 2001): 151–184.

Assembleia da República [Assembly of the Republic], *Regulamentos para a formação e actividades dos partidos políticos. Lei no. 7/91 de 23 de Janeiro, e Diploma Ministerial no. 11/ 91 de 13 de Fevereiro* [Regulations governing the formation and activities of political parties. Law no. 7/91 of January 23 and Ministerial Regulation no. 11/91 of February 13]. Maputo, Imprensa Nacional, 1991.

Atkinson, Doreen. "Brokering a Miracle? The Multi-Party Negotiating Forum." In Steven Friedman and Doreen Atkinson, eds., *The Small Miracle: South Africa's Negotiated Settlement.* Johannesburg: Ravan, 1994.

Ayoade, J. A. A. "States Without Citizens: An Emerging African Phenomenon." In D. Rothchild and N. Chazan, eds., *The Precarious Balance: State and Society in Africa*. Boulder, Colo.: Westview Press, 1988.

Ayittey, George. *Africa in Chaos*. New York: St. Martin's Press, 1998.

Azarya, Victor. "Civil Society and Disengagement in Africa." In John Harbeson, Donald Rothchild, and Naomi Chazan, eds., *Civil Society and the State in Africa*. Boulder, Colo.: Lynne Rienner, 1994.

Bach, D. C. "Indigeneity, Ethnicity, and Federalism." In Larry Diamond, Anthony Kirk-Greene, and Oyeleye Oyediran, eds., *Transition Without End: Nigerian Politics and Civil Society Under Babangida*. Boulder, Colo.: Lynne Rienner, 1997.

Baker, Bruce. "The Class of 1990: How Have the Autocratic Leaders of Sub-Saharan Africa Fared Under Democratization?" *Third World Quarterly* 19, no. 1 (1998): 115–127.

Bako, S. "Muslims, State, and the Struggle for Democratic Transition in Nigeria: From Cooperation to Conflict." In Paul A. Beckett and Crawford Young, eds., *Dilemmas of Democracy in Nigeria*. Rochester: University of Rochester Press, 1997.

Baloi, Obede, et al., eds., *Estudos específicos sobre áreas de direitos humanos e assuntos religiosos: relatório preliminar* [Specific studies on areas of human rights and religious topics: preliminary report]. Maputo, mimeo, June 2000.

Bank of Botswana. *Annual Report*. Gaborone: Government of Botswana, various years.

Barber, Benjamin. *A Place for Us: How to Make Society Civil and Democracy Strong*. New York: Hill and Wang, 1998.

Bardhan, Pranab. *The Political Economy of Development in India*. London: Blackwell, 1984.

Barratt-Brown, Michael, and Pauline Tiffen. *Short Changed: Africa and World Trade*. London: Pluto Press, 1992.

Barry, Norman P. *An Introduction to Modern Political Theory*. London: Macmillan, 1995.

Baskin, Jeremy. *Striking Back: A History of COSATU*. Johannesburg: Ravan, 1991.

Bates, Robert H. *Beyond the Miracle of the Market: Agricultural Politics in Kenya*. Cambridge: Cambridge University Press, 1989.

———. *Markets and States in Tropical Africa: The Political Basis of Agricultural Policies*. Berkeley: University of California Press, 1981.

Bates, Robert H., and Anne Krueger. *Political and Economic Interactions in Economic Policy Reform*. Oxford: Basil Blackwell, 1993.

Bayart, Jean François. "Civil Society in Africa." In Patrick Chabal, ed., *Political Domination in Africa: Reflections on the Limits of Power*. Cambridge: Cambridge University Press, 1986.

———. *L'etat en Afrique*. Paris: Fayard, 1989.

———. *The State in Africa: The Politics of the Belly*. New York: Longman, 1993.

Bayart, Jean François, Stephen Ellis, and Beatrice Hibou. *The Criminalization of the State in Africa*. Oxford: James Currey, 1999.

Beckett, Paul A., and Crawford Young, eds. *Dilemmas of Democracy in Nigeria*. Rochester: University of Rochester Press, 1997.

Bennell, Paul. "Privatization in Sub-Saharan Africa: Progress and Prospects During the 1990s." *World Development* 25, no. 11 (1997): 1785–1803.

Bercovitch, Jacob, and Richard Jackson. *International Conflict: An Encyclopedia of Conflicts and Their Management, 1945–1995*. Washington, D.C.: Congressional Quarterly Press, 1997.

Berdal, Mats, and David Malone, eds. *Greed and Grievance: Economic Agendas in Civil Wars.* Boulder, Colo.: Lynne Rienner, 2000.

Berg, Elliot. "Aid and Public Sector Reform." Paper prepared for the University of Copenhagen conference on aid, October 9–10, 1998.

———. "Privatization in Sub-Saharan Africa: Results, Prospects, and New Approaches." In Jo Ann Paulson, ed., *African Economies in Transition,* vol. 2, *The Reform Experience.* New York: St. Martin's Press, 1999.

Berg, Elliott, and Jeffrey Butler. "Trade Unions." In James S. Coleman and Carl G. Rosberg, eds., *Political Parties and National Integration in Tropical Africa.* Berkeley: University of California Press, 1964.

Berg, Elliot, et al. "Sustaining Private Sector Development in Senegal: Strategic Considerations." Bethesda, Md.: Development Alternatives, June 1997.

Bergen, Geoffrey. "Unions in Senegal." Ph.D. thesis, Department of Political Science, University of California at Los Angeles. Ann Arbor, Mich.: UMI Dissertation Series, 1991.

Berger, Suzanne, ed. *Organizing Interests in Western Europe.* New York: Cambridge University Press, 1981.

Bienen, Henry. "The Politics of Trade Liberalization in Africa." *Economic Development and Cultural Change* 38, no. 4 (1990): 713–732.

Biersteker. Thomas. "The Triumph of Neoclassical Economics in the Developing World: Policy Convergence and Bases of Governance in the International Economic Order." In James Rosenau and Ernst-Otto Czempiel, eds., *Governance Without Government: Order and Change in World Politics.* New York: Cambridge University Press, 1992.

"Big Men, Big Countries, Big Hopes." *Africa Confidential,* January 19, 1998.

Binswanger, Hans Robert Townsend, and Tshikala Tshhibaka. "Spurring Agriculture and Rural Development." Paper presented at the African Development Bank's second research workshop, Abidjan, July 6–11, 1999.

Bolnick, Bruce. "Establishing Fiscal Discipline: The Cash Budget in Zambia." In Merilee S. Grindle, ed., *Getting Good Government: Capacity Building in the Public Sector of Developing Countries.* Cambridge: Harvard Institute for International Development, 1997.

Boone, Catherine. *Merchant Capital and the Roots of State Power in Senegal, 1930–1985.* Cambridge: Cambridge University Press, 1992.

Bost, François. "L'Afrique Subsaharienne: Oubliée par les investisseurs." *Afrique Contemporaine* 189 (1st Trimester 1999): 41–61.

Botswana Central Statistics Office (CSO). *Population and Housing Census Report 1991.* Gaborone: Government Printer, 1992.

———. Ministry of Finance and Development Planning. *Household Income and Expenditure Surveys 1975, 1986.* Gaborone: Government Printer, 1975, 1986.

———. Ministry of Finance and Development Planning. *Labour Survey 1983.* Gaborone: Government Printer, 1984.

———. Ministry of Finance and Development Planning. *Labour Survey 1985.* Gaborone: Government Printer, 1986.

———. Ministry of Finance and Development Planning. *National Development Plans I–V.* Gaborone: Government Printer, 1970, 1973, 1976, 1981, 1986.

———. Ministry of Finance and Development Planning. *National Development Plans VII–IX.* Gaborone: Government Printer, December 1991, August 1997, March 2003.

———. Ministry of Finance and Development Planning. *Planning for the People: Botswana's Human Development Report.* Gaborone: Government of Botswana,

United Nations Development Programme, and United Nations Children's Fund, 1993.

Botswana Department of Labour. *Annual Report 1988.* Gaborone: Ministry of Labour and Home Affairs, 1989.

Botswana Institute for Development Policy Analysis. Ministry of Finance and Development Planning. *Study on Poverty Alleviation in Botswana.* Gaborone: Government Printer, 1997.

Brainard, Lael, Carol Graham, Nigel Purvis, Steven Radelet, and Gayle E. Smith. *The Other Ward: Global Poverty and the Millennium Challenge Account.* Washington, D.C.: Brookings Institution, 2003.

Bratton, Michael. "Beyond the State: Civil Society and Associational Life in Africa." *World Politics* 41, no. 3 (1989): 207–430.

———. "Civil Society and Political Transitions in Africa." In John Harbeson, Donald Rothchild, and Naomi Chazan, eds., *Civil Society and the State in Africa.* Boulder, Colo.: Lynne Rienner, 1994.

———. "The Comrades and the Countryside: The Politics of Agricultural Policy in Zimbabwe." *World Politics* 39, no. 2 (1987): 174–202.

———. "A First Look at Second Elections in Africa." In *Transformation to a Successful Democracy.* Durban: Institute for Federal Democracy, Konrad Adenauer Stiftung, December 1998.

———. "Political Participation in a New Democracy: Institutional Considerations from Zambia." *Comparative Political Studies* 32, no. 5 (August 1999): 549–588.

Bratton, Michael, and Robert Mattes. "Support for Democracy in Africa: Intrinsic or Instrumental?" *British Journal of Political Science* 31 (July 2001): 447–474.

Bratton, Michael, and Nicolas van de Walle. *Democratic Experiments in Africa: Regime Transitions in Comparative Perspective.* New York: Cambridge University Press, 1997.

———. "Neopatrimonial Regimes and Political Transitions in Africa." In Peter Lewis, ed., *Africa: Dilemmas of Development and Change.* Boulder, Colo.: Westview Press, 1998.

Bräutigam, Deborah. "Economic Takeoff in Africa?" *Current History* no. 619 (May 1998).

Breslin, Edward. *Lessons from the Field: Rethinking Community Management for Sustainability—DWAF Revisiting of Water Services Process.* East London: Mvula Trust, 1999.

Brett, Edward. *Providing for the Rural Poor: Institutional Decay and Transformation in Uganda.* Sussex, UK: Institute of Development Studies, 1992.

Brinkerhoff, Derick W. "Assessing Political Will for Anti-Corruption Efforts: An Analytic Framework." *Public Administration and Development* 20, no. 3 (2000): 239–252.

———. "Identifying and Assessing Political Will for Anti-Corruption Efforts." Working Paper no. 13, Implementing Policy Change project, USAID, January 1999.

Buckley, Stephen. "Ethiopia Takes New Ethnic Tack: Deliberately Divisive." *Washington Post,* June 18, 1995.

Budlender, Debbie and Nobayeti Dube. "Starting with What We Have: Basing Development Activities on Local Realities: A Critical Review of Recent Experience." Unpublished paper produced for the Development Bank of Southern Africa, 1997.

Bueno de Mesquita, Bruce, James D. Morrow, Randolph Siverson, and Alastair Smith. "Political Competition and Economic Growth." *Journal of Democracy* 12, no. 1 (January 2001): 58–72.

Cabrillac, Bruno. "La situation macroéconomique des pays africains de la Zone Franc à la fin de l'année 1998." *Afrique Contemporaine* 189 (1st Trimester 1999): 23–29.

Call, Charles, and William Stanley. "A Sacrifice for Peace? Security for the General Public During Implementation of Peace Agreements." In Stephen John Stedman, Donald Rothchild, and Elizabeth Cousens, eds., *Ending Civil Wars: The Implementation of Peace Agreements.* Boulder, Colo.: Lynne Rienner, 2002.

Callaghy, Thomas. "Civil Society, Democracy, and Economic Change." In John Harbeson, Donald Rothchild, and Naomi Chazan, eds., *Civil Society and the State in Africa.* Boulder, Colo.: Lynne Rienner, 1994.

———. "Lost Between State and Market: The Politics of Economic Adjustment in Ghana, Zambia, and Nigeria." In Joan Nelson, ed., *Economic Crisis and Policy Choice: The Politics of Adjustment in the Third World.* Princeton: Princeton University Press, 1990.

———. *The State-Society Struggle: Zaire in Comparative Perspective.* New York: Columbia University Press, 1984.

Carothers, Thomas. *Aiding Democracy Abroad: The Learning Curve.* Washington, D.C.: Carnegie Endowment for International Peace, 1999.

Carter, Gwendolyn, et al. *From the Frontline: Speeches of Sir Seretse Khama.* London: Rex Collings, 1980.

Center for Democracy and Development (CDD). "Elite Attitudes to Democracy and Markets in Ghana." CDD-Ghana Research Paper no. 3. Accra: CDD, August 2000.

Central Bank of Nigeria (CBN). *Annual Report and Statement of Accounts for the Year Ended 31st December 1999.* Abuja: CBN, 2000.

Centre for Policy Studies (CPS). *Quarterly Trends.* Johannesburg: CPS/National Business Initiative, various years.

———. *South Africa Update.* Johannesburg: CPS/Canadian International Development Agency, various years.

Chabal, Patrick. "A Few Considerations on Democracy in Africa." *International Affairs* 74, no. 2 (1998): 289–304.

———, ed. *Political Domination in Africa.* Cambridge: Cambridge University Press, 1986.

———. *Power in Africa: An Essay in Political Interpretation.* London: Macmillan, 1994.

Chabal, Patrick, and Jean-Pascal Daloz. *Africa Works: Disorder as Political Instrument.* Bloomington: Indiana University Press, 1999.

Charney, Craig. *Voices of a New Democracy: African Expectations in the New South Africa.* Johannesburg: Centre for Policy Studies, 1995.

Chazan, Naomi. "Patterns of State-Society Incorporation and Disengagement in Africa." In Donald Rothchild and Naomi Chazan, eds., *The Precarious Balance: State and Society in Africa.* Boulder, Colo.: Westview Press, 1988.

Chazan, Naomi, and Victor Azarya. "Disengagement from the State in Africa: Reflections on the Experience of Ghana and Guinea." *Comparative Studies in Society and History* 29, no. 1 (1987): 106–131.

Chazan, Naomi, Robert Mortimer, John Ravenhill and Donald Rothchild, eds. *Politics and Society in Contemporary Africa.* 2nd ed. Boulder, Colo.: Lynne Rienner, 1992.

Chukwumba, O. "Tension in the Land." *Tell* (Lagos), November 22, 1999.

Citizens' Forum for Constitutional Reform (CFCR). *The Position of the Citizens' Forum for Constitutional Reform on the Review of the 1999 Constitution of the Federal Republic of Nigeria.* Ilupeju, Lagos: CFCR, 2001.

Clapham, Christopher, ed. *African Guerrillas.* London: James Currey, 1998.
———. "Democratization in Africa: Obstacles and Prospects." *Third World Quarterly* 14, no. 3 (1993): 423–438.
———. "Discerning the New Africa." *International Affairs* 74, no. 2 (1998): 263–269.
———. "Rwanda: The Perils of Peacemaking." *Journal of Peace Research* 35, no. 2 (1998): 193–210.
Clement, Jean, et al. *Aftermath of the CFA Franc Devaluation.* International Monetary Fund Occasional Paper no. 138. Washington, D.C.: International Monetary Fund, 1996.
Clough, Michael. *Free at Last: U.S. Policy Toward Africa and the End of the Cold War.* New York: Council on Foreign Relations, 1992.
Cohen, D., and J. Parson, eds. "Politics and Society in Botswana." Department of Political Science, University of Botswana and Swaziland, Gaborone, 1976.
Cohen, J. M. *Ethnic Federalism in Ethiopia.* Development Discussion Paper no. 519. Cambridge: Harvard Institute for International Development, 1995.
Cohen, J., and A. Arato. *Civil Society and Political Theory.* Cambridge: MIT Press, 1992.
Colclough, C., and S. McCarthy. *The Political Economy of Botswana: A Study of Growth and Distribution.* Oxford: Oxford University Press, 1980.
Coleman, James. "Nationalism in Tropical Africa." *American Political Science Review* 48, no. 2 (1954): 404–426.
Collier, Paul. "Explaining African Economic Performance." *Journal of Economic Literature* 37 (March 1999): 64–111.
———. "The Failure of Conditionality." In Catherine Gwin and Joan M. Nelson, eds., *Perspectives on Aid and Development.* Overseas Development Council Policy Essay no. 22. Baltimore: Johns Hopkins University Press, 1997.
———. "Learning from Failure: The International Financial Institutions as Agencies of Restraint in Africa." In Andreas Schedler, Larry Diamond, and Marc F. Plattner, eds., *The Self-Restraining State: Power and Accountability in New Democracies.* Boulder, Colo.: Lynne Rienner, 1999.
———. "Making Aid Smart: Institutional Incentives Facing Donor Organizations and Their Implications for Aid Effectiveness." Paper prepared for the Forum Series on the Role of Institutions in Promoting Economic Growth, directed by the IRIS Center, sponsored by USAID, February 25, 2002.
Comissão Nacional de Eleições [National Electoral Commission]. *Relatório final* [Final report]. Maputo: AWEPA.
Committee for the Defence of Human Rights (CDHR). *2000 Annual Report on the Human Rights Situation in Nigeria.* Ikeja, Lagos: CDHR, May 2001.
Connor, W. "Nation-Building or Nation-Destroying?" *World Politics* 24, no. 3 (1972): 319–315.
Conselho de Ministros [Council of Ministers]. *Linhas de acção para eradicação da pobreza absoluta* [Action steps for the eradication of absolute poverty]. Maputo, April 13, 1999.
Conselho Nacional do Plano [National Planning Council]. *Informação económica* [Economic information]. Maputo, January 1984.
Coolidge, Jacqueline, and Susan Rose-Ackerman. "Kleptocracy and Reform in African Regimes: Theory and Examples." In K. R. Hope Sr. and B. Chikulo, eds., *Corruption and Development in Africa: Lessons from Country Case Studies.* New York: St. Martin's Press, 2000.
Cooper, Richard. *Currency Devaluations in Developing Countries.* Princeton Essays in International Finance no. 86. Princeton: Princeton University Press, 1971.

Cornia, Giovanni, Rolph van der Hoeven, and Thandika Mkandawire, eds. *Africa's Economic Recovery in the 1990s: From Stagnation and Adjustment to Human Development.* New York: St. Martin's Press, 1993.

Courade, Georges, and Véronique Alary. "Les planteurs camerounais ont-ils été réévalués?" *Politique Africaine* no. 54 (1994): 74–87.

Crick, Bernard. *In Defence of Politics.* Reissue. Chicago: University of Chicago Press, 1993.

Datta-Mitra, Jayati. *Fiscal Management in Adjustment Lending.* World Bank Operations Evaluation Study. Washington, D.C.: World Bank, 1997.

Davidson, James Dale, and William Rees-Mogg. *The Sovereign Individual: How to Survive and Thrive During the Collapse of the Welfare State.* New York: Simon and Schuster, 1997.

de Merode, Louis, and Charles Thomas. "Implementing Civil Service Pay and Employment Reform in Africa: The Experiences of Ghana, Gambia, and Guinea." In David L. Lindauer and Barbara Nunberg, eds., *Rehabilitating Government: Pay and Employment Reforms in Africa.* Washington, D.C.: World Bank, 1994.

"Democracy and Development: New Thinking on an Old Question." *Indian Economic Review* 30, no. 1 (1995): 1–18.

Deng, Francis M. "Mediating the Sudanese Conflict: A Challenge for the IGADD." *CSIS Africa Notes* no. 169 (February 1995): 1–7.

Dia, Mamadou. *Africa's Management in the 1990s and Beyond: Reconciling Indigenous and Transplanted Institutions.* Washington, D.C.: World Bank, 1996.

Diamond, Larry. *Class, Ethnicity, and Democracy in Nigeria: The Failure of the First Republic.* London: Macmillan, 1988.

———. "Class Formation in the Swollen African State." *Journal of Modern African Studies* 25, no. 4 (March 1987): 567–596.

———. "Consolidating Democracy in the Americas." *Annals of the American Academy of Political and Social Sciences* 550, no. 34 (March 1997): 12–41.

———. *Developing Democracy: Toward Consolidation.* Baltimore: Johns Hopkins University Press, 1999.

———. "Fostering Institutions to Contain Corruption." *World Bank PREMnotes* 24 (June 1999): 1–4.

———. "Introduction: Roots of Failure, Seeds of Hope." In Larry Diamond, Juan J. Linz, and Seymour Martin Lipset, eds., *Democracy in Developing Countries: Africa.* Boulder, Colo.: Lynne Rienner, 1988.

———. "Is the Third Wave Over?" *Journal of Democracy* 7, no. 3 (July 1996): 20–37.

———. "Nigeria: The Uncivic Society and the Descent into Praetorianism." In Larry Diamond, Juan J. Linz, and Seymour Martin Lipset, eds., *Politics in Developing Countries: Comparing Experiences with Democracy,* 2nd ed. Boulder, Colo.: Lynne Rienner, 1995.

———. "Nigeria's Perennial Struggle." *Journal of Democracy* 2, no. 4 (1991): 73–85.

———. "Nigeria's Search for a New Political Order." *Journal of Democracy* 2, no. 2 (Spring 1991): 54–69.

———. "Preventive Diplomacy for Nigeria: Imperatives for U.S. and International Policy." Paper presented to the U.S. House International Relations Committee, Subcommittee on Africa, Washington, D.C., November 28, 1995.

———. *Prospects for Democratic Development in Africa.* Stanford: Hoover Institution, 1997.

————. "Rethinking Civil Society: Toward Democratic Consolidation." *Journal of Democracy* 5, no. 3 (1994): 4–17.

Diamond, Larry, Anthony Kirk-Greene, and Oyeleye Oyediran, eds. *Transition Without End: Nigerian Politics and Civil Society Under Babangida.* Boulder, Colo.: Lynne Rienner, 1997.

Diamond, Larry, Juan J. Linz, and Seymour Martin Lipset, eds. *Democracy in Developing Countries: Africa.* Boulder, Colo.: Lynne Rienner, 1988.

————, eds. *Politics in Developing Countries: Comparing Experiences with Democracy.* 2nd ed. Boulder, Colo.: Lynne Rienner, 1995.

Diamond, Larry, and Marc Plattner, eds. *Democratization in Africa.* Baltimore: Johns Hopkins University Press, 1999.

Dininio, Phyllis, Sahr Kpundeh, and Robert Leiken. *USAID Handbook for Fighting Corruption.* Technical Publication Series, Center for Democracy and Governance. Washington, D.C.: U.S. Agency for International Development, 1998.

Direcção Nacional de Estatística [National Directorate for Statistics] (DNE). *Informação estatística 1975–1984* [Statistical information, 1975–1984]. Maputo: DNE, 1985.

————. *Informação estatística 1985* [Statistical information, 1985]. Maputo: DNE, May 1986.

Dolan, Chris, and Maxine Reitzes. *The Insider Story? Press Coverage of Illegal Immigrants and Refugees, April 1994–September 1995.* Johannesburg: Centre for Policy Studies, 1996.

Downs, Anthony. *An Economic Theory of Democracy.* New York: Harper and Row, 1957.

Dudley, B. J. *Instability and Political Order: Politics and Crisis in Nigeria.* Ibadan: Ibadan University Press, 1973.

Duncan, T., K. Jefferis, and P. Molutsi. *Social Development in Botswana.* Gaborone: UNICEF, 1994.

Dunn, John, ed. *Democracy: The Unfinished Journey, 508 B.C. to A.D. 1993.* London: Oxford University Press, 1992.

Easterly, William. *The Elusive Quest for Growth: Economists' Adventures and Misadventures in the Tropics.* Cambridge: MIT Press, 2001.

Economist Intelligence Unit. *Country Report: Gabon.* 2nd Quarter 1999. London: the Economist Intelligence Unit, 1999.

Eifert, Benn. "Political Equality and the Performance of African Economies, 1972–1999." Senior honors thesis, Department of Economics, Stanford University, May 2003.

Ekeh, Peter. "Colonialism and the Two Publics in Africa: A Theoretical Statement." *Comparative Studies in Society and History* 17, no. 1 (1975): 91–112.

————. "The Constitution of Civil Society in African History and Politics." In B. Caron, Alex Gboyega, and Eghosa Osaghie, eds., *Democratic Transition in Africa.* Ibadan: CREDU, 1992.

————. "Historical and Cross-Cultural Contexts of Civil Society in Africa." In B. Caron, Alex Gboyega, and Eghosa Osaghie, eds., *Democratic Transition in Africa.* Ibadan: CREDU, 1992.

Elesho, R. "Mr. Integrity." *The News* (Lagos), June 25, 2001.

Ellis, Stephen. *The Mask of Anarchy: The Destruction of Liberia and the Religious Dimensions of an African Civil War.* New York: New York University Press, 1999.

Elungu, P. E. A. *L'éveil philosophique africain* [The African philosophical awakening]. Paris: Éditions l'Harmattan, 1984.

Epstein, Helen. "AIDS: The Lessons of Uganda." *New York Review of Books* 48, no. 11 (2001): 18–23.

Ergas, Zaki, ed. *The African State in Transition*. London: Macmillan, 1987.

Esping-Andersen, Gosta. *The Three Worlds of Welfare Capitalism*. Princeton: Princeton University Press, 1990.

Etzioni, A. "The Evils of Self-Determination." *Foreign Policy* 89 (Winter 1992–1993): 21–35.

Europa Publications. *Africa South of the Sahara*. London: Europa Publications, 1979, 1996.

Falola, Toyin. "Christian Radicalism and Nigerian Politics." In Paul A. Beckett and Crawford Young, eds., *Dilemmas of Democracy in Nigeria*. Rochester: University of Rochester Press, 1997.

Fatton, Robert. "Africa in the Age of Democratization: The Civic Limitations of Civil Society." *African Studies Review* 38, no. 2 (1995): 67–100.

———. *Predatory Rule: State and Civil Society in Africa*. Boulder, Colo.: Lynne Rienner, 1992.

Fauré, Ives A., and Jean François Médard. *Etat et bourgeoisie en Côte d'Ivoire*. Paris: Karthala, 1982.

Fawcus, Peter, with Alan Tilbury. *Botswana: The Road to Independence*. Gaborone: Pula Press, 2000.

Federal Republic of Nigeria. "Constitution of the Federal Republic of Nigeria (Promulgation) Decree 1999." *Official Gazette Extraordinary* 86, no. 27 (May 5, 1999).

———. *The Corrupt Practices and Other Related Offences Act, 2000*. Abuja: Federal Republic of Nigeria, 2000.

———. *Obasanjo's Economic Direction, 1999–2003*. Abuja: Office of the Honourable Minister, Economic Matters, April 2000.

———. *Report of the Political Bureau*. Lagos: Government Printer, 1987.

———. *Report of the Presidential Committee on the Review of the 1999 Constitution*. Vol. 1, *Main Report*. Abuja: Federal Ministry of Information and National Orientation, February 2001.

———. *Report of the Presidential Committee on the Review of the 1999 Constitution: The Constitution of the Federal Republic of Nigeria 1999 (Amendment) Bill, 2001 (Incorporating the Draft of Proposed Amended Constitution)*. Vol. 2. Abuja: Federal Ministry of Information and National Orientation, February 2001.

Fiakpa, L. "Hard Times Are Here . . . as Nigerians Groan Under Economic Hardship." *Tell* (Lagos), June 11, 2001.

Fine, Robert. "Civil Society Theory and the Politics of Transition in South Africa." *Review of African Political Economy* 20, no. 55 (1992): 71–83.

Finifter, Ada, and Ellen Mickiewicz. "Redefining the Political System of the USSR: Mass Support for Political Change." *American Political Science Review* 86, no. 4 (December 1992): 857–874.

Finkel, S. "The Effects of Participation on Political Efficacy and Political Support: Evidence from a West German Panel." *Journal of Politics* 49, no. 2 (1987): 441–464.

Fischer, Stanley, et al. *Africa: Is This the Turning Point?* IMF Papers on Policy Analysis and Assessment. Washington, D.C.: International Monetary Fund, May 1998.

Forrest, Joshua. "The Quest for State 'Hardness' in Africa." *Comparative Politics* 20, no. 4 (1988): 423–442.

Fowler, Alan. "Non-Governmental Organizations and the Promotion of Democracy in Kenya." Ph.D. diss., University of Sussex, December 1993.

Freedom House. *Freedom in the World 2000–2001.* New York: Freedom House, 2001.

Frelimo. *Construímos o futuro com as nossas maos: reabilitação económica, tarefa de todo povo* [Let's build the future with our own hands: economic rehabilitation is a task for the whole people]. Maputo: Partido Frelimo, 1987.

———. *Relatório do Comité Central ao III Congresso* [Report of the Central Committee to the 3rd Congress]. Maputo: Imprensa Nacional, 1977.

———. *Relatório do Comité Central ao IV Congresso* [Report of the Central Committee to the 4th Congress]. Maputo: Imprensa Nacional, 1983.

Frieden, Jeffrey. "Classes, Sectors, and Foreign Debt in Latin America." *Comparative Politics* 21 (October 1988): 1–20.

Friedman, Steven. "Agreeing to Differ: African Democracy—Its Obstacles and Pitfalls." *Social Research* 66, no. 3 (Fall 1999): 940–953.

———. "Bonaparte at the Barricades: The Colonisation of Civil Society." *Theoria* (Durban: University of Natal) 79 (May 1992): 83–96.

———. *Building Tomorrow Today: African Workers in Trade Unions, 1970–1984.* Johannesburg: Ravan, 1987.

———. *Democracy, Inequality, and the Reconstitution of Politics.* Washington, D.C.: Woodrow Wilson Center for International Scholars, 2000.

———. *The Elusive "Community": The Dynamics of Negotiated Urban Development.* Johannesburg: Centre for Policy Studies, 1993.

———. "No Easy Stroll to Dominance: Party Dominance, Opposition, and Civil Society in South Africa." In Hermann Giliomee and Charles Simkins, eds., *The Awkward Embrace: One-Party Domination and Democracy.* Amsterdam: Harwood, 1999.

———. "Society Must Be Brought On Board to Combat AIDS." *Synopsis* (Johannesburg: Centre for Policy Studies) 4, no. 1 (June 2000): 5–6.

———. "South Africa: Divided in a Special Way." In Larry Diamond, Juan J. Linz, and Seymour Martin Lipset, eds., *Politics in Developing Countries: Comparing Experiences with Democracy,* 2nd ed. Boulder, Colo.: Lynne Rienner, 1995.

———. "South Africa: Entering the Post-Mandela Era." *Journal of Democracy* 110, no. 4 (October 1999): 3–18.

———. "Who We Are: Voter Participation, Rationality, and the 1999 Election." *Politikon* (Johannesburg) 26, no. 2 (1999): 213–223.

———. *Yesterday's Pact: Power-Sharing and Legitimate Governance in Post-Settlement South Africa.* Johannesburg: Centre for Policy Studies, 1995.

Friedman, Steven, and Maxine Reitzes. *Democratic Selections? State and Civil Society in Post-Settlement South Africa.* Midrand: Development Bank of Southern Africa, 1995.

Friedman, Steven, and Louise Stack. "The Magic Moment: The 1994 Election." In Steven Friedman and Doreen Atkinson, eds., *South Africa Review 7—The Small Miracle: South Africa's Negotiated Settlement.* Johannesburg: Raven Press, 1994.

Fukuyama, Francis. *Trust: The Social Virtues and the Creation of Prosperity.* New York: Free Press, 1995.

Fumonyoh, Christopher. "Democratization in Fits and Starts." *Journal of Democracy* 12, no. 3 (2001): 37–50.

Galvan, Dennis. "Political Turnover and Social Change in Senegal." *Journal of Democracy* 12, no. 3 (2001): 51–62.

Gibbon, Peter, Kjell J. Havnevik, and Kenneth Hermele. *A Blighted Harvest: The World Bank and African Agriculture in the 1980s.* Trenton, N.J.: Africa World Press, 1993.

Giliomee, Hermann, and Charles Simkins, eds. *The Awkward Embrace: One-Party Domination and Democracy.* Amsterdam: Harwood, 1999.

Gillespie, K., and Gwenn Okruhlik. "The Political Dimensions of Corruption Cleanups: A Framework for Analysis." *Comparative Politics* 23 (October 1991): 77–95.

Goldsmith, Arthur A. "Africa's Overgrown State Reconsidered: Bureaucracy and Economic Growth." *World Politics* 51, no. 4 (July 1999): 520–546.

Goldthorpe, John H., ed. *Order and Conflict in Contemporary Capitalism.* Oxford: Clarendon Press, 1984.

Gordon, David, and Howard Wolpe. "The Other Africa: An End to Afro-Pessimism." *World Policy Journal* 15, no. 1 (1998): 49–59.

Gotz, Graeme. *Buying In, Staying Out: The Politics of Registration for South Africa's First Democratic Local Government Elections.* Johannesburg: Centre for Policy Studies, October 1995.

"Governors Insist on New Revenue Formula." *The Punch* (Lagos), January 26, 2001.

Green, Donald, and Ian Shapiro. *Pathologies of Rational Choice Theory.* New Haven: Yale University Press, 1996.

Gyimah-Boadi, E. "Associational Life, Civil Society, and Democratization in Ghana." In John Harbeson, Donald Rothchild, and Naomi Chazan, eds., *Civil Society and the State in Africa.* Boulder, Colo.: Lynne Rienner, 1994.

———. "Civil Society in Africa." *Journal of Democracy* 7, no. 1 (1996): 118–132.

———. "Debating Democracy Assistance: The Cost of Doing Nothing." *Journal of Democracy* 10, no. 4 (1999): 119–124.

———. "Good Governance and Sustainable Development in Africa." Unpublished remarks prepared for a World Bank Institute seminar in Abidjan, January–February 2000.

———. "Peaceful Political Turnover in Ghana." *Journal of Democracy* 12, no. 2 (2001): 103–117.

———. "The Rebirth of African Liberalism." *Journal of Democracy* 9, no. 2 (1998): 18–31.

Gyimah-Boadi, E., and A. Essuman-Johnson. "PNDC and Organized Labor: An Anatomy of Political Control." In E. Gyimah-Boadi, ed., *Ghana Under PNDC Rule.* Dakar: Codesria, 1993.

Gyimah-Boadi, E., Mike Oquaye, and Kofi Drah. *Civil Society Organizations and Ghanaian Democratization.* Accra: Center for Democracy and Development, 2000.

Habermas, Jürgen. *Direito e democracia entre facticidade e validade* [Between facts and norms: contributions to a discourse theory of law and democracy] vol. 2. Rio de Janeiro: Tempo Brasileiro, 1997.

———. *Pensamento pós-metafísico: estudos filisóficos* [Postmetaphysical thinking: philosophical essays]. Transl. Flávio Beno Siebeneichler. Rio de Janeiro: Tempo Brasileiro, 1990.

Hadenius, Axel. *Institutions and Democratic Citizenship.* Oxford: Oxford University Press, 2001.

Haggard, Stephan, and Steven B. Webb, eds. *Voting for Reform: Economic Adjustment in New Democracies.* New York: Oxford University Press, 1994.

Haile, Minasse. "The New Ethiopian Constitution: Its Impact Upon Unity, Human Rights, and Development." *Suffolk Law Review* 20, no. 1 (1996): 1–84.

Halisi, C. R. D. "Citizenship and Populism in the New South Africa." *Africa Today* 45, nos. 3–4 (1998): 423–438.

Harbeson, John. "Civil Society and Political Renaissance in Africa." In John Harbeson, Donald Rothchild, and Naomi Chazan, eds., *Civil Society and the State in Africa*. Boulder, Colo.: Lynne Rienner, 1994.

Harbeson, John, Donald Rothchild, and Naomi Chazan, eds. *Civil Society and the State in Africa*. Boulder, Colo.: Lynne Rienner, 1994.

Harris, Elliott. "Impact of the Asian Crisis on Sub-Saharan Africa." *Finance and Development* 36, no. 1 (1999): 14–17.

Harris-White, B., and G. White. "Corruption, Liberalization, and Democracy: Editorial Introduction." *IDS [Institute of Development Studies] Bulletin* 27, no. 2 (1996): 1–5.

———, eds. "Liberalization and the New Corruption." *IDS Bulletin* 27, no. 2 (1996): 6–11.

Harsch, Ernest. "Accumulators and Democrats: Challenging State Corruption in Africa." *Journal of Modern African Studies* 31, no. 1 (1993): 31–48.

———. "Structural Adjustment and Africa's Democratic Movements." *Africa Today* 40, no. 4 (1993): 7–29.

Hearns, Julie. *Foreign Aid, Democratization, and Civil Society in Africa: A Study of South Africa, Ghana, and Uganda*. Institute of Development Studies Discussion Paper no. 368. Brighton, UK: Institute of Development Studies, 1999.

———. *Foreign Political Aid, Democratization, and Civil Society in Ghana in the 1990s*. Accra: Center for Democracy and Development, 2000.

"The Heart of the Matter: Africa's Biggest Problems Stem from Its Present Leaders, but They Were Created by African Society and History." *The Economist*, May 13, 2000.

Heidenheimer, Arnold, and Michael Johnston, eds. *Political Corruption: Concepts and Contexts*. 3rd ed. New Brunswick, N.J.: Transaction, 2002.

Heller, Patrick. "Social Capital as a Product of Class Mobilisation and State Intervention: Industrial Workers in Kerala, India." *World Development* 24, no. 6 (June 1996): 1055–1071.

Hellman, Joel. "Winners Take All: The Politics of Partial Reform in Postcommunist Transitions." *World Politics* 50 (January 1998): 203–234.

Hellman, Joel, G. Jones, and D. Kaufmann. "Seize the State, Seize the Day: An Empirical Analysis of State Capture and Corruption in Transition." Paper presented at the World Bank's twelfth ABCDE conference, April 2000.

Herbst, Jeffrey. *The Politics of Reform in Ghana, 1982–1991*. Berkeley: University of California Press, 1993.

———. "Responding to State Failure in Africa." *International Security* 21, no.3 (1996–1997): 120–144.

———. *Securing Peace in Africa: An Analysis of Peacekeeping and Peace Enforcement Potential*. Report no. 17. Cambridge, Mass.: World Peace Foundation, 1998.

———. *State Politics in Zimbabwe*. Berkeley: University of California Press, 1990.

———. "The Structural Adjustment of Politics in Africa." *World Development* 18, no. 7 (1990): 949–958.

Hibou, Béatrice. *L'Afrique est-elle protectioniste?* Paris: Karthala, 1996.

Hill, Polly. *The Migrant Cocoa Farmers of Southern Ghana*. Cambridge: Cambridge University Press, 1963.

Hirschmann, David. "Institutional Development in the Era of Economic Policy Reform: Concerns, Contradictions, and Illustrations from Malawi." *Public Administration and Development* 13, no. 2 (1993): 113–128.

Hodgkin, Thomas. *Nationalism in Colonial Africa.* New York: New York University Press, 1956.

Holm, John, and Patrick Molutsi, eds. *Democracy in Botswana.* Gaborone: Macmillan, 1989.

Hoogvelt, Ankie. *Globalization and the Postcolonial World.* Baltimore: Johns Hopkins University Press, 1997.

Hope, K. R., Sr., and B. Chikulo, eds. *Corruption and Development in Africa: Lessons from Country Case Studies.* New York: St. Martin's Press, 2000.

Human Rights Watch. *Burundi: Human Rights Development.* Human Rights Watch, 1994.

Huntington, Samuel P. *Political Order in Changing Societies.* New Haven: Yale University Press, 1968.

———. *The Third Wave: Democratization in the Late Twentieth Century.* Norman: Oklahoma University Press, 1991.

Husain, Ishrat, and Rashid Faruqee, eds. *Adjustment in Africa: Lessons from Country Case Studies.* Washington, D.C.: World Bank, 1994.

Hutchful, Eboe. "The Civil Society Debate in Africa." *International Journal* 51, no.1 (1996): 54–77.

———. "Demilitarizing the Political Process in Africa: Some Basic Issues." *African Security Review* 6, no. 2 (1997): 3–16.

Hyden, Goran. "Aid and Developmentalism in Southern Africa." In Steven W. Hook, ed., *Foreign Aid Toward the Millennium.* Boulder, Colo.: Lynne Rienner, 1996.

———. "Governance and the Study of Politics." In G. Hyden and M. Bratton, eds., *Governance and Politics in Africa.* Boulder, Colo.: Lynne Rienner, 1992.

Ibrahim, Jibrin. "Obstacles to Democratization in Nigeria." In Paul A. Beckett and Crawford Young, eds., *Dilemmas of Democracy in Nigeria.* Rochester: University of Rochester Press, 1997.

Ibrahim, Saad Eddin. "A Reply to My Accusers." *Journal of Democracy* 11, no. 4 (2000): 58–64.

Idasa Public Opinion Service (POS). *Building a Democratic Culture in KwaZulu-Natal: The Present Terrain.* POS Report no. 9. Cape Town: Idasa, June 1996.

———. *Building a Democratic Culture in the Western Cape: The Present Terrain.* POS Report no. 8. Cape Town: Idasa, May 1996.

———. *Provincial Politics in South Africa: Powers, Performance, and Public Opinion.* POS Report no. 7. Cape Town: Idasa, April 1996.

Instituto Nacional de Estatística [National Statistical Institute]. *II Recenseamento geral da população e habitação, 1997: resultados definitivos* [2nd general population and housing census, 1997: final results]. Maputo: INE, 1997.

International Institute for Democracy and Electoral Assistance (International IDEA). "Building a Culture of Democracy." In *Democracy in Nigeria: Continuing Dialogue(s) for National-Building.* Stockholm: International IDEA, 2001.

———. *Democracy in Nigeria: Continuing Dialogue(s) for National-Building.* Stockholm: International IDEA, 2001.

International Peace Academy. *Civil Society and Conflict Management in Africa.* New York: International Peace Academy, 1996.

Iwenjora, F. "Agonies of Freed MASSOB Leader." *Weekend Vanguard* (Lagos), June 14, 2003.

Jackson, Robert H. *Quasi-States: Sovereignty, International Relations, and the Third World.* Cambridge: Cambridge University Press, 1990.

Jaulin, R. *La decivilisation: politique et pratique de l'ethnocide* [Decivilisation: the politics and practice of ethnocide]. In Mário Mountinho, ed., *Introdução à etnologia* [Introduction to ethnology]. Lisboa: Imprensa Universitária, 1980.

Jayarajah, Carl, and William Branson. *Structural and Sectoral Adjustment: The World Bank Experience, 1980–1992.* Washington, D.C.: World Bank, 1995.

Jega, A., ed. *Identity Transformation and Identity Politics Under Structural Adjustment in Nigeria.* Uppsala, Sweden: Nordic African Institute, 2000.

Jencks, Christopher. *Rethinking Social Policy.* Cambridge: Harvard University Press, 1992.

Johnston, Michael. "Cross-Border Corruption": Points of Vulnerability and Challenges for Reform." In Sahr Kpundeh and Irene Hors, eds., *Corruption and Integrity Improvement Initiatives in Developing Countries.* New York: United Nations Development Programme, 1998.

———. "Fighting Systemic Corruption: Social Foundations for Institutional Reform." In Mark Robinson, ed., *Corruption and Development.* London: Frank Cass, 1998.

———. "Political Will and Corruption." Paper prepared for the World Bank, PREM Division, 1997.

———. "What Can Be Done About Entrenched Corruption?" In Boris Pleskovic, ed., *Annual World Bank Conference on Development Economics 1997.* Washington, D.C.: World Bank, 1998.

Joseph, Richard. "Africa: The Rebirth of Political Freedom." *Journal of Democracy* 2, no. 4 (Fall 1991): 11–21.

———. *Democracy and Prebendal Politics in Nigeria: The Rise and Fall of the Second Republic.* Cambridge: Cambridge University Press, 1987.

———. "A Democratic Nigeria and the Challenges of Leadership in Africa." Public lecture delivered at the Nigerian Institute of International Affairs, Lagos, June 10, 1999.

———. "State, Conflict, and Democracy in Africa." In Richard Joseph, ed., *State, Conflict, and Democracy in Africa.* Boulder, Colo.: Lynne Rienner, 1999.

Joseph, R., S. Taylor, and A. Agbaje. "Nigeria." In W. A. Joseph, M. Kesselman, and J. Krieger, eds., *Third World Politics at the Crossroads.* Lexington, Mass.: D. C. Heath, 1996.

Ka, Samba, and Nicolas van de Walle. "The Political Economy of Structural Adjustment in Senegal, 1980–1991." In Stephan Haggard and Steven B. Webb, eds., *Voting for Reform: Economic Adjustment in New Democracies.* New York: Oxford University Press, 1994.

———. "Senegal: Stalled Reform in Dominant Party System." In Stephen Haggard and Steven B. Webb, eds., *Voting for Reform: Democracy, Political Liberalization, and Economic Adjustment.* New York: Oxford University Press, 1994.

Kaplan, Robert. "The Coming Anarchy: How Scarcity, Crime, Overpopulation, Tribalism, and Disease Are Rapidly Destroying the Social Fabric of Our Planet." *Atlantic Monthly,* February 1994.

———. "Was Democracy Just a Moment?" *Atlantic Monthly* 280, no. 6 (December 1997): 55–80.

Karatnycky, Adrian. "The 2002 Freedom House Survey." *Journal of Democracy* 14, no. 1 (January 2003): 10–25.

Karl, Terry Lynn. "Economic Inequality and Democratic Instability." *Journal of Democracy* 11, no. 1 (2000): 149–156.

———. *The Paradox of Plenty: Oil Booms and Petro-States.* Berkeley: University of California Press, 1997.

Kasfir, Nelson. "The Conventional Notion of Civil Society: A Critique." In Nelson Kasfir, ed., *Civil Society and Democracy in Africa: Critical Perspectives.* London: Frank Cass, 1998.

Kassotche, Florentino Dick. *Globalização: receios dos países em vias de desenvolvimento. Reflexões sobre o caso de Moçambique* [Globalization: fears of the developing countries. Reflections on the Mozambican case]. Maputo: ISRI, 1999.

Katzenstein, Peter, ed. *Between Power and Plenty.* Madison: University of Wisconsin Press, 1978.

Kaufmann, Robert. "Corruption: The Facts." *Foreign Policy* no. 107. Washington, D.C.: Carnegie Endowment for International Peace, Summer 1997.

———. "Corruption in Transition Economies."In *The New Palgrave Dictionary of Economics and the Law.* London: Macmillan, 1998.

Kaufman, Robert, and Barbara Stallings. "The Political Economy of Latin American Populism." In Rudiger Dornbusch and Sebastian Edwards, eds., *The Macroeconomics of Populism in Latin America.* Chicago: University of Chicago Press, 1991.

Kaufmann, Daniel, Aart Kraay, and Pablo Zoido-Lobaton. "Governance Matters." Policy Research Working Paper no. 2196, World Bank, October 1999.

Kaufmann, Daniel, S. Pradhan, and R. Ryterman. "New Frontiers in Diagnosing and Combating Corruption." World Bank *PREMnotes* 7 (October 1998): 1–4.

Keane, John, ed. *Civil Society and the State.* London: Verso, 1988.

———. *Democracy and Civil Society.* London: Verso, 1988.

Kennedy, Paul. *African Capitalism: The Struggle for Ascendancy.* Cambridge: Cambridge University Press, 1988.

Khadiagala, Gilbert. "State Collapse and Reconstruction in Uganda." In I. William Zartman, ed., *Collapsed States: The Disintegration and Restoration of Legitimate Authority.* Boulder, Colo.: Lynne Rienner, 1995.

Kihato, Caroline, and Thabo Rapoo. *An Independent Voice? A Survey of Civil Society Organizations in Africa, Their funding, and Their Influence over the Policy Process.* Research Paper no. 67. Johannesburg: Centre for Policy Studies, 1999.

Killick, Tony. *Aid and the Political Economy of Policy Change.* London: Routledge, 1998.

———. *IMF Programmes in Developing Countries: Design and Impact.* London: Overseas Development Institute, 1996.

Kirk-Greene, A. "The Remedial Imperatives of the Nigerian Constitution, 1922–1992." In Larry Diamond, Anthony Kirk-Greene, and Oyeleye Oyediran, eds., *Transition Without End: Nigerian Politics and Civil Society Under Babangida.* Boulder, Colo.: Lynne Rienner, 1997.

Klitgaard, Robert E. *Controlling Corruption.* Berkeley: University of California Press, 1987.

Knack, Stephen, and P. Keefer. "Institutions and Economic Performance: Cross Country Tests Using Alternative Institutional Measures." *Economics and Politics* 7, no. 3 (1995): 207–227.

Kpundeh, Sahr. "Controlling Corruption in Sierra Leone: An Assessment of Past Efforts and Suggestions for the Future." In K. R. Hope Sr. and B. Chikulo, eds., *Corruption and Development in Africa: Lessons from Country Case Studies.* New York: St. Martin's Press, 2000.

———. "Institutional Reform Efforts in Uganda." In Arnold Heidenheimer and Michael Johnston, eds., *Political Corruption: Concepts and Contexts,* 3rd ed. New Brunswick, N.J.: Transaction, 2002.

———. "Political Will in Fighting Corruption." In Sahr Kpundeh and Irene Hors, eds., *Corruption and Integrity Improvement Initiatives in Developing Countries.* New York: United Nations Development Programme, 1998.

———. *Politics and Corruption in Africa: A Case Study of Sierra Leone.* Lanham, Md.: University Press of America, 1995.

Kpundeh, Sahr, Michael Johnston, and Robert Leiken. *Combating Corruption in Developing and Transitional Countries: A Guidelines Paper for USAID.* Bethesda, Md.: Development Alternatives, 1998.

Lancaster, Carol. *Aid to Africa: So Much to Do, So Little Done.* Chicago: University of Chicago Press, 1999.

Landell-Mills, Pierre. "Governance, Cultural Change, and Empowerment." *Journal of Modern African Studies* 30, no. 4 (1992): 543–567.

Leftwich, Adrian. "Governance, Democracy, and Development in the Third World." *Third World Quarterly* 14, no. 3 (1993): 605–624.

Lemarchand, Rene. "Uncivil States and Civil Societies: How Illusion Became Reality." *Journal of Modern African Studies* 30, no. 2 (1992): 177–191.

Leonard, David. "The Political Realities of African Management." *World Development* 15, no. 7 (1987): 899–910.

Leonard, David K., and Scott Straus. *Africa's Stalled Development: International Causes and Cures.* Boulder, Colo.: Lynne Rienner, 2003.

"Les milliards en l'air du Congo." *L'Autre Afrique,* May 19, 1998.

Lewis, Peter M. "Economic Statism, Private Capital, and the Dilemmas of Accumulation in Nigeria." *World Development* 22, no. 3 (1994): 437–451.

———. "Nigeria: An End to the Permanent Transition?" In Larry Diamond and Marc Plattner, eds., *Democratization in Africa.* Baltimore: Johns Hopkins University Press, 1999.

Lewis, Peter, Pearl T. Robinson, and Barnett R. Rubin. *Stabilizing Nigeria: Sanctions, Incentives, and Support for Civil Society.* New York: Century Foundation Press and the Council for Preventive Action, 1998.

Leys, Colin. "Development Theory and Africa's Future." In *Crises and Reconstruction: African Perspectives,* Nordic Afrika Institute Discussion Paper no. 8. Uppsala, Sweden: Nordic Afrika Institute, 1997.

Lienert, Ian, and Jitendra Modi. "A Decade of Civil Service Reform in Sub-Saharan Africa." Working Paper no. 97/179. Washington, D.C.: International Monetary Fund, Fiscal Affairs Department, December 1997.

Lijphart, A. "South African Democracy: Majoritarian or Consociational?" *Democratization* 5, no. 4 (1998): 144–150.

Lindauer, David L., and Barbara Nunberg, eds. *Rehabilitating Government: Pay and Employment Reforms in Africa.* Washington, D.C.: World Bank, 1994.

Lindberg, Leon N., and Charles Maier. *The Politics of Inflation and Economic Stagnation.* Washington, D.C.: Brookings Institution, 1985.

Link Forum de ONGs [Link NGO Forum]. *Directório de ONGs, Novembro de 2000* [NGO directory, November 2000]. Maputo, 2000.

Linz, Juan. "Democracy, Multinationalism, and Federalism." Paper prepared for the "Conference on Democracy and Federalism," Oxford University, June 5–8, 1997.

Linz, Juan, and Alfred Stepan. *Problems of Democratic Transition and Consolidation: Southern Europe, South America, and Post-Communist Europe.* Baltimore: Johns Hopkins University Press, 1996.

———. "Towards Consolidated Democracies." *Journal of Democracy* 7, no. 2 (April 1996): 14–33.

Lipumba, Nguyuru. *Africa Beyond Adjustment.* Policy Essay no. 15. Washington, D.C.: Overseas Development Council, 1994.

Little, W., and E. Posada-Carbo, eds. *Political Corruption in Europe and Latin America.* London: Macmillan, 1996.

Lofchie, Michael F., and Thomas Callaghy. *Diversity in the Tanzanian Business Community and Its Implications for Growth.* Report to the USAID Mission, Dar es Salaam, Tanzania, December 5, 1995.

Losch, Bruno. "Les agro-exportateurs face à la dévaluation." *Politique Africaine* no. 54 (June 1994): 88–103.

Luckham, Robin. "The Dilemmas of Military Disengagement in Africa." *IDS [Institute of Development Studies] Bulletin* 26, no. 2 (1995): 49–61.

———. "Popular Versus Liberal Democracy in Nicaragua and Tanzania?" *Democratization* 5, no. 3 (Autumn 1998): 92–126.

Lyons, Terrence. "Closing the Transition: The May 1995 Elections in Ethiopia." *Journal of Modern African Studies* 34 (March 1996): 161–190.

———. "The Horn of Africa Regional Politics: A Hobbesian World." In Howard Wriggins, ed., *Dynamics of Regional Politics: Four Systems on the Indian Ocean Rim.* New York: Columbia University Press, 1992.

———. "Implementing Peace and Building Democracy: The Role of Elections." In Stephen John Stedman, Donald Rothchild, and Elizabeth Cousens, eds., *Ending Civil Wars: The Implementation of Peace Agreements.* Boulder, Colo.: Lynne Rienner, 2002.

———. *Voting for Peace: Postconflict Elections in Liberia.* Washington, D.C.: Brookings Institution, 1999.

MacGaffey, Janet. *The Real Economy of Zaire.* Philadelphia: University of Pennsylvania Press, 1991.

Machel, Samora Moisés. *Educar o homem novo para vencer a guerra, criar uma sociedade nova para desenvolver a pátria: mensagem a II Conferência do Departamento da Educação e Cultura* [Educate the new man to win the war, create a new society to develop the motherland: message to the 2nd Conference of the Department of Education and Culture]. N.p.: Frelimo, 1970.

———. *O Partido e as classes trabalhadoras moçambicanas na edificaçaõ da democracia popular: relatório do Comité Central ao III Congresso* [The Party and the Mozambican working class in the building of people's democracy: report of the Central Committee to the III Congress]. Maputo: Departamento do Trabalho Ideológico da Frelimo, 1977.

Mackay, Shaun. "IEC's Sleight of Hand Is Not in Electorate's Long-Term Interest." *Synopsis* (Johannesburg: Centre for Policy Studies) 3, no. 1 (March 1999): 1–3.

"Major Blow for KACA." *Nation Newspaper* (Nairobi), December 23, 2000.

Makumbe, John. "Is There a Civil Society in Africa?" *International Affairs* 74, no. 2 (1998): 305–317.

Mamdani, Mahmood. *Citizen and Subject: Comtemporary Africa and the Legacy of Late Colonialism.* Princeton, NJ: Princeton University Press, 1996.

Mangcu, Xolela. "Why GEAR Is Not Delivering Growth and Jobs." *Synopsis* (Johannesburg: Centre for Policy Studies) 4, no. 2 (August 2000): 2–4.

Manning, Carrie. "Constructing Opposition in Mozambique: Renamo as Political Party." *Journal of Southern African Studies* 24, no. 1 (March 1998): 161–190.

Maqsood Ali, Shaikh, and Susil Sirivardana. "Towards a New Paradigm for Poverty Eradication in South Asia." *UNESCO International Social Science Journal* no. 148 (June 1996): 207–218.

Masland, Tom, and J. Bartholet. "The Lost Billions." *Newsweek,* March 13, 2000.

Mauro, Paolo. "The Effects of Corruption on Growth, Investment, and Government Expenditure: A Cross-Country Analysis." In Kimberly Ann Elliott, ed., *Corruption and the Global Economy.* Washington, D.C.: Institute for International Economics, 1997.

May, Roy, and Arnold Hughes. "Armies on Loan: Toward an Explanation of Transnational Military Intervention Among Black African States: 1960–1985." In

Simon Baynham, ed., *Military Power and Politics in Black Africa*. New York: St. Martin's Press, 1986.

Mazula, Brazão. *A construção da democracia em África: o caso moçambicano* [Building democracy in Africa: the Mozambican case]. Maputo: Ndjira, 2000.

———. *Eleições, democracia e desenvolvimento* [Elections, democracy and development]. Maputo, 1995.

Mbanefoh, G., and F. O. Egwaikhide. "Revenue Allocation in Nigeria: Derivation Principle Revisited." In K. Amuwo et al., eds., *Federalism and Political Restructuring in Nigeria*. Ibadan: Spectrum and IFRA, 1998.

Médard, Jean-François. "The Crisis of Neo-Patrimonial State." In Arnold Heidenheimer and Michael Johnston, eds., *Political Corruption: Concepts and Contexts*, 3rd ed. New Brunswick, N.J.: Transaction, 2002.

Meerman, Jacob. *Reforming Agriculture: The World Bank Goes to Market*. World Bank Operations Evaluation Study. Washington, D.C.: World Bank, 1997.

Mekenkamp, Monique, Paul van Tongeren, and Hans van de Veen, eds. *Searching for Peace in Africa: An Overview of Conflict Prevention and Management Activities*. Utrecht: European Platform on Conflict Prevention and Transformation and the African Centre for the Constructive Resolution of Disputes, 1999.

Mengisteab, Kidane. "Democratization and State Building in Africa: How Compatible Are They?" In Kidane Mengisteab and Cyril Daddieh, eds., *State Building and Democratization in Africa: Faith, Hope, and Realities*. Westport, Conn.: Preager, 1999.

Migdal, Joel S. *Strong Societies and Weak States: State-Society Relations and State Capitalism in the Third World*. Princeton: Princeton University Press, 1988.

Miller, Arthur II., Vicki L. Hesli, and William M. Reisinger. "Conceptions of Democracy Among Mass and Elite in Post-Soviet Societies." *British Journal of Political Science* 27, no. 2 (1997): 157–190.

Ministério de Educação e Cultura [Ministry of Education and Culture]. *Atlas geográfico* [Geographic atlas]. Maputo: Instituto Nacional de Desenvolvimento da Educação, 1983.

———. *Sistema de educação de Moçambique* [The education system in Mozambique]. Maputo: Gabinete do Sistema de Educação, 1980.

Mishler, William, and Richard Rose. "Five Years After the Fall: Trajectories in Support for Democracy in Post-Communist Europe." *Studies in Public Policy* (Glasgow, Scotland: University of Strathclyde, Centre for the Study of Public Policy) 49, no. 5 (1998): 799–823.

Mkandawire, Thandika. "Crisis Management in the Making of 'Choiceless Democracies' in Africa." In Richard Joseph, ed., *State, Conflict, and Democracy in Africa*. Boulder, Colo.: Lynne Rienner, 1999.

———. "The Political Economy of Privatization in Africa." In Giovanni Cornia and Gerry Helleiner, eds., *From Adjustment to Development in Africa: Conflict, Controversy, Convergence, Consensus?* London: Macmillan, 1994.

———. "Shifting Commitments and and National Cohesion in African Countries." In L. Wohlgemuth, S. Gibson, S. Klasen, and E. Rothschild, eds., *Common Security and Civil Society in Africa*. Stockholm: Elanders Gotab, 1999.

Mkandawire, Thandika, and A. Olukoshi, eds. *Between Liberalization and Oppression: The Politics of Structural Adjustment in Africa*. Dakar: Codesria, 1995.

Mkandawire, Thandika, and Charles Soludo. *Our Continent, Our Future: African Perspectives on Structural Adjustment*. Trenton, N.J.: Africa World Press, 1999.

Mogalakwe, M. *The State and Organized Labour in Botswana*. Aldershot, UK: Ashgate, 1997.

Mogalakwe, M., P. Molutsi, and P. Mufune. "The State Legislation and Trade Unions in Botswana." *Journal of Southern African Development* 15, no. 4 (1998).

Molatlhegi, B. "Workers Freedom of Association in Botswana." *Journal of Africa Law* 42, no. 1 (1998): 64–67.

Molutsi, Patrick. "Inequality in Botswana: A Study of Social Stratification, Power, and Distribution of Resources in a Prosperous Country." Unpublished Ph.D. thesis, University of Oxford, 1986.

Molutsi, Patrick, and John Holm. "Developing Democracy When Civil Society Is Weak: The Case of Botswana." *African Affairs* 89 (July 1991): 323–340.

Mondlane, Eduardo. "Tribos ou grupos étnicos moçambicanos. seu significado na luta de liberatação nacional)" [Mozambican tribes or ethnic groups: their significance in the struggle for national liberation]. In João Reis and Armando Pedro Muiuane, eds., *Datas e documentos da história da Frelimo* [Dates and documents from the history of Frelimo], 2nd ed. Maputo: Imprensa Nacional, 1975.

Monga, Celestin. "Civil Society and Democratization in Francophone Africa." *Journal of Modern African Studies* 33, no. 3 (1995): 359–379.

———. "Eight Problems with African Politics." *Journal of Democracy* 8, no. 3 (1997): 156–182.

Mosher, Frederick. *Democracy and the Public Service.* Oxford: Oxford University Press, 1982.

Mosley, Paul, Jane Harrigan, and John Toye. *Aid and Power: The World Bank and Policy Based Lending in the 1980s.* London: Routledge, 1991.

"Mozambique: Funding for Peace." *Africa Confidential,* May 14, 1993.

Mukum, John, and Julius Ihonvbere, eds. *Multi-Party Democracy and Political Change: Constraints to Democratization.* Aldershot, UK: Ashgate, 1998.

Murray, Charles. *Losing Ground: American Social Policy 1950–1980.* New York: Basic Books, 1984.

Mutahaba, Gelase, Rweikiza Baguma, and Mohamed Halfani. *Vitalizing African Public Administration for Recovery and Development.* Hartford, Conn.: Kumarian Press, 1993.

Nash, John. "Trade Policy Reform Implementation in Sub-Saharan Africa: How Much Heat and How Much Light?" World Bank Working Paper. Washington, D.C.: World Bank, 1995.

Nashashibi, Karim, et al. *The Fiscal Dimensions of Adjustment in Low-Income Countries.* IMF Occasional Paper no. 95. Washington, D.C.: International Monetary Fund, April 1992.

Navia, Patricio, and Thomas D. Zweifel, "Democracy, Dictatorship, and Infant Mortality Revisited." *Journal of Democracy* 14 (July 2003): 90–103.

Ndegwa, Stephen. "Citizenship and Ethnicity: An Examination of Two Transition Moments in Kenyan Politics." *American Political Science Review* 91, no. 2 (1997): 559–615.

Nelson, Joan, ed. *Economic Crisis and Policy Choice: The Politics of Economic Adjustment in the Third World.* Princeton: Princeton University Press, 1990.

Newitt, Malyn. *A History of Mozambique.* London: Hurst, 1995.

Ng, F., and A. Yeats. "Open Economies Work Better! Did Africa's Protectionist Policies Cause its Marginalization in World Trade?" World Bank Policy Research Working Paper no. 1636. Washington, D.C.: World Bank, 1996.

Niboro, I. "Lawmakers on the Rampage." *Tell* (Lagos), April 24, 2000.

"Niger: Lassitude pre-electorale." *L'Autre Afrique,* October 12, 1999.

Norris, Pippa, ed. *Critical Citizens: Global Support for Democratic Governance.* New York: Oxford University Press, 1999.

Nunberg, Barbara. "Experiences with Civil Service Pay and Employment Reform: An Overview." In David L. Lindauer and Barbara Nunberg, eds., *Rehabilitating Government: Pay and Employment Reforms in Africa*. Washington, D.C.: World Bank, 1994.

Nwanko, Clement. "Monitoring Nigeria's Elections." *Journal of Democracy* 10, no. 4 (1999): 156–165.

Nyangor'o, Julius, and Timothy Shaw, eds. *Corporatism in Africa*. Boulder, Colo.: Westview Press, 1988.

Obasanjo, Olusegun. "A Balance Sheet of the African Region and the Cold War." In Edmond Keller and Donald Rothchild, eds., *Africa and the New International Order: Rethinking State Sovereignty and Regional Security*. Boulder, Colo.: Lynne Rienner, 1996.

———. "Democracy and Development in Africa: From Transition to Transformation—Address at Harvard University ARCO Forum for Public Affairs, Kennedy School of Government, Cambridge, Massachusetts, USA, October 30, 1999." In *A New Dawn: Selected Speeches by Olusegun Obasanjo, President of the Federal Republic of Nigeria*. Aso Rock, Abuja: Presidential Communications Unit, Office of the President, 2000.

Obi, C. I. "The Impact of Oil on Nigeria's Revenue Allocation System: Problems and Prospects for National Reconstruction." In K. Amuwo et al., eds., *Federalism and Political Restructuring in Nigeria*. Ibadan: Spectrum and IFRA, 1998.

Obidigbo, S. "IMF Scores Government Low, CBN Gives Self Pass Mark." *The Guardian* (Lagos), August 7, 2001.

O'Brien, Cruise D. "Modernization, Order, and the Erosion of the Democratic Ideal." *Journal of Development Studies* 7 (July 1971): 141–160.

Oche, J. "Budget Scandal." *Tell* (Lagos), May 22, 2000.

Odion, L., et al. "How Do Oil Governors Spend Their Money?" *Thisday* (Lagos), June 2, 2001.

O'Donnell, Guillermo. "Do Economists Really Know Best?" In Larry Diamond and Marc Plattner, eds., *The Global Resurgence of Democracy*, 2nd ed. Baltimore: Johns Hopkins University Press, 1999.

O'Donnell, Guillermo, and Philippe Schmitter. *Transitions from Authoritarian Rule: Tentative Conclusions About Uncertain Democracies*. Baltimore: Johns Hopkins University Press, 1987.

Offi, S. "Governors Would Use State Police to Fight Their Opponents." *Tell* (Lagos), May 14, 2001.

Ogidan, A. "Group Faults Obasanjo over Lingering Unemployment Crisis." *The Guardian* (Lagos), August 7, 2001.

Ohlson, Thomas, and Stephen John Stedman, with Robert Davies: *The New Is Not Yet Born: Conflict Resolution in Southern Africa*. Washington, D.C.: Brookings Institution, 1994.

Olowononi, G. D. "Revenue Allocation and Economics of Federalism." In K. Amuwo et al., eds., *Federalism and Political Restructuring in Nigeria*. Ibadan: Spectrum and IFRA, 1998.

Olowu, Bamidele. "Redesigning African Civil Service Reforms." *Journal of Modern African Studies* 37, no. 1 (1999): 1–23.

Olowu, Dele. "Roots and Remedies of Governmental Corruption in Africa." *Corruption and Reform* 7, no. 3 (1993): 227–236.

Olson, Mancur. "Dictatorship, Democracy, and Development." *American Political Science Review* 87, no. 3 (September 1993): 567–575.

Omenuwa, O. "At the Mercy of Armed Robbers." *The News* (Lagos), July 2, 2001.

Onimode, B. "How Twenty-Three Nations Control Their Resources: Case Studies for Nigeria." *Sunday Tribune* (Lagos), April 8, 2001.

Onyeacholem, G. "A Collapsible Entity." *Tell* (Lagos), June 5, 2000.

Osayimwese, I., and S. Iyare. "The Economics of Nigerian Federalism: Selected Issues in Economic Management." *Publius: The Journal of Federalism* 21, no. 4 (Fall 1991): 89–102.

Oseni, T., S. Sambo, and K. Samuel. *Nigeria: Path to Sustainable Democracy.* Lagos: Obafemi Awolowo, 2000.

Osifo-Whiskey, Onome, et al. "My Conscience Is Clear." *Tell* (Lagos), May 21, 2001.

Ottaway, Marina. "African Democratization and the Leninist Option." *Journal of Modern African Studies* 35, no. 1 (1997): 1–15.

———. "Angola's Failed Elections." In Chetan Kumar, ed., *Postconflict Elections and International Assistance.* Boulder, Colo.: Lynne Rienner, 1998.

———. *Democratization and Ethnic Nationalism: African and Eastern European Experiences.* Washington, D.C.: Overseas Development Council, 1994.

———. "Democratization in Collapsed States." In I. William Zartman, ed., *Collapsed States: The Disintegration and Restoration of Legitimate Authority.* Boulder, Colo.: Lynne Rienner, 1995.

———. "Less Is Better: An Agenda for Africa." *Policy Brief* (Carnegie Endowment for International Peace) 1, no. 2 (December 2000): 1–7.

Ottaway, Marina, and Theresa Chung. "Debating Democracy Assistance: Toward a New Paradigm." *Journal of Democracy* 10, no. 4 (1999): 99–113.

Owoeye-Wyse, L. "Dashed Hopes." *The News* (Lagos), May 14, 2001.

———. "The Face of Shame." *The News,* June 11, 2001.

Owoeye-Wise, L., and O. Omenuwa. "End of Road for Derico." *The News* (Lagos), July 23, 2001.

Owusu, Maxwell. "Democracy and Africa: The View from the Village." *Journal of Modern African Studies* 30, no. 3 (1992): 369–396.

Oyediran, O., and A. Agbaje. *Nigeria: Politics of Transition and Governance, 1986–1996.* Dakar: Codesria, 1999.

Paden, John N. "Nigerian Unity and the Tensions of Democracy: Geo-Cultural Zones and North-South Legacies." In Paul A. Beckett and Crawford Young, eds., *Dilemmas of Democracy in Nigeria.* Rochester: University of Rochester Press, 1997.

Padgen, A. "The Genesis of Governance and Enlightenment Conceptions of the Cosmopolitan World Order." *International Social Science Journal* 155 (March 1998): 7–15.

Parsons, N. "The Economic History of Khama's Country in Botswana, 1844–1930." In R. Palmer and N. Parsons, eds., *The Roots of Rural Poverty in Central and Southern Africa.* Oxford: Oxford University Press, 1977.

Parsons, N., et al. *Seretse Khama.* Oxford: Oxford University Press, 1997.

Phillips, A. "Managing Fiscal Federalism: Revenue Allocation Issues." *Publius: The Journal of Federalism* 21, no. 4 (Fall 1991): 7–15.

Pinto-Duschinsky, Michael. "The Rise of Political Aid." In Larry Diamond, Marc Plattner, and Hung-mao Tien, eds., *Consolidating the Third Wave Democracies: Regional Challenges.* Baltimore: Johns Hopkins University Press, 1997.

Piven, Frances Fox, and Richard Cloward. *Why Americans Don't Vote.* New York: Pantheon, 1988.

Polan, A. J. *Lenin and the End of Politics.* London: Methuen, 1984.

Post, Ken. "State, Civil Society, and Democracy in Africa: Some Theoretical Considerations." In R. Cohen and H. Gouldbourne, eds., *Democracy and Socialism in Africa*. Boulder, Colo.: Westview Press, 1991.

Prendergast, John, and Emily Plumb. "Civil Society Organizations and Peace Agreement Implementation." In Stephen John Stedman, Donald Rothchild, and Elizabeth Cousens, eds., *Ending Civil Wars: The Implementation of Peace Agreements*. Boulder, Colo.: Lynne Rienner, 2002.

Project Manzi. Unpublished focus group study of consumer responses to water delivery and payment commissioned by Rand Water, May 1995.

Przeworksi, Adam. *Capitalism and Social Democracy*. Cambridge: Cambridge University Press, 1987.

———. *Democracy and the Market: Political and Economic Reforms in Eastern Europe and Latin America*. New York: Cambridge University Press, 1991.

Przeworski, Adam, Michael E. Alvarez, Jose Antonio Cheibub, and Fernando Limongi. *Democracy and Development: Political Institutions and Well-Being in the World, 1950–1990*. Cambridge: Cambridge University Press, 2000.

Przeworski, Adam, and Fernando Limongi. "Modernization: Theories and Facts." *World Politics* 49, no. 2 (January 1997): 155–183.

———. "Political Regimes and Economic Growth." *Journal of Economic Literature* 7, no. 3 (1993): 51–69.

Putnam, Robert. "Bowling Alone: America's Declining Social Capital." *Journal of Democracy* 6, no. 1 (January 1995): 65–78.

———. *Bowling Alone: The Collapse and Revival of American Community*. New York: Simon and Schuster, 2000.

———. *Making Democracy Work: Civic Traditions in Modern Italy*. Princeton: Princeton University Press, 1993.

Raczynski, Dagmar, ed. *Strategies for Combatting Poverty in Latin America*. Washington, D.C.: Inter-American Development Bank, 1995.

Radelet, Steven. "Bush and Foreign Aid." *Foreign Affairs* 82, no. 5 (September–October 2003): 104–117.

———. "The Millennium Challenge Account." Testimony for the House International Relations Committee, March 6, 2003.

Rakner, Lise, Nicolas van de Walle, and Dominic Mulaisho. "Aid and Reform in Zambia." Unpublished report for the World Bank project on aid and reform, Washington, D.C., 1999.

Ramachadran, Vijaya. *Investing in Africa*. Policy Essay no. 25. Washington, D.C.: Overseas Development Council, 2001.

Ramos de Almeida, Pedro. *Historia do colonialismo português em África: cronologia. Séc. XX* [A history of Portuguese colonialism in Africa: chronology. Twentieth century]. Lisbon: Estampa, Imprensa Universitária, 1979.

Rantete, Johannes, and Mark Swilling. "Organization and Strategies of the Major Resistance Movements in the Negotiation Era." In Robin Lee and Lawrence Schlemmer, eds., *Transition to Democracy: Policy Perspectives 1991*. Cape Town: Oxford University Press, 1991.

Rapoo, Thabo. *Twist in the Tail? The ANC and the Appointment of Provincial Premiers*. Policy Brief no. 7. Johannesburg: Centre for Policy Studies, October 1998.

Ravenhill, John. "Adjustment with Growth: A Fragile Consensus." *Journal of Modern African Studies* 26, no. 2 (1988): 179–210.

Reitzes, Maxine. *Divided on the "Demon": Immigration Policy Since the Election*. Johannesburg: Centre for Policy Studies, 1995.

Remmer, Karen. "Exclusionary Democracy." *Studies in Comparative International Development* 20, no. 4 (1986).

Reno, William. *Corruption and State Politics in Sierra Leone.* New York: Cambridge University Press, 1995.

Republic of South Africa. Department of Water Affairs and Forestry. *Water Supply and Sanitation Policy White Paper.* Cape Town: Republic of South Africa, 1994.

Riley, Stephen. "The Political Economy of Anti-Corruption Strategies in Africa." In Mark Robinson, ed., *Corruption and Development.* London: Frank Cass, 1998.

Robertson, Claire. "Contesting the Contest: Negotiating the Electoral Machinery." In Steven Friedman and Doreen Atkinson, eds., *The Small Miracle: South Africa's Negotiated Settlement.* Johannesburg: Ravan Books, 1995.

Robinson, Derek. *Civil Service Pay in Africa.* Geneva: International Labour Organization, 1990.

Robinson, Mark. "Corruption and Development: An Introduction." In Mark Robinson, ed., *Corruption and Development.* London: Frank Cass, 1998.

———, ed. *Corruption and Development.* London: Frank Cass, 1998.

———. "Privatizing the Voluntary Sector: NGOs as Public Service Contracters?" In David Hulme and Michael Edwards, eds., *NGOs, States, and Donors: Too Close for Comfort?* New York: St. Martin's Press, 1997.

Robinson, Mark, and Gordon White. "The Role of Civic Organizations in the Provision of Social Services." United Nations University WIDER Research for Action Paper no. 37, Helsinki, July 1997.

Robinson, Pearl. "The National Conference Phenomenon in Francophone Africa." *Comparative Studies in Society and History* 36, no. 3(1994): 575–610.

Rodrik, Dani. *The New Global Economy and Developing Countries: Making Openness Work.* Washington, D.C.: Overseas Development Council, 1999.

———. "Understanding Economic Policy Reform." *Journal of Economic Literature* 34 (March 1996): 9–41.

———. "Why Is Trade Reform so Difficult in Africa?" *Journal of African Economies* 7, no. 1 (1998): 43–69.

Roll, Richard, and John R. Talbott, "Political Freedom, Economic Liberty, and Prosperity." *Journal of Democracy* 14, no. 3 (July 2003): 75–89.

Romão, Antonio et al. *Moçambique: um país do futuro* [Mozambique: a country of the future]. Lisbon: Montepio Geral, 1998.

Rose, Richard, William Mishler, and Christian Haerpfer. *Democracy and Its Alternatives: Understanding Post-Communist Societies.* Baltimore: Johns Hopkins University Press, 1998.

Rose-Ackerman, Susan. *Corruption and Government: Causes, Consequences, and Reform.* New York: Cambridge University Press, 1999.

———. "The Political Economy of Corruption." In Kimberly Elliott, ed., *Corruption and the Global Economy.* Washington, D.C.: Institute for International Economics, 1997.

Rothchild, Donald, ed. "Ethnic Bargaining and State Breakdown in Africa." *Nationalism and Ethnic Politics* 1, no.1 (Spring 1995): 54–72.

———. *Ghana: The Political Economy of Recovery.* Boulder, Colo.: Lynne Rienner, 1991.

———. "Reconfiguring State-Ethnic Relations in Africa: Liberalization and the Search for New Routines of Interaction." In Peter Lewis, ed., *Africa: Dilemmas of Change and Development.* Boulder, Colo.: Westview Press, 1998.

Rothchild, Donald, and Naomi Chazan, eds. *The Precarious Balance: State and Society in Africa.* Boulder, Colo.: Westview Press, 1988.

Rouis, Mustapha. "Senegal: Stabilization, Partial Adjustment, and Stagnation." In Ishrat Husain and Rashid Faruqee, eds., *Adjustment in Africa: Lessons from Country Case Studies.* Washington, D.C.: World Bank, 1994.

Roux, Edward. *Time Longer Than Rope: A History of the Black Man's Struggle for Freedom in South Africa.* Madison: University of Wisconsin Press, 1964.

Rupert, James. "U.S. Troops Teach Peacekeeping to Africans." *Washington Post,* September 26, 1997.

Sachs, Jeff. "Foreign Direct Investment in Africa." In *The Africa Competitiveness Report, 1998.* Geneva: World Economic Forum, 1998.

Sachs, Jeff, and Warner, Andrew. "Economic Reform and the Process of Global Integration." *Brookings Papers on Economic Activity* no.1 (1995).

Sadig, Rasheed, and David Fasholé Luke, eds. *Development Management in Africa: Towards Dynamism, Empowerment, and Entrepreneurship.* Boulder, Colo.: Westview Press, 1995.

Sagay, I. "Nigeria: Federalism, the Constitution, and Resource Control." 3 parts. *The Guardian* (Lagos), May 23–25, 2001.

Sahn, David E. "Public Expenditures in Sub-Saharan Africa During a Period of Economic Reform." *World Development* 20, no. 5 (May 1992): 673–693.

Sahn, David E., Paul A. Dorosh, and Stephen D. Younger. *Structural Adjustment Reconsidered: Economic Policy and Poverty in Africa.* New York: Cambridge University Press, 1997.

Salamon, M. *Industrial Relations: Theory and Practice.* London: Prentice Hall, 1987.

Sandbrook, Richard. *The Politics of Africa's Economic Stagnation.* Cambridge: Cambridge University Press, 1985.

Sandbrook, Richard, and Robin Cohen. *The Development of the African Working Class: Studies in Class Formation and Action.* London: Longman, 1975.

Sandbrook, Richard, and Jay Oelbaum. *Reforming the Political Kingdom: Governance in Ghana's Fourth Republic.* Accra: Center for Democracy and Development, 1999.

Saul, John. "For Fear of Being Condemned as Old Fashioned: Liberal Democracy vs. Popular Democracy in Sub-Saharan Africa." *Review of African Political Economy* 24, no. 73 (1997): 339–353.

Schedler, Andreas. "Conceptualizing Accountability." In Andreas Schedler, Larry Diamond, and Marc F. Plattner, eds., *The Self-Restraining State: Power and Accountability in New Democracies.* Boulder, Colo.: Lynne Rienner, 1999.

Schedler, Andreas, Larry Diamond, and Marc F. Plattner, eds. *The Self-Restraining State: Power and Accountability in New Democracies.* Boulder, Colo.: Lynne Rienner, 1999.

Schmitter, Philippe. "Dangers and Dilemmas of Democracy." *Journal of Democracy* 5 (April 1994): 57–74.

Schmitter, Philippe, and Terry Karl. "What Democracy Is . . . and Is Not." *Journal of Democracy* 2 (Summer 1991): 75–88.

Schmitz, Tobias. *Rethinking Delivery? A Review of the Efforts of the Department of Water Affairs, 1994–9.* Johannesburg: Centre for Policy Studies, 1999.

Semboja, Joseph, and Ole Therkildsen, eds. *Service Provision Under Stress in East Africa.* London: James Currey, 1995.

Semenitari, I. "Paying for Civil Rule." *Tell* (Lagos), June 18, 2001.

Sen, Amartya. "Democracy as a Universal Value." *Journal of Democracy* 10, no. 3 (July 1999): 1–17.

Seppälä, Pekka. "Food Marketing Reconsidered: An Assessment of the Liberalization of Food Marketing in Sub-Saharan Africa." United Nations University WIDER Research for Action Paper no. 34, Helsinki, 1997.

Sharer, Robert, Hema De Zoysa, and Calvin McDonald. *Uganda: Adjustment with Growth, 1987–94.* IMF Occasional Paper no. 121. Washington, D.C.: International Monetary Fund, 1995.

Shepherd, Andrew, and Stefano Farolfi. *Export Crop Liberalization in Africa: A Review.* FAO Agricultural Services Bulletin no. 135. Rome: Food and Agriculture Organization, 1999.

Shils, Edward. "The Virtue of Civil Society." *Government and Opposition* 26, no. 1 (1991): 3–20.

Shivji, Issa. "The Democracy Debate in Africa: Tanzania." *Review of African Political Economy* 18, no. 50 (Spring 1991): 79–91.

Simon, Janos. "Popular Conceptions of Democracy in Post-Communist Europe." In Samuel H. Barnes and Janos Simon, eds., *The Post-Communist Citizen.* Budapest: Erasmus Foundation and Institute for Political Science, Hungarian Academy of Sciences, 1993.

Sisk, Timothy. "Elections and Conflict Management in Africa: Conclusions and Recommendations." In Timothy Sisk and Andrew Reynolds, eds., *Elections and Conflict Management in Africa.* Washington, D.C.: United States Institute of Peace Press, 1998.

Sisk, Timothy, and Andrews Reynolds, eds. *Elections and Conflict Management in Africa.* Washington, D.C.: U.S. Institute of Peace Press, 1998.

Sithole, Masipula. "Fighting Authoritarianism in Zimbabwe." *Journal of Democracy* 12, no. 1 (2001): 160–169.

Skalnes, Tor. *The Politics of Economic Reform in Zimbabwe.* New York: St. Martin's Press, 1995.

Sklar, Richard. "Developmental Democracy." *Comparative Studies in Society and History* 29, no. 4 (1987): 686–671.

———. "Finding Peace Through Democracy in Sahelian Africa." *Current History* 91, no. 565 (May 1992): 224–229.

———. *Nigerian Political Parties: Power in an Emergent African Nation.* Princeton: Princeton University Press, 1963.

———. "Nigerian Politics in Perspective." *Government and Opposition* 5, no.1 (May 1967): 1–11.

Skocpol, Theda, and Ira Katznelson. *Social Policy in the U.S.: Future Possibilities in Historical Perspective.* Princeton: Princeton University Press, 1996.

Soludu, Charles. "Trade Policy Reforms and Supply Responses in Africa." Geneva: UNCTAD, September 1998.

Sommer, J. G. *Hope Restored? Humanitarian Aid in Somalia, 1990–1994.* Washington, D.C.: RPG, 1994.

Soremekun, K., and Agbaje, A. "Developing Conflict Management Capabilities for Sustainable Democracy." In T. Oseni, A. Sambo, and K. Samuel, eds., *Nigeria: Path to Sustainable Democracy.* Lagos: Obafemi Awolowo Foundation, 2000.

"South-South Empowerment Front (SSEF) Sues Federal Government on Derivation." *The Guardian* (Lagos), September 21, 2000.

Spear, Joanna. "Demobilization and Disarmament: Key Implementation Issues." In Stephen John Stedman, Donald Rothchild, and Elizabeth Cousens, eds., *Ending Civil Wars: The Implementation of Peace Agreements.* Boulder, Colo.: Lynne Rienner, 2002.

Stacey, Simon. *New Capacities for Old? Public-Private Partnerships and Universal Service Delivery in South Africa, Angola, and Mozambique.* Johannesburg: Centre for Policy Studies, 1997.

Stapenhurst, R., and Sahr Kpundeh. *Curbing Corruption: Toward a Model for Building National Integrity.* Washington, D.C.: World Bank, 1999.

Stasavage, David, and Dambisa Moyo. *Are Cash Budgets a Cure for Excess Fiscal Deficits (and at What Cost)?* Center for the Study of African Economies Paper no. WPS/99-11. Oxford: Oxford University Press, May 1999.

Stedman, Stephen John, ed. *Botswana: The Political Economy of Democractic Development.* Aldershot, UK: Ashgate, 1992.

———. "Conflict and Conciliation in Sub-Saharan Africa." In Michael E. Brown, ed., *The International Dimensions of Internal Conflict.* Cambridge: MIT Press, 1996.

———. "Spoiler Problems in Peace Processes." *International Security* 22, no. 3 (Fall 1997): 5–53.

Stedman, Stephen John, Donald Rothchild, and Elizabeth Cousens, eds. *Ending Civil Wars: The Implementation of Peace Agreements.* Boulder, Colo.: Lynne Rienner, 2002.

Stepan, Alfred "Towards a New Comparative Analysis for Democracy and Federalism." Background paper for the "Conference on Democracy and Federalism," Oxford University, June 5–8, 1997.

Stevens, Mike. "Public Expenditure and Civil Service Reform in Tanzania." In David L. Lindauer and Barbara Nunberg, eds., *Rehabilitating Government: Pay and Employment Reforms in Africa.* Washington, D.C.: World Bank, 1994.

Stoker, G. "Governance as Theory: Five Propositions." *International Social Science Journal* 50, no. 155 (March 1998): 17–27.

Suberu, R. T. "Can Nigeria's New Democracy Survive?" *Current History* 100, no. 646 (May 2001): 207–212.

———. "Federalism, Ethnicity, and Regionalism in Nigeria." In Paul A. Beckett and Crawford Young, eds., *Dilemmas of Democracy in Nigeria.* Rochester: University of Rochester Press, 1997.

Suberu, R. T., and A. Agbaje. "The Future of Nigeria's Federalism." In K. Amuwo et al., eds., *Federalism and Political Restructuring in Nigeria.* Ibadan: Spectrum and IFRA, 1998.

Synge, Richard. *Mozambique: UN Peacekeeping in Action, 1992–1994.* Washington, D.C.: U.S. Institute of Peace Press, 1997.

Tangri, Roger. *The Politics of Patronage in Africa.* Oxford: James Currey, 2000.

Tanner, Michael. *The End of Welfare: Fighting Poverty in the Civil Society.* Washington, D.C.: Cato Institute, 1996.

———. "Liberia: Railroading Peace." *Review of African Political Economy* 25, no. 75 (March 1998): 133–147.

Taylor, Helen, and Robert Mattes. *Public Evaluations of and Demands on Local Government.* POS Report no 3. Cape Town: Idasa Public Opinion Service, February 1998.

Tempels, Placide. *La philosophie bantoue* [English edition published as *Bantu philosophy,* 1969]. Paris: Presence africaine, 1961.

Thioub, Ibrahima, Momar-Coumba Diop, and Catherine Boone. "Economic Liberalization in Senegal: Shifting Politics in Indigenous Business Interests." *African Studies Review* 41, no. 2 (September 1998): 63–89.

Tomlinson, Mary R. *From Institution-Building to House-Building: The Second Year of the Government's Housing Subsidy Scheme.* Johannesburg: Centre for Policy Studies, 1996.

———. *From Rejection to Resignation: Beneficiaries' Views of the Government's Housing Subsidy Scheme.* Johannesburg: Centre for Policy Studies, 1997.

Touraine, Alain. *O que é a democracia?* [What is democracy?]. Rio de Janeiro: Petrópolis, Vozes, 1996.

Transparency International. *Global Corruption Report 2001.* Berlin: Transparency International, 2001.

————. *Global Corruption Report 2003*. London: Profile Books, 2003.

Tripp, Aili Mari. *Changing the Rules: The Politics of Liberalization and the Urban Informal Economy in Tanzania*. Berkeley: University of California Press, 1997.

————. "New Political Activism in Africa." *Journal of Democracy* 12, no. 3 (2001): 141–155.

Turner, J. Michael, Sue Nelson, and Kimberly Mahling-Clark. "Mozambique's Vote for Democratic Governance." In Chetan Kumar, ed., *Postconflict Elections and International Assistance*. Boulder, Colo.: Lynne Rienner, 1998.

United Nations Development Programme (UNDP). *Human Development Report: Millennium Development Goals: A Compact Among Nations to End Human Poverty*. New York: Oxford University Press, 2003.

————. *Human Development Report 1997*. New York: UNDP, 1997.

————. *Moçambique: crescimento económico e desenvolvimento humano: progresso, obstaculos e desafios* [Mozambique: economic growth and human development: progress, obstacles and challenges]. Maputo: UNDP, 1999.

————. *Moçambique: relatório nacional de desenvolvimento humano, 1998. Paz e crescimento económico: oportunidades para desenvolvimento humano* [Mozambique national human development report, 1998. Peace and economic growth: opportunities for human development]. Maputo: UNDP, 1999.

U.S. Agency for International Development (USAID). *Foreign Aid in the National Interest: Promoting Freedom, Security, and Opportunity*. Washington, D.C.: USAID, 2002. Available at www.usaid.gov/fani.

Uwugiaren, I. "Stinking Senate." *The News* (Lagos), May 7, 2001.

Vambe, Maurice Taonezvi. "Popular Songs and Social Realities in Post-Independence Zimbabwe." *African Studies Review* 43, no. 2 (September 2000): 73–86.

van de Walle, Nicolas. *African Economies and the Politics of Permanent Crisis, 1979–1999*. New York: Cambridge University Press, 2001.

————. "Aid's Crisis of Legitimacy: Current Proposals and Future Prospects." *African Affairs* 98 (July 1999): 337–352.

————. "A Comment on the MCA Proposal." Center for Global Development, January 9, 2003. Available at www.cgdev.org/briefs/vandewalle_20030109.pdf.

————. "The Decline of the Franc Zone: Monetary Politics in Francophone Africa." *African Affairs* 90 (July 1991): 383–405.

————. *The Politics of Permanent Crisis*. New York: Cambridge University Press, 2001.

van de Walle, Nicolas, and Kimberly Butler. "Political Parties and Party Systems in Africa's Illiberal Democracies." *Cambridge Review of International Affairs* 14, no. 1 (1999): 14–28.

van de Walle, Nicolas, and Timothy Johnston. *Improving Aid to Africa*. Baltimore: Johns Hopkins University Press for the Overseas Development Council, 1996.

Vines, Alex. *Renamo: From Terrorism to Democracy in Mozambique?* London: James Currey, 1996.

Walker, J. A. "Civil Society, the Challenge to the Authoritarian State, and the Consolidation of Democracy in Nigeria." *Issue* 27, no. 1 (1999).

Walton, John, and David Seddon. *Free Markets and Food Riots: the Politics of Global Adjustment*. London: Blackwell, 1994.

Watts, R., ed. "Federalism." *International Social Science Journal* 53, no. 1 (March 2001).

Weber, Max. *Economy and Society*. New York: Bedminster Press, 1968.

Wei, Shang-Jin. "How Taxing Is Corruption on International Investors." Cambridge: Kennedy School of Government, Harvard University, 1997. Mimeo.

Weingast, B. R. "The Political Foundations of Democracy and the Rule of Law." *American Political Science Review* 91, no. 2 (June 1997): 245–263.

Whitaker, C. S. "The Unfinished State of Nigeria." *Worldview* 27, no. 6 (March 1984).

White, Caroline. *Makhulu Padroni? Patron-Clientelism in Shack Areas and Some Italian Lessons for South Africa.* Johannesburg: Centre for Policy Studies, 1993.

White, Gordon. Civil Society, Democratization, and Development: Clearing the Analytical Ground." *Democratization* 1, no. 3 (1994): 375–390.

White, Howard. "Foreign Aid, Taxes, and Public Investment: A Further Comment." *Journal of Development Economics* 45 (1994): 155–163.

Widner, Jennifer A., ed. *Economic Change and Political Liberalization in Sub-Saharan Africa.* Baltimore: Johns Hopkins University Press, 1994.

Williamson, J. "Democracy and the Washington Consensus." *World Development* 21, no. 8 (1993): 1329–1336.

Wiredu, Kwasi. "Democracy and Consensus in Traditional Politics: A Plea for a Non-Party Polity." In P. H. Cotzee and A. P. J. Roux, eds., *Philosophy from Africa.* Johannesburg: International Thompson, 1998.

Wohlgemuth, L., et al., eds. *Common Security and Civil Society in Africa.* Stockholm: Nordic Institute for African Studies, 1999.

World Bank. *Adjustment in Africa: Reforms, Results, and the Road Ahead.* Washington, D.C.: World Bank, 1994.

———. *African Development Indicators 1997.* Washington, D.C.: World Bank, 1997.

———. *Botswana: A Case Study of Economic Policy Prudence and Growth.* Washington D.C.: World Bank, August 31, 1999

———. *Bureaucrats in Business: The Economics and Politics of Government Ownership.* Washington, D.C.: World Bank, 1995.

———. *A Continent in Transition: Sub-Saharan Africa in the Mid-1990s.* Washington, D.C.: World Bank, November 1995.

———. *Global Economic Prospects and the Developing Countries.* Washington, D.C.: World Bank, 1997.

———. *The Impact of Public Expenditure Reviews: An Evaluation.* Operations Evaluation Department Report no. 18573. Washington, D.C.: World Bank, November 13, 1998.

———. *Operations Evaluation Study.* Washington, D.C.: World Bank, 1995.

———. *Poverty Reduction and the World Bank: Progress and Challenges in the 1990s.* Washington, D.C.: World Bank, 1996.

———. *Poverty Reduction and the World Bank: Progress in Fiscal 1996 and 1997.* Washington, D.C.: World Bank, 1997.

———. *Recommendations for Strengthening the Anti-Corruption Program in Uganda.* PRSD (Africa Region) Anti-Corruption Series no. 1. Washington, D.C.: World Bank, 1998.

———. *World Development Report 1997: The State in a Changing World.* New York: Oxford University Press 1997.

———. *World Development Report 1998: Knowledge for Development.* New York: Oxford University Press, 1998.

———. *World Development Report 2002: Building Institutions for Markets.* New York: Oxford University Press, 2002.

———. *World Development Report 2003: Sustainable Development in a Dynamic World.* New York: Oxford University Press, 2003.

Wunsch, James, and Dele Olowu, eds. *The Failure of the Centralized State: Institutions and Self-Governance in Africa.* Boulder, Colo.: Westview Press, 1990.

Young, Crawford. *Ideology and Development in Africa.* New Haven: Yale University Press, 1982.

————. "In Search of Civil Society." In John Harbeson, Donald Rothchild, and Naomi Chazan, eds., *Civil Society and the State in Africa.* Boulder, Colo.: Lynne Rienner, 1994.

————. "The Third Wave of Democratization in Africa: Ambiguities and Contradictions." In Richard Joseph, ed., *State, Conflict, and Democracy in Africa.* Boulder, Colo.: Lynne Rienner, 1999.

"Zambia Finalizes Sale of State Copper Mine Group." *Financial Times,* April 4, 2000.

Zangor, Dane. *The Non-Profit Sector in South Africa.* Kent: Charities Aid Foundation, 1997.

Zartman, I. William, ed. *Collapsed States: The Disintegration and Restoration of Legitimate Authority.* Boulder, Colo.: Lynne Rienner, 1995.

————. "Dynamics and Constraints in Negotiations in Internal Conflicts." In I. William Zartman, ed., *Elusive Peace: Negotiating an End to Civil Wars.* Washington, D.C.: Brookings Institution, 1995.

————, ed. *Governance as Conflict Management: Politics and Violence in West Africa.* Washington, D.C.: Brookings Institution, 1996.

————. "Posing the Problem of State Collapse." In I. William Zartman, ed., *Collapsed States: The Disintegration and Restoration of Legitimate Authority.* Boulder, Colo.: Lynne Rienner, 1995.

Zweifel, Thomas D., and Patricio Navia, "Democracy, Dictatorship, and Infant Mortality." *Journal of Democracy* 11, no. 2 (April 2000): 99–114.

The Contributors

Adigun Agbaje is professor of political science at the University of Ibadan, Nigeria.

Michael Bratton is professor of political science, Michigan State University, East Lansing, and codirector of Afrobarometer.

Larry Diamond is senior fellow at Stanford University's Hoover Institution; coeditor of the Journal of Democracy and codirector of the International Forum for Democratic Studies.

Steven Friedman is senior research fellow at the Center for Policy Studies, based in Johannesburg.

E. Gyimah-Boadi is professor of political science at the University of Ghana, Legon; head of the Ghana Center for Democratic Development (CDD-Ghana), Accra; and codirector of Afrobarometer.

Sahr J. Kpundeh is senior public sector specialist in the World Bank working with the Poverty Reduction Unit in the World Bank Institute and the Bank's Africa Region's Public Sector and Capacity Building Group on Governance and Public Sector Reforms.

Terrence Lyons is an assistant professor at the Institute for Conflict Analysis and Resolution of the George Mason University. He is also a senior associate with the Africa program at the Center for Strategic and International Studies.

Robert Mattes is director of the Democracy Research Unit in the Center for Social Science Research and associate professor of political science at the University of Cape Town. He is also codirector of Afrobarometer.

Brazão Mazula is rector of the Eduardo Mondlane University, Maputo, Mozambique.

Patrick Molutsi is executive secretary of the Botswana Tertiary Education Council. He was until recently director of programs at the Institute for Democracy and Electoral Assistance (Stockholm).

Stephen John Stedman is senior fellow at the Institute for International Studies at Stanford University and head of research for the UN's High-Level Panel on Threats, Challenges, and Change.

Nicolas van de Walle is professor of international studies and director of the Mario Einaudi Center for International Studies at Cornell University.

Index

Abacha, Sani, 73, 132, 148, 208, 216, 223
Abiola, M. K. O., 208
Aboyade Commission, 210
Abubakar, Abdulsalam, 208–209
Abuja process, 152
Accountability: causes of corruption, 123–125; of elected officials, 267–268; enforcing for better governance, 274–275; international community monitoring governance, 278–286; Nigeria's government, 216–217; South Africa's diminishing, 235–236; as tool against corruption, 121–122, 129–130, 134–136
Acheampong regime, 115
Adams, Ganiyu, 218
Adjustment policies. *See* Structural adjustment
Africa Economic Research Consortium, 107
Africa Growth and Opportunity Act (AGOA), 288–289
African Association, 184
African Crisis Response Initiative, 152
African Development Bank, 271, 291(n40)
African Development Foundation, 136–137
African Development Report, 271
African Leadership Forum, 151
African National Congress (ANC), 235, 237–240, 242, 244

African Peer Review Mechanism (APRM), 276–278
African renaissance, 29, 275
African Security Dialogue and Research (Ghana), 20, 26(n33)
African Union (AU), 23–24, 229, 275
Afrobarometer, 2, 65, 70–71
Afropessimism, 1
AGOA. *See* Africa Growth and Opportunity Act
Agricultural production: Botswana's economic decline and development programs, 171, 173–174; decline in, 35, 60(n23); economic development of civil society, 105–106; Nigeria's need to improve, 225; obstacles to economic liberalization and agricultural reform, 37; rentier economy, 273; stimulating growth by curtailing subsidies, 284; structural adjustment policies, 36
Aid: African aid levels, 290(n4); anticorruption efforts, 131–132, 137–138; Botswana's development programs, 166–167; civil service reform, 40; civil society attracting donor support, 113; Cold War era recipients, 147; contributing to corruption, 127, 272–275; demilitarization of Mozambique's politics, 157; economic policy reform and, 30–31; embezzlement of, 111, 119(n24); global aid levels, 290(n3); good governance as condition for,

Party system: Botswana's distribution
of seats, 167(table); Botswana's
election reforms, 167–168; Mozam-
bique's Political Parties Law, 196;
multiparty systems, 148, 190–192,
195, 239; unitary systems, 11–12,
72, 73, 204, 211; weak development
of, 11–12
Patrimonialism and patronage, 11,
22, 26(n45), 166, 274. *See also*
Neopatrimonialism
Peace agreements. *See* Negotiated
peace
Peacekeeping operations, 150, 154
Peer review process, 276–278
People's Democratic Party (Nigeria),
217
Pluralism, 5
Police reform, 151
Policy learning, 53
Policymaking, 7–8
Political aristocracy, 46–47
Political economy, 55
Political factors in development, 160
Political good of democracy, 69
Political openness, 266–267
Political Parties Law (Mozambique),
196
Political reform: advances made in, 2;
Botswana's election reforms, 168–
169; Botswana under Mogae, 169–
170; citizenship issues, 21; civil-
military relations, 20–21; civil
society's contribution to, 107–108;
democratic development, 6–9;
enlisting the aid of internal reformers,
283; failures in, 9–13; HIV/AIDS
pandemic as threat to, 18–20;
importance of political will in
combating corruption, 133–137;
public opinion, 65–66; relationship
between politics and economic
reform, 88–90; state- and nation-
building, 13–17
Political society, 183
Political will, 133–138, 150, 275,
278–280, 283
Population: Botswana, 180(n25);
Mozambique, 185; Nigeria, 204;
relative development performance of
Africa, 264(table)

Populist anticorruption initiatives,
131
Portuguese colonies, 142, 157(n6), 184,
186–189
Postal voting, 168
Postcolonialism, 14–15
Poverty: Africa's statistics on, 60(n24),
263–264; aid's failure to relieve,
285–286; Botswana, 180(n26);
excluding the poor from decision-
making, 254–255; increase through
lack of public investment, 34–35;
Mozambique, 186; Nigeria's allevia-
tion programs, 224, 228–229
Prebendalism, 44
Presidential systems, 45
Prevention of Corruption Bureau
(Tanzania), 128, 134
Price fixing, 37
Price liberalization, 36
Private Enterprise Foundation (Ghana),
107
Private responsibility, 81–83
Private sector, 183, 276, 283
Privatization: implementation, 42;
inadequacy of, 2; Nigeria, 224–225;
public enterprise reform, 38–40;
public opinion of, 84–85
Property rights, 8
Provincial governance, South Africa's,
240, 258(n9)
Provisional National Defense Council,
100
Public Complaints Commission
(Nigeria), 131
Public enterprise reform, 38–40
Public Expenditure Review, 53
Public health systems, 35
Public Investment Program, 53
Public opinion: Afrobarometer, 65–66;
Botswana's government performance, 175–176; of democracy,
66–72, 68(table), 74–78; distributive
justice, 92–93; rejecting nondemocratic regimes, 72–74; relationship
between politics and economic
reform, 88–90; South Africa's need
for public participation in governance, 247–251, 255–256; structural
adjustment, 78–81, 83–87; support
for market values, 81–83

About the Book

After more than a decade of reform efforts in Africa, much of the optimism over the continent's prospects has been replaced by a widespread "Afropessimism." But to what extent is either view well founded? *Democratic Reform in Africa* plumbs the key issues in the contemporary African experience—including intrastate conflict, corruption, and the development of civil society—highlighting the challenges and evaluating the progress of political and economic change. Case studies of Botswana, Mozambique, Nigeria, and South Africa complement the thematic chapters in this exploration of the complex interactions between democracy and development in Africa.

E. Gyimah-Boadi is professor of political science at the University of Ghana and executive director of the Center for Democratic Development, Accra.